SIX M.

Aeschylus (525–456 B. ... ...
was an aristocrat by b... ...
His masterpiece, the *Oresteia*, is composed of *Agamemnon*,
The Libation Bearers, and *The Euminides*.

Sophocles (496–406 B.C.) was praised above all other tragic
poets by Aristotle, who declared *Oedipus Rex* to be the
highest model of Greek tragedy.

Christopher Marlowe (1564–1593) is considered Shakespeare's
most important contemporary. His best-known plays include
Doctor Faustus, Tamburlaine, and *The Jew of Malta.*

William Shakespeare (1564–1616) is widely considered to
be the greatest of all playwrights. His most powerful tragedies
include *King Lear, Macbeth, Othello,* and *Hamlet.*

Henrik Ibsen (1828–1906) opened new frontiers and challenged
the unwritten taboos of nineteenth-century drama. This
Norwegian playwright began by writing social satire and then
moved into the more experimental realm of the "drama of
ideas" with plays such as *Hedda Gabler, A Doll's House,*
and *An Enemy of the People.*

Eugene O'Neill (1888–1953), the first American dramatist to
treat the stage as a literary medium, won four Pulitzer Prizes
for *Beyond the Horizon, Anna Christie, Strange Interlude,*
and *Long Day's Journey into Night.* He is the most widely
translated and produced playwright after Shakespeare and
George Bernard Shaw.

———————

William Packard teaches playwrighting at H. B. Studio in
New York and poetry at the Washington Square Writing Center
of New York University. He is the author of the acclaimed
novel *Saturday at San Marcos* and a translation of Racine's
Phèdre.

Bantam Classics
Ask your bookseller for these other World Classics

THE BHAGAVAD-GITA (translated by Barbara Stoler Miller)

CHEKHOV: FIVE MAJOR PLAYS, Anton Chekhov
A DOCTOR'S VISIT: SHORT STORIES by Anton Chekhov

THE INFERNO, Dante (translated by Allen Mandelbaum)
PURGATORIO, Dante (translated by Allen Mandelbaum)
PARADISO, Dante (translated by Allen Mandelbaum)

THE BROTHERS KARAMAZOV, Fyodor Dostoevsky
CRIME AND PUNISHMENT, Fyodor Dostoevsky
THE IDIOT, Fyodor Dostoevsky
NOTES FROM UNDERGROUND, Fyodor Dostoevsky

THE COUNT OF MONTE CRISTO, Alexandre Dumas
THE THREE MUSKETEERS, Alexandre Dumas

MADAME BOVARY, Gustave Flaubert

FAUST, Johann Wolfgang von Goethe

THE COMPLETE FAIRYTALES OF THE BROTHERS GRIMM
   (translated by Jack Zipes)

THE HUNCHBACK OF NOTRE DAME, Victor Hugo

FOUR GREAT PLAYS, Henrik Ibsen

THE METAMORPHOSIS, Franz Kafka

LES LIAISONS DANGEREUSES, Pierre Choderlos de Laclos

THE PRINCE, Machiavelli

CYRANO DE BERGERAC, Edmond Rostand

THE RED AND THE BLACK by Marie-Henri Beyle de Stendhal

ANNA KARENINA, Leo Tolstoy
THE DEATH OF IVAN ILYICH, Leo Tolstoy

FATHERS AND SONS, Ivan Turgenev

AROUND THE WORLD IN EIGHTY DAYS, Jules Verne
20,000 LEAGUES UNDER THE SEA, Jules Verne

CANDIDE, Voltaire

DEATH IN VENICE, Thomas Mann (translated by David Luke)

SIX MAJOR TRAGEDIES

AGAMEMNON *by Aeschylus*
OEDIPUS THE KING *by Sophocles*
DOCTOR FAUSTUS
by Christopher Marlowe
KING LEAR *by William Shakespeare*
HEDDA GABLER *by Henrik Ibsen*
THE EMPEROR JONES
by Eugene O'Neill

Edited and with an Introduction
by William Packard

BANTAM BOOKS
NEW YORK • TORONTO • LONDON • SYDNEY • AUCKLAND

SIX MAJOR TRAGEDIES

A Bantam Classic Book / October 1989

PRINTING HISTORY

Aeschylus: AGAMEMNON, translated by Richard Lattimore, copyright 1947 by Richmond Lattimore, copyright © 1953 by the University of Chicago.

Sophocles: OEDIPUS REX, translated by Richard Green from Greek Plays in Modern Translation, copyright 1947 Dudley Fitts. (Dial Press)

Christopher Marlowe: DOCTOR FAUSTUS, adapted by William Packard, copyright © 1989 by William Packard.

William Shakespeare: KING LEAR, edited by David Bevington, Bantam 1988, footnotes copyright © 1980, 1973 by Scott, Foresman and Company.

Henrik Ibsen: HEDDA GABLER, adapted by Aloha Brown based on a translation by William Archer and Edmund Gosse, copyright © 1988 by Aloha Brown.

Eugene O'Neill: THE EMPEROR JONES, copyright © 1953 by Eugene O'Neill, copyright 1932 by Liveright, Inc., copyright renewed 1954 by Carlotta Monterey O'Neill.

ISBN 0-553-21364-4

Published simultaneously in the United States and Canada

Bantam Books are published by Bantam Books, a division of Bantam Doubleday Dell Publishing Group, Inc. Its trademark, consisting of the words "Bantam Books" and the portrayal of a rooster, is Registered in U.S. Patent and Trademark Office and in other countries. Marca Registrada. Bantam Books, 666 Fifth Avenue, New York, New York 10103.

PRINTED IN THE UNITED STATES OF AMERICA

O   0 9 8 7 6 5 4 3 2 1

CONTENTS

INTRODUCTION

A student gets a low grade on a term paper . . . a couple of high school kids get killed in an automobile accident . . . a marriage of twenty-three years hits the divorce courts . . . an earthquake in Armenia devastates hundreds of thousands of people.

All these things are sad happenings, but strictly speaking none of them is "tragic." Call them disasters or catastrophes if you like, and feel pity for the victims if you will, but understand that you are not yet entering into that special experience that we call "tragedy."

Then what *is* tragedy?

Tragedy almost always involves a conflict between a leading character, or protagonist, and some higher power outside of himself. During the course of this struggle, the hero makes some crucial realization about his being and the world he lives in. And although the hero is almost always ennobled by his tragic insight, his new awareness does not significantly alter the course of his destiny, which almost always ends in some kind of catastrophe.

Okay, then, why bother to pay attention to tragedy?

The numbing humdrum of our everyday lives tends to anesthetize us to the larger emotional and spiritual realities that surround us. We spend most of our time wandering around in a self-induced daze state, unaware of who we really are or why we are the way we are. We need something to return us to reality, if only for short intervals, so we can get some true bearing on what this life is all about.

We need tragedy to remind us of the universe we live in. When we enter the very special arena of tragedy, we witness someone not too unlike ourselves go through a series of sudden shocks and reversals of fortune, in order for us to see, if only for an instant, the way things really are. And by sharing in this person's tragic realization, we may also undergo our own profound catharsis for having lived and suffered and seen things as they really are.

In this book we are presenting six of the greatest tragedies ever written: the *Agamemnon* of Aeschylus, the *Oedipus Rex* of Sophocles, *Doctor Faustus* of Christopher Marlowe, *King Lear* of William Shakespeare, *Hedda Gabler* of Henrik Ibsen, and *The Emperor Jones* of Eugene O'Neill. From the ancient classical world of Greece to Renaissance England, from the nineteenth-century revolution in European drama to twentieth-century American theater, these six tragedies offer a very special way of being and seeing and knowing that is as relevant to us today as when the plays were first written.

The oracle of Apollo at Delphi told the ancient Greeks that their highest destiny on earth was *gnothi seuton,* to know oneself, which is what we've just been discussing. So it is no wonder that the art of tragedy began with these same ancient Greeks—in the year 534 B.C., when the actor Thespis began the first drama in Greece, which was called *tragoidia,* or "goat song," and was written for only one actor who interacted with a chorus. This earliest tragedy was a combination of song, dance, poetry, and dramatic action. It was a celebration of human fertility. It was also a religious ritual, with a statue of the god Dionysos onstage; animals were sacrificed before each performance of the play. Because of the presence of Dionysos, there could be no violence onstage. Any death or disaster had to occur offstage and be reported to the onstage characters by means of a messenger.

Later in the fifth century B.C., when tragedies were written for more than one actor, the ruler Pericles persuaded democratic Athens to vote for the right of each citizen to attend the plays and games that took place in the major outdoor amphitheaters. There were similar theaters at nearby Epidaurus, Delphi, and Syracuse. The great Dionysian theater in Athens seated some fifteen thousand people, and it was not unusual for five plays to be performed in one day, from dawn to dusk. There were only male actors, and they wore masks, had raised boots to elevate their height onstage, and could project their voices to the farthest row of the amphitheater. By and large the audiences already knew the stories that were told in the plays; as one commentator explains:

> The subject of a Greek tragedy is, without exception, taken from history, and almost always from remote and legendary history, away from the tyranny of exact information. It is never invented by the poet.
> —Gilbert Murray, *The Classical Tradition in Poetry*

The major tragic Greek playwrights were Aeschylus, Sophocles, and Euripides—Aeschylus wrote ninety plays of which seven are extant; Sophocles wrote one hundred twenty plays of which seven are extant; and Euripides wrote between eighty and ninety plays of which eighteen are extant.

The Greeks knew exactly what they were doing with this tragic art form. Aristotle gives a precise definition for the classical view of tragedy:

> A tragedy, then, is the imitation of an action that is serious, complete, and of a certain magnitude; in language having pleasurable accessories, each kind brought in separately in the different parts of the work; in dramatic, and not narrative form; with incidents arousing pity and fear, wherewith to accomplish the catharsis of these emotions.
>
> —Aristotle, *Poetics*

There are several elements in Aristotle's definition that we ought to look at more closely:

• *imitation:* this comes from the word *mimesis,* from which we get our modern word *mime;* it means we are not presenting the real thing but the semblance of the thing. We do not actually kill people onstage, we only perform it so that they appear to be killed.

• *action:* the Greek word for it is *praxis,* and it is the heart and soul of drama. A character's *praxis* is the same thing as his objective, what he wants, or what he has to do.

• *serious:* this means the action is concerned with important matters, and not just accidental events.

• *complete:* this means the action has a beginning and a middle and an end.

• *of a certain magnitude:* this means that the stakes of the action are significant, usually life and death, and involve a reconciliation with the gods.

• *language having pleasurable accessories:* this means the text of tragedy will have various types of poetry. Generally there are three kinds of language in a Greek tragedy: the long character speeches explaining motivation and feeling, the rapid back-and-forth dialogue, or *stichomythia,* and finally the long choral passages that are made up of *strophes* and *antistrophes* and *epodes.*

• *in dramatic, and not narrative form:* this means the action of the tragedy does not merely *tell* us something, it also *shows* it to us. This is the principal difference between narrative and dramatic. Narrative tells, dramatic shows.

• *pity and fear:* these are the two tragic emotions, "pity" being *eleos* in ancient Greek (from which we get our modern word *elegy*) and meaning a profound feeling toward something; and "fear" meaning terror, awe, and profound reverence for something.

• *catharsis:* this is from the Greek word *katharsis* and means a cleansing or purging of the emotions.

There are also the following technical terms that are useful to know in approaching classical tragedy:

1. *anagnorisis:* a sudden recognition or discovery, as when Oedipus realizes that he himself is the moral pollution he has been seeking to uncover.

2. *peripeteia:* a sudden reversal of fortunes, usually from happiness to misery, as when Agamemnon goes from being conquering hero to being helpless victim in just a few minutes of time.

3. *hamartia:* a tragic flaw, some error or sin on the part of the protagonist, as when Agamemnon pays no attention to the past sacrifice of his daughter Iphigeneia or the effect of this sacrifice on his wife, Clytaemestra.

4. *hubris:* self-deluding pride, the most common kind of tragic flaw, as when Oedipus reveals his blinding sense of importance in the opening line, "I, Oedipus, whom all men call the Great."

5. *nemesis:* retribution of the gods, a divine punishment, usually against the sin of hubris or pride, as when Oedipus has to cut down the body of his wife/mother, Jocasta, and use her brooches to blind himself.

6. *pharmakos:* a scapegoat, someone who is chosen to bear the sins of a whole people, usually unintentionally; Oedipus Rex is such a *pharmakos,* which accounts for why he is considered both a taboo figure and an object of un-earthly reverence in the later play by Sophocles, *Oedipus at Colonus.*

The tragedies contained in this book have some or all of the above ingredients of classical tragedy. But each one has at least the following elements: a protagonist who must experience some struggle with a higher power outside him-self, a protagonist who must go through a series of sudden reversals that cause him to have a tragic realization in which he sees things as they really are, and finally, a protagonist who is overwhelmed in the final catastrophe.

Aeschylus (525–456 B.C.) is credited with adding a second actor to the original single actor of Thespis and later adding a third. By introducing more actors, Aeschylus made dramatic dialogue and action possible. He also made use of the cho-rus, which sang and danced to express their reflections on the action. Actors could play more than one role by switch-ing masks.

Aeschylus wrote the *Oresteia,* a trilogy, in 458 B.C., of which the *Agamemnon* is the opening play. The three plays trace the curse of the House of Atreus, from its origins in Tantalos, Pelops, and Atreus through its eruption in mayhem in the lives of the characters Agamemnon and Orestes, until it is finally purged by the goddess Athena. It illustrates the Greek belief that violence is carried on from generation to generation, in much the same way as family feuds such as the Montagues and the Capulets continue in *Romeo and Juliet* or the Hatfields and the McCoys in American mythology.

The story of *Agamemnon* opens with the beginning of the Trojan War, when Agamemnon sacrifices his daughter Iphigeneia to help get strong winds for his ships that are bound for Troy. In the Aeschylus play, Agamemnon's wife, Clytaemnestra, has been awaiting her husband's return from war in order to get revenge for the slaying of her daughter.

Together with her consort/lover Aegisthus, she has been planning Agamemnon's murder for ten years. The story of Agamemnon is a very ancient one: the ghost of Agamemnon tells it in Book XI of Homer's *Odyssey,* which was written at least four hundred years before the play by Aeschylus.

An interesting twist in the Aeschylus play is that the *anagnorisis,* or discovery, is made, not by Agamemnon himself, but by the chorus of old men. They are the only ones who are able to see things as they really are. The other characters are in shock after witnessing the murder of Agamemnon. Usually in Greek tragedy a chorus is confined to commenting on the tragic action, but in this play the chorus suddenly becomes aware that Clytaemnestra was lying during the first part of the play. The chorus comes close to actually fighting with Aegisthus at the end of the play. Because Agamemnon and Cassandra have both been murdered the chorus is raised to the status of dramatic character, and the tragic realization is almost more than these old men of Argos can bear.

The *peripeteia,* or reversal, in the play takes place during Cassandra's long speech when she foresees the ruin of Agamemnon, which is taking place that very moment behind the palace doors. The *hamartias,* or tragic flaws, are Agamemnon's failure to realize the devastating effect his sacrifice of Iphigeneia has had on Clytaemnestra and his ignoring the bloodstream curse on the house of Atreus that he carries. Agamemnon's *hubris,* or pride, lies in his having led the Achaian forces to victory over the Trojans in the recent war, which blinds him to what is in store for him back home. The *nemesis,* or swift retribution of the gods, comes when he is killed inside his own palace. Agamemnon thus becomes a *pharmakos,* or scapegoat, for crimes that were committed generations ago by his ancestors in the house of Atreus, as Cassandra reveals in her prophetic speeches just before she herself is murdered.

It has been said that the Greek playwright Sophocles (496–406 B.C.) experienced "the happiest life that anyone ever lived." He lived during the great period of Athenian glory, when cultural and political activity was surging after Athens defeated Persia. He was wealthy and handsome, politically prominent, and the winner of many dramatic awards. Yet Sophocles concluded in his last play, *Oedipus at Colonus*, "Never to have lived is best, ancient writers say: never to have seen the bright light of day. . . . The second best's a gay good night, and quickly turn away."

The play *Oedipus Rex* is part of a trilogy that includes *Oedipus Rex, Oedipus at Colonus,* and *Antigone*. The story of Oedipus, like the story of Agamemnon, is ancient. We know there was a man named Oedipus who actually lived in Thebes around 1250 B.C., and Homer refers to Oedipus in Book XI of the *Odyssey* as follows:

> "I saw the mother of Oedipus, Jocasta,
> whose unconscious conquest it was
> to marry her own son—he took this wife
> from a slain father, but soon the gods
> brought all to light to make the ancient story."
> —Homer, *Odyssey,* Book XI (trans. William Packard)

As the play *Oedipus Rex* unfolds onstage, the audience is confronted with a series of major revelations that lead to Oedipus's discovery of the awful truth that he has unwittingly killed his father and married his mother. First, the character of Creon brings news from the priest of Apollo that the plague in Thebes is caused by a moral pollution; second, the blind seer Teiresias tells Oedipus that he is the pollution; third, a messenger reports the death of Polybus in Corinth, with the news that Oedipus is unrelated to this king who was purported to be his father; fourth, the old shepherd tells how a newborn baby was given to him by Jocasta; and finally, a second messenger comes onstage and reports to the audience that Jocasta has hanged herself, and Oedipus has cut down her body and blinded himself with her brooches.

These five revelations in the play constitute the *peripeteia,* or turning points, whereby Oedipus's state changes from happiness to misery. The *anagnorisis,* or discovery, occurs when Oedipus finally learns the truth about himself and, in a fit of despair, goes offstage to find that his wife/mother has already discovered the truth. Oedipus blinds himself and comes back onstage, fully aware of the *nemesis,* or divine punishment, that has been visited on him for his *hamartia,* or tragic flaw, of ignorance and more particularly for his *hubris,* or pride, in thinking that he could solve all the riddles of existence. From proud ruler, Oedipus has been transformed into a *pharmakos,* or scapegoat, for the sins of his people, and he must leave Thebes in search of his final expiation.

In the *Agamemnon* of Aeschylus and the *Oedipus Rex* of Sophocles, we can see a slight shift in the view of tragedy. Aeschylus seems to believe tragedy is the result of some moral flaw in the tragic hero that has to be punished by laws that are built into the nature of things; Sophocles, on the other hand, believes there is some kind of predetermined karma or bloodstream design that one can never quite grasp consciously even though one tries one's utmost to comprehend it. As Moses Hadas writes:

> To resist fate is hopeless; what the Sophoclean hero does is to wrest what human dignity and what beauty he can from a world in which, as his characters say, best of all things it is never to have been born.
> —Moses Hadas, *Introduction to Classical Drama*

After the period of classical Greek tragedy (roughly the fifth century B.C.), the Western world lapsed into the desolate Dark Ages (roughly A.D. 500–1000), which was followed by the medieval Age of Faith. The medieval world no longer believed in the idea of tragedy. The worldview of the Middle Ages was like some great Gothic cathedral, scholastic and symmetrical and soaring skyward. This mathematical architecture is reflected in the perfect triple rhymes and the monochromatic moral universe of Dante's *Commedia.* Classical concerns about personal fate and individual destiny were no longer of any moment—all that mattered in the Middle Ages was one's ultimate salvation and one's relation to the priestly hierarchy of the Catholic Church.

Instead of tragedies, the medieval world produced miracle plays (plays that showed events of biblical faith, such as *Noah* and *Abraham*), mystery plays (plays that showed the secret teachings of incarnation and nativity, such as *The Second Shepherd's Play*), and morality plays (plays that showed the perilous adventure of the human soul as a pilgrim in a corrupt world, such as *Everyman*). As medievalism began to waver and disintegrate under the weight of its own authoritarianism, a new groundswell of skepticism, free thinking, and interest in science began to challenge the

Catholic worldview, thus preparing the way for Martin Luther's eventual Protestant Reformation in 1517.

And thus, the English Renaissance came into being.

The Faust legend as depicted in Christopher Marlowe's *Doctor Faustus* is a key to this transition from medievalism to the Renaissance and our modern world. The notion of someone's selling his soul to the devil is a metaphor for turning away from the established religious and moral order and opting for secularism, witchcraft, and black magic, which stand for materialism and science—all of which came into prominence in the sixteenth century. Faustus's lust for worldly power thus becomes the original sin of eating from the forbidden tree of knowledge in the Garden of Eden.

Christopher Marlowe (1564–1593) was dazzlingly brilliant and precocious. He wrote *Doctor Faustus* at the age of twenty-four, and he thought nothing of flaunting his atheism with such blasphemous statements as "The New Testament is filthily written." Educated at Cambridge University, Marlowe created the most powerful early Elizabethan plays, offering a strong rivalry to the young Shakespeare, who was the same age. Marlowe wrote *Tamburlaine* in 1587, *The Jew of Malta* in 1588, *Doctor Faustus* in 1588, and the history play *Edward II* in 1593. Had Marlowe lived longer, there is no telling what the English Renaissance would have been like with both Shakespeare and Marlowe writing great plays. But Marlowe was fated to die early. There is a strong probability he was living a double life as a spy in the service of Sir Thomas Walsingham, and this probably accounts for Marlowe's life having been abruptly cut off, when he was murdered at the age of twenty-nine at a tavern in Deptford.

In the opening scene of *Doctor Faustus*, Faustus rejects book after book of official learning—Aristotle's *Physics*, Galen's *Medicine*, Jerome's Bible, and Justinian's *Laws*—until he finally settles on necromancy, black magic, for his life study. Mephistophilis appears to him, and Faustus agrees to sell his soul to him for twenty-four years, during which time Faustus can do whatever he chooses. At the end of the period, however, Faustus's soul will belong to Lucifer.

The rest of the play shows how Faustus exercises his new supernatural power over this twenty-four-year period. Toward the end of the play, Faustus asks for the most beautiful woman in the history of the world (Helen of Troy), and she appears to him in a vision, which occasions these soaring lines of poetry:

> "Was this the face that launched a thousand ships
> And burnt the topless towers of Ilium?
> Sweet Helen, make me immortal with a kiss.
>
> . . . .
>
> "O, thou art fairer than the evening's air,
> Clad in the beauty of a thousand stars."

Here Marlowe reaches his height of power as a poet, blending lyrical airy lilt with strong vowel music, assonance, and a liquid sense of ascension.

It is only at the end of the play that we begin to feel the staggering dimensions of the tragedy of *Doctor Faustus*. When Faustus realizes for the first time what his damnation means to him. In one of the most heartrending passages in all poetry, Faustus wakes up to the total hopelessness of his situation:

> "O, I'll leap up to my God! Who pulls me down?
> See, see, where Christ's blood streams in the firmament!
> One drop would save my soul, half a drop! Ah, my
> Christ!
> Rend not my heart for naming of my Christ!"

In this play the *anagnorisi,* or discovery, takes place when Faustus realizes that his damnation is in earnest, and there will be no reprieve. The *peripeteia,* or sudden reversal, takes place when Faustus goes from the height of power, summoning Helen to appear before him, to being dragged down to hell by Mephistophilis. Faustus's *hamartia,* or tragic flaw, lies in his greed, boredom, and lust for material power, more especially in his *hubris,* or pride, which keeps him from believing that his damnation can be eternal. In other words, Faustus does not want to accept the consequences of his actions, and his pride deludes him into thinking he can escape the damnation he has pledged to Lucifer. The *nemesis,* or divine retribution, takes place when Faustus is taken down into hell, all the while screaming and pleading for mercy from Christ's blood, which "streams in the firmament."

The power of the play lies in the fact that Faustus becomes a *pharmakos,* or scapegoat. The final chorus holds Faustus up as an example to us in the modern world—and indeed, the play is frighteningly modern in its implications. In Faustus's tragic realization of his own hopelessness, he speaks for all modern men and women who live their entire lives without any thought of their final hour until, suddenly, it is too late.

When we come to the plays of William Shakespeare, we sense another slight shift in the idea of tragedy. To be sure, there is a restatement of the classical ideas of *hubris,* or pride, and *nemesis,* or fate. As Aristotle wrote in the *Poetics,* an individual is confronted with some higher power outside himself that occasions a struggle that leads to some catastrophe. Romeo and Juliet are "star-crossed lovers," Othello is a man who "loved not wisely but too well," and Hamlet is a man who ends up "thinking too precisely upon th' event."

But also working in Shakespearean tragedy is a sense of the accidental, an individual pitted against random destiny. The protagonist's *hamartia,* or tragic flaw, is usually one weakness that triggers the Furies in a particular situation. As Hamlet says to Horatio,

> "So, oft it chances in particular men,
> That for some vicious mole of nature in them,
> As in their birth—wherein they are not guilty,
> Since nature cannot choose his origin—
> By the o'ergrowth of some complexion,
> Oft breaking down the pales and forts of reason,
> Or by some habit that too much o'erleavens
> The form of plausive manners, that these men,
> Carrying, I say, the stamp of one defect,
> Being nature's livery, or fortune's star,
> His virtues else, be they as pure as grace,
> As infinite as man may undergo,
> Shall in the general censure take corruption
> From that particular fault. . . ."
>
> —William Shakespeare, *Hamlet,* I, iv

William Shakespeare (1564–1616) wrote some thirty-six plays, of roughly four types: histories, comedies, tragedies, and romances. It's impossible to say anything adequate about the mind of Shakespeare; he was, quite simply, one of the greatest intelligences that ever lived. If one wants to get some measure of his achievement, one can look at the years 1605–1606 when he was at the height of his so-called dark period, writing both *Macbeth* and *King Lear* back to back. It is staggering to think of what must have been going on inside the mind of that quiet Stratford gentleman during those seemingly uneventful months.

In writing *King Lear*, Shakespeare drew on the ancient legend of Lear that was part of English mythology and existed in various written Tudor versions, such as *The First Part of the Mirror for Magistrates* (1574) and Holinshed's *Chronicles* (1587). In Edmund Spenser's poem *The Faerie Queene* (1590), Cordelia ends her own life by hanging herself. We also know there was an anonymous play, *King Leir*, that was registered on May 14, 1594, and which Shakespeare surely must have known; the play's authorship has been variously ascribed to the playwrights Thomas Kyd, Thomas Lodge, George Peele, and Robert Greene.

Shakespeare's *King Lear* is a harlequin mockery of an aging monarch whose headstrong pride mistakes the sincerity of his three daughters. Lear announces at the beginning of the play that he intends to divide up his kingdom among his daughters, according to their profession of their love for him. Goneril and Regan both assert undying love for Lear and receive large portions of his kingdom in return. Cordelia, however, refuses to make a false statement of her love, and she is thereby banished and disinherited. In the ensuing scenes of the play, Lear is rebuffed by both Goneril and Regan, who turn him away from their castles on the grounds that he is attended by too many knights. It is ruthlessly cruel of them to treat their aged father in this way, and Lear is so brokenhearted he, in the middle of a terrible storm, begins to rave. Only his Fool, the blind Gloucester, Edgar, and the disguised Kent remain loyal to him. At the end of the play, Cordelia is hanged, Goneril poisons Regan and then stabs herself, and the broken Lear carries the dead body of Cordelia onstage, having awoken, too late, to the tragic realization that Cordelia was the only daughter who really loved him.

The awful tragedy of Lear lies in the aged monarch's heartfelt awareness of his error and his general inability to deal with the real world; the *anagnorisis,* or discovery, takes place toward the end of the play, when Lear says:

> "Pray, do not mock me.
> I am a very foolish fond old man,
> Fourscore and upward, not an hour more nor less;
> And, to deal plainly,
> I fear I am not in my perfect mind."
> —William Shakespeare, *King Lear,* IV, vii

The following is a nineteenth-century medical doctor's assessment of the nature of Lear's insanity; it is taken from the *American Journal of Insanity* for July 1844:

> Lear's is a genuine case of insanity from the beginning to the end; such as we often see in aged persons. On reading it we cannot divest ourselves of the idea that it is a real case of insanity correctly reported. . . . The general belief is, that the insanity of Lear originated solely from the ill-treatment of his daughters, while in truth he was insane before that, from the beginning of the play, when he gave his kingdom away, and banished, as it were, Cordelia and Kent, and abused his servants. The ill-usage of his daughters only aggravated the disease, and drove him to raving madness. . . .
>
> In the storm scene he becomes violently enraged, exhibiting what may be seen daily in a mad-house, a paroxysm of rage and violence. It is not until he has seen and conversed with Edgar, "the philosopher and learned Theban" as he calls him, that he becomes a real maniac. After this, aided by a proper course of treatment, he falls asleep, and sleep, as in all similar cases, partially restores him. But the violence of his disease and his sufferings are too great for his feeble system, and he dies, and dies deranged.
> —A. Brigham, M.D., "Shakespeare's Illustrations of Insanity"
> (From the Variorum edition of *King Lear,* Dover, 1963, ed. Horace Howard Furness)

It is one peculiarity of *King Lear* that the *peripeteia,* or reversal, takes place in the very opening scene, when Lear

divests himself of his kingdom and causes the reversal of his
fortunes. The *hamartia,* or tragic flaw, in Lear is his inability
to see what a viper's nest he has spawned in his own family,
and his *hubris,* or pride, leads him to reward the more
hypocritical of his daughters, Goneril and Regan, and punish
the more straightforward and virtuous daughter, Cordelia.
The *nemesis,* or divine retribution, takes place during the
hearth scene when Lear tries to outshout the full fury of the
storm, and, of course, the full catastrophe occurs when he
discovers the dead body of his daughter, Cordelia. Lear in
his final agony becomes pure *pharmakos,* or scapegoat, not
only for his own people, but, one senses, for all the defense-
less creatures of the world who are unhoused and open to
the stormy blasts of the angry skies. The play is awesome in
its power and scope, as well as in its majesty of suffering.

The English Renaissance is divided into the Elizabethan
and Jacobean periods: after Queen Elizabeth's death in 1603,
James I ascended the throne, at about the same time that
Shakespeare was entering into his so-called dark period,
when he would write his great tragedies *Hamlet, Othello,
Macbeth,* and *King Lear.* As the Jacobean period continued,
the tragedies became darker and more sinister and macabre:
John Webster's *The Duchess of Malfi* (1614) opened the
floodgates of doubt on a world that was still reeling from the
Copernican displacement of man as the center of the universe. In Webster's play, Antonio gives voice to the endless
emptiness of a godless universe:

> "I do love these ancient ruines:
> We never tread upon them, but we set
> Our foot upon some reverend History.
> And questionless, here in this open Court
> (Which now lies naked to the injuries
> Of stormy weather) some men lie Enter'd
> Loved the Church so well, and gave so largely to it. . . .
> But all things have their end:
> Churches, and Cities (which have diseases like to men)
> Must have like death that we have."
> —John Webster, *The Duchess of Malfi,* V, iii

And a few years later, in France under Louis XIV, the neoclassic theater saw playwrights such as Molière and Corneille developing a theater of high style, heroic satire, and declamation. In 1677 Jean Racine wrote his tragic masterpiece, *Phèdre,* which contains a terrible subtext of incest, violence, and monstrosity lurking just beneath the surface politeness of classically formal alexandrine verse.

The eighteenth-century theater begins with the Restoration in 1660, when the English aristocracy ended its long exile in France and returned to England bearing the legacy of Molière: unrivaled wit and merciless high satire of hypocrisy, pretension, and affectation. Restoration playwrights such as George Etherege, William Wycherley, John Dryden, and George Farquhar turned out witty plays filled with bon mots and an inflated sense of gallantry. Who gets to bed with whom is about the gist of Restoration theater. It left behind the idea of tragedy in favor of a sentimental comedy of manners, in much the same way that the Middle Ages managed to obliterate the idea of tragedy in favor of plays that embodied the medieval Catholic catechism. When you take away the seriousness of an isolated individual struggling with some higher power outside himself, then you've taken away the very foundation of tragedy. Nonetheless, there are three Restoration plays that can lay claim to being masterpieces of their genre: William Congreve's *The Way of the World* (1700), Oliver Goldsmith's *She Stoops to Conquer* (1773), and Richard Brinsley Sheridan's *The School for Scandal* (1777).

The nineteenth century saw the return of tragedy and the birth of modern drama. The three giants of modern tragedy in this period were August Strindberg, Anton Chekhov, and Henrik Ibsen.

August Strindberg (1849–1912), a Swedish dramatist, explored the lethal subterranean power struggles that take place between man and woman, between servant and master, and between man and himself. Strindberg's dark pessimism is often relentless and intense in such plays as *The Father* (1887), *Miss Julie* (1888), and *A Dream Play* (1902).

Anton Chekhov (1860–1904), a Russian doctor and short story writer, recorded the ironic awareness of the wearing away of our will to live, in such plays as *The Sea Gull* (1896), *Uncle Vanya* (1897), *The Three Sisters* (1901), and *The*

Cherry Orchard (1904). Chekhov's insistence that these plays were "comedies" caused only consternation in the great Russian director Stanislavsky and in other directors who tried to stage these great tragic commentaries on modern daily life.

The third giant of modern tragic drama is Henrik Ibsen (1828–1906), who left his native Norway in 1864 to live abroad in Rome, Dresden, and Munich. Ibsen's early play *Peer Gynt* (1867) may be more well known to us as the incidental music of the same name, provided for the play by the young Edvard Grieg. The play itself is a lyrical allegory of the seductions of materialism, not unlike the parable play *Marco Millions* (1927) by the American playwright Eugene O'Neill. But Ibsen's later plays—*A Doll's House* (1879), *Ghosts* (1881), and *An Enemy of the People* (1882)—reveal an interest in social issues that led to the creation of our modern realistic drama.

In *Hedda Gabler* (1890) Ibsen presents a woman who seems normal and well adjusted on the surface but who is actually hopelessly bored, desperately restless, and so utterly benumbed by the pointlessness of her own life, she is driven to creating mayhem all around her. Never before had there been such a devastating portrait of such a bewildering and bewildered woman—Tolstoy's *Anna Karenina* (1875–1877) hints at this type of woman but only in incipient form.

Hedda Gabler is childless and trapped in a conventional marriage that has neither purpose nor personality. And she is driven to subtly destructive and castrating behavior toward everyone around her. Her only tragic realization is her weary awareness that she is living a lie: she is a shallow figure in a meaningless charade, trying to act out a shadow life that has no value to anyone, least of all to herself. She is a study in nihilism; she seems determined to perpetrate as much pain on others as she can in protest against the absence of any moral universe.

One would say that the *anagnorisis,* or discovery, in this play is Hedda's realization that she is trapped and about to be blackmailed into an affair with Judge Brack. The *peripeteia,* or reversal, is her burning of Eilert Lövborg's manuscript. Hedda's *hamartia,* or tragic flaw, is her envy of anyone else's freedom or meaning, such as Lövborg's life work; and her *hubris,* or pride, is represented by her father's horse pistols, which she keeps playing with. At the end of the play, her *nemesis,* or retribution, comes with her realization that she has no recourse but to shoot herself.

One translator of *Hedda Gabler,* Una Ellis-Fermor, describes Hedda's tragic flaw thus: "Hedda refuses to discover herself, and her conflict and her tragedy are the result of this refusal." To Eva Le Gallienne, the celebrated actress and translator: "There is a 'fallen angel' quality about her [Hedda], and that, in spite of our dislike for her, fills us with pity—we are appalled at such tragic waste." And Michael Meyer, another translator of Ibsen, sums it up: "[Ibsen] intended the play as a tragedy of the purposelessness of life."

Some people might question whether *Hedda Gabler* is indeed a tragedy based on classical principles; but there can be no denying that Ibsen has used the tragic form to present us with a dramatic portrait that is relevant to our lives. Surely Hedda ends up as pure *pharmakos,* or scapegoat, for all the meaninglessness of the middle class, the leisure class that has come into existence as a result of the Industrial Revolution.

The Emperor Jones (1920) is an early work of Eugene O'Neill (1888–1953). O'Neill went on to write more ambitious plays, such as *Beyond the Horizon* (1920), *Desire under the Elms* (1924), *Strange Interlude* (1926–27), *Mourning Becomes Electra* (1929–31), and the soaring and soul-searing autobiographical play *Long Day's Journey into Night* (1941). But none of these later O'Neill plays has the stark simplicity and sheer expressionist terror of *The Emperor Jones.* From the early dislodgement of Jones in the play, the action heads like an arrow toward the final target catastrophe. There are only eight scenes in the play: the first is about fourteen pages long; thereafter the scenes are relatively short—two to four pages each—until the play reaches its final denouement.

The play takes place in the West Indies "palace" where Jones keeps his "trash niggers" in their place through his cool contempt and a pearl-handled revolver. Jones himself once worked as a Pullman car porter in the service of the white man, and he boasts he has come "from stowaway to Emperor in two years." But one also senses that Jones has more contempt for himself than he has for others: his two first names, Emperor and Brutus, indicate his own profound adversarial attitude toward himself. Thus Jones becomes a metaphor for modern man who is divided against himself and cannot resolve his ambivalence.

The white man, Smithers, with his slick cynicism and his riding whip, seems to be a chorus figure modeled after the chorus in Greek tragedy, and he is there as a witness and commentator on the tragedy that Jones himself is about to undergo. The offstage beating of the tom-tom, with its insistent throbbing pulse beat, is another chorus element that remains through the rest of the play. Once Jones flees from the palace, the play becomes an exercise in atavism; Jones is driven back to his primal roots, through the dark unconscious forest where he faces the Little Formless Fears—until finally he sheds his clothes and the last vestiges of civilization, as he is taken back to the African slave trade, then back to the Congo, and at last all the way back to his past as a reptile. It is all back, back, back, until Jones himself has his tragic discovery, or *anagnorisis,* his realization of the grim agony of his own origin.

The *peripeteia,* or reversal, takes place with the tom-toms and the Emperor's escape from the palace, to begin his long journey downward into himself. His *hamartia,* or tragic flaw, is his contempt for others and for himself, and his *hubris,* or pride, is represented by the pearl-handled revolver that has six bullets in it—a symbol for Jones's delusion that he can control his own destiny. The *nemesis,* or punishment, comes with the Little Formless Fears, which are like the Eumenides, or Furies, that haunt characters in Greek tragedy. By the end of the play, Jones has become *pharmakos,* or scapegoat, for the whole of Western civilization, the exploiters and the exploited.

Eugene O'Neill was very concerned that Americans should have the ability to rise to the heights of tragic awareness. He insisted on the development of an American theater that would provide some insight into the contemporary human condition:

The playwright today must dig at the roots of the sickness of today as he feels it—the death of the old God and the failure of science and materialism to give any

satisfying new one for the surviving primitive religious
instinct to find a meaning for life in and to comfort its
fears of death with. It seems to me that anyone trying to
do big work nowadays must have this big subject behind
all the little subjects of his plays or novels, or he is
simply scribbling around the surface of things and has
no more real status than a parlor entertainer.

—Eugene O'Neill, Letter to George Jean Nathan

In these six great tragedies, we see how heroes struggle
with some higher power outside themselves and achieve
some tragic insight into themselves and their world before
being overwhelmed in some final catastrophe. And we also
see how tragedy usually consists of six key elements—*anagnorisis* (discovery), *peripeteia* (reversal), *hamartia* (tragic
flaw), *hubris* (pride), *nemesis* (retribution), and *pharmakos*
(scapegoat). The circumstances may vary but the principles
remain the same.

The ambition of this book and, as we said at the outset, the
effect of tragedies in general is to shake or shock us so that
we may come to realize, if only for an instant, who we are
and why we are the way we are.

WILLIAM PACKARD

NEW YORK
JANUARY 1989

AGAMEMNON

BY
Aeschylus

TRANSLATED BY
Richmond Lattimore

CHARACTERS

WATCHMAN

CLYTAEMNESTRA

HERALD

AGAMEMNON

CASSANDRA

AEGISTHUS

CHORUS *of Argive elders*

*Attendants of Clytaemnestra, Attendants of Agamemnon;
Bodyguard of Aegisthus (all silent parts)*

TIME: *directly after the fall of Troy.*

SCENE: ARGOS, *before the palace of* KING AGAMEMNON. *The* WATCHMAN, *who speaks the opening lines, is posted on the roof of the palace.* CLYTAEMNESTRA'S *entrances are made from a door in the center of the stage; all others, from the wings.*

[*The* WATCHMAN, *alone.*]
I ask the gods some respite from the weariness
of this watchtime measured by years I lie awake
elbowed upon the Atreidae's roof dogwise to mark
the grand processionals of all the stars of night
burdened with winter and again with heat for men,   5
dynasties in their shining blazoned on the air,
these stars, upon their wane and when the rest
    arise.

I wait; to read the meaning in that beacon light,
a blaze of fire to carry out of Troy the rumor
and outcry of its capture; to such end a lady's   10
male strength of heart in its high confidence
    ordains.
Now as this bed stricken with night and drenched
    with dew
I keep, nor ever with kind dreams for company:
since fear in sleep's place stands forever at my head
against strong closure of my eyes, or any rest: 15
I mince such medicine against sleep failed: I sing,
only to weep again the pity of this house
no longer, as once, administered in the grand way.
Now let there be again redemption from distress,
the flare burning from the blackness in good augury.   20

[*A light shows in the distance.*]
Oh, hail, blaze of the darkness, harbinger of day's
shining, and of processionals and dance and choirs
of multitudes in Argos for this day of grace.
Ahoy!

I cry the news aloud to Agamemnon's queen,   25
that she may rise up from her bed of state with
    speed
to raise the rumor of gladness welcoming this
    beacon,
and singing rise, if truly the citadel of Ilium
has fallen, as the shining of this flare proclaims.
I also, I, will make my choral prelude, since   30
my lord's dice cast aright are counted as my own,
and mine the tripled sixes of this torchlit throw.

May it only happen. May my king come home, and I
take up within this hand the hand I love. The rest
I leave to silence; for an ox stands huge upon   35
my tongue. The house itself, could it take voice,
    might speak
aloud and plain. I speak to those who understand,
but if they fail, I have forgotten everything.

                    [*Exit. The* CHORUS *enters, speaking.*]
Ten years since the great contestants   40
of Priam's right,
Menelaus and Agamemnon, my lord,
twin throned, twin sceptered, in twofold power
of kings from God, the Atreidae,
put forth from this shore   45
the thousand ships of the Argives,
the strength and the armies.
Their cry of war went shrill from the heart,
as eagles stricken in agony
for young perished, high from the nest   50
eddy and circle
to bend and sweep of the wings' stroke,
lost far below
the fledglings, the nest, and the tendance.
Yet someone hears in the air, a god,   55
Apollo, Pan, or Zeus, the high
thin wail of these sky-guests, and drives
late to its mark
the Fury upon the transgressors.
So drives Zeus the great guest god   60

the Atreidae against Alexander:
for one woman's promiscuous sake
the struggling masses, legs tired,
knees grinding in dust,
spears broken in the onset.   65
Danaans and Trojans
they have it alike. It goes as it goes
now. The end will be destiny.
You cannot burn flesh or pour unguents,
not innocent cool tears,   70
that will soften the gods' stiff anger.

But we; dishonored, old in our bones,
cast off even then from the gathering horde,
stay here, to prop up
on staves the strength of a baby.   75
Since the young vigor that urges
inward to the heart
is frail as age, no warcraft yet perfect,
while beyond age, leaf
withered, man goes three footed   80
no stronger than a child is,
a dream that falters in daylight.

[CLYTAEMNESTRA *enters quietly. The* CHORUS
            continues to speak.]

But you, lady,
daughter of Tyndareus, Clytaemnestra, our queen:
What is there to be done? What new thing have you
      heard?
In persuasion of what   85
report do you order such sacrifice?
To all the gods of the city,
the high and the deep spirits,
to them of the sky and the marketplaces,   90
the altars blaze with oblations.
The staggered flame goes sky high
one place, then another,
drugged by the simple soft
persuasion of sacred unguents,   95

the deep stored oil of the kings.
Of these things what can be told
openly, speak.
Be healer to this perplexity
that grows now into darkness of thought,   100
while again sweet hope shining from the flames
beats back the pitiless pondering
of sorrow that eats my heart.

I have mastery yet to chant the wonder at the
    wayside
given to kings. Still by God's grace there surges
    within me   105
singing magic
grown to my life and power,
how the wild bird portent
hurled forth the Achaeans'
twin-stemmed power single-hearted,   110
lords of the youth of Hellas,
with spear and hand of strength
to the land of Teucrus.
Kings of birds to the kings of the ships,
one black, one blazed with silver,   115
clear seen by the royal house
on the right, the spear hand,
they lighted; watched by all
tore a hare, ripe, bursting with young unborn yet,
stayed from her last fleet running.   120
Sing sorrow, sorrow: but good win out in the end.

Then the grave seer of the host saw through to the
    hearts divided,
knew the fighting sons of Atreus feeding on the hare
with the host, their people.
Seeing beyond, he spoke: 125
"With time, this foray
shall stalk the castle of Priam.
Before then, under
the walls, Fate shall spoil
in violence the rich herds of the people.   130
Only let no doom of the gods darken
upon this huge iron forged to curb Troy—

from inward. Artemis the undefiled
is angered with pity
at the flying hounds of her father   135
eating the unborn young in the hare and the
    shivering mother.
She is sick at the eagles' feasting.
Sing sorrow, sorrow: but good win out in the end.

"Lovely you are and kind   140
to the tender young of ravening lions.
For sucklings of all the savage
beasts that lurk in the lonely places you have
    sympathy.
Grant meaning to these appearances
good, yet not without evil.   145
Healer Apollo, I pray you
let her not with crosswinds
bind the ships of the Danaans
to time-long anchorage   150
forcing a second sacrifice unholy, untasted,
working bitterness in the blood
and faith lost. For the terror returns like sickness to
    lurk in the house;
the secret anger remembers the child that shall be
    avenged."   155
Such, with great good things beside, rang out in the
    voice of Calchas,
these fatal signs from the birds by the way to the
    house of the princes,
wherewith in sympathy
sing sorrow, sorrow: but good win out in the end.

Zeus: whatever he may be, if this name   160
pleases him in invocation,
thus I call upon him.
I have pondered everything
yet I cannot find a way,
only Zeus, to cast this dead weight of ignorance   165
finally from out my brain.

He who in time long ago was great,
throbbing with gigantic strength,

shall be as if he never were, unspoken.   170
He who followed him has found
his master, and is gone.
Cry aloud without fear the victory of Zeus,
you will not have failed the truth: 175

Zeus, who guided men to think,
who has laid it down that wisdom
comes alone through suffering.
Still there drips in sleep against the heart
grief of memory; against   180
our pleasure we are temperate.
From the gods who sit in grandeur
grace comes somehow violent.

On that day the elder king
of the Achaean ships, no more
strict against the prophet's word,   185
turned with the crosswinds of fortune,
when no ship sailed, no pail was full,
and the Achaean people sulked
fast against the shore at Aulis
facing Chalcis, where the tides ebb and surge: 190

and winds blew from the Strymon, bearing
sick idleness, ships tied fast, and hunger,
distraction of the mind, carelessness
for hull and cable;   195
with time's length bent to double measure
by delay crumbled the flower and pride
of Argos. Then against the bitter wind
the seer's voice clashed out
another medicine   200
more hateful yet, and spoke of Artemis, so that the
    kings
dashed their staves to the ground and could not
    hold their tears.

The elder lord spoke aloud before them: 205
"My fate is angry if I disobey these,
but angry if I slaughter

this child, the beauty of my house,
with maiden blood shed staining
these father's hands beside the altar.   210
What of these things goes now without disaster?
How shall I fail my ships
and lose my faith of battle?
For them to urge such sacrifice of innocent blood   215
angrily, for their wrath is great—it is right. May all
   be well yet."

But when necessity's yoke was put upon him
he changed, and from the heart the breath came   220
   bitter
and sacrilegious, utterly infidel,
to warp a will now to be stopped at nothing.
The sickening in men's minds, tough,
reckless in fresh cruelty brings daring. He endured
   then
to sacrifice his daughter
to stay the strength of war waged for a woman,   225
first offering for the ships' sake.

Her supplications and her cries of father
were nothing, nor the child's lamentation
to kings passioned for battle.   230
The father prayed, called to his men to lift her
with strength of hand swept in her robes aloft
and prone above the altar, as you might lift
a goat for sacrifice, with guards
against the lips' sweet edge, to check   235
the curse cried on the house of Atreus
by force of bit and speech drowned in strength.

Pouring then to the ground her saffron mantle
she struck the sacrificers with   240
the eyes' arrows of pity,
lovely as in a painted scene, and striving
to speak—as many times
at the kind festive table of her father
she had sung, and in the clear voice of a stainless
   maiden   245

with love had graced the song
of worship when the third cup was poured.

What happened next I saw not, neither speak it.
The crafts of Calchas fail not of outcome.
Justice so moves that those only learn   250
who suffer; and the future
you shall know when it has come; before then,
    forget it.
It is grief too soon given.
All will come clear in the next dawn's sunlight.
Let good fortune follow these things as   255
she who is here desires,
our Apian land's single-hearted protectress.

[*The* CHORUS *now turns toward* CLYTAEMNESTRA,
                    and the leader speaks to her.]
I have come in reverence, Clytaemnestra, of your
    power.
For when the man is gone and the throne void, his
    right
falls to the prince's lady, and honor must be given.   260
Is it some grace—or otherwise—that you have
    heard
to make you sacrifice at messages of good hope?
I should be glad to hear, but must not blame your
    silence.

CLYTAEMNESTRA
As it was said of old, may the dawn child be born
to be an angel of blessing from the kindly night.   265
You shall know joy beyond all you ever hoped to
    hear.
The men of Argos have taken Priam's citadel.

CHORUS
What have you said? Your words escaped my
    unbelief.

CLYTAEMNESTRA
The Achaeans are in Troy. Is that not clear enough?

CHORUS
  This slow delight steals over me to bring forth tears.   270

CLYTAEMNESTRA
  Yes, for your eyes betray the loyal heart within.

CHORUS
  Yet how can I be certain? Is there some evidence?

CLYTAEMNESTRA
  There is, there must be; unless a god has lied to me.

CHORUS
  Is it dream visions, easy to believe, you credit?

CLYTAEMNESTRA
  I accept nothing from a brain that is dull with sleep.   275

CHORUS
  The charm, then, of some rumor, that made rich
    your hope?

CLYTAEMNESTRA
  Am I some young girl, that you find my thoughts so
    silly?

CHORUS
  How long, then, is it since the citadel was stormed?

CLYTAEMNESTRA
  It is the night, the mother of this dawn I hailed.

CHORUS
  What kind of messenger could come in speed like
    this?   280

CLYTAEMNESTRA
  Hephaestus, who cast forth the shining blaze from
    Ida.
  And beacon after beacon picking up the flare
  carried it here; Ida to the Hermaean horn

of Lemnos, where it shone above the isle, and next
the sheer rock face of Zeus on Athos caught it up;   285
and plunging skyward to arch the shoulders of the
    sea
the strength of the running flare in exultation,
pine timbers flaming into gold, like the sunrise,
brought the bright message to Macistus' sentinel
    cliffs,
who, never slow nor in the carelessness of sleep   290
caught up, sent on his relay in the courier chain,
and far across Euripus' streams the beacon flare
carried to signal watchmen on Messapion.
These took it again in turn, and heaping high a pile
of silvery brush flamed it to throw the message on.   295
And the flare sickened never, but grown stronger
    yet
outleapt the river valley of Asopus like
the very moon for shining, to Cithaeron's scar
to waken the next station of the flaming post.
These watchers, not contemptuous of the far-
    thrown blaze,   300
kindled another beacon vaster than commanded.
The light leaned high above Gorgopis' staring
    marsh,
and striking Aegyplanctus' mountaintop, drove on
yet one more relay, lest the flare die down in speed.
Kindled once more with stintless heaping force,
    they send   305
the beard of flame to hugeness, passing far beyond
the promontory that gazes on the Saronic strait
and flaming far, until it plunged at last to strike
the steep rock of Arachnus near at hand, our
    watchtower.
And thence there fell upon this house of Atreus'
    sons   310
the flare whose fathers mount to the Idaean beacon.
These are the changes on my torchlight
    messengers,
one from another running out the laps assigned.
The first and the last sprinters have the victory.
By such proof and such symbol I announce to you   315
my lord at Troy has sent his messengers to me.

CHORUS
The gods, lady, shall have my prayers and thanks
straightway.
And yet to hear your story till all wonder fades
would be my wish, could you but tell it once again.

CLYTAEMNESTRA
The Achaeans have got Troy, upon this very day. 320
I think the city echoes with a clash of cries.
Pour vinegar and oil into the selfsame bowl,
you could not say they mix in friendship, but fight
on.
Thus variant sound the voices of the conquerors
and conquered, from the opposition of their fates. 325
Trojans are stooping now to gather in their arms
their dead, husbands and brothers; children lean to
clasp
the aged who begot them, crying upon the death
of those most dear, from lips that never will be free.
The Achaeans have their midnight work after the
fighting 330
that sets them down to feed on all the city has,
ravenous, headlong, by no rank and file assigned,
but as each man has drawn his shaken lot by
chance.
And in the Trojan houses that their spears have
taken
they settle now, free of the open sky, the frosts 335
and dampness of the evening; without sentinels set
they sleep the sleep of happiness the whole night
through.
And if they reverence the gods who hold the city
and all the holy temples of the captured land,
they, the despoilers, might not be despoiled in turn. 340
Let not their passion overwhelm them; let no lust
seize on these men to violate what they must not.
The run to safety and home is yet to make; they
must turn
the pole, and run the backstretch of the double
course.
Yet, though the host come home without offense to
high 345

gods, even so the anger of these slaughtered men
may never sleep. Oh, let there be no fresh wrong
    done!

Such are the thoughts you hear from me, a woman
    merely.
Yet may the best win through, that none may fail to
    see.
Of all good things to wish this is my dearest choice.   350

CHORUS
My lady, no grave man could speak with better
    grace.
I have listened to the proofs of your tale, and I
    believe,
and go to make my glad thanksgivings to the gods.
This pleasure is not unworthy of the grief that gave
    it.

O Zeus our lord and Night beloved,   355
bestower of power and beauty,
you slung above the bastions of Troy
the binding net, that none, neither great
nor young, might outleap
the gigantic toils   360
of enslavement and final disaster.
I gaze in awe on Zeus of the guests
who wrung from Alexander such payment.
He bent the bow with slow care, that neither
the shaft might hurdle the stars, nor fall   365
spent to the earth, short driven.

They have the stroke of Zeus to tell of.
This thing is clear and you may trace it.
He acted as he had decreed. A man thought
the gods deigned not to punish mortals   370
who trampled down the delicacy of things
inviolable. That man was wicked.
The curse on great daring
shines clear; it wrings atonement   375
from those high hearts that drive to evil,
from houses blossoming to pride

and peril. Let there be
wealth without tears; enough for
the wise man who will ask no further.   380
There is not any armor
in gold against perdition
for him who spurns the high altar
of Justice down to the darkness.

Persuasion the persistent overwhelms him,   385
she, strong daughter of designing Ruin.
And every medicine is vain; the sin
smolders not, but burns to evil beauty.
As cheap bronze tortured   390
at the touchstone relapses
to blackness and grime, so this man
tested shows vain
as a child that strives to catch the bird flying
and wins shame that shall bring down his city.   395
No god will hear such a man's entreaty,
but whoso turns to these ways
they strike him down in his wickedness.
This was Paris: he came
to the house of the sons of Atreus,   400
stole the woman away, and shamed
the guest's right of the board shared.

She left among her people the stir and clamor
of shields and of spearheads,   405
the ships to sail and the armor.
She took to Ilium her dowry, death.
She stepped forth lightly between the gates
daring beyond all daring. And the prophets
about the great house wept aloud and spoke:
"Alas, alas for the house and for the champions,   410
alas for the bed signed with their love together.
Here now is silence, scorned, unreproachful.
The agony of his loss is clear before us.
Longing for her who lies beyond the sea
he shall see a phantom queen in his household.   415
Her images in their beauty
are bitterness to her lord now

where in the emptiness of eyes
all passion has faded."

Shining in dreams the sorrowful   420
memories pass; they bring him
vain delight only.
It is vain, to dream and to see splendors,
and the image slipping from the arms' embrace
escapes, not to return again,   425
on wings drifting down the ways of sleep.
Such have the sorrows been in the house by the
    hearthside;
such have there been, and yet there are worse than
    these.
In all Hellas, for those who swarmed to the host
the heartbreaking misery   430
shows in the house of each.
Many are they who are touched at the heart by
    these things.
Those they sent forth they knew;
now, in place of the young men
urns and ashes are carried home   435
to the houses of the fighters.

The god of war, money changer of dead bodies,
held the balance of his spear in the fighting,
and from the corpse-fires at Ilium   440
sent to their dearest the dust
heavy and bitter with tears shed
packing smooth the urns with
ashes that once were men.
They praise them through their tears, how this man 445
knew well the craft of battle, how another
went down splendid in the slaughter:
and all for some strange woman.
Thus they mutter in secrecy,
and the slow anger creeps below their grief   450
at Atreus' sons and their quarrels.
There by the walls of Ilium
the young men in their beauty keep
graves deep in the alien soil
they hated and they conquered.   455

The citizens speak: their voice is dull with hatred.
The curse of the people must be paid for.
There lurks for me in the hooded night
terror of what may be told me.   460
The gods fail not to mark
those who have killed many.
The black Furies stalking the man
fortunate beyond all right
wrench back again the set of his life   465
and drop him to darkness. There among
the ciphers there is no more comfort
in power. And the vaunt of high glory
is bitterness; for God's thunderbolts
crash on the towering mountains.   470
Let me attain no envied wealth,
let me not plunder cities,
neither be taken in turn, and face
life in the power of another.

> [*Various members of the* CHORUS, *speaking
> severally.*]

From the beacon's bright message   475
the fleet rumor runs
through the city. If this be real
who knows? Perhaps the gods have sent some lie to
    us.

Who of us is so childish or so reft of wit
that by the beacon's messages   480
his heart flamed must despond again
when the tale changes in the end?

It is like a woman indeed
to take the rapture before the fact has shown for
    true.

They believe too easily, are too quick to shift   485
from ground to ground; and swift indeed
the rumor voiced by a woman dies again.

Now we shall understand these torches and their
    shining,

the beacons, and the interchange of flame and
   flame.   490
They may be real; yet bright and dreamwise ecstasy
in light's appearance might have charmed our hearts
   awry.
I see a herald coming from the beach, his brows
shaded with sprigs of olive; and upon his feet
the dust, dry sister of the mire, makes plain to me   495
that he will find a voice, not merely kindle flame
from mountain timber, and make signals from the
   smoke,
but tell us outright, whether to be happy, or—
but I shrink back from naming the alternative.
That which appeared was good; may yet more good
   be given.   500

And any man who prays that different things befall
the city, may he reap the crime of his own heart.

> [*The* HERALD *enters, and speaks.*]

Soil of my fathers, Argive earth I tread upon,
in daylight of the tenth year I have come back to
   you.
All my hopes broke but one, and this I have at last.   505
I never could have dared to dream that I might die
in Argos, and be buried in this beloved soil.
Hail to the Argive land and to its sunlight, hail
to its high sovereign, Zeus, and to the Pythian king.
May you no longer shower your arrows on our   510
   heads.
Beside Scamandrus you were grim; be satisfied
and turn to savior now and healer of our hurts,
my lord Apollo. Gods of the marketplace
   assembled,
I greet you all, and my own patron deity
Hermes, beloved herald, in whose right all heralds   515
are sacred; and you heroes that sent forth the host,
propitiously take back all that the spear has left.
O great hall of the kings and house beloved; seats
of sanctity; divinities that face the sun:
if ever before, look now with kind and glowing eyes   520
to greet our king in state after so long a time.

He comes, Lord Agamemnon, bearing light in
   gloom
to you, and to all that are assembled here.
Salute him with good favor, as he well deserves,
the man who has wrecked Ilium with the spade of
   Zeus   525
vindictive, whereby all their plain has been laid
   waste.
Gone are their altars, the sacred places of the gods
are gone, and scattered all the seed within the
   ground.
With such a yoke as this gripped to the neck of
   Troy
he comes, the king, Atreus' elder son, a man   530
fortunate to be honored far above all men
alive; not Paris nor the city tied to him
can boast he did more than was done him in return.
Guilty of rape and theft, condemned, he lost the
   prize
captured, and broke to sheer destruction all the   535
   house
of his fathers, with the very ground whereon it
   stood.
Twice over the sons of Priam have atoned their sins.

CHORUS
Hail and be glad, herald of the Achaean host.

HERALD
I am happy; I no longer ask the gods for death.

CHORUS
Did passion for your country so strip bare your   540
   heart?

HERALD
So that the tears broke in my eyes, for happiness.

CHORUS
You were taken with that sickness, then, that brings
   delight.

HERALD
  How? I cannot deal with such words until I
    understand.

CHORUS
  Struck with desire of those who loved as much
    again.

HERALD
  You mean our country longed for us, as we for   545
    home?

CHORUS
  So that I sighed, out of the darkness of my heart.

HERALD
  Whence came this black thought to afflict the mind
    with fear?

CHORUS
  Long since it was my silence kept disaster off.

HERALD
  But how? There were some you feared when the
    kings went away?

CHORUS
  So much that as you said now, even death were   550
    grace.

HERALD
  Well: the end has been good. And in the length of
    time
  part of our fortune you could say held favorable,
  but part we cursed again. And who, except the
    gods,
  can live time through forever without any pain?
  Were I to tell you of the hard work done, the nights 555
  exposed, the cramped sea-quarters, the foul beds—
    what part
  of day's disposal did we not cry out loud?

Ashore, the horror stayed with us and grew. We lay
against the ramparts of our enemies, and from
the sky, and from the ground, the meadow dews
   came out   560
to soak our clothes and fill our hair with lice. And if
I were to tell of winter time, when all birds died,
the snows of Ida past endurance she sent down,
or summer heat, when in the lazy noon the sea
fell level and asleep under a windless sky—   565
but why live such grief over again? That time is
   gone
for us, and gone for those who died. Never again
need they rise up, nor care again for anything.
Why must a live man count the numbers of the
   slain,
why grieve at fortune's wrath that fades to break
   once more?'   570
I call a long farewell to all our unhappiness.
For us, survivors of the Argive armament,
the pleasure wins, pain casts no weight in the
   opposite scale.
And here, in this sun's shining, we can boast aloud,
whose fame has gone with wings across the land
   and sea: 575
"Upon a time the Argive host took Troy, and on
the houses of the gods who live in Hellas nailed
the spoils, to be the glory of days long ago."
And they who hear such things shall call this city
   blest
and the leaders of the host; and high the grace of
   God   580
shall be exalted, that did this. You have the story.

CHORUS

I must give way; your story shows that I was wrong.
Old men are always young enough to learn, with
   profit.
But Clytaemnestra and her house must hear, above
others, this news that makes luxurious my life.   585

[CLYTAEMNESTRA *comes forward and*
speaks.]

I raised my cry of joy, and it was long ago
when the first beacon flare of message came by
    night
to speak of capture and of Ilium's overthrow.
But there was one who laughed at me, who said:
    "You trust   590
in beacons so, and you believe that Troy has fallen?
How like a woman, for the heart to lift so light."
Men spoke like that; they thought I wandered in my
    wits;
yet I made sacrifice, and in the womanish strain
voice after voice caught up the cry along the city   595
to echo in the temples of the gods and bless
and still the fragrant flame that melts the sacrifice.

Why should you tell me then the whole long tale at
    large
when from my lord himself I shall hear all the
    story?
But now, how best to speed my preparation to   600
receive my honored lord come home again—what
    else
is light more sweet for woman to behold than this,
to spread the gates before her husband home from
    war
and saved by God's hand?—take this message to
    the king:
Come, and with speed, back to the city that longs
    for him,   605
and may he find a wife within his house as true
as on the day he left her, watchdog of the house
gentle to him alone, fierce to his enemies,
and such a woman in all her ways as this, who has
not broken the seal upon her in the length of days.   610
With no man else have I known delight, nor any
    shame
of evil speech, more than I know how to temper
    bronze.

[CLYTAEMNESTRA *goes to the back of the*
stage.]

HERALD
A vaunt like this, so loaded as it is with truth,
it well becomes a highborn lady to proclaim.

CHORUS
Thus has she spoken to you, and well you
understand,   615
words that impress interpreters whose thought is
clear.
But tell me, herald; I would learn of Menelaus,
that power beloved in this land. Has he survived
also, and come with you back to his home again?

HERALD
I know no way to lie and make my tale so fair   620
that friends could reap joy of it for any length of
time.

CHORUS
Is there no means to speak us fair, and yet tell the
truth?
It will not hide, when truth and good are torn
asunder.

HERALD
He is gone out of the sight of the Achaean host,
vessel and man alike. I speak no falsehood there.   625

CHORUS
Was it when he had put out from Ilium in your
sight,
or did a storm that struck you both whirl him away?

HERALD
How like a master bowman you have hit the mark
and in your speech cut a long sorrow to brief
stature.

CHORUS
But then the rumor in the host that sailed beside,   630
was it that he had perished, or might yet be living?

HERALD
> No man knows. There is none could tell us that for
>   sure
> except the Sun, from whom this earth has life and
>   increase.

CHORUS
> How did this storm, by wrath of the divinities,
> strike on our multitude at sea? How did it end?   635

HERALD
> It is not well to stain the blessing of this day
> with speech of evil weight. Such gods are honored
>   apart.
> And when the messenger of a shaken host, sad
>   faced,
> brings to his city news it prayed never to hear,
> this scores one wound upon the body of the people;   640
> and that from many houses many men are slain
> by the two-lashed whip dear to the War God's hand,
>   this turns
> disaster double-bladed, bloodily made two.
> The messenger so freighted with a charge of tears
> should make his song of triumph at the Furies'
>   door.   645
> But, carrying the fair message of our hopes'
>   salvation,
> come home to a glad city's hospitality,
> how shall I mix my gracious news with foul, and tell
> of the storm on the Achaeans by God's anger sent?
> For they, of old the deepest enemies, sea and fire,   650
> made a conspiracy and gave the oath of hand
> to blast in ruin our unhappy Argive army.
> At night the sea began to rise in waves of death.
> Ship against ship the Thracian stormwind shattered
>   us,
> and gored and split, our vessels, swept in violence   655
> of storm and whirlwind, beaten by the breaking
>   rain,
> drove on in darkness, spun by the wicked
>   shepherd's hand.

But when the sun came up again to light the dawn,
we saw the Aegaean Sea blossoming with dead
    men,
the men of Achaea, and the wreckage of their ships.   660
For us, and for our ship, some god, no man, by
    guile
or by entreaty's force prevailing, laid his hand
upon the helm and brought us through with hull
    unscarred.
Life-giving fortune deigned to take our ship in
    charge
that neither riding in deep water she took the surf   665
nor drove to shoal and break upon some rocky
    shore.
But then, delivered from death at sea, in the pale
    day,
incredulous of our own luck, we shepherded
in our sad thoughts the fresh disaster of the fleet
so pitifully torn and shaken by the storm.   670
Now of these others, if there are any left alive
they speak of us as men who perished, must they
    not?
Even as we, who fear that they are gone. But may
it all come well in the end. For Menelaus: be sure
if any of them come back that he will be the first.   675
If he is still where some sun's gleam can track him
    down,
alive and open-eyed, by blessed hand of God
who willed that not yet should his seed be utterly
    gone,
there is some hope that he will still come home
    again.
You have heard all; and be sure, you have heard the
    truth.   680

           [*The* HERALD *goes out.*]

CHORUS
Who is he that named you so
fatally in every way?
Could it be some mind unseen

in divination of your destiny
shaping to the lips that name   685
for the bride of spears and blood,
Helen, which is death? Appropriately
death of ships, death of men and cities
from the bower's soft curtained   690
and secluded luxury she sailed then,
driven on the giant west wind,
and armored men in their thousands came,
huntsmen down the oar blade's fading footprint   695
to struggle in blood with those
who by the banks of Simoeis
beached their hulls where the leaves break.

And on Ilium in truth
in the likeness of the name   700
the sure purpose of the Wrath drove
marriage with death: for the guest board
shamed, and Zeus kindly to strangers,
the vengeance wrought on those men
who graced in too loud voice the bride-song   705
fallen to their lot to sing,
the kinsmen and the brothers.
And changing its song's measure
the ancient city of Priam   710
chants in high strain of lamentation,
calling Paris him of the fatal marriage;
for it endured its life's end
in desolation and tears
and the piteous blood of its people.   715

Once a man fostered in his house
a lion cub, from the mother's milk
torn, craving the breast given.
In the first steps of its young life   720
mild, it played with children
and delighted the old.
Caught in the arm's cradle
they pampered it like a newborn child,
shining-eyed and broken to the hand   725
to stay the stress of its hunger.

But it grew with time, and the lion
in the blood strain came out; it paid
grace to those who had fostered it
in blood and death for the sheep flocks,   730
a grim feast forbidden.
The house reeked with blood run
nor could its people beat down the bane,
the giant murderer's onslaught.
This thing they raised in their house was blessed   735
by God to be priest of destruction.

And that which first came to the city of Ilium,
call it a dream of calm
and the wind dying,
the loveliness and luxury of much gold,   740
the melting shafts of the eyes' glances,
the blossom that breaks the heart with longing.
But she turned in midstep of her course to make
bitter the consummation,   745
whirling on Priam's people
to blight with her touch and nearness.
Zeus hospitable sent her,
a vengeance to make brides weep.

It has been made long since and grown old among
    men,   750
this saying: human wealth
grown to fullness of stature
breeds again nor dies without issue.
From high good fortune in the blood   755
blossoms the quenchless agony.
Far from others I hold my own
mind; only the act of evil
breeds others to follow,
young sins in its own likeness.   760
Houses clear in their right are given
children in all loveliness.

But Pride aging is made
in men's dark actions
ripe with the young pride   765
late or soon when the dawn of destiny

comes and birth is given
to the spirit none may fight nor beat down,
sinful Daring; and in those halls
the black-visaged Disasters stamped   770
in the likeness of their fathers.

And Righteousness is a shining in
the smoke of mean houses.
Her blessing is on the just man.   775
From high halls starred with gold by reeking hands
she turns back
with eyes that glance away to the simple in heart,
spurning the strength of gold
stamped false with flattery.   780
And all things she steers to fulfilment.

[AGAMEMNON *enters in a chariot, with* CASSANDRA
            beside him. The CHORUS *speaks to him.*]
Behold, my king: sacker of Troy's citadel,
own issue of Atreus.
How shall I hail you? How give honor   785
not crossing too high nor yet bending short
of this time's graces?
For many among men are they who set high
the show of honor, yet break justice.
If one be unhappy, all else are fain   790
to grieve with him: yet the teeth of sorrow
come nowise near to the heart's edge.
And in joy likewise they show joy's semblance,
and torture the face to the false smile.
Yet the good shepherd, who knows his flock,   795
the eyes of men cannot lie to him,
that with water of feigned
love seem to smile from the true heart.
But I: when you marshaled this armament
for Helen's sake, I will not hide it,   800
in ugly style you were written in my heart
for steering aslant the mind's course
to bring home by blood
sacrifice and dead men that wild spirit.
But now, in love drawn up from the deep heart,   805
not skimmed at the edge, we hail you.

You have won, your labor is made gladness.
Ask all men: you will learn in time
which of your citizens have been just
in the city's sway, which were reckless.   810

AGAMEMNON

To Argos first, and to the gods within the land,
I must give due greeting; they have worked with me
    to bring
me home; they helped me in the vengeance I have
    wrought
on Priam's city. Not from the lips of men the gods
heard justice, but in one firm cast they laid their   815
    votes
within the urn of blood that Ilium must die
and all her people; while above the opposite vase
the hand hovered and there was hope, but no vote
    fell.
The stormclouds of their ruin live; the ash that dies
upon them gushes still in smoke their pride of   820
    wealth.
For all this we must thank the gods with grace of
    much
high praise and memory, we who fenced within our
    toils
of wrath the city; and, because one woman strayed,
the beast of Argos broke them, the fierce young
    within
the horse, the armored people who marked out   825
    their leap
against the setting of the Pleiades. A wild
and bloody lion swarmed above the towers of Troy
to glut its hunger lapping at the blood of kings.

This to the gods, a prelude strung to length of
    words.
But, for the thought you spoke, I heard and I
    remember   830
and stand behind you. For I say that it is true.
In few men is it part of nature to respect
a friend's prosperity without begrudging him,
as envy's wicked poison settling to the heart

piles up the pain in one sick with unhappiness,   835
who, staggered under sufferings that are all his own,
winces again to the vision of a neighbor's bliss.
And I can speak, for I have seen, I know it well,
this mirror of companionship, this shadow's ghost,
these men who seemed my friends in all sincerity.   840
One man of them all, Odysseus, he who sailed
    unwilling,
once yoked to me carried his harness, nor went
    slack.
Dead though he be or living, I can say it still.

Now in the business of the city and the gods
we must ordain full conclave of all citizens   845
and take our counsel. We shall see what element
is strong, and plan that it shall keep its virtue still.
But that which must be healed—we must use
    medicine,
or burn, or amputate, with kind intention, take
all means at hand that might beat down corruption's
    pain.   850
So to the king's house and the home about the
    hearth
I take my way, with greeting to the gods within
who sent me forth, and who have brought me home
    once more.
My prize was conquest; may it never fail again.

[CLYTAEMNESTRA *comes forward and*
                                speaks.]

Grave gentlemen of Argolis assembled here,   855
I take no shame to speak aloud before you all
the love I bear my husband. In the lapse of time
modesty fades; it is human.
                        What I tell you now
I learned not from another; this is my own sad life
all the long years this man was gone at Ilium.   860
It is evil and a thing of terror when a wife
sits in the house forlorn with no man by, and hears
rumors that like a fever die to break again,
and men come in with news of fear, and on their
    heels

another messenger, with worse news to cry aloud   865
here in this house. Had Agamemnon taken all
the wounds the tale whereof was carried home to
      me,
he had been cut full of gashes like a fishing net.
If he had died each time that rumor told his death,
he must have been some triple-bodied Geryon   870
back from the dead with threefold cloak of earth
      upon
his body, and killed once for every shape assumed.
Because such tales broke out forever on my rest,
many a time they cut me down and freed my throat   875
from the noose overslung where I had caught it fast.
And therefore is your son, in whom my love and
      yours
are sealed and pledged, not here to stand with us
      today,
Orestes. It were right; yet do not be amazed.
Strophius of Phocis, comrade in arms and faithful
      friend   880
to you, is keeping him. He spoke to me of peril
on two counts; of your danger under Ilium,
and here, of revolution and the clamorous people
who might cast down the council—since it lies in
      men's
nature to trample on the fighter already down.   885
Such my excuse to you, and without subterfuge.

For me: the rippling springs that were my tears
      have dried
utterly up, nor left one drop within. I keep
the pain upon my eyes where late at night I wept
over the beacons long ago set for your sake,   890
untended left forever. In the midst of dreams
the whisper that a gnat's thin wings could winnow
      broke
my sleep apart. I thought I saw you suffer wounds
more than the time that slept with me could ever
      hold.

Now all my suffering is past, with griefless heart   895
I hail this man, the watchdog of the fold and hall;

the stay that keeps the ship alive; the post to grip
groundward the towering roof; a father's single
   child;
land seen by sailors after all their hope was gone;
splendor of daybreak shining from the night of
   storm;   900
the running spring a parched wayfarer strays upon.
Oh, it is sweet to escape from all necessity!

Such is my greeting to him, that he well deserves.
Let none bear malice; for the harm that went before
I took, and it was great.
                    Now, my beloved one,   905
step from your chariot; yet let not your foot, my
   lord,
sacker of Ilium, touch the earth. My maidens there!
Why this delay? Your task has been appointed you,
to strew the ground before his feet with tapestries.
Let there spring up into the house he never hoped   910
to see, where Justice leads him in, a crimson path.

In all things else, my heart's unsleeping care shall
   act
with the gods' aid to set aright what fate ordained.

[CLYTAEMNESTRA'S *handmaidens spread a bright
carpet between the chariot and the door.*]

AGAMEMNON
Daughter of Leda, you who kept my house for me,
there is one way your welcome matched my
   absence well.   915
You strained it to great length. Yet properly to
   praise
me thus belongs by right to other lips, not yours.
And all this—do not try in woman's ways to make
me delicate, nor, as if I were some Asiatic,
bow down to earth and with wide mouth cry out to   920
   me,
nor cross my path with jealousy by strewing the
   ground

with robes. Such state becomes the gods, and none
   beside.
I am a mortal, a man; I cannot trample upon
these tinted splendors without fear thrown in my
   path.
I tell you, as a man, not god, to reverence me.   925
Discordant is the murmur at such treading down
of lovely things; while God's most lordly gift to man
is decency of mind. Call that man only blest
who has in sweet tranquillity brought his life to
   close.
If I could only act as such, my hope is good.   930

CLYTAEMNESTRA
Yet tell me this one thing, and do not cross my will.

AGAMEMNON
My will is mine. I shall not make it soft for you.

CLYTAEMNESTRA
It was in fear surely that you vowed this course to
   God.

AGAMEMNON
No man has spoken knowing better what he said.

CLYTAEMNESTRA
If Priam had won as you have, what would he have   935
   done?

AGAMEMNON
I well believe he might have walked on tapestries.

CLYTAEMNESTRA
Be not ashamed before the bitterness of men.

AGAMEMNON
The people murmur, and their voice is great in
   strength.

CLYTAEMNESTRA
Yet he who goes unenvied shall not be admired.

AGAMEMNON
  Surely this lust for conflict is not womanlike?   940

CLYTAEMNESTRA
  Yet for the mighty even to give way is grace.

AGAMEMNON
  Does such a victory as this mean so much to you?

CLYTAEMNESTRA
  Oh, yield! The power is yours. Give way of your
    free will.

AGAMEMNON
  Since you must have it—here, let someone with all
    speed
  take off these sandals, slaves for my feet to tread
    upon.   945
  And as I crush these garments stained from the rich
    sea
  let no god's eyes of hatred strike me from afar.
  Great the extravagance, and great the shame I feel
  to spoil such treasure and such silver's worth of
    webs.

  So much for all this. Take this stranger girl within   950
  now, and be kind. The conqueror who uses softly
  his power, is watched from far in the kind eyes of
    God,
  and this slave's yoke is one no man will wear from
    choice.
  Gift of the host to me, and flower exquisite
  from all my many treasures, she attends me here.   955

  Now since my will was bent to listen to you in this
  my feet crush purple as I pass within the hall.

CLYTAEMNESTRA
  The sea is there, and who shall drain its yield? It
    breeds
  precious as silver, ever of itself renewed,

the purple ooze wherein our garments shall be
   dipped.   960
And by God's grace this house keeps full
   sufficiency
of all. Poverty is a thing beyond its thought.
I could have vowed to trample many splendors
   down
had such decree been ordained from the oracles
those days when all my study was to bring home
   your life.   965
For when the root lives yet the leaves will come
   again
to fence the house with shade against the Dog
   Star's heat,
and now you have come home to keep your hearth
   and house
you bring with you the symbol of our winter's
   warmth;
but when Zeus ripens the green clusters into wine 970
there shall be coolness in the house upon those
   days
because the master ranges his own halls once more.

Zeus, Zeus accomplisher, accomplish these my
   prayers.
Let your mind bring these things to pass. It is your
   will.

     [AGAMEMNON *and* CLYTAEMNESTRA *enter the*
        house. CASSANDRA *remains in the chariot.*
                   The CHORUS *speaks.*]
Why must this persistent fear   975
beat its wings so ceaselessly
and so close against my mantic heart?
Why this strain unwanted, unrepaid, thus
   prophetic?
Nor can valor of good hope   980
seated near the chambered depth
of the spirit cast it out
as dreams of dark fancy; and yet time
has buried in the mounding sand

the sea cables since that day   985
when against Ilium
the army and the ships put to sea.

Yet I have seen with these eyes
Agamemnon home again.
Still the spirit sings, drawing deep   990
from within this unlyric threnody of the Fury.
Hope is gone utterly,
the sweet strength is far away.
Surely this is not fantasy.   995
Surely it is real, this whirl of drifts
that spin the stricken heart.
Still I pray; may all this
expectation fade as vanity
into unfulfilment, and not be.   1000

Yet it is true: the high strength of men
knows no content with limitation. Sickness
chambered beside it beats at the wall between.
Man's fate that sets a true   1005
course yet may strike upon
the blind and sudden reefs of disaster.
But if before such time, fear
throw overboard some precious thing
of the cargo, with deliberate cast,   1010
not all the house, laboring
with weight of ruin, shall go down,
nor sink the hull deep within the sea.
And great and affluent the gift of Zeus
in yield of plowed acres year on year   1015
makes void again sick starvation.

But when the black and mortal blood of man
has fallen to the ground before his feet, who then   1020
can sing spells to call it back again?
Did Zeus not warn us once
when he struck to impotence
that one who could in truth charm back the dead
    men?
Had the gods not so ordained   1025
that fate should stand against fate

to check any man's excess,
my heart now would have outrun speech
to break forth the water of its grief.
But this is so; I murmur deep in darkness   1030
sore at heart; my hope is gone now
ever again to unwind some crucial good
from the flames about my heart.

[CLYTAEMNESTRA *comes out from the house
again and speaks to* CASSANDRA.]

Cassandra, you may go within the house as well,   1035
since Zeus in no unkindness has ordained that you
must share our lustral water, stand with the great
    throng
of slaves that flock to the altar of our household
    god.
Step from this chariot, then, and do not be so
    proud.
And think—they say that long ago Alcmena's son   1040
was sold in bondage and endured the bread of
    slaves.
But if constraint of fact forces you to such fate,
be glad indeed for masters ancient in their wealth.
They who have reaped success beyond their dreams
    of hope
are savage above need and standard toward their
    slaves.   1045
From us you shall have all you have the right to ask.

CHORUS
What she has spoken is for you, and clear enough.
Fenced in these fatal nets wherein you find yourself
you should obey her if you can; perhaps you can
    not.

CLYTAEMNESTRA
Unless she uses speech incomprehensible,   1050
barbarian, wild as the swallow's song, I speak
within her understanding, and she must obey.

CHORUS
Go with her. What she bids is best in circumstance

that rings you now. Obey, and leave this carriage
   seat.

CLYTAEMNESTRA
   I have no leisure to stand outside the house and
      waste   1055
   time on this woman. At the central altarstone
   the flocks are standing, ready for the sacrifice
   we make to this glad day we never hoped to see.
   You: if you are obeying my commands at all, be
      quick.
   But if in ignorance you fail to comprehend,   1060
   speak not, but make with your barbarian hand
      some sign.

CHORUS
   I think this stranger girl needs some interpreter
   who understands. She is like some captive animal.

CLYTAEMNESTRA
   No, she is in the passion of her own wild thoughts.
   Leaving her captured city she has come to us   1065
   untrained to take the curb, and will not understand
   until her rage and strength have foamed away in
      blood.
   I shall throw down no more commands for her
      contempt.

      [CLYTAEMNESTRA *goes back into the house*.]

CHORUS
   I, though, shall not be angry, for I pity her.
   Come down, poor creature, leave the empty car.
      Give way   1070
   to compulsion and take up the yoke that shall be
      yours.

      [CASSANDRA *descends from the chariot and
                        cries out loud*.]
   Oh, shame upon the earth!
   Apollo, Apollo!

CHORUS
>You cry on Loxias in agony? He is not
>of those immortals the unhappy supplicate. 1075

CASSANDRA
>Oh, shame upon the earth!
>Apollo, Apollo!

CHORUS
>Now once again in bitter voice she calls upon
>this god, who has not part in any lamentation.

CASSANDRA
>Apollo, Apollo! 1080
>Lord of the ways, my ruin.
>You have undone me once again, and utterly.

CHORUS
>I think she will be prophetic of her own disaster.
>Even in the slave's heart the gift divine lives on.

CASSANDRA
>Apollo, Apollo! 1085
>Lord of the ways, my ruin.
>Where have you led me now at last? What house is
>   this?

CHORUS
>The house of the Atreidae. If you understand
>not that, I can tell you; and so much at least is true.

CASSANDRA
>No, but a house that God hates, guilty within 1090
>of kindred blood shed, torture of its own,
>the shambles for men's butchery, the dripping floor.

CHORUS
>The stranger is keen scented like some hound upon
>the trail of blood that leads her to discovered death.

CASSANDRA
>Behold there the witnesses to my faith. 1095

The small children wail for their own death
and the flesh roasted that their father fed upon.

CHORUS
We had been told before of this prophetic fame
of yours: we want no prophets in this place at all.

CASSANDRA
Ah, for shame, what can she purpose now?   1100
What is this new and huge
stroke of atrocity she plans within the house
to beat down the beloved beyond hope of healing?
Rescue is far away.

CHORUS
I can make nothing of these prophecies. The rest   1105
I understood; the city is full of the sound of them.

CASSANDRA
So cruel then, that you can do this thing?
The husband of your own bed
to bathe bright with water—how shall I speak the
    end?
This thing shall be done with speed. The hand
    gropes now, and the other   1110
hand follows in turn.

CHORUS
No, I am lost. After the darkness of her speech
I go bewildered in a mist of prophecies.

CASSANDRA
No, no, see there! What is that thing that shows?
Is it some net of death?   1115
Or is the trap the woman there, the murderess?
Let now the slakeless Fury in the race
rear up to howl aloud over this monstrous death.

CHORUS
Upon what demon in the house do you call, to raise
the cry of triumph? All your speech makes dark my
    hope.   1120

And to the heart below trickles the pale drop
as in the hour of death
timed to our sunset and the mortal radiance.
Ruin is near, and swift.

CASSANDRA
See there, see there! Keep from his mate the bull.   1125
Caught in the folded web's
entanglement she pinions him and with the black
    horn
strikes. And he crumples in the watered bath.
Guile, I tell you, and death there in the caldron
    wrought.

CHORUS
I am not proud in skill to guess at prophecies,   1130
yet even I can see the evil in this thing.
From divination what good ever has come to men?
Art, and multiplication of words
drifting through tangled evil bring
terror to them that hear.   1135

CASSANDRA
Alas, alas for the wretchedness of my ill-starred
    life.
This pain flooding the song of sorrow is mine alone.
Why have you brought me here in all unhappiness?
Why, why? Except to die with him? What else
    could be?

CHORUS
You are possessed of God, mazed at heart   1140
to sing your own death
song, the wild lyric as
in clamor for Itys, Itys over and over again
her long life of tears weeping forever grieves
the brown nightingale.   1145

CASSANDRA
Oh, for the nightingale's pure song and a fate like
    hers.
With fashion of beating wings the gods clothed her
    about

and a sweet life gave her and without lamentation.
But mine is the sheer edge of the tearing iron.

CHORUS
Whence come, beat upon beat, driven of God,   1150
vain passions of tears?
Whence your cries, terrified, clashing in horror,
in wrought melody and the singing speech?
Whence take you the marks to this path of
        prophecy
and speech of terror?   1155

CASSANDRA
Oh, marriage of Paris, death to the men beloved!
Alas, Scamandrus, water my fathers drank.
There was a time I too at your springs
drank and grew strong. Ah me,
for now beside the deadly rivers, Cocytus   1160
and Acheron, I must cry out my prophecies.

CHORUS
What is this word, too clear, you have uttered now?
A child could understand.
And deep within goes the stroke of the dripping
        fang
as mortal pain at the trebled song of your agony   1165
shivers the heart to hear.

CASSANDRA
O sorrow, sorrow of my city dragged to uttermost
        death.
O sacrifices my father made at the wall.
Flocks of the pastured sheep slaughtered there.
And no use at all   1170
to save our city from its pain inflicted now.
And I too, with brain ablaze in fever, shall go down.

CHORUS
This follows the run of your song.
Is it, in cruel force of weight,
some divinity kneeling upon you brings   1175
the death song of your passionate suffering?
I can not see the end.

CASSANDRA

No longer shall my prophecies like some young girl
new-married glance from under veils, but bright and
strong
as winds blow into morning and the sun's uprise   1180
shall wax along the swell like some great wave, to
burst
at last upon the shining of this agony.
Now I will tell you plainly and from no cryptic
speech;
bear me then witness, running at my heels upon
the scent of these old brutal things done long ago.   1185
There is a choir that sings as one, that shall not
again
leave this house ever; the song thereof breaks harsh
with menace.
And drugged to double fury on the wine of men's
blood shed, there lurks forever here a drunken rout
of ingrown vengeful spirits never to be cast forth.   1190
Hanging above the hall they chant their song of hate
and the old sin; and taking up the strain in turn
spit curses on that man who spoiled his brother's
bed.
Did I go wide, or hit, like a real archer? Am I
some swindling seer who hawks his lies from door
to door?   1195
Upon your oath, bear witness that I know by heart
the legend of ancient wickedness within this house.

CHORUS

And how could an oath, though cast in rigid
honesty,
do any good? And still we stand amazed at you,
reared in an alien city far beyond the sea,   1200
how can you strike, as if you had been there, the
truth.

CASSANDRA

Apollo was the seer who set me to this work.

CHORUS

Struck with some passion for you, and himself a
god?

CASSANDRA
  There was a time I blushed to speak about these
    things.

CHORUS
  True; they who prosper take on airs of vanity.   1205

CASSANDRA
  Yes, then; he wrestled with me, and he breathed
    delight.

CHORUS
  Did you come to the getting of children then, as
    people do?

CASSANDRA
  I promised that to Loxias, but I broke my word.

CHORUS
  Were you already ecstatic in the skills of God?

CASSANDRA
  Yes; even then I read my city's destinies.   1210

CHORUS
  So Loxias' wrath did you no harm? How could that
    be?

CASSANDRA
  For this my trespass, none believed me ever again.

CHORUS
  But we do; all that you foretell seems true to us.

CASSANDRA
  But this is evil, see!
  Now once again the pain of grim, true prophecy   1215
  shivers my whirling brain in a storm of things
    foreseen.
  Look there, see what is hovering above the house,
  so small and young, imaged as in the shadow of
    dreams,

like children almost, killed by those most dear to
     them,
and their hands filled with their own flesh, as food
     to eat.   1220
I see them holding out the inward parts, the vitals,
oh, pitiful, that meat their father tasted of. . . .
I tell you: There is one that plots vengeance for
     this,
the strengthless lion rolling in his master's bed,
who keeps, ah me, the house against his lord's
     return;   1225
my lord too, now that I wear the slave's yoke on my
     neck.
King of the ships, who tore up Ilium by the roots,
what does he know of this accursed bitch, who
     licks
his hand, who fawns on him with lifted ears, who
     like
a secret death shall strike the coward's stroke, nor
     fail?   1230
No, this is daring when the female shall strike down
the male. What can I call her and be right? What
     beast
of loathing? Viper double-fanged, or Scylla witch
holed in the rocks and bane of men that range the
     sea;
smoldering mother of death to smoke relentless
     hate   1235
on those most dear. How she stood up and howled
     aloud
and unashamed, as at the breaking point of battle,
in feigned gladness for his salvation from the sea!
What does it matter now if men believe or no?
What is to come will come. And soon you too will
     stand   1240
beside, to murmur in pity that my words were true.

CHORUS
     Thyestes' feast upon the flesh of his own children
     I understand in terror at the thought, and fear
     is on me hearing truth and no tale fabricated.

The rest: I heard it, but wander still far from the
   course.   1245

CASSANDRA
  I tell you, you shall look on Agamemnon dead.

CHORUS
  Peace, peace, poor woman; put those bitter lips to
    sleep.

CASSANDRA
  Useless; there is no god of healing in this story.

CHORUS
  Not if it must be; may it somehow fail to come.

CASSANDRA
  Prayers, yes; they do not pray; they plan to strike,
    and kill.   1250

CHORUS
  What man is it who moves this beastly thing to be?

CASSANDRA
  What man? You did mistake my divination then.

CHORUS
  It may be; I could not follow through the schemer's
    plan.

CASSANDRA
  Yet I know Greek; I think I know it far too well.

CHORUS
  And Pythian oracles are Greek, yet hard to read.   1255

CASSANDRA
  Oh, flame and pain that sweeps me once again! My
    lord,
  Apollo, King of Light, the pain, aye me, the pain!
  This is the woman-lioness, who goes to bed
  with the wolf, when her proud lion ranges far away,

and she will cut me down; as a wife mixing drugs   1260
she wills to shred the virtue of my punishment
into her bowl of wrath as she makes sharp the blade
against her man, death that he brought a mistress
    home.
Why do I wear these mockeries upon my body,
this staff of prophecy, these flowers at my throat?   1265
At least I will spoil you before I die. Out, down,
break, damn you! This for all that you have done to
    me.
Make someone else, not me, luxurious in
    disaster. . . .
Lo now, this is Apollo who has stripped me here
of my prophetic robes. He watched me all the time   1270
wearing this glory, mocked of all, my dearest ones
who hated me with all their hearts, so vain, so
    wrong;
called like some gypsy wandering from door to
    door
beggar, corrupt, half-starved, and I endured it all.
And now the seer has done with me, his
    prophetess,   1275
and led me into such a place as this, to die.
Lost are my father's altars, but the block is there
to reek with sacrificial blood, my own. We two
must die, yet die not vengeless by the gods. For
    there
shall come one to avenge us also, born to slay   1280
his mother, and to wreak death for his father's
    blood.
Outlaw and wanderer, driven far from his own land,
he will come back to cope these stones of inward
    hate.
For this is a strong oath and sworn by the high
    gods,
that he shall cast men headlong for his father felled.   1285
Why am I then so pitiful? Why must I weep?
Since once I saw the citadel of Ilium
die as it died, and those who broke the city,
    doomed
by the gods, fare as they have fared accordingly,
I will go through with it. I too will take my fate.   1290

I call as on the gates of death upon these gates
to pray only for this thing, that the stroke be true,
and that with no convulsion, with a rush of blood
in painless death, I may close up these eyes, and
   rest.

                              •

CHORUS
O woman much enduring and so greatly wise,   1295
you have said much. But if this thing you know be
   true,
this death that comes upon you, how can you,
   serene,
walk to the altar like a driven ox of God?

CASSANDRA
Friends, there is no escape for any longer time.

CHORUS
Yet longest left in time is to be honored still.   1300

CASSANDRA
The day is here and now; I can not win by flight.

CHORUS
Woman, be sure your heart is brave; you can take
   much.

CASSANDRA
None but the unhappy people ever hear such
   praise.

CHORUS
Yet there is a grace on mortals who so nobly die.

CASSANDRA
Alas for you, father, and for your lordly sons.   1305
Ah!

CHORUS
What now? What terror whirls you backward from
   the door?

CASSANDRA
  Foul, foul!

CHORUS
  What foulness then, unless some horror in the
    mind?

CASSANDRA
  That room within reeks with blood like a slaughter
    house.

CHORUS
  What then? Only these victims butchered at the
    hearth.   1310

CASSANDRA
  There is a breath about it like an open grave.

CHORUS
  This is no Syrian pride of frankincense you mean.

CASSANDRA
  So. I am going in, and mourning as I go
  my death and Agamemnon's. Let my life be done.
  Ah friends,   1315
  truly this is no wild bird fluttering at a bush,
  nor vain my speech. Bear witness to me when I die,
  when falls for me, a woman slain, another woman,
  and when a man dies for this wickedly mated man.
  Here in my death I claim this stranger's grace of
    you.   1320

CHORUS
  Poor wretch, I pity you the fate you see so clear.

CASSANDRA
  Yet once more will I speak, and not this time my
    own
  death's threnody. I call upon the Sun in prayer
  against that ultimate shining when the avengers
    strike

these monsters down in blood, that they avenge as
     well   1325
one simple slave who died, a small thing, lightly
     killed.

Alas, poor men, their destiny. When all goes well
a shadow will overthrow it. If it be unkind
one stroke of a wet sponge wipes all the picture
     out;
and that is far the most unhappy thing of all.   1330

[CASSANDRA *goes slowly into the house*.]

CHORUS
     High fortune is a thing slakeless
     for mortals. There is no man who shall point
     his finger to drive it back from the door
     and speak the words: "Come no longer."
     Now to this man the blessed ones have given   1335
     Priam's city to be captured
     and return in the gods' honor.
     Must he give blood for generations gone,
     die for those slain and in death pile up
     more death to come for the blood shed,   1340
     what mortal else who hears shall claim
     he was born clear of the dark angel?

[AGAMEMNON, *inside the house*.]
     Ah, I am struck a deadly blow and deep within!

CHORUS
     Silence: who cried out that he was stabbed to death
         within the house?

AGAMEMNON
     Ah me, again, they struck again. I am wounded   1345
         twice.

CHORUS
     How the king cried out aloud to us! I believe the
         thing is done.
     Come, let us put our heads together, try to find
         some safe way out.

[The members of the CHORUS *go about
distractedly, each one speaking in turn.]*

Listen, let me tell you what I think is best to do.
Let the herald call all citizens to rally here.

No, better to burst in upon them now, at once,   1350
and take them with the blood still running from
    their blades.

I am with this man and I cast my vote to him.
Act now. This is the perilous and instant time.

Anyone can see it, by these first steps they have
    taken,
they purpose to be tyrants here upon our city.   1355

Yes, for we waste time, while they trample to the
    ground
deliberation's honor, and their hands sleep not.

I can not tell which counsel of yours to call my
    own.
It is the man of action who can plan as well.

I feel as he does; nor can I see how by words   1360
we shall set the dead man back upon his feet again.

Do you mean, to drag our lives out long, that we
    must yield
to the house shamed, and leadership of such as
    these?

No, we can never endure that; better to be killed.
Death is a softer thing by far than tyranny.   1365

Shall we, by no more proof than that he cried in
    pain,
be sure, as by divination, that our lord is dead?

Yes, we should know what is true before we break
    our rage.

Here is sheer guessing and far different from sure
   knowledge.

From all sides the voices multiply to make me   1370
   choose
this course; to learn first how it stands with
   Agamemnon.

[*The doors of the palace open, disclosing the
      bodies of* AGAMEMNON *and* CASSANDRA,
      with CLYTAEMNESTRA *standing over them.*]

CLYTAEMNESTRA
   Much have I said before to serve necessity,
   but I will take no shame now to unsay it all.
   How else could I, arming hate against hateful men
   disguised in seeming tenderness, fence high the
      nets   1375
   of ruin beyond overleaping? Thus to me
   the conflict born of ancient bitterness is not
   a thing new thought upon, but pondered deep in
      time.
   I stand now where I struck him down. The thing is
      done.
   Thus have I wrought, and I will not deny it now.   1380
   That he might not escape nor beat aside his death,
   as fishermen cast their huge circling nets, I spread
   deadly abundance of rich robes, and caught him
      fast.
   I struck him twice. In two great cries of agony
   he buckled at the knees and fell. When he was
      down   1385
   I struck him the third blow, in thanks and reverence
   to Zeus the lord of dead men underneath the
      ground.
   Thus he went down, and the life struggled out of
      him;
   and as he died he spattered me with the dark red
   and violent driven rain of bitter savored blood   1390
   to make me glad, as gardens stand among the
      showers
   of God in glory at the birthtime of the buds.

These being the facts, elders of Argos assembled
      here,
be glad, if it be your pleasure; but for me, I glory.
Were it religion to pour wine above the slain,   1395
this man deserved, more than deserved, such
      sacrament.
He filled our cup with evil things unspeakable
and now himself come home has drunk it to the dregs.

CHORUS
We stand here stunned. How can you speak this
      way, with mouth
so arrogant, to vaunt above your fallen lord?   1400

CLYTAEMNESTRA
You try me out as if I were a woman and vain;
but my heart is not fluttered as I speak before you.
You know it. You can praise or blame me as you
      wish;
it is all one to me. That man is Agamemnon,
my husband; he is dead; the work of this right hand   1405
that struck in strength of righteousness. And that is
      that.

CHORUS
Woman, what evil thing planted upon the earth
or dragged from the running salt sea could you have
      tasted now
to wear such brutality and walk in the people's
      hate?
You have cast away, you have cut away. You shall go
      homeless now,   1410
crushed with men's bitterness.

CLYTAEMNESTRA
Now it is I you doom to be cast out from my city
with men's hate heaped and curses roaring in my
      ears.
Yet look upon this dead man; you would not cross
      him once
when with no thought more than as if a beast had
      died,   1415

when his ranged pastures swarmed with the deep
    fleece of flocks,
he slaughtered like a victim his own child, my pain
grown into love, to charm away the winds of Thrace.
Were you not bound to hunt him then clear of this
    soil
for the guilt stained upon him? Yet you hear what I   1420
have done, and lo, you are a stern judge. But I say
    to you:
go on and threaten me, but know that I am ready,
if fairly you can beat me down beneath your hand,
for you to rule; but if the god grant otherwise,
you shall be taught—too late, for sure—to keep
    your place.   1425

CHORUS
Great your design, your speech is a clamor of pride.
Swung to the red act drives the fury within your
    brain
signed clear in the splash of blood over your eyes.
Yet to come is stroke given for stroke
vengeless, forlorn of friends.   1430

CLYTAEMNESTRA
Now hear you this, the right behind my sacrament:
By my child's Justice driven to fulfilment, by
her Wrath and Fury, to whom I sacrificed this man,
the hope that walks my chambers is not traced with
    fear
while yet Aegisthus makes the fire shine on my
    hearth,   1435
my good friend, now as always, who shall be for us
the shield of our defiance, no weak thing; while he,
this other, is fallen, stained with this woman you
    behold,
plaything of all the golden girls at Ilium;
and here lies she, the captive of his spear, who saw   1440
wonders, who shared his bed, the wise in
    revelations
and loving mistress, who yet knew the feel as well
of the men's rowing benches. Their reward is not
unworthy. He lies there; and she who swanlike
    cried

aloud her lyric mortal lamentation out   1445
is laid against his fond heart, and to me has given
a delicate excitement to my bed's delight.

CHORUS
O that in speed, without pain
and the slow bed of sickness
death could come to us now, death that forever   1450
carries sleep without ending, now that our lord is
     down,
our shield, kindest of men,
who for a woman's grace suffered so much,
struck down at last by a woman.

Alas, Helen, wild heart   1455
for the multitudes, for the thousand lives
you killed under Troy's shadow,
you alone, to shine in man's memory
as blood flower never to be washed out. Surely a
     demon then   1460
of death walked in the house, men's agony.

CLYTAEMNESTRA
No, be not so heavy, nor yet draw down
in prayer death's ending,
neither turn all wrath against Helen
for men dead, that she alone killed   1465
all those Danaan lives, to work
the grief that is past all healing.

CHORUS
Divinity that kneel on this house and the two
strains of the blood of Tantalus,
in the hands and hearts of women you steer   1470
the strength tearing my heart.
Standing above the corpse, obscene
as some carrion crow she sings
the crippled song and is proud.

CLYTAEMNESTRA
Thus have you set the speech of your lips   1475
straight, calling by name
the spirit thrice glutted that lives in this race.

From him deep in the nerve is given
the love and the blood drunk, that before
the old wound dries, it bleeds again.   1480

CHORUS
  Surely it is a huge
  and heavy spirit bending the house you cry;
  alas, the bitter glory
  of a doom that shall never be done with;
  and all through Zeus, Zeus,   1485
  first cause, prime mover.
  For what thing without Zeus is done among
       mortals?
  What here is without God's blessing?

  O king, my king,
  how shall I weep for you?   1490
  What can I say out of my heart of pity?
  Caught in this spider's web you lie,
  your life gasped out in indecent death,
  struck prone to this shameful bed
  by your lady's hand of treachery   1495
  and the stroke twin edged of the iron.

CLYTAEMNESTRA
  Can you claim I have done this?
  Speak of me never
  more as the wife of Agamemnon.
  In the shadow of this corpse's queen   1500
  the old stark avenger
  of Atreus for his revel of hate
  struck down this man,
  last blood for the slaughtered children.

CHORUS
  What man shall testify   1505
  your hands are clean of this murder?
  How? How? Yet from his father's blood
  might swarm some fiend to guide you.
  The black ruin that shoulders
  through the streaming blood of brothers   1510
  strides at last where he shall win requital
  for the children who were eaten.

O king, my king,
how shall I weep for you?
What can I say out of my heart of pity?   1515
Caught in this spider's web you lie,
your life gasped out in indecent death,
struck prone to this shameful bed
by your lady's hand of treachery
and the stroke twin edged of the iron.   1520

CLYTAEMNESTRA

No shame, I think, in the death given
this man. And did he not
first of all in this house wreak death
by treachery?
The flower of this man's love and mine,   1525
Iphigeneia of the tears
he dealt with even as he has suffered.
Let his speech in death's house be not loud.
With the sword he struck,
with the sword he paid for his own act.

CHORUS

My thoughts are swept away and I go bewildered.   1530
Where shall I turn the brain's
activity in speed when the house is falling?
There is fear in the beat of the blood rain breaking
wall and tower. The drops come thicker.
Still fate grinds on yet more stones the blade   1535
for more acts of terror.

Earth, my earth, why did you not fold me under
before ever I saw this man lie dead
fenced by the tub in silver?   1540
Who shall bury him? Who shall mourn him?
Shall you dare this who have killed
your lord? Make lamentation,
render the graceless grace to his soul   1545
for huge things done in wickedness?
Who over this great man's grave shall lay
the blessing of tears
worked soberly from a true heart?   1550

CLYTAEMNESTRA
Not for you to speak of such tendance.
Through us he fell,
by us he died; we shall bury.
There will be no tears in this house for him.
It must be Iphigeneia   1555
his child, who else,
shall greet her father by the whirling stream
and the ferry of tears
to close him in her arms and kiss him.

CHORUS
Here is anger for anger. Between them   1560
who shall judge lightly?
The spoiler is robbed; he killed, he has paid.
The truth stands ever beside God's throne
eternal: he who has wrought shall pay; that is law.
Then who shall tear the curse from their blood?   1565
The seed is stiffened to ruin.

CLYTAEMNESTRA
You see truth in the future
at last. Yet I wish
to seal my oath with the Spirit
in the house: I will endure all things as they stand   1570
now, hard though it be. Hereafter
let him go forth to make bleed with death
and guilt the houses of others.
I will take some small
measure of our riches, and be content
that I swept from these halls   1575
the murder, the sin, and the fury.

[AEGISTHUS enters, followed at a
little distance by his armed bodyguard.]

AEGISTHUS
O splendor and exaltation of this day of doom!
Now I can say once more that the high gods look
    down
on mortal crimes to vindicate the right at last,
now that I see this man—sweet sight—before me
    here   1580

sprawled in the tangling nets of fury, to atone
the calculated evil of his father's hand.
For Atreus, this man's father, King of Argolis—
I tell you the clear story—drove my father forth,
Thyestes, his own brother, who had challenged him   1585
in his king's right—forth from his city and his home.
Yet sad Thyestes came again to supplicate
the hearth, and win some grace, in that he was not
    slain
nor soiled the doorstone of his fathers with blood
    spilled.
Not his own blood. But Atreus, this man's godless
    sire,   1590
angrily hospitable set a feast for him,
in seeming a glad day of fresh meat slain and good
cheer; then served my father his own children's
    flesh
to feed on. For he carved away the extremities,
hands, feet, and cut the flesh apart, and covered
    them   1595
served in a dish to my father at his table apart,
who with no thought for the featureless meal before
    him ate
that ghastly food whose curse works now before
    your eyes.
But when he knew the terrible thing that he had
    done,
he spat the dead meat from him with a cry, and
    reeled   1600
spurning the table back to heel with strength the
    curse:
"Thus crash in ruin all the seed of Pleisthenes."
Out of such acts you see this dead man stricken
    here,
and it was I, in my right, who wrought this murder,
    I
third born to my unhappy father, and with him   1605
driven, a helpless baby in arms, to banishment.
Yet I grew up, and justice brought me home again,
till from afar I laid my hands upon this man,
since it was I who pieced together the fell plot.
Now I can die in honor again, if die I must,   1610

having seen him caught in the cords of his just
   punishment.

CHORUS
   Aegisthus, this strong vaunting in distress is vile.
   You claim that you deliberately killed the king,
   you, and you only, wrought the pity of this death.
   I tell you then: There shall be no escape, your head   1615
   shall face the stones of anger from the people's
      hands.

AEGISTHUS
   So loud from you, stooped to the meanest rowing
      bench
   with the ship's masters lordly on the deck above?
   You are old men; well, you shall learn how hard it is
   at your age, to be taught how to behave yourselves.   1620
   But there are chains, there is starvation with its
      pain,
   excellent teachers of good manners to old men,
   wise surgeons and exemplars. Look! Can you not
      see it?
   Lash not at the goads for fear you hit them, and be
      hurt.

CHORUS
   So then you, like a woman, waited the war out   1625
   here in the house, shaming the master's bed with
      lust,
   and planned against the lord of war this treacherous
      death?

AEGISTHUS
   It is just such words as these will make you cry in
      pain.
   Not yours the lips of Orpheus, no, quite otherwise,
   whose voice of rapture dragged all creatures in his
      train.   1630
   You shall be dragged, for baby whimperings sobbed
      out
   in rage. Once broken, you will be easier to deal
      with.

CHORUS

How shall you be lord of the men of Argos, you
who planned the murder of this man, yet could not
    dare
to act it out, and cut him down with your own
    hand?   1635

AEGISTHUS

No, clearly the deception was the woman's part,
and I was suspect, that had hated him so long.
Still with his money I shall endeavor to control
the citizens. The mutinous man shall feel the yoke
drag at his neck, no cornfed racing colt that runs   1640
free traced; but hunger, grim companion of the dark
dungeon shall see him broken to the hand at last.

CHORUS

But why, why then, you coward, could you not have
    slain
your man yourself? Why must it be his wife who
    killed,
to curse the country and the gods within the
    ground?   1645
Oh, can Orestes live, be somewhere in sunlight
    still?
Shall fate grown gracious ever bring him back again
in strength of hand to overwhelm these murderers?

AEGISTHUS

You shall learn then, since you stick to
    stubbornness of mouth and hand.
Up now from your cover, my henchmen: here is
    work for you to do.   1650

CHORUS

Look, they come! Let every man clap fist upon his
    hilted sword.

AEGISTHUS

I too am sword-handed against you; I am not afraid
    of death.

CHORUS
    Death you said and death it shall be; we take up the
        word of fate.

CLYTAEMNESTRA
    No, my dearest, dearest of all men, we have done
        enough. No more
    violence. Here is a monstrous harvest and a bitter
        reaping time.   1655
    There is pain enough already. Let us not be bloody
        now.
    Honored gentlemen of Argos, go to your homes
        now and give way
    To the stress of fate and season. We could not do
        otherwise
    than we did. If this is the end of suffering, we can
        be content
    broken as we are by the brute heel of angry destiny.   1660
    Thus a woman speaks among you. Shall men deign
        to understand?

AEGISTHUS
    Yes, but think of these foolish lips that blossom into
        leering gibes,
    think of the taunts they spit against me daring
        destiny and power,
    sober opinion lost in insults hurled against my
        majesty.

CHORUS
    It was never the Argive way to grovel at a vile man's
        feet.   1665

AEGISTHUS
    I shall not forget this; in the days to come I shall be
        there.

CHORUS
    Nevermore, if God's hand guiding brings Orestes
        home again.

AEGISTHUS
   Exiles feed on empty dreams of hope. I know it. I
      was one.

CHORUS
   Have your way, gorge and grow fat, soil justice,
      while the power is yours.

AEGISTHUS
   You shall pay, make no mistake, for this misguided
      insolence.   1670

CHORUS
   Crow and strut, brace cockerel by your hen; you
      have no threats to fear.

CLYTAEMNESTRA
   These are howls of impotent rage; forget them,
      dearest; you and I
   have the power; we two shall bring good order to
      our house at last.

> [*They enter the house. The doors close. All
>   persons leave the stage.*]

OEDIPUS THE KING

BY
Sophocles

TRANSLATED BY
David Grene

CHARACTERS

OEDIPUS, *King of Thebes*

JOCASTA, *his wife*

CREON, *his brother-in-law*

TEIRESIAS, *an old blind prophet*

A PRIEST

FIRST MESSENGER

SECOND MESSENGER

A HERDSMAN

CHORUS *of old men of Thebes*

In front of the palace of OEDIPUS *at Thebes. To the right of the stage near the altar stands the* PRIEST *with a crowd of children.* OEDIPUS *emerges from the central door.*

OEDIPUS

Children, young sons and daughters of old Cadmus,
why do you sit here with your suppliant crowns?
The town is heavy with a mingled burden
of sounds and smells, of groans and hymns and
   incense;
I did not think it fit that I should hear   5
of this from messengers but came myself—
I, Oedipus, whom all men call the Great.

                    [*He turns to the* PRIEST.]
You're old and they are young; come, speak for
   them.
What do you fear or want, that you sit here
suppliant? Indeed I'm willing to give all   10
that you may need; I would be very hard
should I not pity suppliants like these.

PRIEST

O ruler of my country, Oedipus,
you see our company around the altar;
you see our ages; some of us, like these,   15
who cannot yet fly far, and some of us
heavy with age; these children are the chosen
among the young, and I the priest of Zeus.
Within the marketplace sit others crowned
with suppliant garlands, at the double shrine   20
of Pallas and the temple where Ismenus
gives oracles by fire. King, you yourself
have seen our city reeling like a wreck
already; it can scarcely lift its prow
out of the depths, out of the bloody surf.   25

A blight is on the fruitful plants of the earth,
A blight is on the cattle in the fields,
a blight is on our women that no children
are born to them; a God that carries fire,
a deadly pestilence, is on our town,   30
strikes us and spares not, and the house of Cadmus
is emptied of its people while black Death
grows rich in groaning and in lamentation.
We have not come as suppliants to this altar
because we thought of you as of a God,   35
but rather judging you the first of men
in all the chances of this life and when
we mortals have to do with more than man.
You came and by your coming saved our city,
freed us from tribute which we paid of old   40
to the Sphinx, cruel singer. This you did
in virtue of no knowledge we could give you,
in virtue of no teaching; it was God
that aided you, men say, and you are held
with God's assistance to have saved our lives.   45
Now, Oedipus, greatest in all men's eyes,
here falling at your feet we all entreat you,
find us some strength for rescue.
Perhaps you'll hear a wise word from some God,
perhaps you will learn something from a man   50
(for I have seen that for the skilled of practice
the outcome of their counsels live the most).
Noblest of men, go, and raise up our city,
go—and give heed. For now this land of ours
calls you its savior since you saved it once.   55
So, let us never speak about your reign
as of a time when first our feet were set
secure on high, but later fell to ruin.
Raise up our city, save it and raise it up.
Once you have brought us luck with happy omen;   60
be no less now in fortune.
If you will rule this land, as now you rule it,
better to rule it full of men than empty.
For neither tower nor ship is anything
when empty, and none live in it together.   65

OEDIPUS

I pity you, children. You have come full of longing,
but I have known the story before you told it
only too well. I know you are all sick,
yet there is not one of you, sick though you are,
that is as sick as I myself. 70
Your several sorrows each have single scope
and touch but one of you. My spirit groans
for city and myself and you at once.
You have not roused me like a man from sleep;
know that I have given many tears to this, 75
gone many ways wandering in thought,
but as I thought I found only one remedy
and that I took. I sent Menoeceus' son
Creon, Jocasta's brother, to Apollo,
to his Pythian temple, 80
that he might learn there by what act or word
I could save this city. As I count the days,
it vexes me what ails him; he is gone
far longer than he needed for the journey.
But when he comes, then, may I prove a villain 85
if I shall not do all the God commands.

PRIEST

Thanks for your gracious words. Your servants here
signal that Creon is this moment coming.

OEDIPUS

His face is bright. O holy Lord Apollo,
grant that his news too may be bright for us 90
and bring us safety.

PRIEST

It is happy news,
I think, for else his head would not be crowned
with sprigs of fruitful laurel.

OEDIPUS

We will know soon;
he's within hail. Lord Creon, my good brother,
what is the word you bring us from the God? 95

[CREON *enters.*]

CREON
A good word—for things hard to bear themselves
if in the final issue all is well
I count complete good fortune.

OEDIPUS
                                    What do you mean?
What you have said so far
leaves me uncertain whether to trust or fear.   100

CREON
If you will hear my news before these others
I am ready to speak, or else to go within.

OEDIPUS
Speak it to all;
the grief I bear, I bear it more for these
than for my own heart.

CREON
                                    I will tell you, then,   105
what I heard from the God.
King Phoebus in plain words commanded us
to drive out a pollution from our land,
pollution grown ingrained within the land;
drive it out, said the God, not cherish it,   110
till it's past cure.

OEDIPUS
                                    What is the right
of purification? How shall it be done?

CREON
By banishing a man, or expiation
of blood by blood, since it is murder guilt
which holds our city in this destroying storm.   115

OEDIPUS
Who is this man whose fate the God pronounces?

CREON
  My lord, before you piloted the state
  we had a king called Laius.

OEDIPUS
  I know of him by hearsay. I have not seen him.

CREON
  The God commanded clearly: let some one   120
  punish with force this dead man's murderers.

OEDIPUS
  Where are they in the world? Where would a trace
  of this old crime be found? It would be hard
  to guess where.

CREON
                    The clue is in this land;
  that which is sought is found;   125
  the unheeded thing escapes:
  so said the God.

OEDIPUS
                    Was it at home,
  or in the country that death came upon him,
  or in another country traveling?

CREON
  He went, he said himself, upon an embassy,   130
  but never returned when he set out from home.

OEDIPUS
  Was there no messenger, no fellow traveler
  who knew what happened? Such a one might tell
  something of use.

CREON
  They were all killed save one. He fled in terror   135
  and he could tell us nothing in clear terms
  of what he knew, nothing, but one thing only.

OEDIPUS
>What was it?
>If we could even find a slim beginning
>in which to hope, we might discover much.   140

CREON
>This man said that the robbers they encountered
>were many and the hands that did the murder
>were many; it was no man's single power.

OEDIPUS
>How could a robber dare a deed like this
>were he not helped with money from the city,   145
>money and treachery?

CREON
>   That indeed was thought.
>But Laius was dead and in our trouble
>there was none to help.

OEDIPUS
>What trouble was so great to hinder you
>inquiring out the murder of your king?   150

CREON
>The riddling Sphinx induced us to neglect
>mysterious crimes and rather seek solution
>of troubles at our feet.

OEDIPUS
>I will bring this to light again. King Phoebus
>fittingly took this care about the dead,   155
>and you, too, fittingly.
>And justly you will see in me an ally,
>a champion of my country and the God.
>For when I drive pollution from the land
>I will not serve a distant friend's advantage,   160
>but act in my own interest. Whoever
>he was that killed the king may readily
>wish to dispatch me with his murderous hand;
>so helping the dead king I help myself.

Come, children, take your suppliant boughs and go; 165
up from the altars now. Call the assembly
and let it meet upon the understanding
that I'll do everything. God will decide
whether we prosper or remain in sorrow.

PRIEST
Rise, children—it was this we came to seek, 170
which of himself the king now offers us.
May Phoebus who gave us the oracle
come to our rescue and stay the plague.

[*Exeunt all but the* CHORUS.]

CHORUS
Strophe
What is the sweet spoken word of God from the
   shrine of Pytho rich in gold
that has come to glorious Thebes? 175
I am stretched on the rack of doubt, and terror and
   trembling hold
my heart, O Delian Healer, and I worship full of
   fears
for what doom you will bring to pass, new or
   renewed in the revolving years.
Speak to me, immortal voice,
child of golden Hope. 180

Antistrophe
First I call on you, Athene, deathless daughter of
   Zeus,
and Artemis, Earth Upholder,
who sits in the midst of the marketplace in the
   throne which men call Fame,
and Phoebus, the Far Shooter, three averters of
   Fate,
come to us now, if ever before, when ruin rushed 185
   upon the state,
you drove destruction's flame away
out of our land.

Strophe
Our sorrows defy number;

all the ship's timbers are rotten;
taking of thought is no spear for the driving away of   190
   the plague.
There are no growing children in this famous land;
there are no women bearing the pangs of childbirth.
You may see them one with another, like birds swift
   on the wing,
quicker than fire unmastered,
speeding away to the coast of the Western God.   195

   Antistrophe
In the unnumbered deaths
of its people the city dies;
those children that are born lie dead on the naked
   earth
unpitied, spreading contagion of death; and gray-
   haired mothers and wives
everywhere stand at the altar's edge, suppliant,   200
   moaning;
the hymn to the healing God rings out but with it
   the wailing voices are blended.
From these our sufferings grant us, O golden
   Daughter of Zeus,
glad-faced deliverance.

   Strophe
There is no clash of brazen shields but our fight is
   with the War God,
a War God ringed with the cries of men, a savage   205
   God who burns us;
grant that he turn in racing course backward out of
   our country's bounds
to the great palace of Amphitrite or where the
   waves of the Thracian sea
deny the stranger safe anchorage.
Whatsoever escapes the night
at last the light of day revisits;   210
so smite the War God, Father Zeus,
beneath your thunderbolt,
for you are the lord of the lightning, the lightning
   that carries fire.

Antistrophe
And your unconquered arrow shafts, winged by the
   golden corded bow,
Lycean King, I beg to be at our side for help;   215
and the gleaming torches of Artemis with which she
   scours the Lycean hills,
and I call on the God with the turban of gold, who
   gave his name to this country of ours,
the Bacchic God with the wind-flushed face,
Evian One, who travel
with the Maenad company,   220
combat the God that burns us
with your torch of pine;
for the God that is our enemy is a God unhonored
   among the gods.

[OEDIPUS *returns.*]

OEDIPUS
For what you ask me—if you will hear my words,
and hearing welcome them and fight the plague,   225
you will find strength and lightening of your load.

Hark to me; what I say to you, I say
as one that is a stranger to the story
as stranger to the deed. For I would not
be far upon the track if I alone   230
were tracing it without a clue. But now,
since after all was finished, I became
a citizen among you, citizens—
now I proclaim to all the men of Thebes:
who so among you knows the murderer   235
by whose hand Laius, son of Labdacus,
died—I command him to tell everything
to me—yes, though he fears himself to take the
   blame
on his own head; for bitter punishment
he shall have none, but leave this land unharmed.   240
Or if he knows the murderer, another,
a foreigner, still let him speak the truth.
For I will pay him and be grateful, too.

But if you shall keep silence, if perhaps
some one of you, to shield a guilty friend,   245
or for his own sake shall reject my words—
hear what I shall do then:
I forbid that man, whoever he be, my land,
my land where I hold sovereignty and throne;
and I forbid any to welcome him   250
or cry him greeting or make him a sharer
in sacrifice or offering to the gods,
or give him water for his hands to wash.
I command all to drive him from their homes,
since he is our pollution, as the oracle   255
of Pytho's God proclaimed him now to me.
So I stand forth a champion of the God
and of the man who died.
Upon the murderer I invoke this curse—
whether he is one man and all unknown,   260
or one of many—may he wear out his life
in misery to miserable doom!
If with my knowledge he lives at my hearth
I pray that I myself may feel my curse.
On you I lay my charge to fulfill all this   265
for me, for the God, and for this land of ours
destroyed and blighted, by the God forsaken.

Even were this no matter of God's ordinance
it would not fit you so to leave it lie,
unpurified, since a good man is dead   270
and one that was a king. Search it out.
Since I am now the holder of his office,
and have his bed and wife that once was his,
and had his line not been unfortunate
we would have common children—(fortune leaped   275
upon his head)—because of all these things,
I fight in his defense as for my father,
and I shall try all means to take the murderer
of Laius the son of Labdacus
the son of Polydorus and before him   280
of Cadmus and before him of Agenor.
Those who do not obey me, may the gods
grant no crops springing from the ground they plow
nor children to their women! May a fate

like this, or one still worse than this consume them! 285
For you whom these words please, the other
    Thebans,
may Justice as your ally and all the gods
live with you, blessing you now and forever!

CHORUS
    As you have held me to my oath, I speak:
    I neither killed the king nor can declare   290
    the killer; but since Phoebus set the quest
    it is his part to tell who the man is.

OEDIPUS
    Right; but to put compulsion on the gods
    against their will—no man can do that.

CHORUS
    May I then say what I think second best?   295

OEDIPUS
    If there's a third best, too, spare not to tell it.

CHORUS
    I know that what the Lord Teiresias
    sees, is most often what the Lord Apollo
    sees. If you should inquire of this from him
    you might find out most clearly.   300

OEDIPUS
    Even in this my actions have not been sluggard.
    On Creon's word I have sent two messengers,
    and why the prophet is not here already
    I have been wondering.

CHORUS
                         His skill apart
    there is besides only an old faint story.   305

OEDIPUS
    What is it?
    I look at every story.

CHORUS
                              It was said
    that he was killed by certain wayfarers.

OEDIPUS
    I heard that, too, but no one saw the killer.

CHORUS
    Yet if he has a share of fear at all,   310
    his courage will not stand firm, hearing your curse.

OEDIPUS
    The man who in the doing did not shrink
    will fear no word.

CHORUS
                          Here comes his prosecutor:
    led by your men the godly prophet comes
    in whom alone of mankind truth is native.   315

                [*Enter* TEIRESIAS, *led by a little boy.*]

OEDIPUS
    Teiresias, you are versed in everything,
    things teachable and things not to be spoken,
    things of the heaven and earth-creeping things.
    You have no eyes but in your mind you know
    with what a plague our city is afflicted.   320
    My lord, in you alone we find a champion,
    in you alone one that can rescue us.
    Perhaps you have not heard the messengers,
    but Phoebus sent in answer to our sending
    an oracle declaring that our freedom   325
    from this disease would only come when we
    should learn the names of those who killed King
        Laius,
    and kill them or expel from our country.
    Do not begrudge us oracles from birds,
    or any other way of prophecy   330
    within your skill; save yourself and the city,
    save me; redeem the debt of our pollution
        that lies on us because of this dead man.

We are in your hands; pains are most nobly taken
to help another when you have means and power.   335

TEIRESIAS

Alas, how terrible is wisdom when
it brings no profit to the man that's wise!
This I knew well, but had forgotten it,
else I would not have come here.

OEDIPUS   What is this?   340
How sad you are now you have come!

TEIRESIAS

Let me
go home. It will be easiest for us both
to bear our several destinies to the end
if you will follow my advice.

OEDIPUS

You'd rob us
of this your gift of prophecy? You talk   345
as one who had no care for law nor love
for Thebes who reared you.

TEIRESIAS

Yes, but I see that even your own words
miss the mark; therefore I must fear for mine.

OEDIPUS

For God's sake, if you know of anything,   350
do not turn from us; all of us kneel to you,
all of us here, your suppliants.

TEIRESIAS

All of you here know nothing. I will not
bring to the light of day my troubles, mine—
rather than call them yours.

OEDIPUS

What do you mean?   355
You know of something but refuse to speak.
Would you betray us and destroy the city?

TEIRESIAS

  I will not bring this pain upon us both,
neither on you nor on myself. Why is it
you question me and waste your labor? I   360
will tell you nothing.

OEDIPUS

  You would provoke a stone! Tell us, you villain,
tell us, and do not stand there quietly
unmoved and balking at the issue.

TEIRESIAS

  You blame my temper but you do not see   365
your own that lives within you; it is me
you chide.

OEDIPUS

  Who would not feel his temper rise
at words like these with which you shame our city?

TEIRESIAS

  Of themselves things will come, although I hide
    them   370
and breathe no word of them.

OEDIPUS

                         Since they will come
tell them to me.

TEIRESIAS

                  I will say nothing further.
Against this answer let your temper rage
as wildly as you will.

OEDIPUS

             Indeed I am
so angry I shall not hold back a jot   375
of what I think. For I would have you know
I think you were complotter of the deed
and doer of the deed save in so far
as for the actual killing. Had you had eyes
I would have said alone you murdered him.   380

TEIRESIAS

Yes? Then I warn you faithfully to keep
the letter of your proclamation and
from this day forth to speak no word of greeting
to these nor me; you are the land's pollution.

OEDIPUS

How shamelessly you started up this taunt! 385
How do you think you will escape?

TEIRESIAS

I have.
I have escaped; the truth is what I cherish
and that's my strength.

OEDIPUS

And who has taught you
truth?
Not your profession surely!

TEIRESIAS

You have taught me,
for you have made me speak against my will. 390

OEDIPUS

Speak what? Tell me again that I may learn it
better.

TEIRESIAS

Did you not understand before or would you
provoke me into speaking?

OEDIPUS

I did not grasp it,
not so to call it known. Say it again.

TEIRESIAS

I say you are the murderer of the king 395
whose murderer you seek.

OEDIPUS

Not twice you shall
say calumnies like this and stay unpunished.

TEIRESIAS
   Shall I say more to tempt your anger more?

OEDIPUS
   As much as you desire; it will be said
   in vain.

TEIRESIAS
            I say that with those you love best   400
   you live in foulest shame unconsciously
   and do not see where you are in calamity.

OEDIPUS
   Do you imagine you can always talk
   like this, and live to laugh at it hereafter?

TEIRESIAS
   Yes, if the truth has anything of strength.   405

OEDIPUS
   It has, but not for you; it has no strength
   for you because you are blind in mind and ears
   as well as in your eyes.

TEIRESIAS
                     You are a poor wretch
   to taunt me with the very insults which
   everyone soon will heap upon yourself.   410

OEDIPUS
   Your life is one long night so that you cannot
   hurt me or any other who sees the light.

TEIRESIAS
   It is not fate that I should be your ruin,
   Apollo is enough; it is his care
   to work this out.

OEDIPUS
              Was this your own design
   or Creon's?   415

TEIRESIAS
                    Creon is no hurt to you,
   but you are to yourself.

OEDIPUS
   Wealth, sovereignty, and skill outmatching skill
   for the contrivance of an envied life!
   Great store of jealousy fill your treasury chests,   420
   if my friend Creon, friend from the first and loyal,
   thus secretly attacks me, secretly
   desires to drive me out, and secretly
   suborns this juggling, trick-devising quack,
   this wily beggar who has only eyes   425
   for his own gains, but blindness in his skill.
   For, tell me, where have you seen clear, Teiresias,
   with your prophetic eyes? When the dark singer,
   the Sphinx, was in your country, did you speak
   word of deliverance to its citizens?   430
   And yet the riddle's answer was not the province
   of a chance comer. It was a prophet's task
   and plainly you had no such gift of prophecy
   from birds nor otherwise from any God
   to glean a word of knowledge. But I came,   435
   Oedipus, who knew nothing, and I stopped her.
   I solved the riddle by my wit alone.
   Mine was no knowledge got from birds. And now
   you would expel me,
   because you think that you will find a place   440
   by Creon's throne. I think you will be sorry,
   both you and your accomplice, for your plot
   to drive me out. And did I not regard you
   as an old man, some suffering would have taught
         you
   that what was in your heart was treason.   445

CHORUS
   We look at this man's words and yours, my king,
   and we find both have spoken them in anger.
   We need no angry words but only thought
   how we may best hit the God's meaning for us.

TEIRESIAS
　　If you are king, at least I have the right   450
　　no less to speak in my defense against you.
　　Of that much I am master. I am no slave
　　of yours, by Loxias', and so I shall not
　　enroll myself with Creon for my patron.
　　Since you have taunted me with being blind,   455
　　here is my word for you.
　　You have your eyes but see not where you are
　　in sin, nor where you live, nor whom you live with.
　　Do you know who your parents are? Unknowing
　　you are an enemy to kith and kin   460
　　in death, beneath the earth, and in this life.
　　A deadly-footed, double-striking curse,
　　from father and mother both, shall drive you forth
　　out of this land, with darkness on your eyes,
　　that now have such straight vision. Shall there be   465
　　a place will not be harbor to your cries,
　　a corner of Cithaeron will not ring
　　in echo to your cries, soon, soon—
　　when you shall learn the secret of your marriage,
　　which steered you to a haven in this house—   470
　　haven no haven, after lucky voyage?
　　And of the multitude of other evils
　　establishing a grim equality
　　between you and your children, you know nothing.
　　So, muddy with contempt my words and Creon's!   475
　　Misery shall grind no man as it will you.

OEDIPUS
　　Is it endurable that I should hear
　　such words from him? Go, and a curse go with you!
　　Quick, home with you! Out of my house at once!

TEIRESIAS
　　I would not have come either had you not called
　　　　me.   480

OEDIPUS
　　I did not know then you would talk like a fool—
　　or it would have been long before I called you.

TEIRESIAS
   I am a fool then, as it seems to you—
   but to the parents who have bred you, wise.

OEDIPUS
   What parents? Stop! Who are they of all the world?   485

TEIRESIAS
   This day will show your birth and will destroy you.

OEDIPUS
   How needlessly your riddles darken everything.

TEIRESIAS
   But it's in riddle answering you are strongest.

OEDIPUS
   Yes. Taunt me where you will find me great.

TEIRESIAS
   It is this very luck that has destroyed you.   490

OEDIPUS
   I do not care, if it has saved this city.

TEIRESIAS
   Well, I will go. Come, boy, lead me away.

OEDIPUS
   Yes, lead him off. So long as you are here,
   you'll be a stumbling block and a vexation;
   once gone, you will not trouble me again.

TEIRESIAS
                        I have said   495
   what I came here to say not fearing your
   countenance: there is no way you can hurt me.
   I tell you, King, this man, this murderer
   (whom you have long declared you are in search of,
   indicting him in threatening proclamation   500
   as murderer of Laius)—he is here.

In name he is a stranger among citizens
but soon he will be shown to be a citizen
true native Theban, and he'll have no joy
of the discovery: blindness for sight   505
and beggary for riches his exchange,
he shall go journeying to a foreign country
tapping his way before him with a stick.
He shall be proved father and brother both
to his own children in his house; to her   510
that gave him birth, a son and husband both;
a fellow sower in his father's bed
with that same father that he murdered.
Go within, reckon that out, and if you find me
mistaken, say I have no skill in prophecy.   515

[*Exeunt separately* TEIRESIAS *and* OEDIPUS.]

CHORUS
    Strophe
Who is the man proclaimed
by Delphi's prophetic rock
as the bloody-handed murderer,
the doer of deeds that none dare name?
Now is the time for him to run   520
with a stronger foot
than Pegasus,
for the child of Zeus leaps in arms upon him
with fire and the lightning bolt,
and terribly close on his heels   525
are the Fates that never miss.

    Antistrophe
Lately from snowy Parnassus
clearly the voice flashed forth,
bidding each Theban track him down,
the unknown murderer.   530
In the savage forests he lurks and in
the caverns like
the mountain bull.
He is sad and lonely, and lonely his feet
that carry him far from the navel of earth;   535

but its prophecies, ever living,
flutter around his head.

Strophe
The augur has spread confusion,
terrible confusion;
I do not approve what was said 540
nor can I deny it.
I do not know what to say;
I am in a flutter of foreboding;
I never heard in the present
nor past of a quarrel between 545
the sons of Labdacus and Polybus,
that I might bring as proof
in attacking the popular fame
of Oedipus, seeking
to take vengeance for undiscovered 550
death in the line of Labdacus.

Antistrophe
Truly Zeus and Apollo are wise
and in human things all knowing;
but amongst men there is no
distinct judgment, between the prophet 555
and me—which of us is right.
One man may pass another in wisdom
but I would never agree
with those that find fault with the king
till I should see the word 560
proved right beyond doubt. For once
in visible form the Sphinx
came on him and all of us
saw his wisdom and in that test
he saved the city. So he will not be condemned by
my mind. 565

[*Enter* CREON.]

CREON
Citizens, I have come because I heard
deadly words spread about me, that the king

accuses me. I cannot take that from him.
If he believes that in these present troubles
he has been wronged by me in word or deed   570
I do not want to live on with the burden
of such a scandal on me. The report
injures me doubly and most vitally—for I'll be
    called a traitor to my city
and traitor also to my friends and you.

CHORUS
Perhaps it was a sudden gust of anger   575
that forced that insult from him, and no judgment.

CREON
But did he say that it was in compliance
with schemes of mine that the seer told him lies?

CHORUS
Yes, he said that, but why, I do not know.

CREON
Were his eyes straight in his head? Was his mind
    right   580
when he accused me in this fashion?

CHORUS
I do not know; I have no eyes to see
what princes do. Here comes the king himself.

[*Enter* OEDIPUS.]

OEDIPUS
You, sir, how is it you come here? Have you so
    much
brazen-faced daring that you venture in   585
my house although you are proved manifestly
the murderer of that man, and though you tried,
openly, highway robbery of my crown?
For God's sake, tell me what you saw in me,
what cowardice or what stupidity,   590
that made you lay a plot like this against me?
Did you imagine I should not observe
the crafty scheme that stole upon me, or

seeing it, take no means to counter it?
Was it not stupid of you to make the attempt,   595
to try to hunt down royal power without
the people at your back or friends? For only
with the people at your back or money can
the hunt end in the capture of a crown.

CREON

Do you know what you're doing? Will you listen   600
to words to answer yours, and then pass judgment?

OEDIPUS

You're quick to speak, but I am slow to grasp you,
for I have found you dangerous—and my foe.

CREON

First of all hear what I shall say to that.

OEDIPUS

At least don't tell me that you are not guilty.   605

CREON

If you think obstinacy without wisdom
a valuable possession, you are wrong.

OEDIPUS

And you are wrong if you believe that one,
a criminal, will not be punished only
because he is my kinsman.

CREON

                        This is but just—   610
but tell me, then, of what offense I'm guilty?

OEDIPUS

Did you or did you not urge me to send
to this prophetic mumbler?

CREON

                        I did indeed,
and I shall stand by what I told you.

OEDIPUS

How long ago is it since Laius. . . .   615

CREON
  What about Laius? I don't understand.

OEDIPUS
  Vanished—died—was murdered?

CREON
                          It is long,
  a long, long time to reckon.

OEDIPUS
                          Was this prophet
  in the profession then?

CREON
                          He was, and honored
  as highly as he is today.   620

OEDIPUS
  At that time did he say a word about me?

CREON
  Never, at least when I was near him.

OEDIPUS
  You never made a search for the dead man?

CREON
  We searched, indeed, but never learned of anything.

OEDIPUS
  Why did our wise old friend not say this then?

CREON
  I don't know; and when I know nothing, I   625
  usually hold my tongue.

OEDIPUS
                          You know this much,
  and can declare this much if you are loyal.

CREON
  What is it? If I know, I'll not deny it.

OEDIPUS
That he would not have said that I killed Laius
had he not met you first.

CREON
                              You know yourself   630
whether he said this, but I demand that I
should hear as much from you as you from me.

OEDIPUS
Then hear—I'll not be proved a murderer.

CREON
Well, then. You're married to my sister.

OEDIPUS
                              Yes,
that I am not disposed to deny.

CREON
                              You rule   635
this country giving her an equal share
in the government?

OEDIPUS
                        Yes, everything she wants
she has from me.

CREON
                  And I, as thirdsman to you,
am rated as the equal of you two?

OEDIPUS
Yes, and it's there you've proved yourself false
    friend.   640

CREON
Not if you will reflect on it as I do.
Consider, first, if you think anyone
would choose to rule and fear rather than rule
and sleep untroubled by a fear if power
were equal in both cases. I, at least,   645

I was not born with such a frantic yearning
to be a king—but to do what kings do.
And so it is with everyone who has learned
wisdom and self-control. As it stands now,
the prizes are all mine—and without fear.   650
But if I were the king myself, I must
do much that went against the grain.
How should despotic rule seem sweeter to me
than painless power and an assured authority?
I am not so besotted yet that I   655
want other honors than those that come with profit.
Now every man's my pleasure; every man greets
    me;
now those who are your suitors fawn on me—
success for them depends upon my favor.
Why should I let all this go to win that?   660
My mind would not be traitor if it's wise;
I am no treason lover, of my nature,
nor would I ever dare to join a plot.
Prove what I say. Go to the oracle
at Pytho and inquire about the answers,   665
if they are as I told you. For the rest,
if you discover I laid any plot
together with the seer, kill me, I say,
not only by your vote but by my own.
But do not charge me on obscure opinion   670
without some proof to back it. It's not just
lightly to count your knaves as honest men,
nor honest men as knaves. To throw away
an honest friend is, as it were, to throw
your life away, which a man loves the best.   675
In time you will know all with certainty;
time is the only test of honest men,
one day is space enough to know a rogue.

CHORUS
    His words are wise, King, if one fears to fall.
    Those who are quick of temper are not safe.   680

OEDIPUS
    When he that plots against me secretly
    moves quickly, I must quickly counterplot.

If I wait taking no decisive measure
his business will be done, and mine be spoiled.

CREON

What do you want to do then? Banish me?   685

OEDIPUS

No, certainly; kill you, not banish you.[1]

CREON

I do not think that you've your wits about you.

OEDIPUS

For my own interests, yes.

CREON

               But for mine, too,
you should think equally.

OEDIPUS

                  You are a rogue.

CREON

Suppose you do not understand?

OEDIPUS

                  But yet   690
I must be ruler.

CREON

                 Not if you rule badly.

OEDIPUS

O, city, city!

1. Two lines omitted here owing to the confusion in the dialogue
consequent on the loss of a third line. The lines as they stand in
Jebb's edition (1902) are:

OED.: That you may show what manner of thing is envy.
CREON: You speak as one that will not yield or trust.
[OED. lost line.]

CREON
> I, too, have some share
> in the city; it is not yours alone.

CHORUS
> Stop, my lords! Here—and in the nick of time
> I see Jocasta coming from the house;   695
> with her help lay the quarrel that now stirs you.

> [*Enter* JOCASTA.]

JOCASTA
> For shame! Why have you raised this foolish
>   squabbling
> brawl? Are you not ashamed to air your private
> griefs when the country's sick? Go in, you,
>   Oedipus,
> and you, too, Creon, into the house. Don't magnify   700
> your nothing troubles.

CREON
> Sister, Oedipus,
> your husband, thinks he has the right to do
> terrible wrongs—he has but to choose between
> two terrors: banishing or killing me.

OEDIPUS
> He's right, Jocasta; for I find him plotting   705
> with knavish tricks against my person.

CREON
> That God may never bless me! May I die
> accursed if I have been guilty of
> one tittle of the charge you bring against me!

JOCASTA
> I beg you, Oedipus, trust him in this,   710
> spare him for the sake of this his oath to God,
> for my sake, and the sake of those who stand here.

CHORUS
> Be gracious, be merciful,
> we beg of you.

OEDIPUS
    In what would you have me yield?   715

CHORUS
    He has been no silly child in the past.
    He is strong in his oath now.
    Spare him.

OEDIPUS
    Do you know what you ask?

CHORUS
    Yes.   720

OEDIPUS
    Tell me then.

CHORUS
    He has been your friend before all men's eyes; do not
    cast him away dishonored on an obscure conjecture.

OEDIPUS
    I would have you know that this request of yours
    really requests my death or banishment.   725

CHORUS
    May the Sun God, king of gods, forbid! May I die
    without God's blessing, without friends' help, if I had
    any such thought. But my spirit is broken by my
    unhappiness for my wasting country; and this would
    but add troubles amongst ourselves to the other
    troubles.   730

OEDIPUS
    Well, let him go then—if I must die ten times for it,
    or be sent out dishonored into exile.
    It is your lips that prayed for him I pitied,
    not his; wherever he is, I shall hate him.

CREON
    I see you sulk in yielding and you're dangerous   735
    when you are out of temper; natures like yours
    are justly heaviest for themselves to bear.

OEDIPUS
Leave me alone! Take yourself off, I tell you.

CREON
I'll go, you have not known me, but they have,
and they have known my innocence.   740

[*Exit.*]

CHORUS
Won't you take him inside, lady?

JOCASTA
Yes, when I've found out what was the matter.

CHORUS
There was some misconceived suspicion of a story,
and on the other side the sting of injustice.

JOCASTA
So, on both sides?   745

CHORUS
Yes.

JOCASTA
What was the story?

CHORUS
I think it best, in the interests of the country, to leave
it where it ended.

OEDIPUS
You see where you have ended, straight of judgment   750
although you are, by softening my anger.

CHORUS
Sir, I have said before and I say again—be sure that I
would have been proved a madman, bankrupt in sane
council, if I should put you away, you who steered
the country I love safely when she was crazed with   755

troubles. God grant that now, too, you may prove a
fortunate guide for us.

JOCASTA
Tell me, my lord, I beg of you, what was it
that roused your anger so?

OEDIPUS
                              Yes, I will tell you.
I honor you more than I honor them.   760
It was Creon and the plots he laid against me.

JOCASTA
Tell me—if you can clearly tell the quarrel—

OEDIPUS
                              Creon says
that I'm the murderer of Laius.

JOCASTA
Of his own knowledge or on information?

OEDIPUS
He sent this rascal prophet to me, since   765
he keeps his own mouth clean of any guilt.

JOCASTA
Do not concern yourself about this matter;
listen to me and learn that human beings
have no part in the craft of prophecy.
Of that I'll show you a short proof.   770
There was an oracle once that came to Laius—
I will not say that it was Phoebus' own,
but it was from his servants—and it told him
that it was fate that he should die a victim
at the hands of his own son, a son to be born   775
of Laius and me. But, see now, he,
the king, was killed by foreign highway robbers
at a place where three roads meet—so goes the
     story;
and for the son—before three days were out

after his birth King Laius pierced his ankles   780
and by the hands of others cast him forth
upon a pathless hillside. So Apollo
failed to fulfill his oracle to the son,
that he should kill his father, and to Laius
also proved false in that the thing he feared,   785
death at his son's hands, never came to pass.
So clear in this case were the oracles,
so clear and false. Give them no heed, I say;
what God discovers need of, easily
he shows to us himself.

OEDIPUS
                                O dear Jocasta,   790
as I hear this from you, there comes upon me
a wandering of the soul—I could run mad.

JOCASTA
What trouble is it, that you turn again
and speak like this?

OEDIPUS
                        I thought I heard you say
that Laius was killed at a crossroads.   795

JOCASTA
Yes, that was how the story went and still
that word goes round.

OEDIPUS
                            Where is this place, Jocasta,
where he was murdered?

JOCASTA
                            Phocis is the country
and the road splits there, one of two roads from
    Delphi,
another comes from Daulia.

OEDIPUS
                                How long ago is this?   800

JOCASTA

> The news came to the city just before
> you became king and all men's eyes looked to you.
> What is it, Oedipus, that's in your mind?

OEDIPUS

> What have you designed, O Zeus, to do with me?

JOCASTA

> What is the thought that troubles your heart?   805

OEDIPUS

> Don't ask me yet—tell me of Laius—
> How did he look? How old or young was he?

JOCASTA

> He was a tall man and his hair was grizzled
> already—nearly white—and in his form
> not unlike you.

OEDIPUS

>   O God, I think I have   810
> called curses on myself in ignorance.

JOCASTA

> What do you mean? I am terrified
> when I look at you.

OEDIPUS

>   I have a deadly fear
> that the old seer had eyes. You'll show me more
> if you can tell me one more thing.

JOCASTA

>   I will.   815
> I'm frightened—but if I can understand,
> I'll tell you all you ask.

OEDIPUS

>   How was his company?
> Had he few with him when he went this journey,
> or many servants, as would suit a prince?

JOCASTA
In all there were but five, and among them   820
a herald; and one carriage for the king.

OEDIPUS
It's plain—it's plain—who was it told you this?

JOCASTA
The only servant that escaped safe home.

OEDIPUS
Is he at home now?

JOCASTA   No, when he came home again
and saw you king and Laius was dead,   825
he came to me and touched my hand and begged
that I should send him to the fields to be
my shepherd and so he might see the city
as far off as he might. So I
sent him away. He was an honest man,   830
as slaves go, and was worthy of far more
than what he asked of me.

OEDIPUS
O, how I wish that he could come back quickly!

JOCASTA
He can. Why is your heart so set on this?

OEDIPUS
O dear Jocasta, I am full of fears   835
that I have spoken far too much; and therefore
I wish to see this shepherd.

JOCASTA
                    He will come;
but, Oedipus, I think I'm worthy, too,
to know what it is that disquiets you.

OEDIPUS
It shall not be kept from you, since my mind   840
has gone so far with its forebodings. Whom

should I confide in rather than you, who is there
of more importance to me who have passed
through such a fortune?
Polybus was my father, king of Corinth,   845
and Merope, the Dorian, my mother.
I was held greatest of the citizens
in Corinth till a curious chance befell me
as I shall tell you—curious, indeed,
but hardly worth the store I set upon it.   850
There was a dinner and at it a man,
a drunken man, accused me in his drink
of being bastard. I was furious
but held my temper under for that day.
Next day I went and taxed my parents with it;   855
they took the insult very ill from him,
the drunken fellow who had uttered it.
So I was comforted for their part, but
still this thing rankled always, for the story
crept about widely. And I went at last   860
to Pytho, though my parents did not know.
But Phoebus sent me home again unhonored
in what I came to learn, but he foretold
other and desperate horrors to befall me,
that I was fated to lie with my mother,   865
and show to daylight an accursed breed
which men would not endure, and I was doomed
to be murderer of the father that begot me.
When I heard this I fled, and in the days
that followed I would measure from the stars   870
the whereabouts of Corinth—yes, I fled
to somewhere where I should not see fulfilled
the infamies told in that dreadful oracle.
And as I journeyed I came to the place
where, as you say, this king met with his death.   875
Jocasta, I will tell you the whole truth.
When I was near the branching of the crossroads,
going on foot, I was encountered by
a herald and a carriage with a man in it,
just as you tell me. He that led the way   880
and the old man himself wanted to thrust me
out of the road by force. I became angry
and struck the coachman who was pushing me.

When the old man saw this he watched his moment,
and as I passed he struck me from his carriage,   885
full on the head with his two-pointed goad.
But he was paid in full and presently
my stick had struck him backward from the car
and he rolled out of it. And then I killed them
all. If it happened there was any tie   890
of kinship twixt this man and Laius,
who is then now more miserable than I,
what man on earth so hated by the gods,
since neither citizen nor foreigner
may welcome me at home or even greet me,   895
but drive me out of doors? And it is I,
I and no other have so cursed myself.
And I pollute the bed of him I killed
by the hands that killed him. Was I not born evil?
Am I not utterly unclean? I had to fly   900
and in my banishment not even see
my kindred nor set foot in my own country,
or otherwise my fate was to be yoked
in marriage with my mother and kill my father,
Polybus who begot me and had reared me.   905
Would not one rightly judge and say that on me
these things were sent by some malignant God?
O, no, no, no—O holy majesty
of God on high, may I not see that day!
May I be gone out of men's sight before   910
I see the deadly taint of this disaster
come upon me.

CHORUS
  Sir, we, too, fear these things. But until you see this
  man face to face and hear his story, hope.

OEDIPUS
  Yes, I have just this much of hope—to wait until the   915
  herdsman comes.

JOCASTA
  And when he comes, what do you want with him?

OEDIPUS
  I'll tell you; if I find that his story is the same as
  yours, I at least will be clear of this guilt.

JOCASTA
  Why, what so particularly did you learn from my   920
  story?

OEDIPUS
  You said that he spoke of highway *robbers* who
  killed Laius. Now if he uses the same number, it was
  not I who killed him. One man cannot be the same
  as many. But if he speaks of a man traveling alone,
  then clearly the burden of the guilt inclines toward
  me.   925

JOCASTA
  Be sure, at least, that this was how he told the story.
  He cannot unsay it now, for everyone in the city
  heard it—not I alone. But, Oedipus, even if he di-
  verges from what he said then, he shall never prove
  that the murder of Laius squares rightly with the   930
  prophecy—for Loxias declared that the king should
  be killed by his own son. And that poor creature did
  not kill him surely—for he died himself first. So as
  far as prophecy goes, henceforward I shall not look
  to the right hand or the left.   935

OEDIPUS
  Right. But yet, send someone for the peasant to
  bring him here; do not neglect it.

JOCASTA
  I will send quickly. Now let me go indoors. I will do
  nothing except what pleases you.

                                              [*Exeunt.*]

CHORUS
    Strophe
  May destiny ever find me   940
  pious in word and deed

prescribed by the laws that live on high:
laws begotten in the clear air of heaven,
whose only father is Olympus;
no mortal nature brought them to birth,   945
no forgetfulness shall lull them to sleep;
for God is great in them and grows not old.

Antistrophe
Insolence breeds the tyrant, insolence
if it is glutted with a surfeit, unseasonable,
    unprofitable,
climbs to the rooftop and plunges   950
sheer down to the ruin that must be,
and there its feet are no service.
But I pray that the God may never
abolish the eager ambition that profits the state.
For I shall never cease to hold the God as our
    protector.   955

Strophe
If a man walks with haughtiness
of hand or word and gives no heed
to Justice and the shrines of gods
despises—may an evil doom
smite him for his ill-starred pride of heart!—   960
if he reaps gains without justice
and will not hold from impiety
and his fingers itch for untouchable things.
When such things are done, what man shall
    contrive
to shield his soul from the shafts of the God?   965
When such deeds are held in honor,
why should I honor the gods in the dance?

Antistrophe
No longer to the holy place,
to the navel of earth I'll go
to worship, nor to Abae   970
nor to Olympia,
unless the oracles are proved to fit,
for all men's hands to point at.
O Zeus, if you are rightly called

the sovereign lord, all-mastering,   975
let this not escape you nor your ever-living power!
The oracles concerning Laius
are old and dim and men regard them not.
Apollo is nowhere clear in honor; God's service
  perishes.

[*Enter* JOCASTA, *carrying garlands.*]

JOCASTA
Princes of the land, I have had the thought to go   980
to the gods' temples, bringing in my hand
garlands and gifts of incense, as you see.
For Oedipus excites himself too much
at every sort of trouble, not conjecturing,
like a man of sense, what will be from what was,   985
but he is always at the speaker's mercy,
when he speaks terrors. I can do no good
by my advice, and so I came as suppliant
to you, Lycaean Apollo, who are nearest.
These are the symbols of my prayer and this   990
my prayer: grant us escape free of the curse.
Now when we look to him we are all afraid;
he's pilot of our ship and he is frightened.

[*Enter* MESSENGER.]

MESSENGER
Might I learn from you, sirs, where is the house of
Oedipus? Or best of all, if you know, where is the   995
king himself?

CHORUS
This is his house and he is within doors. This lady is
his wife and mother of his children.

MESSENGER
God bless you, lady, and God bless your household!
God bless Oedipus' noble wife!   1000

JOCASTA
God bless you, sir, for your kind greeting! What do

you want of us that you have come here? What have
you to tell us?

MESSENGER
Good news, lady. Good for your house and for your
husband.   1005

JOCASTA
What is your news? Who sent you to us?

MESSENGER
I come from Corinth and the news I bring will give
you pleasure. Perhaps a little pain, too.

JOCASTA
What is this news of double meaning?

MESSENGER
The people of the Isthmus will choose Oedipus to be   1010
their king. That is the rumor there.

JOCASTA
But isn't their king still old Polybus?

MESSENGER
No. He is in his grave. Death has got him.

JOCASTA
Is that the truth? Is Oedipus' father dead?

MESSENGER
May I die myself if it be otherwise!   1015

JOCASTA [*To a servant*]
Be quick and run to the king with the news! O
oracles of the gods, where are you now? It was from
this man Oedipus fled, lest he should be his murderer! And now he is dead, in the course of nature,
and not killed by Oedipus.   1020

[*Enter* OEDIPUS.]

OEDIPUS
Dearest Jocasta, why have you sent for me?

JOCASTA
Listen to this man and when you hear reflect what is
the outcome of the holy oracles of the gods.

OEDIPUS
Who is he? What is his message for me?

JOCASTA
He is from Corinth and he tells us that your father   1025
Polybus is dead and gone.

OEDIPUS
What's this you say, sir? Tell me yourself.

MESSENGER
Since this is the first matter you want clearly told:
Polybus has gone down to death. You may be sure of
it.

OEDIPUS
By treachery or sickness?   1030

MESSENGER
A small thing will put old bodies asleep.

OEDIPUS
So he died of sickness, it seems—poor old man!

MESSENGER
Yes, and of age—the long years he had measured.

OEDIPUS
Ha! Ha! O dear Jocasta, why should one
look to the Pythian hearth? Why should one look   1035
to the birds screaming overhead? They prophesied
that I should kill my father! But he's dead,
and hidden deep in earth, and I stand here
who never laid a hand on spear against him—

unless perhaps he died of longing for me, 1040
and thus I am his murderer. But they,
the oracles, as they stand—he's taken them
away with him, they're dead as he himself is,
and worthless.

JOCASTA

That I told you before now.

OEDIPUS
You did, but I was misled by my fear. 1045

JOCASTA
Then lay no more of them to heart, not one.

OEDIPUS
But surely I must fear my mother's bed?

JOCASTA
Why should man fear since chance is all in all
for him, and he can clearly foreknow nothing?
Best to live lightly, as one can, unthinkingly. 1050
As to your mother's marriage bed—don't fear it.
Before this, in dreams, too, as well as oracles,
many a man has lain with his own mother.
But he to whom such things are nothing bears
his life most easily. 1055

OEDIPUS
All that you say would be said perfectly
if she were dead; but since she lives I must
still fear, although you talk so well, Jocasta.

JOCASTA
Still in your father's death there's light of comfort?

OEDIPUS
Great light of comfort; but I fear the living. 1060

MESSENGER
Who is the woman that makes you afraid?

OEDIPUS
    Merope, old man, Polybus' wife.

MESSENGER
    What about her frightens the queen and you?

OEDIPUS
    A terrible oracle, stranger, from the gods.

MESSENGER
    Can it be told? Or does the sacred law   1065
    forbid another to have knowledge of it?

OEDIPUS
    O, no! Once on a time Loxias said
    that I should lie with my own mother and
    take on my hands the blood of my own father.
    And so for these long years I've lived away   1070
    from Corinth; it has been to my great happiness;
    but yet it's sweet to see the face of parents.

MESSENGER
    This was the fear which drove you out of Corinth?

OEDIPUS
    Old man, I did not wish to kill my father.

MESSENGER
    Why should I not free you from this fear, sir,   1075
    since I have come to you in all goodwill?

OEDIPUS
    You would not find me thankless if you did.

MESSENGER
    Why, it was just for this I brought the news—
    to earn your thanks when you had come safe home.

OEDIPUS
    No, I will never come near my parents.

MESSENGER

                                      Son,   1080
  it's very plain you don't know what you're doing.

OEDIPUS
  What do you mean, old man? For God's sake, tell
    me.

MESSENGER
  If your homecoming is checked by fears like these.

OEDIPUS
  Yes, I'm afraid that Phoebus may prove right.

MESSENGER
  The murder and the incest?

OEDIPUS
                          Yes, old man;
  that is my constant terror.

MESSENGER
                          Do you know   1085
  that all your fears are empty?

OEDIPUS
                          How is that,
  if they are father and mother and I their son?

MESSENGER
  Because Polybus was no kin to you in blood.

OEDIPUS
  What, was not Polybus my father?

MESSENGER
  No more than I but just so much.

OEDIPUS
                          How can   1090
  my father be my father as much as one
  that's nothing to me?

MESSENGER

Neither he nor I
begat you.

OEDIPUS

Why then did he call me son?

MESSENGER
A gift he took you from these hands of mine.

OEDIPUS
Did he love so much what he took from another's
hand?   1095

MESSENGER
His childlessness before persuaded him.

OEDIPUS
Was I a child you bought or found when I
was given to him?

MESSENGER

On Cithaeron's slopes
in the twisting thickets you were found.

OEDIPUS

And why
were you a traveler in those parts?

MESSENGER

I was   1100
in charge of mountain flocks.

OEDIPUS

You were a shepherd?
A hireling vagrant?

MESSENGER

Yes, but at least at that time
the man that saved your life, son.

OEDIPUS
What ailed me when you took me in your arms?

MESSENGER
  In that your ankles should be witnesses.   1105

OEDIPUS
  Why do you speak of that old pain?

MESSENGER
                        I loosed you;
  the tendons of your feet were pierced and fettered—

OEDIPUS
  My swaddling clothes brought me a rare disgrace.

MESSENGER
  So that from this you're called your present name.

OEDIPUS
  Was this my father's doing or my mother's?   1110
  For God's sake, tell me.

MESSENGER
                    I don't know, but he
  who gave you to me has more knowledge than I.

OEDIPUS
  You yourself did not find me then? You took me
  from someone else?

MESSENGER
                    Yes, from another shepherd.

OEDIPUS
  Who was he? Do you know him well enough   1115
  to tell?

MESSENGER
                    He was called Laius' man.

OEDIPUS
  You mean the king who reigned here in the old
  days?

MESSENGER
    Yes, he was that man's shepherd.

OEDIPUS
                              Is he alive
    still, so that I could see him?

MESSENGER
                        You who live here
    would know that best.

OEDIPUS
                        Do any of you here   1120
    know of this shepherd whom he speaks about
    in town or in the fields? Tell me. It's time
    that this was found out once for all.

CHORUS
    I think he is none other than the peasant
    whom you have sought to see already; but   1125
    Jocasta here can tell us best of that.

OEDIPUS
    Jocasta, do you know about this man
    whom we have sent for? Is he the man he
        mentions?

JOCASTA
    Why ask of whom he spoke? Don't give it heed;
    nor try to keep in mind what has been said.   1130
    It will be wasted labor.

OEDIPUS
                        With such clues
    I could not fail to bring my birth to light.

JOCASTA
    I beg you—do not hunt this out—I beg you,
    if you have any care for your own life.
    What I am suffering is enough.

OEDIPUS
                                    Keep up   1135
your heart, Jocasta. Though I'm proved a slave,
thrice slave, and though my mother is thrice slave,
you'll not be shown to be of lowly lineage.

JOCASTA
O, be persuaded by me, I entreat you;
do not do this.   1140

OEDIPUS
I will not be persuaded to let be
the chance of finding out the whole thing clearly.

JOCASTA
It is because I wish you well that I
give you this counsel—and it's the best counsel.

OEDIPUS
Then the best counsel vexes me, and has   1145
for some while since.

JOCASTA
                          O Oedipus, God help you!
God keep you from the knowledge of who you are!

OEDIPUS
Here, someone, go and fetch the shepherd for me;
and let her find her joy in her rich family!

JOCASTA
O Oedipus, unhappy Oedipus!   1150
that is all I can call you, and the last thing
that I shall ever call you.

                                        [*Exit.*]

CHORUS
Why has the queen gone, Oedipus, in wild
grief rushing from us? I am afraid that trouble
will break out of this silence.   1155

OEDIPUS

Break out what will! I at least shall be
willing to see my ancestry, though humble.
Perhaps she is ashamed of my low birth,
for she has all a woman's high-flown pride.   1160
But I account myself a child of Fortune,
beneficent Fortune, and I shall not be
dishonored. She's the mother from whom I spring;
the months, my brothers, marked me, now as small,
and now again as mighty. Such is my breeding,   1165
and I shall never prove so false to it,
as not to find the secret of my birth.

CHORUS

Strophe

If I am a prophet and wise of heart
you shall not fail, Cithaeron,
by the limitless sky, you shall not!—   1170
to know at tomorrow's full moon
that Oedipus honors you,
as native to him and mother and nurse at once;
and that you are honored in dancing by us, as
    finding favor in sight of our king.   1175
Apollo, to whom we cry, find these things pleasing!

Antistrophe

Who was it bore you, child? One of
the long-lived nymphs who lay with Pan—
the father who treads the hills?
Or was she a bride of Loxias, your mother? The
    grassy slopes   1180
are all of them dear to him. Or perhaps Cyllene's
    king
or the Bacchants' God that lives on the tops
of the hills received you a gift from some
one of the Helicon Nymphs, with whom he mostly
    plays?

[*Enter an old man, led by* OEDIPUS' *servants.*]

OEDIPUS

If someone like myself who never met him   1185

may make a guess—I think this is the herdsman,
whom we were seeking. His old age is consonant
with the other. And besides, the men who bring
    him
I recognize as my own servants. You
perhaps may better me in knowledge since   1190
you've seen the man before.

CHORUS

                        You can be sure
I recognize him. For if Laius
had ever an honest shepherd, this was he.

OEDIPUS

You, sir, from Corinth, I must ask you first,
is this the man you spoke of?

MESSENGER

                        This is he   1195
before your eyes.

OEDIPUS

                Old man, look here at me
and tell me what I ask you. Were you ever
a servant of King Laius?

HERDSMAN

                I was—
no slave he bought but reared in his own house.

OEDIPUS

What did you do as work? How did you live?   1200

HERDSMAN

Most of my life was spent among the flocks.

OEDIPUS

In what part of the country did you live?

HERDSMAN

Cithaeron and the places near to it.

OEDIPUS
And somewhere there perhaps you knew this man?

HERDSMAN
What was his occupation? Who?

OEDIPUS
                              This man here,   1205
have you had any dealings with him?

HERDSMAN
                        No—
not such that I can quickly call to mind.

MESSENGER
That is no wonder, master. But I'll make him remember what he does not know. For I know, that he
well knows the country of Cithaeron, how he with   1210
two flocks, I with one kept company for three
years—each year half a year—from spring till autumn time and then when winter came I drove my
flocks to our fold home again and he to Laius' stead-
ings. Well—am I right or not in what I said we did?   1215

HERDSMAN
You're right—although it's a long time ago.

MESSENGER
Do you remember giving me a child
to bring up as my foster child?

HERDSMAN
                        What's this?
Why do you ask this question?

MESSENGER
                        Look, old man,
here he is—here's the man who was that child!   1220

HERDSMAN
Death take you! Won't you hold your tongue?

OEDIPUS
                                                        No, no,
do not find fault with him, old man. Your words
are more at fault than his.

HERDSMAN
                              O best of masters,
how do I give offense?

OEDIPUS
                         When you refuse
to speak about the child of whom he asks you.   1225

HERDSMAN
He speaks out of his ignorance, without meaning.

OEDIPUS
If you'll not talk to gratify me, you
will talk with pain to urge you.

HERDSMAN
                                    O, please, sir,
don't hurt an old man, sir.

OEDIPUS [*To the servants*]
                              Here, one of you,
twist his hands behind him.

HERDSMAN
                           Why, God help me, why?   1230
What do you want to know?

OEDIPUS
                          You gave a child
to him—the child he asked you of?

HERDSMAN
                                  I did.
I wish I'd died the day I did.

OEDIPUS
                          You will
unless you tell me truly.

HERDSMAN

> And I'll die
> far worse if I should tell you.

OEDIPUS

> This fellow   1235
> is bent on more delays, as it would seem.

HERDSMAN

> O, no, no! I have told you that I gave it.

OEDIPUS

> Where did you get this child from? Was it your own
> or did you get it from another?

HERDSMAN

> Not
> my own at all; I had it from someone.   1240

OEDIPUS

> One of these citizens? Or from what house?

HERDSMAN

> O master, please—I beg you, master, please
> don't ask me more.

OEDIPUS

> You're a dead man if I
> ask you again.

HERDSMAN

> It was one of the children
> of Laius.

OEDIPUS

> A slave? Or born in wedlock?   1245

HERDSMAN

> O God, I am on the brink of frightful speech.

OEDIPUS

> And I of frightful hearing. But I must hear.

HERDSMAN

The child was called his child; but she within,
your wife would tell you best how all this was.

OEDIPUS

She gave it to you?

HERDSMAN

                                Yes, she did, my lord.   1250

OEDIPUS

To do what with it?

HERDSMAN

                            Make away with it.

OEDIPUS

She was so hard—its mother?

HERDSMAN

                                Aye, through fear
of evil oracles.

OEDIPUS

                Which?

HERDSMAN

                            They said that he
should kill his parents.

OEDIPUS

                            How was it that you
gave it away to this old man?

HERDSMAN

                                O master,   1255
I pitied it, and thought that I could send it
off to another country, and this man
was from another country. But he saved it
for the most terrible troubles. If you are
the man he says you are, you're bred to misery.   1260

OEDIPUS

O, O, O, they will all come,
all come out clearly! Light of the sun, let me
look upon you no more after today!

I who first saw the light bred of a match
accursed, and accursed in my living   1265
with them I lived with, cursed in my killing.

[Exeunt all but the CHORUS.*]*

CHORUS
    Strophe
O generations of men, how I
count you as equal with those who live
not at all!
What man, what man on earth wins more   1270
of happiness than a seeming
and after that turning away?
Oedipus, you are my pattern of this,
Oedipus, you and your fate!
Luckless Oedipus, whom of all men   1275
I envy not at all.

    Antistrophe
In as much as he shot his bolt
beyond the others and won the prize
of happiness complete—
O Zeus—and killed and reduced to nought   1280
the hooked-taloned maid of the riddling speech,
standing a tower against death for my land:
hence he was called my king and hence
was honored the highest of all
honors; and hence he ruled   1285
in the great city of Thebes.

    Strophe
But now whose tale is more miserable?
Who is there lives with a savager fate?
Whose troubles so reverse his life as his?

O Oedipus, the famous prince   1290
for whom a great haven
the same both as father and son
sufficed for generation,
how, O, how, have the furrows plowed
by your father endured to bear you, poor wretch, 1295
and hold their peace so long?

Antistrophe
Time who sees all has found you out
against your will; judges your marriage accursed,
begetter and begot at one in it.

O child of Laius,
would I had never seen you.   1300
I weep for you and cry
a dirge of lamentation.

To speak directly, I drew my breath
from you at the first and so now I lull
my mouth to sleep with your name.   1305

[*Enter a* SECOND MESSENGER.]

SECOND MESSENGER
O princes always honored by our country,
what deeds you'll hear of and what horrors see,
what grief you'll feel, if you as trueborn Thebans
care for the house of Labdacus's sons.
Phasis nor Ister cannot purge this house,   1310
I think, with all their streams, such things
it hides, such evils shortly will bring forth
into the light, whether they will or not;
and troubles hurt the most
when they prove self-inflicted.   1315

CHORUS
What we had known before did not fall short
of bitter groaning's worth; what's more to tell?

SECOND MESSENGER
Shortest to hear and tell—our glorious queen
Jocasta's dead.

CHORUS
                    Unhappy woman! How?

SECOND MESSENGER
By her own hand. The worst of what was done   1320
you cannot know. You did not see the sight.
Yet in so far as I remember it

you'll hear the end of our unlucky queen.
When she came raging into the house she went
straight to her marriage bed, tearing her hair 1325
with both her hands, and crying upon Laius
long dead—Do you remember, Laius,
that night long past which bred a child for us
to send you to your death and leave
a mother making children with her son? 1330
And then she groaned and cursed the bed in which
she brought forth husband by her husband, children
by her own child, an infamous double bond.
How after that she died I do not know—
for Oedipus distracted us from seeing. 1335
He burst upon us shouting and we looked
to him as he paced frantically around,
begging us always: Give me a sword, I say,
to find this wife no wife, this mother's womb,
this field of double sowing whence I sprang 1340
and where I sowed my children! As he raved
some god showed him the way—none of us there.
Bellowing terribly and led by some
invisible guide he rushed on the two doors—
wrenching the hollow bolts out of their sockets, 1345
he charged inside. There, there, we saw his wife
hanging, the twisted rope around her neck.
When he saw her, he cried out fearfully
and cut the dangling noose. Then, as she lay,
poor woman, on the ground, what happened after 1350
was terrible to see. He tore the brooches—
the gold chased brooches fastening her robe—
away from her and lifting them up high
dashed them on his own eyeballs, shrieking out
such things as: they will never see the crime 1355
I have committed or had done upon me!
Dark eyes, now in the days to come look on
forbidden faces, do not recognize
those whom you long for—with such imprecations
he struck his eyes again and yet again 1360
with the brooches. And the bleeding eyeballs
    gushed
and stained his beard—no sluggish oozing drops
but a black rain and bloody hail poured down.

So it has broken—and not on one head
but troubles mixed for husband and for wife.
The fortune of the days gone by was true   1365
good fortune—but today groans and destruction
and death and shame—of all ills can be named
not one is missing.

CHORUS
Is he now in any ease from pain?

SECOND MESSENGER
                              He shouts
for someone to unbar the doors and show him   1370
to all the men of Thebes, his father's killer,
his mother's—no, I cannot say the word,
it is unholy—for he'll cast himself
out of the land, he says, and not remain
to bring a curse upon his house, the curse   1375
he called upon it in his proclamation. But
he wants for strength, aye, and someone to guide
    him;
his sickness is too great to bear. You, too,
will be shown that. The bolts are opening.
Soon you will see a sight to waken pity   1380
even in the horror of it.

                [*Enter the blinded* OEDIPUS.]

CHORUS
This is a terrible sight for men to see!
I never found a worse!
Poor wretch, what madness came upon you!
What evil spirit leaped upon your life   1385
to your ill-luck—a leap beyond man's strength!
Indeed I pity you, but I cannot
look at you, though there's much I want to ask
and much to learn and much to see.
I shudder at the sight of you.   1390

OEDIPUS
O, O,
where am I going? Where is my voice
borne on the wind to and fro?
Spirit, how far have you sprung?

CHORUS
  To a terrible place whereof men's ears
  may not hear, nor their eyes behold it.   1395

OEDIPUS
  Darkness!
  Horror of darkness enfolding, resistless,
    unspeakable visitant sped by an ill wind in haste!
  madness and stabbing pain and memory
  of evil deeds I have done!

CHORUS
  In such misfortunes it's no wonder   1400
  if double weighs the burden of your grief.

OEDIPUS
  My friend,
  you are the only one steadfast, the only one that
    attends on me;
  you still stay nursing the blind man.
  Your care is not unnoticed. I can know   1405
  your voice, although this darkness is my world.

CHORUS
  Doer of dreadful deeds, how did you dare
  so far to do despite to your own eyes?
  What spirit urged you to it?

OEDIPUS
  It was Apollo, friends, Apollo   1410
  that brought this bitter bitterness, my sorrows to
    completion.
  But the hand that struck me
  was none but my own.
  Why should I see
  whose vision showed me nothing sweet to see?   1415

CHORUS
  These things are as you say.

OEDIPUS
  What can I see to love?
  What greeting can touch my ears with joy?

Take me away, and haste—to a place out of the way!
Take me away, my friends, the greatly miserable,   1420
the most accursed, whom God, too, hates
above all men on earth!

CHORUS
Unhappy in your mind and your misfortune,
would I had never known you!

OEDIPUS
Curse on the man who took   1425
the cruel bonds from off my legs, as I lay in the
   field.
He stole me from death and saved me,
no kindly service.
Had I died then
I would not be so burdensome to friends.   1430

CHORUS
I, too, could have wished it had been so.

OEDIPUS
Then I would not have come
to kill my father and marry my mother infamously.
Now I am godless and child of impurity,
begetter in the same seed that created my wretched
   self.   1435
If there is any ill worse than ill,
that is the lot of Oedipus.

CHORUS
I cannot say your remedy was good;
you would be better dead than blind and living.

OEDIPUS
What I have done here was best done—don't tell me   1440
otherwise, do not give me further counsel.
I do not know with what eyes I could look
upon my father when I die and go
under the earth, nor yet my wretched mother—
those two to whom I have done things deserving   1445
worse punishment than hanging. Would the sight
of children, bred as mine are, gladden me?

No, not these eyes, never. And my city,
its towers and sacred places of the gods,
of these I robbed my miserable self   1450
when I commanded all to drive *him* out,
the criminal since proved by God impure
and of the race of Laius.
To this guilt I bore witness against myself—
with what eyes shall I look upon my people?   1455
No. If there were a means to choke the fountain
of hearing I would not have stayed my hand
from locking up my miserable carcass,
seeing and hearing nothing; it is sweet
to keep our thoughts out of the range of hurt.   1460

Cithaeron, why did you receive me? Why
having received me did you not kill me straight?
And so I had not shown to men my birth.

O Polybus and Corinth and the house,
the old house that I used to call my father's—   1465
what fairness you were nurse to, and what foulness
festered beneath! Now I am found to be
a sinner and a son of sinners. Crossroads,
and hidden glade, oak and the narrow way
at the crossroads, that drank my father's blood   1470
offered you by my hands, do you remember
still what I did as you looked on, and what
I did when I came here? O marriage, marriage!
you bred me and again when you had bred
bred children of your child and showed to men   1475
brides, wives, and mothers and the foulest deeds
that can be in this world of ours.

Come—it's unfit to say what is unfit
to do.—I beg of you in God's name hide me
somewhere outside your country, yes, or kill me,   1480
or throw me into the sea, to be forever
out of your sight. Approach and deign to touch me
for all my wretchedness, and do not fear.
No man but I can bear my evil doom.

CHORUS
     Here Creon comes in fit time to perform   1485

or give advice in what you ask of us.
Creon is left sole ruler in your stead.

OEDIPUS
    Creon! Creon! What shall I say to him?
    How can I justly hope that he will trust me?
    In what is past I have been proved toward him   1490
    an utter liar.

                                    [*Enter* CREON.]

CREON
                    Oedipus, I've come
    not so that I might laugh at you nor taunt you
    with evil of the past. But if you still
    are without shame before the face of men
    reverence at least the flame that gives all life,   1495
    our lord the Sun, and do not show unveiled
    to him pollution such that neither land
    nor holy rain nor light of day can welcome.

                                    [*To a servant.*]
    Be quick and take him in. It is most decent
    that only kin should see and hear the troubles   1500
    of kin.

OEDIPUS
            I beg you, since you've torn me from
    my dreadful expectations and have come
    in a most noble spirit to a man
    that has used you vilely—do a thing for me.
    I shall speak for your own good, not for my own.   1505

CREON
    What do you need that you would ask of me?

OEDIPUS
    Drive me from here with all the speed you can
    to where I may not hear a human voice.

CREON
    Be sure, I would have done this had not I
    wished first of all to learn from the God the course   1510
    of action I should follow.

OEDIPUS
                    But his word
has been quite clear to let the parricide,
the sinner, die.

CREON
                Yes, that indeed was said.
But in the present need we had best discover
what we should do.

OEDIPUS
                        And will you ask about   1515
a man so wretched?

CREON
                            Now even you will trust
the God.

OEDIPUS
        So. I command you—and will beseech you—
to her that lies inside that house give burial
as you would have it; she is yours and rightly   1520
you will perform the rites for her. For me—
never let this my father's city have me
living a dweller in it. Leave me live
in the mountains where Cithaeron is, that's called
my mountain, which my mother and my father   1525
while they were living would have made my tomb.
So I may die by their decree who sought
indeed to kill me. Yet I know this much:
no sickness and no other thing will kill me.
I would not have been saved from death if not   1530
for some strange evil fate. Well, let my fate
go where it will.
Creon, you need not care
about my sons; they're men and so wherever
they are, they will not lack a livelihood.
But my two girls—so sad and pitiful—   1535
whose table never stood apart from mine,
and everything I touched they always shared—
O Creon, have a thought for them! And most
I wish that you might suffer me to touch them
and sorrow with them.   1540

[*Enter* ANTIGONE *and* ISMENE, OEDIPUS' *two*
                                           daughters.]

O my lord! O true noble Creon! Can I
really be touching them, as when I saw?
What shall I say?
Yes, I can hear them sobbing—my two darlings!
and Creon has had pity and has sent me   1545
what I loved most?
Am I right?

CREON

You're right: it was I gave you this
because I knew from old days how you loved them
as I see now.

OEDIPUS

              God bless you for it, Creon,   1550
and may God guard you better on your road
than he did me!
                O children,
where are you? Come here, come to my hands,
a brother's hands which turned your father's eyes,
those bright eyes you knew once, to what you see,   1555
a father seeing nothing, knowing nothing,
begetting you from his own source of life.
I weep for you—I cannot see your faces—
I weep when I think of the bitterness
there will be in your lives, how you must live   1560
before the world. At what assemblages
of citizens will you make one? To what
gay company will you go and not come home
in tears instead of sharing in the holiday?
And when you're ripe for marriage, who will he be,   1565
the man who'll risk to take such infamy
as shall cling to my children, to bring hurt
on them and those that marry with them? What
curse is not there? "Your father killed his father
and sowed the seed where he had sprung himself   1570
and begot you out of the womb that held him."
These insults you will hear. Then who will marry
    you?
No one, my children; clearly you are doomed

to waste away in barrenness unmarried.
Son of Menoeceus, since you are all the father   1575
left these two girls, and we, their parents, both
are dead to them—do not allow them wander
like beggars, poor and husbandless.
They are of your own blood.
And do not make them equal with myself   1580
in wretchedness; for you can see them now
so young, so utterly alone, save for you only.
Touch my hand, noble Creon, and say yes.
If you were older, children, and were wiser,
there's much advice I'd give you. But as it is,   1585
let this be what you pray: give me a life
wherever there is opportunity
to live, and better life than was my father's.

CREON

Your tears have had enough of scope; now go
   within the house.   1590

OEDIPUS

I must obey, though bitter of heart.

CREON

In season, all is good.

OEDIPUS

Do you know on what conditions I obey?

CREON

                        You tell me them,
and I shall know them when I hear.

OEDIPUS

                   That you shall send me out
to live away from Thebes.

CREON

               That gift you must ask of the God.   1595

OEDIPUS

But I'm now hated by the gods.

CREON
                    So quickly you'll obtain your prayer.

OEDIPUS
  You consent then?

CREON
              What I do not mean, I do not use to say.

OEDIPUS
  Now lead me away from here.

CREON
                Let go the children, then, and come.

OEDIPUS
  Do not take them from me.

CREON
              Do not seek to be master in everything,
  for the things you mastered did not follow you
      throughout your life.   1600

                [As CREON and OEDIPUS go out.]

CHORUS
  You that live in my ancestral Thebes, behold this
      Oedipus—
  him who knew the famous riddles and was a man
      most masterful;
  not a citizen who did not look with envy on his
      lot—
  see him now and see the breakers of misfortune
      swallow him!
  Look upon that last day always. Count no mortal
      happy till   1605
  he has passed the final limit of his life secure from
      pain.

THE TRAGICAL HISTORY
OF THE LIFE AND DEATH
OF DOCTOR FAUSTUS

BY

Christopher Marlowe

◆

CHARACTERS

THE CHORUS

DOCTOR FAUSTUS

WAGNER, *his student and servant*

VALDES

CORNELIUS

THREE SCHOLARS

AN OLD MAN

POPE ADRIAN

RAYMOND, *King of Hungary*

BRUNO, *the rival pope*

TWO CARDINALS

THE ARCHBISHOP OF RHEIMS

CHARLES V, *emperor of Germany*

MARTINO ⎫
FREDERICK ⎬ *Gentlemen of the Emperor's court*
BENVOLIO ⎭

BEËLZEBUB

DUKE OF SAXONY

DUKE OF ANHOLT

DUCHESS OF ANHOLT

ROBIN, *the clown, an hostler*

DICK

A VINTNER

A HORSECORSER

A CARTER

HOSTESS

GOOD ANGEL

BAD ANGEL

LUCIFER

MEPHISTOPHILIS

PRIDE ⎫
COVETOUSNESS ⎪
ENVY ⎪
WRATH ⎬ *The Seven Deadly Sins*
GLUTTONY ⎪
SLOTH ⎪
LECHERY ⎭

ALEXANDER THE GREAT

HIS PARAMOUR

DARIUS, KING OF PERSIA

HELEN OF TROY

TWO CUPIDS

Devils, Bishops, Monks, Friars, Soldiers

PROLOGUE

Enter CHORUS.

CHORUS

Not marching in the fields of Trasimene
Where Mars did mate the warlike Carthagens,
Nor sporting in the dalliance of love
In courts of kings where state is overturned,
Nor in the pomp of proud audacious deeds   5
Intends our muse to vaunt his heavenly verse.
Only this, gentles: we must now perform
The form of Faustus' fortunes, good or bad.
And now to patient judgments we appeal,
And speak for Faustus in his infancy.   10
Now is he born, of parents base of stock,
In Germany, within a town called Rhode.
At riper years to Wittenberg he went,
Whereas his kinsmen chiefly brought him up.
So much he profits in divinity.   15
The fruitful plot of scholarism graced,
That shortly he was graced with doctor's name,
Excelling all whose sweet delight disputes
In th' heavenly matters of theology,
Till swoll'n with cunning of a self-conceit,   20
His waxen wings did mount above his reach,
And melting, heavens conspired his overthrow;
For, falling to a devilish exercise
And glutted now with learning's golden gifts,
He surfeits upon cursèd necromancy.   25
Nothing so sweet as magic is to him,
Which he prefers before his chiefest bliss;
And this the man that in his study sits.

2 **Carthagens** Carthaginians; alluding to the Carthaginian Hannibal, who crossed the Alps to make war on Rome
21 **waxen wings** of Icarus, who flew too near the sun and fell into the sea when his wings melted

ACT ONE
Scene One

FAUSTUS *in his study.*

FAUSTUS
   Settle thy studies, Faustus, and begin
   To sound the depth of that thou wilt profess.
   Having commenced, be a divine in show;
   Yet level at the end of every art,
   And live and die in Aristotle's works.   5
   Sweet Analytics, 'tis thou hast ravished me!
   Bene disserere est finis logices.
   Is to dispute well logic's chiefest end?
   Affords this art no greater miracle?
   Then read no more; thou hast attained that end.   10
   A greater subject fitteth Faustus' wit!
   Bid *On cay mae on* farewell; Galen come.
   Seeing *ubi desinit philosophus ibi incipit medicus,*
   Be a physician, Faustus; heap up gold,
   And be eternized for some wondrous cure.   15
   Summum bonum medicinae sanitas.
   The end of physic is our body's health.
   Why, Faustus, hast thou not attained that end?
   Is not thy common talk sound aphorisms?
   Are not thy bills hung up as monuments   20
   Whereby whole cities have escaped the plague
   And divers desperate maladies been cured?
   Yet art thou still but Faustus and a man.
   Couldst thou make men to live eternally,
   Or, being dead, raise them to life again,   25
   Then this profession were to be esteemed.
   Physic, farewell! Where is Justinian?
   [*He reads.*] *Si una eademque res legatus duobus,*
   Alter rem, alter valorem rei, etc.
   A petty case of paltry legacies!   30
   [*He reads.*] *Exhæreditare filium non potest pater*
     nisi—
   Such is the subject of the Institute
   And universal body of the law.

7 Bene . . . logices to dispute well is logic's chief aim
27 Justinian Roman emperor who laid down Roman law

This study fits a mercenary drudge
Who aims at nothing but external trash,   35
Too servile and illiberal for me.
When all is done, divinity is best.
Jeromè's Bible, Faustus, view it well:
[*He reads.*] *Stipendium peccati mors est*. Ha!
   Stipendium, etc.
The reward of sin is death. That's hard.   40
[*He reads.*] *Si peccasse negamus, fallimur
Et nulla est in nobis veritas.*
If we say that we have no sin,
We deceive ourselves, and there's no truth in us.
Why then belike we must sin,   45
And so consequently die.
Ay, we must die an everlasting death.
What doctrine call you this? *Che serà, serà:*
What will be, shall be! Divinity, adieu!
These metaphysics of magicians   50
And necromantic books are heavenly.
Lines, circles, signs, letters, and characters—
Ay, these are those that Faustus most desires.
O, what a world of profit and delight,
Of power, of honor, of omnipotence   55
Is promised to the studious artisan!
All things that move between the quiet poles
Shall be at my command. Emperors and kings
Are but obeyed in their several provinces,
Nor can they raise the wind or rend the clouds,   60
But his dominion that exceeds in this
Stretcheth as far as doth the mind of man.
A sound magician is a demigod.
Here try thy brains to get a deity!
Wagner!

Enter WAGNER.

         Commend me to my dearest friends,   65
The German Valdes and Cornelius;
Request them earnestly to visit me.
WAGNER
I will, sir.   *Exit.*

FAUSTUS
    Their conference will be a greater help to me
    Than all my labors, plod I ne'er so fast.   70

Enter the GOOD ANGEL *and the* EVIL ANGEL.

GOOD ANGEL
    O, Faustus, lay that damnèd book aside,
    And gaze not on it, lest it tempt thy soul
    And heap God's heavy wrath upon thy head.
    Read, read the Scriptures. That is blasphemy.
BAD ANGEL
    Go forward, Faustus, in that famous art   75
    Wherein all nature's treasury is contained.
    Be thou on earth as Jove is in the sky,
    Lord and commander of these elements.

                                    Exeunt ANGELS.

FAUSTUS
    How am I glutted with conceit of this!
    Shall I make spirits fetch me what I please,   80
    Resolve me of all ambiguities,
    Perform what desperate enterprise I will?
    I'll have them fly to India for gold,
    Ransack the ocean for orient pearl,
    And search all corners of the new-found world   85
    For pleasant fruits and princely delicates.
    I'll have them read me strange philosophy
    And tell the secrets of all foreign kings:
    I'll have them wall all Germany with brass
    And make swift Rhine circle fair Wittenberg.   90
    I'll have them fill the public schools with silk
    Wherewith the students shall be bravely clad.
    I'll levy soldiers with the coin they bring
    And chase the Prince of Parma from our land
    And reign sole king of all the provinces.   95
    Yea, stranger engines for the brunt of war
    Than was the fiery keel at Antwerp's bridge
    I'll make my servile spirits to invent.

79 conceit the conception of attaining   **81 Resolve me of** explain to me

[*He calls within.*] Come, German Valdes and
   Cornelius,
And make me blessed with your sage conference!   100

Enter VALDES *and* CORNELIUS.

Valdes, sweet Valdes, and Cornelius,
Know that your words have won me at the last
To practice magic and concealèd arts;
Yet not your words only, but mine own fantasy
That will receive no object, for my head   105
But ruminates on necromantic skill.
Philosophy is odious and obscure;
Both law and physic are for petty wits;
Divinity is basest of the three.
Unpleasant, harsh, contemptible, and vile.   110
'Tis magic, magic, that hath ravished me.
Then, gentle friends, aid me in this attempt,
And I, that have with subtle syllogisms
Graveled the pastors of the German church,
And made the flowering pride of Wittenberg   115
Swarm to my problems as th' infernal spirits
On sweet Musaeus when he came to hell,
Will be as cunning as Agrippa was,
Whose shadows made all Europe honor him.

VALDES
Faustus, these books, thy wit, and our experience   120
Shall make all nations to canonize us.
As Indian Moors obey their Spanish lords,
So shall the spirits of every element
Be always serviceable to us three.
Like lions shall they guard us when we please,   125
Like Almain rutters with their horsemen's staves
Or Lapland giants trotting by our sides,
Sometimes like women or unwedded maids,
Shadowing more beauty in their airy brows
Than in the white breasts of the queen of love.   130
From Venice shall they drag huge argosies,
And from America the golden fleece
That yearly stuffs old Philip's treasury,
If learnèd Faustus will be resolute.

FAUSTUS

    Valdes, as resolute am I in this   135
    As thou to live; therefore object it not.

CORNELIUS

    The miracles that magic will perform
    Will make thee vow to study nothing else.
    He that is grounded in astrology,
    Enriched with tongues, well seen in minerals,   140
    Hath all the principles magic doth require.
    Then doubt not, Faustus, but to be renowned
    And more frequented for this mystery
    Than heretofore the Delphian oracle.
    The spirits tell me they can dry the sea   145
    And fetch the treasure of all foreign wracks,
    Yea, all the wealth that our forefathers hid
    Within the massy entrails of the earth.
    Then tell me, Faustus, what shall we three want?

FAUSTUS

    Nothing, Cornelius. O, this cheers my soul!   150
    Come, show me some demonstrations magical,
    That I may conjure in some lusty grove
    And have these joys in full possession.

VALDES

    Then haste thee to some solitary grove,
    And bear wise Bacon's and Abanus' works,   155
    The Hebrew Psalter, and New Testament;
    And whatsoever else is requisite
    We will inform thee ere our conference cease.

CORNELIUS

    Valdes, first let him know the words of art,
    And then, all other ceremonies learned,   160
    Faustus may try his cunning by himself.

VALDES

    First I'll instruct thee in the rudiments,
    And then wilt thou be perfecter than I.

FAUSTUS

    Then come and dine with me, and after meat
    We'll canvass every quiddity thereof,   165
    For ere I sleep I'll try what I can do.
    This night I'll conjure, though I die therefore.

                                      Exeunt.

Scene Two

Enter two SCHOLARS.

FIRST SCHOLAR   I wonder what's become of Faustus, that was wont to make our schools ring with *sic probo*.

Enter WAGNER.

SECOND SCHOLAR   That shall we presently know; here comes his boy.   5

FIRST SCHOLAR   How now, sirrah! Where's thy master?

WAGNER   God in heaven knows.

SECOND SCHOLAR   Why, dost not thou know then?

WAGNER   Yes, I know, but that follows not.   10

FIRST SCHOLAR   Go to, sirrah! Leave your jesting and tell us where he is.

WAGNER   That follows not by force of argument, which you, being licentiates, should stand upon; therefore acknowledge your error and be attentive.   15

SECOND SCHOLAR   Then you will not tell us?

WAGNER   You are deceived, for I will tell you. Yet if you were not dunces, you would never ask me such a question. For is he not *corpus naturale,* and is not that *mobile*? Then wherefore should you ask me   20
such a question? But that I am by nature phlegmatic, slow to wrath, and prone to lechery—to love, I would say—it were not for you to come within forty foot of the place of execution, although I do not doubt but to see you both hanged the next sessions.   25
Thus having triumphed over you, I will set my countenance like a precisian and begin to speak thus: Truly, my dear brethren, my master is within at dinner with Valdes and Cornelius, as this wine, if it could speak, would inform your worships. And so,   30
the Lord bless you, preserve you, and keep you, my dear brethren.   *Exit.*

FIRST SCHOLAR
   O Faustus, then I fear that which I have long
      suspected.
   That thou art fall'n into that damnèd art
   For which they two are infamous through the world.   35
SECOND SCHOLAR
   Were he a stranger, not allied to me,
   The danger of his soul would make me mourn.
   But come, let us go and inform the rector.
   It may be his grave counsel may reclaim him.
FIRST SCHOLAR
   I fear me nothing will reclaim him now.   40
SECOND SCHOLAR
   Yet let us see what we can do.   *Exeunt.*

Scene Three

Thunder. Enter [above] LUCIFER *and four* DEVILS.
Enter FAUSTUS *to conjure.*

FAUSTUS
   Now that the gloomy shadow of the night,
   Longing to view Orion's drizzling look,
   Leaps from th' Antarctic world unto the sky
   And dims the welkin with her pitchy breath,
   Faustus begin thine incantations,   5
   And try if devils will obey thy hest,
   Seeing thou hast prayed and sacrificed to them.
   Within this circle is Jehovah's name,
   Forward and backward anagrammatized,
   Th' abbreviated names of holy saints,   10
   Figures of every adjunct to the heavens,
   And characters of signs and erring stars,
   By which the spirits are enforced to rise.
   Then fear not, Faustus, to be resolute,
   And try the utmost magic can perform.   *Thunder.*   15
   Sint mihi Dei Acherontis propitii! Valeat numen tri-
   plex Jehovae. Ignei, aerii, aquatani spiritus,
   salvete! Orientis princeps, Beëlzebub, inferni arden-
   tis monarcha, et Demogorgon, propitiamus vos, ut
   appareat et surgat Mephistophilis. Quid tu moraris?   20
   Per Jehovam Gehennam, et consecratam aquam
   quam nunc spargo, signumque crucis quod nunc

facio, et per vota nostra, ipse nunc surgat nobis
dicatus Mephistophilis.

Enter [MEPHISTOPHILIS,] *a devil.*

I charge thee to return and change thy shape;   25
Thou art too ugly to attend on me.
Go, and return an old Franciscan friar;
That holy shape becomes a devil best.

                                Exit DEVIL.

I see there's virtue in my heavenly words.
Who would not be proficient in this art?   30
How pliant is this Mephistophilis,
Full of obedience and humility.
Such is the force of magic and my spells.
Now, Faustus, thou art conjuror laureate,
That canst command great Mephistophilis.   35
Quin redis Mephistophilis fratris imagine.

Enter MEPHISTOPHILIS [*dressed like a Franciscan*
friar].

MEPHISTOPHILIS
Now, Faustus, what wouldst thou have me do?
FAUSTUS
I charge thee wait upon me whilst I live,
To do whatever Faustus shall command,
Be it to make the moon drop from her sphere   40
Or the ocean to overwhelm the world.
MEPHISTOPHILIS
I am a servant to great Lucifer
And may not follow thee without his leave.
No more than he commands must we perform.
FAUSTUS
Did not he charge thee to appear to me?   45
MEPHISTOPHILIS
No, I came hither of mine own accord.
FAUSTUS
Did not my conjuring speeches raise thee? Speak.
MEPHISTOPHILIS
That was the cause, but yet *per accidens*,
For when we hear one rack the name of God,

    Abjure the Scriptures and his Savior Christ,   50
    We fly in hope to get his glorious soul;
    Nor will we come unless he use such means
    Whereby he is in danger to be damned.
    Therefore the shortest cut for conjuring
    Is stoutly to abjure the Trinity   55
    And pray devoutly to the prince of hell.

FAUSTUS
    So Faustus hath
    Already done, and holds this principle:
    There is no chief but only Beëlzebub,
    To whom Faustus doth dedicate himself.   60
    This word "damnation" terrifies not me,
    For I confound hell in Elysium.
    My ghost be with the old philosophers!
    But leaving these vain trifles of men's souls,
    Tell me what is that Lucifer thy lord?   65

MEPHISTOPHILIS
    Archregent and commander of all spirits.

FAUSTUS
    Was not that Lucifer an angel once?

MEPHISTOPHILIS
    Yes, Faustus, and most dearly loved of God.

FAUSTUS
    How comes it then that he is prince of devils?

MEPHISTOPHILIS
    O, by aspiring pride and insolence,   70
    For which God threw him from the face of heaven.

FAUSTUS
    And what are you that live with Lucifer?

MEPHISTOPHILIS
    Unhappy spirits that fell with Lucifer,
    Conspired against our God with Lucifer,
    And are forever damned with Lucifer.   75

FAUSTUS
    Where are you damned?

MEPHISTOPHILIS
    In hell.

FAUSTUS
    How comes it then that thou art out of hell?

MEPHISTOPHILIS
    Why, this is hell, nor am I out of it.

Think'st thou that I who saw the face of God
And tasted the eternal joys of heaven   80
Am not tormented with ten thousand hells
In being deprived of everlasting bliss?
O Faustus, leave these frivolous demands
Which strike a terror to my fainting soul.

FAUSTUS

What, is great Mephistophilis so passionate   85
For being deprivèd of the joys of heaven?
Learn thou of Faustus manly fortitude,
And scorn those joys thou never shalt possess.
Go bear these tidings to great Lucifer:
Seeing Faustus hath incurred eternal death   90
By desperate thoughts against Jove's deity,
Say he surrenders up to him his soul,
So he will spare him four-and-twenty years,
Letting him live in all voluptuousness,
Having thee ever to attend on me,   95
To give me whatsoever I shall ask,
To tell me whatsoever I demand,
To slay mine enemies, and aid my friends,
And always be obedient to my will.
Go, and return to mighty Lucifer,   100
And meet me in my study at midnight,
And then resolve me of thy master's mind.

MEPHISTOPHILIS

I will, Faustus.   *Exit.*

FAUSTUS

Had I as many souls as there be stars,
I'd give them all for Mephistophilis.   105
By him I'll be great emperor of the world,
And make a bridge through the moving air,
To pass the ocean with a band of men.
I'll join the hills that bind the Afric shore,
And make that country continent to Spain,   110
And both contributory to my crown.
The Emperor shall not live but by my leave,
Nor any potentate of Germany.
Now that I have obtained what I desire,
I'll live in speculation of this art   115
Till Mephistophilis return again.   *Exit.*

Scene Four

Enter WAGNER *and* [ROBIN,] *the Clown.*

WAGNER   Come hither, sirrah boy.

ROBIN   Boy! O disgrace to my person. Zounds, boy in
your face! You have seen many boys with such pick-
edevants, I am sure.

WAGNER   Sirrah, hast thou no comings in?   5

ROBIN   Yes, and goings out too, you may see, sir.

WAGNER   Alas, poor slave! See how poverty jests in
his nakedness. I know the villain's out of service, and
so hungry that I know he would give his soul to the
devil for a shoulder of mutton, though it were blood-   10
raw.

ROBIN   Not so neither. I had need to have it well
roasted, and good sauce to it, if I pay so dear, I can
tell you.

WAGNER   Sirrah, wilt thou be my man and wait on me,   15
and I will make thee go like *Qui mihi discipulus?*

ROBIN   What, in verse?

WAGNER   No, slave; in beaten silk and stavesacre.

ROBIN   Stavesacre? That's good to kill vermin. Then,
belike, if I serve you I shall be lousy.   20

WAGNER   Why, so thou shalt be, whether thou dost it
or no; for, sirrah, if thou dost not presently bind
thyself to me for seven years, I'll turn all the lice
about thee into familiars and make them tear thee in
pieces.   25

ROBIN   Nay, sir, you may save yourself a labor, for
they are as familiar with me as if they paid for their
meat and drink, I can tell you.

WAGNER   Well, sirrah, leave your jesting and take
these guilders.   30

ROBIN   Yes, marry, sir, and I thank you too.

WAGNER   So, now thou art to be at an hour's
warning, whensoever and wheresoever the devil
shall fetch thee.

ROBIN   Here, take your guilders again. I'll none of   35
'em.

WAGNER   Not I. Thou art pressed. Prepare thyself,

for I will presently raise up two devils to carry thee
away. Banio! Belcher!

ROBIN   Belcher? And Belcher come here, I'll belch   40
him. I am not afraid of a devil.

Enter two DEVILS.

WAGNER   How now, sir? Will you serve me now?
ROBIN   Ay, good Wagner; take away the devil then.
WAGNER   Spirits away! Now, sirrah, follow me.
                                        [*Exeunt* DEVILS.]
ROBIN   I will, sir. But hark you, master, will you teach   45
me this conjuring occupation?
WAGNER   Ay, sirrah. I'll teach thee to turn thyself to a
dog, or a cat, or a mouse, or a rat, or anything.
ROBIN   A dog, or a cat, or a mouse, or a rat! O brave
Wagner!   50
WAGNER   Villain, call me Master Wagner, and see
that you walk attentively, and let your right eye be
always diametrally fixed upon my left heel, that
thou may'st *quasi vestigias nostras insistere*.
ROBIN   Well, sir, I warrant you.   *Exeunt*.   55

ACT TWO
Scene One

Enter FAUSTUS *in his study.*

FAUSTUS
Now, Faustus, must thou needs be damned,
And canst thou not be saved.
What boots it then to think on God or heaven?
Away with such vain fancies, and despair;
Despair in God, and trust in Beëlzebub.   5
Now go not backward; Faustus, be resolute.
Why waver'st thou? O, something soundeth in mine
    ear:
"Abjure this magic; turn to God again."
Ay, and Faustus will turn to God again!
To God? He loves thee not.   10
The God thou serv'st is thine own appetite,

Wherein is fixed the love of Beëlzebub.
To him I'll build an altar and a church,
And offer lukewarm blood of newborn babes.

Enter the two ANGELS.

BAD ANGEL   Go forward, Faustus, in that famous art.   15
GOOD ANGEL   Sweet Faustus, leave that execrable
art.
FAUSTUS   Contrition, prayer, repentance—what of
these?
GOOD ANGEL   O, they are means to bring thee unto
heaven.
BAD ANGEL   Rather illusions, fruits of lunacy,
That make men foolish that do use them most.   20
GOOD ANGEL   Sweet Faustus, think of heaven and
heavenly things.
BAD ANGEL   No, Faustus; think of honor and wealth.
                              Exeunt ANGELS.

FAUSTUS
Wealth? Why, the signory of Emden shall be mine.
When Mephistophilis shall stand by me,
What power can hurt me? Faustus, thou art safe.   25
Cast no more doubts. Mephistophilis, come
And bring glad tidings from great Lucifer.
Is't not midnight? Come, Mephistophilis.
Veni, veni, Mephistophile.

Enter MEPHISTOPHILIS.

Now tell me what saith Lucifer, thy lord?   30
MEPHISTOPHILIS
That I shall wait on Faustus whilst he lives,
So he will buy my service with his soul.
FAUSTUS
Already Faustus hath hazarded that for thee.
MEPHISTOPHILIS
But now thou must bequeath it solemnly
And write a deed of gift with thine own blood,   35
For that security craves great Lucifer.
If thou deny it, I must back to hell.

FAUSTUS
   Stay, Mephistophilis! Tell me what good
   Will my soul do thy lord.
MEPHISTOPHILIS   Enlarge his kingdom.
FAUSTUS   Is that the reason why he tempts us thus?   40
MEPHISTOPHILIS   *Solamen miseris socios habuisse*
   doloris.
FAUSTUS   Why, have you any pain that torture
   others?
MEPHISTOPHILIS
   As great as have the human souls of men.
   But tell me, Faustus, shall I have thy soul?
   And I will be thy slave and wait on thee   45
   And give thee more than thou hast wit to ask.
FAUSTUS   Ay, Mephistophilis, I'll give it him.
MEPHISTOPHILIS
   Then, Faustus, stab thy arm courageously,
   And bind thy soul that at some certain day
   Great Lucifer may claim it as his own,   50
   And then be thou as great as Lucifer.
FAUSTUS [*stabbing his arm*]
   Lo, Mephistophilis, for love of thee,
   I cut mine arm, and with my proper blood
   Assure my soul to be great Lucifer's,
   Chief lord and regent of perpetual night.   55
   View here this blood that trickles from mine arm,
   And let it be propitious for my wish.
MEPHISTOPHILIS
   But, Faustus,
   Write it in manner of a deed of gift.
FAUSTUS
   Ay, so I do. [*He writes.*] But, Mephistophilis,   60
   My blood congeals, and I can write no more.
MEPHISTOPHILIS
   I'll fetch thee fire to dissolve it straight.   *Exit.*
FAUSTUS
   What might the staying of my blood portend?
   Is it unwilling I should write this bill?
   Why streams it not that I may write afresh?   65
   "Faustus gives to thee his soul." Ah, there it stayed.
   Why shouldst thou not? Is not thy soul thine own?
   Then write again: "Faustus gives to thee his soul."

Enter MEPHISTOPHILIS *with the chafer of fire.*

MEPHISTOPHILIS
    See, Faustus, here is fire. Set it on.
FAUSTUS
    So. Now the blood begins to clear again.   70
    Now will I make an end immediately. [*He writes.*]
MEPHISTOPHILIS   [*Aside*]
    What will not I do to obtain his soul?
FAUSTUS
    Consummatum est; this bill is ended,
    And Faustus hath bequeathed his soul to Lucifer.
    But what is this inscription on mine arm?   75
    Homo fuge! Whither should I fly?
    If unto God, he'll throw me down to hell.
    My senses are deceived: here's nothing writ.
    O, yes, I see it plain. Even here is writ
    Homo fuge! Yet shall not Faustus fly.   80
MEPHISTOPHILIS [*Aside*]
    I'll fetch him somewhat to delight his mind.   *Exit.*

    Enter DEVILS, *giving crowns and rich apparel to*
    FAUSTUS. *They dance and then depart. Enter*
    MEPHISTOPHILIS.

FAUSTUS
    What means this show? Speak, Mephistophilis.
MEPHISTOPHILIS
    Nothing, Faustus, but to delight thy mind
    And let thee see what magic can perform.
FAUSTUS
    But may I raise such spirits when I please?   85
MEPHISTOPHILIS
    Ay, Faustus, and do greater things than these.
FAUSTUS
    Then, Mephistophilis, receive this scroll,
    A deed of gift of body and of soul,
    But yet conditionally that thou perform
    All covenants and articles between us both.   90

73 **Consummatum est** "it is finished," last words of Christ on the cross

MEPHISTOPHILIS
Faustus, I swear by hell and Lucifer
To effect all promises between us made.
FAUSTUS
Then hear me read it, Mephistophilis.
On these conditions following:
First, that Faustus may be a spirit in form and
substance;   95
Secondly, that Mephistophilis shall be his servant
and be at his command;
Thirdly, that Mephistophilis shall do for him and
bring him whatsoever;
Fourthly, that he shall be in his chamber or house
invisible;   100
Lastly, that he shall appear to the said John Faustus
at all times, in what form or shape soever he
please:
I, John Faustus, of Wittenberg, doctor, by these
presents, do give both body and soul to Lucifer,
Prince of the East, and his minister, Mephi-
stophilis; and furthermore grant unto them that
four-and-twenty years being expired, the   105
articles above written inviolate, full power to fetch
or carry the said John Faustus, body and soul,
flesh, blood, or goods, into their habitation
wheresoever.

By me, John Faustus.   110
MEPHISTOPHILIS   Speak, Faustus. Do you deliver this
as your deed?
FAUSTUS   Ay, take it, and the devil give thee good of
it.
MEPHISTOPHILIS   So now, Faustus, ask me what thou
wilt.
FAUSTUS
First will I question with thee about hell.
Tell me, where is the place that men call hell?
MEPHISTOPHILIS   Under the heavens.   115
FAUSTUS   Ay, so are all things else. But whereabouts?
MEPHISTOPHILIS
Within the bowels of these elements,
Where we are tortured and remain forever.

Hell hath no limits, nor is circumscribed
In one self place, but where we are is hell,   120
And where hell is, there must we ever be.
And, to be short, when all the world dissolves
And every creature shall be purified,
All places shall be hell that is not heaven.

FAUSTUS   I think hell's a fable.

MEPHISTOPHILIS   Ay, think so still, till experience   125
change thy mind.

FAUSTUS   Why, dost thou think that Faustus shall be
damned?

MEPHISTOPHILIS
Ay, of necessity, for here's the scroll
In which thou hast given thy soul to Lucifer.

FAUSTUS
Ay, and body too. But what of that?   130
Think'st thou that Faustus is so fond to imagine
That after this life there is any pain?
No, these are trifles and mere old wives' tales.

MEPHISTOPHILIS
But I am an instance to prove the contrary,
For I tell thee I am damned and now in hell.   135

FAUSTUS
Nay, and this be hell, I'll willingly be damned.
What? Sleeping, eating, walking, and disputing?
But, leaving off this, let me have a wife,
The fairest maid in Germany,
For I am wanton and lascivious,   140
And cannot live without a wife.

MEPHISTOPHILIS   I prithee, Faustus, talk not of a
wife.

FAUSTUS   Nay, sweet Mephistophilis, fetch me one,
for I will have one.

MEPHISTOPHILIS
Well, Faustus, thou shalt have a wife.
Sit there till I come.   [*Exit.*]   145

Enter [MEPHISTOPHILIS] *with a* DEVIL *dressed like a
woman, with fireworks.*

FAUSTUS   What sight is this?

MEPHISTOPHILIS   Now, Faustus, how dost thou like
  thy wife?
FAUSTUS   Here's a hot whore indeed! No, I'll no wife.
MEPHISTOPHILIS
  Marriage is but a ceremonial toy,
  And if thou lovest me, think no more of it.   150
  I'll cull thee out the fairest courtesans
  And bring them every morning to thy bed.
  She whom thine eye shall like, thy heart shall have,
  Were she as chaste as was Penelope,
  As wise as Saba, or as beautiful   155
  As was bright Lucifer before his fall.
  Hold; take this book; peruse it thoroughly.
  The iterating of these lines brings gold;
  The framing of this circle on the ground
  Brings thunder, whirlwinds, storm, and lightning.   160
  Pronounce this thrice devoutly to thyself,
  And men in harness shall appear to thee,
  Ready to execute what thou command'st.
FAUSTUS
  Thanks, Mephistophilis, for this sweet book.
  This will I keep as chary as my life.   *Exeunt.*   165

Scene Two

Enter FAUSTUS *in his study and* MEPHISTOPHILIS.
FAUSTUS
  When I behold the heavens, then I repent
  And curse thee, wicked Mephistophilis,
  Because thou hast deprived me of those joys.
MEPHISTOPHILIS
  'Twas thine own seeking, Faustus; thank thyself.
  But think'st thou heaven is such a glorious thing?   5
  I tell thee, Faustus, 'tis not half so fair
  As thou, or any man that breathes on earth.
FAUSTUS   How prov'st thou that?
MEPHISTOPHILIS
  'Twas made for man; then he's more excellent.
FAUSTUS
  If heaven was made for man, 'twas made for me.   10
  I will renounce this magic and repent.

Enter the two ANGELS.

GOOD ANGEL   Faustus, repent; yet God will pity thee.
BAD ANGEL   Thou art a spirit; God cannot pity thee.
FAUSTUS
    Who buzzeth in mine ears I am a spirit?
    Be I a devil, yet God may pity me;   15
    Yea, God will pity me if I repent.
BAD ANGEL   Ay, but Faustus never shall repent.
                                    Exeunt ANGELS.
FAUSTUS
    My heart is hardened; I cannot repent.
    Scarce can I name salvation, faith, or heaven,
    But fearful echoes thunder in mine ears: 20
    "Faustus, thou art damned!" Then swords and knives,
    Poison, guns, halters, and envenomed steel
    Are laid before me to dispatch myself;
    And long ere this I should have done the deed,
    Had not sweet pleasure conquered deep despair.   25
    Have not I made blind Homer sing to me
    Of Alexander's love and Oenon's death?
    And hath not he, that built the walls of Thebes
    With ravishing sound of his melodious harp,
    Made music with my Mephistophilis?   30
    Why should I die then, or basely despair?
    I am resolved; Faustus shall not repent.
    Come, Mephistophilis, let us dispute again
    And reason of divine astrology.
    Speak; are there many spheres above the moon?   35
    Are all celestial bodies but one globe,
    As is the substance of this centric earth?
MEPHISTOPHILIS
    As are the elements, such are the heavens,
    Even from the moon unto the empyreal orb,
    Mutually folded in each others' spheres,   40
    And jointly move upon one axletree,
    Whose terminè is termed the world's wide pole;
    Nor are the names of Saturn, Mars, or Jupiter
    Feigned, but are erring stars.
FAUSTUS
                            But have they all
    One motion, both *situ et tempore*?   45

MEPHISTOPHILIS   All move from east to west in four-
and-twenty hours upon the poles of the world, but
differ in their motions upon the poles of the zodiac.

FAUSTUS
These slender questions Wagner can decide.
Hath Mephistophilis no greater skill?   50
Who knows not the double motion of the planets?
That the first is finished in a natural day?
The second thus? Saturn in thirty years?
Jupiter in twelve; Mars in four; the sun, Venus, and
Mercury in a year; the moon in twenty-eight days?   55
These are freshmen's suppositions. But tell me, hath
every sphere a dominion or *intelligentia*?

MEPHISTOPHILIS   Ay.

FAUSTUS   How many heavens or spheres are there?

MEPHISTOPHILIS   Nine—the seven planets, the firmament, and the empyreal heaven.   60

FAUSTUS   But is there not *coelum igneum, et crys-
tallinum*?

MEPHISTOPHILIS   No, Faustus, they be but fables.

FAUSTUS   Resolve me then in this one question: why   65
are not conjunctions, oppositions, aspects, eclipses
all at one time, but in some years we have more, in
some less?

MEPHISTOPHILIS   *Per inaequalem motum respectu
totius.*   70

FAUSTUS   Well, I am answered. Now tell me who
made the world.

MEPHISTOPHILIS   I will not.

FAUSTUS   Sweet Mephistophilis, tell me.

MEPHISTOPHILIS   Move me not, Faustus.   75

FAUSTUS   Villain, have not I bound thee to tell me
anything?

MEPHISTOPHILIS   Ay, that is not against our kingdom.
This is. Thou art damned. Think thou of hell.   80

FAUSTUS   Think, Faustus, upon God that made the
world.

MEPHISTOPHILIS   Remember this.   *Exit*.

FAUSTUS
Ay, go accursèd spirit to ugly hell.
'Tis thou hast damned distressèd Faustus' soul.   85
Is't not too late?

Enter the two ANGELS.

BAD ANGEL   Too late.
GOOD ANGEL   Never too late, if Faustus will repent.
BAD ANGEL   If thou repent, devils will tear thee in
pieces.   90
GOOD ANGEL   Repent, and they shall never raze thy
skin.   *Exeunt* ANGELS.
FAUSTUS
O Christ, my Savior, my Savior,
Help to save distressèd Faustus' soul.

Enter LUCIFER, BEËLZEBUB, *and* MEPHISTOPHILIS.

LUCIFER
Christ cannot save thy soul, for he is just.   95
There's none but I have interest in the same.
FAUSTUS   O, what art thou that look'st so terribly?
LUCIFER   I am Lucifer,
And this is my companion in hell.
FAUSTUS   O, Faustus, they are come to fetch thy soul.   100
BEËLZEBUB   We are come to tell thee thou dost injure
us.
LUCIFER   Thou call'st on Christ, contrary to thy prom-
ise.
BEËLZEBUB   Thou shouldst not think on God.
LUCIFER   Think on the devil.
BEËLZEBUB   And his dam too.   105
FAUSTUS
Nor will I henceforth. Pardon me in this,
And Faustus vows never to look to heaven,
Never to name God, or to pray to him,
To burn his Scriptures, slay his ministers,
And make my spirits pull his churches down.   110
LUCIFER
So shalt thou show thyself an obedient servant,
And we will highly gratify thee for it.
BEËLZEBUB   Faustus, we are come from hell in person
to show thee some pastime. Sit down, and thou shalt
behold the Seven Deadly Sins appear to thee in their   115
own proper shapes and likeness.

FAUSTUS   That sight will be as pleasant to me as Paradise was to Adam the first day of his creation.

LUCIFER   Talk not of Paradise or creation, but mark the show. Go Mephistophilis, fetch them in.   120

[*Exit* MEPHISTOPHILIS.]

Enter the Seven Deadly Sins, [with MEPHISTOPHILIS, *led by a* PIPER].

BEËLZEBUB   Now, Faustus, question them of their names and dispositions.

FAUSTUS   That shall I soon. What art thou, the first?

PRIDE   I am Pride. I disdain to have any parents. I am like to Ovid's flea: I can creep into every corner of a   125 wench. Sometimes, like a periwig, I sit upon her brow. Next, like a necklace, I hang about her neck. Then, like a fan of feathers, I kiss her lips, and then, turning myself to a wrought smock, do what I list. But fie, what a smell is here! I'll not speak another   130 word unless the ground be perfumed and covered with cloth of Arras.

FAUSTUS   Thou art a proud knave indeed. What art thou, the second?

COVETOUSNESS   I am Covetousness, begotten of an old churl in a leather bag, and might I now obtain my   135 wish, this house, you and all, should turn to gold, that I might lock you safe into my chest. O my sweet gold!

FAUSTUS   And what art thou, the third?

ENVY   I am Envy, begotten of a chimney sweeper and   140 an oyster-wife. I cannot read and therefore wish all books burned. I am lean with seeing others eat. O, that there would come a famine over all the world, that all might die, and I live alone; then thou shouldst see how fat I'd be. But must thou sit and I   145 stand? Come down, with a vengeance.

FAUSTUS   Out envious wretch! But what are thou, the fourth?

WRATH   I am Wrath. I had neither father nor mother. I leaped out of a lion's mouth when I was scarce an   150 hour old, and ever since have run up and down the

world with this case of rapiers, wounding myself
when I could get none to fight withal. I was born in
hell, and look to it, for some of you shall be my
father.   155

FAUSTUS   And what are you, the fifth?

GLUTTONY   I am Gluttony. My parents are all dead,
and the devil a penny they have left me but a small
pension, and that buys me thirty meals a day and ten
bevers—a small trifle to suffice nature. I come of a   160
royal pedigree. My father was a gammon of bacon,
and my mother was a hogshead of claret wine. My
godfathers were these: Peter Pickled-herring and
Martin Martlemas-beef. But my godmother, O, she
was a jolly gentlewoman, and well beloved in every   165
good town and city; her name was Mistress Margery
March-beer. Now, Faustus, thou hast heard all my
progeny; wilt thou bid me to a supper.

FAUSTUS   Not I. Thou wilt eat up all my victuals.

GLUTTONY   Then the devil choke thee.   170

FAUSTUS   Choke thyself, glutton. What art thou, the
sixth?

SLOTH   Heigh ho! I am Sloth. I was begotten on a
sunny bank, where I have lain ever since, and you
have done me great injury to bring me from thence.   175
Let me be carried thither again by Gluttony and
Lechery. Heigh ho! I'll not speak a word more for a
king's ransom.

FAUSTUS   And what are you, Mistress Minx, the sev-
enth and last?   180

LECHERY   Who, I, sir? I am one that loves an inch of
raw mutton better than an ell of fried stockfish, and
the first letter of my name begins with lechery.

LUCIFER   Away to hell! Away! On, piper!
                    Exeunt the Seven Sins [and the PIPER].

FAUSTUS   O, how this sight doth delight my soul!   185

LUCIFER   But, Faustus, in hell is all manner of delight.

FAUSTUS   O, might I see hell and return again safe,
how happy were I then!

LUCIFER   Faustus, thou shalt. At midnight I will send
for thee. Meanwhile peruse this book and view it   190
thoroughly, and thou shalt turn thyself into what
shape thou wilt.

FAUSTUS   Thanks, mighty Lucifer.
  This will I keep as chary as my life.
LUCIFER   Now, Faustus, farewell.   195
FAUSTUS   Farewell, great Lucifer. Come, Mephis-
  tophilis.   *Exeunt, several ways.*

Scene Three

Enter the clown [ROBIN, *holding a book*].

ROBIN   What, Dick, look to the horses there till I
  come again. I have gotten one of Doctor Faustus'
  conjuring books, and now we'll have such knavery
  as't passes.

Enter DICK.

DICK   What, Robin, you must come away and walk the   5
  horses.
ROBIN   I walk the horses? I scorn't, 'faith. I have other
  matters in hand. Let the horses walk themselves and
  they will. [*He reads.*] *A per se a; t, h, e, the; o per se
  o; deny orgon, gorgon.* Keep further from me, O   10
  thou illiterate and unlearned hostler.
DICK   'Snails, what hast thou got there? A book?
  Why, thou canst not tell ne'er a word on't.
ROBIN   That thou shalt see presently. Keep out of the
  circle, I say, lest I send you into the hostry with a   15
  vengeance.
DICK   That's like, 'faith. You had best leave your fool-
  ery, for an my master come, he'll conjure you, 'faith.
ROBIN   My master conjure me? I'll tell thee what: an
  my master come here, I'll clap as fair a pair of horns   20
  on's head as e'er thou sawest in thy life.
DICK   Thou needst not do that, for my mistress hath
  done it.
ROBIN   Ay, there be of us here that have waded as
  deep into matters as other men, if they were dis-   25
  posed to talk.
DICK   A plague take you! I thought you did not sneak
  up and down after her for nothing. But I prithee, tell
  me in good sadness, Robin, is that a conjuring book?

ROBIN   Do but speak what thou'lt have me to do, and   30
  I'll do't. If thou'lt dance naked, put off thy clothes,
  and I'll conjure thee about presently. Or if thou'lt go
  but to the tavern with me, I'll give thee white wine,
  red wine, claret wine, sack, muscadine, malmesey,
  and whippincrust. Hold belly, hold, and we'll not pay   35
  one penny for it.
DICK   O, brave! Prithee let's to it presently, for I am as
  dry as a dog.
ROBIN   Come then, let's away.   *Exeunt*.

PROLOGUE

Enter the CHORUS.

CHORUS
  Learnèd Faustus,
  To find the secrets of astronomy
  Graven in the book of Jove's high firmament,
  Did mount him up to scale Olympus' top,
  Where, sitting in a chariot burning bright   5
  Drawn by the strength of yokèd dragons' necks,
  He views the clouds, the planets, and the stars,
  The tropics, zones, and quarters of the sky,
  From the bright circle of the hornèd moon
  Even to the height of *Primum Mobile*.   10
  And whirling round with this circumference,
  Within the concave compass of the pole,
  From east to west his dragons swiftly glide
  And in eight days did bring him home again.
  Not long he stayed within his quiet house   15
  To rest his bones after his weary toil,
  But new exploits do hale him out again,
  And mounted then upon a dragon's back,
  That with his wings did part the subtle air,
  He now is gone to prove cosmography,   20
  That measures coasts and kingdoms of the earth,
  And, as I guess, will first arrive at Rome
  To see the Pope and manner of his court
  And take some part of holy Peter's feast,   25
  The which this day is highly solemnized.   *Exit*.

ACT THREE
Scene One

Enter FAUSTUS *and* MEPHISTOPHILIS.

FAUSTUS
Having now, my good Mephistophilis,
Passed with delight the stately town of Trier,
Environed round with airy mountaintops,
With walls of flint, and deep entrenchèd lakes,
Not to be won by any conquering prince;   5
From Paris next, coasting the realm of France,
We saw the river Main fall into Rhine,
Whose banks are set with groves of fruitful vines;
Then up to Naples, rich Campania,
Whose buildings fair and gorgeous to the eye,   10
The streets straight forth and paved with finest brick,
Quarters the town in four equivalents.
There saw we learnèd Maro's golden tomb,
The way he cut, an English mile in length,
Through a rock of stone in one night's space.   15
From thence to Venice, Padua, and the rest,
In midst of which a sumptuous temple stands,
That threats the stars with her aspiring top,
Whose frame is paved with sundry colored stones,
And roofed aloft with curious work in gold.   20
Thus hitherto hath Faustus spent his time.
But tell me now, what resting-place is this?
Hast thou, as erst I did command,
Conducted me within the walls of Rome?
MEPHISTOPHILIS
I have, my Faustus, and for proof thereof   25
This is the goodly palace of the Pope;
And 'cause we are no common guests,
I choose his privy chamber for our use.
FAUSTUS   I hope his holiness will bid us welcome.
MEPHISTOPHILIS
All's one, for we'll be bold with his venison.   30
But now, my Faustus, that thou may'st perceive
What Rome contains for to delight thine eyes,
Know that this city stands upon seven hills

That underprop the groundwork of the same.
Just through the midst runs flowing Tiber's stream,   35
With winding banks that cut it in two parts,
Over the which four stately bridges lean,
That make safe passage to each part of Rome.
Upon the bridge called Ponte Angelo
Erected is a castle passing strong,   40
Where thou shalt see such store of ordinance
As that the double cannons, forged of brass,
Do match the number of the days contained
Within the compass of one complete year;
Beside the gates and high pyramidès   45
That Julius Caesar brought from Africa.

FAUSTUS

Now, by the kingdoms of infernal rule,
Of Styx, of Acheron, and the fiery lake
Of ever-burning Phlegethon, I swear
That I do long to see the monuments   50
And situation of bright-splendent Rome.
Come, therefore, let's away.

MEPHISTOPHILIS

Nay, stay, my Faustus. I know you'd see the Pope
And take some part of holy Peter's feast,
The which, in state and high solemnity,   55
This day is held through Rome and Italy
In honor of the Pope's triumphant victory.

FAUSTUS

Sweet Mephistophilis, thou pleasest me.
Whilst I am here on earth, let me be cloyed
With all things that delight the heart of man.   60
My four-and-twenty years of liberty
I'll spend in pleasure and in dalliance,
That Faustus' name, whilst this bright frame doth stand,
May be admirèd through the furthest land.

MEPHISTOPHILIS

'Tis well said, Faustus. Come then, stand by me   65
And thou shalt see them come immediately.

FAUSTUS

Nay, stay, my gentle Mephistophilis,
And grant me my request, and then I go.
Thou know'st within the compass of eight days
We viewed the face of heaven, of earth, and hell.   70

So high our dragons soared into the air,
That looking down, the earth appeared to me
No bigger than my hand in quantity.
There did we view the kingdoms of the world,
And what might please mine eye I there beheld.   75
Then in this show let me an actor be,
That this proud Pope may Faustus' cunning see.

MEPHISTOPHILIS
Let it be so, my Faustus. But, first stay
And view their triumphs as they pass this way,
And then devise what best contents thy mind   80
By cunning in thine art to cross the Pope
Or dash the pride of this solemnity,
To make his monks and abbots stand like apes
And point like antics at his triple crown,
To beat the beads about the friars' pates   85
Or clap huge horns upon the cardinals' heads,
Or any villainy thou canst devise,
And I'll perform it, Faustus. Hark, they come.
This day shall make thee be admired in Rome.

Enter the CARDINALS *and* BISHOPS, *some bearing
crosiers, some the pillars;* MONKS *and* FRIARS *singing their procession. Then the* POPE, *and* RAYMOND,
KING OF HUNGARY, *with* BRUNO, *led in chains.*

POPE   Cast down our footstool.
RAYMOND   Saxon Bruno, stoop,   90
Whilst on thy back his holiness ascends
Saint Peter's chair and state pontifical.

BRUNO
Proud Lucifer, that state belongs to me,
But thus I fall to Peter, not to thee.

POPE
To me and Peter shalt thou groveling lie   95
And crouch before the papal dignity.
Sound trumpets then, for thus Saint Peter's heir
From Bruno's back ascends Saint Peter's chair.
                         A flourish while he ascends.
Thus, as the gods creep on with feet of wool
Long ere with iron hands they punish men,   100

So shall our sleeping vengeance now arise
And smite with death thy hated enterprise.
Lord cardinals of France and Padua,
Go forthwith to our holy consistory,
And read amongst the Statutes Decretal   105
What, by the holy council held at Trent,
The sacred synod hath decreed for him
That doth assume the papal government
Without election and a true consent.
Away, and bring us word with speed.   110

FIRST CARDINAL   We go, my lord.

                              Exeunt CARDINALS.
POPE   Lord Raymond.   [*They talk apart.*]

FAUSTUS
Go, haste thee, gentle Mephistophilis,
Follow the cardinals to the consistory,
And as they turn their superstitious books,   115
Strike them with sloth and drowsy idleness,
And make them sleep so sound that in their shapes
Thyself and I may parley with this Pope,
This proud confronter of the Emperor,
And in despite of all his holiness   120
Restore this Bruno to his liberty
And bear him to the states of Germany.

MEPHISTOPHILIS   Faustus, I go.

FAUSTUS
Dispatch it soon.
The Pope shall curse that Faustus came to Rome.   125

                  Exeunt FAUSTUS *and* MEPHISTOPHILIS.

BRUNO
Pope Adrian, let me have some right of law.
I was elected by the Emperor.

POPE
We will depose the Emperor for that deed
And curse the people that submit to him.
Both he and thou shalt stand excommunicate   130
And interdict from church's privilege
And all society of holy men.
He grows too proud in his authority,
Lifting his lofty head above the clouds,
And like a steeple overpeers the church.   135
But we'll pull down his haughty insolence,

And as Pope Alexander, our progenitor,
Trod on the neck of German Frederick,
Adding this golden sentence to our praise,
"That Peter's heirs should tread on emperors   140
And walk upon the dreadful adder's back,
Treading the lion and the dragon down
And fearless spurn the killing basilisk,"
So will we quell that haughty schismatic,
And by authority apostolical   145
Depose him from his regal government.

BRUNO
Pope Julius swore to princely Sigismond,
For him and the succeeding popes of Rome,
To hold the emperors their lawful lords.

POPE
Pope Julius did abuse the church's rites,   150
And therefore none of his decrees can stand.
Is not all power on earth bestowed on us?
And therefore, though we would, we cannot err.
Behold this silver belt, whereto is fixed
Seven golden keys fast sealed with seven seals   155
In token of our sevenfold power from heaven,
To bind or loose, lock fast, condemn or judge,
Resign, or seal, or whatso pleaseth us.
Then he and thou and all the world shall stoop,
Or be assurèd of our dreadful curse   160
To light as heavy as the pains of hell.

Enter FAUSTUS *and* MEPHISTOPHILIS, *like the* CAR-
DINALS.

MEPHISTOPHILIS   Now tell me, Faustus, are we not
fitted well?

FAUSTUS
Yes, Mephistophilis, and two such cardinals
Ne'er served a holy pope as we shall do.
But whilst they sleep within the consistory,   165
Let us salute his reverend fatherhood.

RAYMOND   Behold, my lord, the cardinals are
returned.

POPE
Welcome, grave fathers. Answer presently:

What have our holy council there decreed
Concerning Bruno and the Emperor,   170
In quittance of their late conspiracy
Against our state and papal dignity?

FAUSTUS
Most sacred patron of the church of Rome,
By full consent of all the synod
Of priests and prelates it is thus decreed: 175
That Bruno and the German Emperor
Be held as Lollards and bold schismatics
And proud disturbers of the church's peace.
And if that Bruno by his own assent,
Without enforcement of the German peers,   180
Did seek to wear the triple diadem
And by your death to climb Saint Peter's chair,
The Statutes Decretal have thus decreed:
He shall be straight condemned of heresy
And on a pile of fagots burned to death.   185

POPE
It is enough. Here, take him to your charge,
And bear him straight to Ponte Angelo,
And in the strongest tower enclose him fast.
Tomorrow, sitting in our consistory
With all our college of grave cardinals,   190
We will determine of his life or death.
Here, take his triple crown along with you,
And leave it in the church's treasury.
Make haste again, my good lord cardinals,
And take our blessing apostolical.   195

MEPHISTOPHILIS   So, so. Was never devil thus
blessed before.

FAUSTUS
Away, sweet Mephistophilis, be gone.
The cardinals will be plagued for this anon.
            Exeunt FAUSTUS *and* MEPHISTOPHILIS
                          [*with* BRUNO].

POPE
Go presently and bring a banquet forth,
That we may solemnize Saint Peter's feast,   200
And with Lord Raymond, King of Hungary,
Drink to our late and happy victory.   *Exeunt.*

Scene Two

*A sennet [is sounded] while the banquet is brought
in; and then enter* FAUSTUS *and* MEPHISTOPHILIS *in
their own shapes.*

MEPHISTOPHILIS
    Now, Faustus, come, prepare thyself for mirth.
    The sleepy cardinals are hard at hand
    To censure Bruno, that is posted hence,
    And on a proud-paced steed, as swift as thought,
    Flies o'er the Alps to fruitful Germany,   5
    There to salute the woeful Emperor.
FAUSTUS
    The Pope will curse them for their sloth today,
    That slept both Bruno and his crown away.
    But now, that Faustus may delight his mind
    And by their folly make some merriment,   10
    Sweet Mephistophilis, so charm me here
    That I may walk invisible to all
    And do whate'er I please unseen of any.
MEPHISTOPHILIS
    Faustus, thou shalt. Then kneel down presently:
        Whilst on thy head I lay my hand   15
        And charm thee with this magic wand.
        First wear this girdle; then appear
        Invisible to all are here.
        The planets seven, the gloomy air,
        Hell and the Furies' forkèd hair,   20
        Pluto's blue fire, and Hecate's tree,
        With magic spells so compass thee
        That no eye may thy body see.
    So, Faustus. Now, for all their holiness,
    Do what thou wilt, thou shalt not be discerned.   25
FAUSTUS
    Thanks, Mephistophilis. Now friars take heed
    Lest Faustus make your shaven crowns to bleed.
MEPHISTOPHILIS
    Faustus, no more. See where the cardinals come.

Enter POPE *and all the* LORDS. *Enter the* CARDINALS
with a book.

POPE
    Welcome, lord cardinals. Come, sit down.
    Lord Raymond, take your seat. Friars, attend,   30
    And see that all things be in readiness,
    As best beseems this solemn festival.

FIRST CARDINAL
    First, may it please Your Sacred Holiness
    To view the sentence of the reverend synod
    Concerning Bruno and the Emperor?   35

POPE
    What needs this question? Did I not tell you
    Tomorrow we would sit i' th' consistory
    And there determine of his punishment?
    You brought us word even now: it was decreed
    That Bruno and the cursèd Emperor   40
    Were by the holy council both condemned
    For loathèd Lollards and base schismatics.
    Then wherefore would you have me view that book?

FIRST CARDINAL
    Your Grace mistakes. You gave us no such charge.

RAYMOND
    Deny it not. We all are witnesses   45
    That Bruno here was late delivered you,
    With his rich triple crown to be reserved
    And put into the church's treasury.

BOTH CARDINALS
    By holy Paul, we saw them not.

POPE
    By Peter, you shall die   50
    Unless you bring them forth immediately.
    Hale them to prison. Lade their limbs with gyves.
    False prelates, for this hateful treachery
    Cursed be your souls to hellish misery.
        [*Exeunt the two* CARDINALS *with* ATTENDANTS.]

FAUSTUS
    So, they are safe. Now, Faustus, to the feast.   55
    The Pope had never such a frolic guest.

POPE
    Lord Archbishop of Rheims, sit down with us.

ARCHBISHOP   I thank Your Holiness.

FAUSTUS   Fall to. The devil choke you an you spare.

POPE   Who's that spoke? Friar, look about.   60
FRIAR   Here's nobody, if it like Your Holiness.
POPE
   Lord Raymond, pray fall to. I am beholding
   To the Bishop of Milan for this so rare a present.
FAUSTUS   I thank you, sir.   [*He snatches the dish.*]
POPE
   How now? Who snatched the meat from me?   65
   Villains, why speak you not?
   My good Lord Archbishop, here's a most dainty
     dish
   Was sent me from a cardinal in France.
FAUSTUS   I'll have that too.   [*He snatches the dish.*]
POPE
   What Lollards do attend Our Holiness,   70
   That we receive such great indignity?
   Fetch me some wine.
FAUSTUS   Ay, pray do, for Faustus is a-dry.
POPE   Lord Raymond, I drink unto Your Grace.
FAUSTUS   I pledge Your Grace. [*He snatches the cup.*]   75
POPE
   My wine gone too? Ye lubbers, look about
   And find the man that doth this villainy,
   Or by our sanctitude, you all shall die.
   I pray, my lords, have patience at this
   Troublesome banquet.   80
ARCHBISHOP   Please it Your Holiness, I think it be
   some ghost crept out of purgatory, and now is come
   unto Your Holiness for his pardon.
POPE   It may be so.
   Go then, command our priests to sing a dirge
   To lay the fury of this same troublesome ghost.   85
                 [*Exit an* ATTENDANT.]
   Once again, my lord, fall to.
               The POPE *crosseth himself.*
FAUSTUS
   How now?
   Must every bit be spicèd with a cross?
   Nay then, take that.   [*He strikes the* POPE.]
POPE
   O, I am slain. Help me, my lords.   90

O, come and help to bear my body hence.
Damned be this soul forever for this deed.
              Exeunt the POPE *and his train.*
MEPHISTOPHILIS   Now, Faustus, what will you do
now? For I can tell you you'll be cursed with bell,
book, and candle.
FAUSTUS
Bell, book, and candle; candle, book, and bell,   95
Forward and backward, to curse Faustus to hell.

Enter the FRIARS *with bell, book, and candle for the
dirge.*

FIRST FRIAR   Come, brethren, let's about our business
with good devotion.
                           [*They chant.*]
*Cursed be he that stole his holiness' meat from the
    table.*
          Maledicat Dominus!   100
*Cursed be he that struck his holiness a blow on the
    face.*
          Maledicat Dominus!
*Cursed be he that struck Friar Sandelo a blow on
    the pate.*
          Maledicat Dominus!
Cursed be he that disturbeth our holy dirge.   105
          Maledicat Dominus!
Cursed be he that took away his holiness' wine.
          Maledicat Dominus! Et omnes sancti.
          Amen.
     [FAUSTUS *and* MEPHISTOPHILIS] *beat the* FRIARS,
          fling fireworks among them, and exeunt.

                    Scene Three

Enter [ROBIN,] *the clown, and* DICK, *with a cup.*

DICK   Sirrah Robin, we were best look that your devil
can answer the stealing of this same cup, for the
vintner's boy follows us at the hard heels.

94 Bell, book, and candle used in the office of excommunication

ROBIN   'Tis no matter. Let him come. An he follow us, 5
I'll so conjure him as he was never conjured in his
life, I warrant him. Let me see the cup.

Enter VINTNER.

DICK   Here 'tis. Yonder he comes. Now, Robin, now
or never show thy cunning.

VINTNER   Oh, are you here? I am glad I have found
you. You are a couple of fine companions. Pray, 10
where's the cup you stole from the tavern?

ROBIN   How, how? We steal a cup? Take heed what
you say. We look not like cup stealers, I can tell you.

VINTNER   Never deny't, for I know you have it, and
I'll search you. 15

ROBIN   Search me? Ay, and spare not. [*Aside to*
DICK.] Hold the cup, Dick. [*To* VINTNER.] Come,
come, search me, search me.

[*The* VINTNER *searches* ROBIN.]

VINTNER [*To* DICK]   Come on, sirrah, let me search
you now. 20

DICK   Ay, ay, do, do. [*Aside to* ROBIN.] Hold the cup,
Robin. [*To* VINTNER.] I fear not your searching. We
scorn to steal your cups, I can tell you.

[*The* VINTNER *searches* DICK.]

VINTNER   Never outface me for the matter, for sure
the cup is between you two. 25

ROBIN   Nay, there you lie. 'Tis beyond us both.

VINTNER   A plague take you! I thought 'twas your
knavery to take it away. Come, give it me again.

ROBIN   Ay, much. When? Can you tell? Dick, make
me a circle, and stand close at my back, and stir not 30
for thy life. Vintner, you shall have your cup anon.
Say nothing, Dick, *O per se, O Demogorgon,
Belcher and Mephistophilis.*

Enter MEPHISTOPHILIS. [*Exit the* VINTNER, *in
fright.*]

MEPHISTOPHILIS
Monarch of hell, under whose black survey
Great potentates do kneel with awful fear, 35

Upon whose altars thousand souls do lie,
How am I vexèd by these villains' charms!
From Constantinople have they brought me now,
Only for pleasure of these damnèd slaves.

ROBIN   By Lady, sir, you have had a shrewd journey of   40
it. Will it please you to take a shoulder of mutton to
supper and a tester in your purse, and go back again?

DICK   Ay, I pray you heartily, sir, for we called you but
in jest, I promise you.

MEPHISTOPHILIS
To purge the rashness of this cursèd deed,   45
First be thou turnèd to this ugly shape,
For apish deeds transformèd to an ape.

ROBIN   O, brave, an ape! I pray, sir, let me have the
carrying of him about to show some tricks.

MEPHISTOPHILIS   And so thou shalt. Be thou trans-   50
formed to a dog, and carry him upon thy back. Away,
be gone!

ROBIN   A dog? That's excellent. Let the maids look
well to their porridge pots, for I'll into the kitchen
presently. Come, Dick, come.   55

Exeunt [ROBIN *and* DICK,] *the two clowns.*

MEPHISTOPHILIS
Now with the flames of ever-burning fire,
I'll wing myself and forthwith fly amain
Unto my Faustus, to the great Turk's court.   *Exit.*

PROLOGUE

Enter CHORUS.

CHORUS
When Faustus had with pleasure ta'en the view
Of rarest things and royal courts of kings,
He stayed his course and so returnèd home;
Where such as bare his absence but with grief—
I mean his friends and nearest companions—   5
Did gratulate his safety with kind words,
And in their conference of what befell,
Touching his journey through the world and air,
They put forth questions of astrology,

Which Faustus answered with such learnèd skill   10
As they admired and wondered at his wit.
Now is his fame spread forth in every land.
Amongst the rest, the Emperor is one—
Carolus the Fifth—at whose palace now
Faustus is feasted 'mongst his noblemen.   15
What there he did in trial of his art
I leave untold, your eyes shall see performed.

Exit.

ACT FOUR
Scene One

Enter MARTINO *and* FREDERICK, *at several doors.*

MARTINO
What ho, officers, gentlemen,
Hie to the presence to attend the Emperor.
Good Frederick, see the rooms be voided straight;
His Majesty is coming to the hall.
Go back, and see the state in readiness.   5
FREDERICK
But where is Bruno, our elected pope,
That on a fury's back came post from Rome?
Will not His Grace consort the Emperor?
MARTINO
O, yes, and with him comes the German conjurer,
The learnèd Faustus, fame of Wittenberg,   10
The wonder of the world for magic art;
And he intends to show great Carolus
The race of all his stout progenitors,
And bring in presence of his majesty
The royal shapes and warlike semblances   15
Of Alexander and his beauteous paramour.
FREDERICK   Where is Benvolio?
MARTINO   Fast asleep, I warrant you.
He took his rouse with stoups of Rhenish wine
So kindly yesternight to Bruno's health   20
That all this day the sluggard keeps his bed.
FREDERICK   See, see, his window's ope. We'll call to
him.
MARTINO   What ho, Benvolio!

Enter BENVOLIO *above at a window, in his nightcap,*
buttoning.

BENVOLIO   What a devil ail you two?
MARTINO
   Speak softly, sir, lest the devil hear you,   25
   For Faustus at the court is late arrived,
   And at his heels a thousand furies wait
   To accomplish whatsoever the doctor please.
BENVOLIO   What of this?
MARTINO
   Come, leave thy chamber first, and thou shalt see   30
   This conjurer perform such rare exploits
   Before the Pope and royal Emperor
   As never yet was seen in Germany.
BENVOLIO
   Has not the Pope enough of conjuring yet?
   He was upon the devil's back late enough,   35
   And if he be so far in love with him,
   I would he would post with him to Rome again.
FREDERICK
   Speak, wilt thou come and see this sport?
BENVOLIO   Not I.
MARTINO   Wilt thou stand in thy window and see it
   then?   40
BENVOLIO   Ay, and I fall not asleep i' th' meantime.
MARTINO
   The Emperor is at hand, who comes to see
   What wonders by black spells may compassed be.
BENVOLIO   Well, go you attend the Emperor. I am
   content for this once to thrust my head out at a   45
   window, for they say if a man be drunk overnight the
   devil cannot hurt him in the morning. If that be true,
   I have a charm in my head shall control him as well
   as the conjurer, I warrant you.
              Exit [FREDERICK, *with* MARTINO. BENVOLIO
                     remains at the window above].

Scene Two

A sennet [is sounded. Enter] CHARLES, *the German emperor,* BRUNO, [*the Duke of*] *Saxony,* FAUSTUS, MEPHISTOPHILIS, FREDERICK, MARTINO, *and* ATTENDANTS.

EMPEROR
Wonder of men, renowned magician,
Thrice-learnèd Faustus, welcome to our court.
This deed of thine, in setting Bruno free
From his and our professèd enemy,
Shall add more excellence unto thine art   5
Than if by powerful necromantic spells
Thou couldst command the world's obedience.
Forever be beloved of Carolus,
And if this Bruno thou hast late redeemed
In peace possess the triple diadem   10
And sit in Peter's chair despite of chance,
Thou shalt be famous through all Italy
And honored of the German Emperor.

FAUSTUS
These gracious words, most royal Carolus,
Shall make poor Faustus to his utmost power   15
Both love and serve the German Emperor
And lay his life at holy Bruno's feet.
For proof whereof, if so Your Grace be pleased,
The doctor stands prepared by power of art
To cast his magic charms that shall pierce through   20
The ebon gates of ever-burning hell,
And hale the stubborn Furies from their caves
To compass whatsoe'er Your Grace commands.

BENVOLIO [*Above*] Blood, he speaks terribly, but for all
that, I do not greatly believe him. He looks as like a   25
conjurer as the Pope to a costermonger.

EMPEROR
Then, Faustus, as thou late did'st promise us,
We would behold that famous conqueror,
Great Alexander, and his paramour
In their true shapes and state majestical,   30
That we may wonder at their excellence.

FAUSTUS
  Your Majesty shall see them presently.
  Mephistophilis, away,
  And with a solemn noise of trumpets' sound
  Present before this royal Emperor,   35
  Great Alexander and his beauteous paramour.
MEPHISTOPHILIS   Faustus, I will.   [*Exit*.]
BENVOLIO   Well, master doctor, an your devils come
  not away quickly, you shall have me asleep presently.
  Zounds, I could eat myself for anger to think I have   40
  been such an ass all this while, to stand gaping after
  the devil's governor and can see nothing.
FAUSTUS   I'll make you feel something anon, if my art
  fail me not.
  My lord, I must forewarn Your Majesty   45
  That when my spirits present the royal shapes
  Of Alexander and his paramour,
  Your Grace demand no questions of the king,
  But in dumb silence let them come and go.
EMPEROR   Be it as Faustus please; we are content.   50
BENVOLIO   Ay, ay, and I am content too. And thou
  bring Alexander and his paramour before the Em-
  peror, I'll be Actaeon and turn myself to a stag.
FAUSTUS   And I'll play Diana and send you the horns
  presently.   55

  [*A*] *sennet* [*is sounded*]. *Enter at one* [*door*] *the*
  EMPEROR ALEXANDER, *at the other* DARIUS. *They*
  meet [*in combat*]. DARIUS *is thrown down*; ALEX-
  ANDER *kills him, takes off his crown, and, offering to*
  go out, his paramour meets him. He embraceth her
  and sets DARIUS' *crown upon her head; and coming*
  back, both salute the EMPEROR, *who, leaving his*
  state, offers to embrace them, which FAUSTUS
  seeing, suddenly stays him. Then trumpets cease
  and music sounds.

  My gracious lord, you do forget yourself.
  These are but shadows, not substantial.
EMPEROR
  O, pardon me. My thoughts are so ravishèd
  With sight of this renownèd emperor,

That in mine arms I would have compassed him. 60
But, Faustus, since I may not speak to them,
To satisfy my longing thoughts at full,
Let me this tell thee: I have heard it said
That this fair lady, whilst she lived on earth,
Had on her neck a little wart or mole; 65
How may I prove that saying to be true?

FAUSTUS   Your Majesty may boldly go and see.

EMPEROR
Faustus, I see it plain,
And in this sight thou better pleasest me
Than if I gained another monarchy. 70

FAUSTUS   Away! Be gone!   *Exit show.*
See, see, my gracious lord, what strange beast is
yon, that thrusts his head out at window?

EMPEROR
O, wondrous sight! See, Duke of Saxony,
Two spreading horns most strangely fastenèd 75
Upon the head of young Benvolio.

SAXONY   What? Is he asleep or dead?

FAUSTUS   He sleeps, my lord, but dreams not of his
horns.

EMPEROR   This sport is excellent. We'll call and wake 80
him.
What ho, Benvolio!

BENVOLIO   A plague upon you! Let me sleep a while.

EMPEROR   I blame thee not to sleep much, having
such a head of thine own. 85

SAXONY   Look up, Benvolio: 'tis the Emperor calls.

BENVOLIO   The Emperor? Where? Oh, zounds, my
head!

EMPEROR   Nay, and thy horns hold, 'tis no matter for
thy head, for that's armed sufficiently. 90

FAUSTUS   Why, how now, sir knight! What, hanged by
the horns? This is most horrible. Fie, fie, pull in your
head for shame. Let not all the world wonder at you.

BENVOLIO   Zounds, doctor, is this your villainy?

FAUSTUS
O, say not so, sir. The doctor has no skill, 95
No art, no cunning, to present these lords
Or bring before this royal Emperor
The mighty monarch, warlike Alexander.

If Faustus do it, you are straight resolved
In bold Actaeon's shape to turn a stag.   100
And therefore, my lord, so please Your Majesty,
I'll raise a kennel of hounds shall hunt him so
As all his footmanship shall scarce prevail
To keep his carcass from their bloody fangs.
Ho, Belimote, Argiron, Asterote!   105

BENVOLIO   Hold, hold! Zounds, he'll raise up a kennel
of devils, I think, anon. Good, my lord, entreat for
me. 'Sblood, I am never able to endure these tor-
ments.

EMPEROR   Then, good master doctor,   110
Let me entreat you to remove his horns.
He has done penance now sufficiently.

FAUSTUS   My gracious lord, not so much for injury
done to me, as to delight Your Majesty with some
mirth, hath Faustus justly requited this injurious   115
knight; which being all I desire, I am content to
remove his horns. Mephistophilis, transform him.
              [MEPHISTOPHILIS *removes the horns.*]
And hereafter, sir, look you speak well of scholars.

BENVOLIO [*Aside*] Speak well of ye? 'Sblood, and
scholars be such cuckold makers to clap horns of   120
honest men's heads o' this order, I'll ne'er trust
smooth faces and small ruffs more. But an I be not
revenged for this, would I might be turned to a
gaping oyster and drink nothing but salt water.
                                          [*Exit* BENVOLIO *above.*]

EMPEROR
Come, Faustus. While the Emperor lives,   125
In recompense of this thy high desert,
Thou shalt command the state of Germany
And live beloved of mighty Carolus.   *Exeunt.*

Scene Three

Enter BENVOLIO, MARTINO, FREDERICK, *and* SOL-
DIERS.

MARTINO
Nay, sweet Benvolio, let us sway thy thoughts
From this attempt against the conjurer.

BENVOLIO
    Away! You love me not to urge me thus.
    Shall I let slip so great an injury,
    When every servile groom jests at my wrongs   5
    And in their rustic gambols proudly say,
    "Benvolio's head was graced with horns today"?
    O, may these eyelids never close again
    Till with my sword I have that conjurer slain.
    If you will aid me in this enterprise,   10
    Then draw your weapons and be resolute.
    If not, depart. Here will Benvolio die,
    But Faustus' death shall quit my infamy.
FREDERICK
    Nay, we will stay with thee, betide what may,
    And kill that doctor if he come this way.   15
BENVOLIO
    Then, gentle Frederick, hie thee to the grove,
    And place our servants and our followers
    Close in an ambush there behind the trees.
    By this, I know, the conjurer is near.
    I saw him kneel and kiss the Emperor's hand   20
    And take his leave, laden with rich rewards.
    Then, soldiers, boldly fight. If Faustus die,
    Take you the wealth: leave us the victory.
FREDERICK
    Come, soldiers. Follow me unto the grove.
    Who kills him shall have gold and endless love.   25
               Exit FREDERICK *with the* SOLDIERS.
BENVOLIO
    My head is lighter than it was by th' horns,
    But yet my heart's more ponderous than my head
    And pants until I see that conjurer dead.
MARTINO   Where shall we place ourselves, Benvolio?
BENVOLIO
    Here will we stay to bide the first assault.   30
    O, were that damnèd hellhound but in place,
    Thou soon shouldst see me quit my foul disgrace.

Enter FREDERICK.

FREDERICK
    Close, close, the conjurer is at hand

And all alone comes walking in his gown.
Be ready then, and strike the peasant down.   35

BENVOLIO
  Mine be that honor then. Now, sword, strike home.
  For horns he gave I'll have his head anon.

Enter FAUSTUS *with the false head.*

MARTINO   See, see, he comes.
BENVOLIO
                              No words! This blow
    ends all.
  Hell take his soul; his body thus must fall.
                              [*He stabs* FAUSTUS.]

FAUSTUS [*Falling*] O!   40
FREDERICK   Groan you, master doctor?
BENVOLIO
  Break may his heart with groans! Dear Frederick,
    see,
  Thus will I end his griefs immediately.

MARTINO
  Strike with a willing hand. His head is off.
            [BENVOLIO *strikes off* FAUSTUS' *false head.*]

BENVOLIO   The devil's dead. The Furies now may
  laugh.   45

FREDERICK
  Was this that stern aspèct, that awful frown,
  Made the grim monarch of infernal spirits
  Tremble and quake at his commanding charms?

MARTINO
  Was this that damnèd head whose heart conspired
  Benvolio's shame before the Emperor?   50

BENVOLIO
  Ay, that's the head, and here the body lies,
  Justly rewarded for his villainies.

FREDERICK
  Come, let's devise how we may add more shame
  To the black scandal of his hated name.

BENVOLIO
  First, on his head, in quittance of my wrongs,   55
  I'll nail huge forkèd horns and let them hang

Within the window where he yoked me first,
That all the world may see my just revenge.

MARTINO   What use shall we put his beard to?

BENVOLIO   We'll sell it to a chimney sweeper. It will   60
wear out ten birchen brooms, I warrant you.

FREDERICK   What shall eyes do?

BENVOLIO   We'll put out his eyes, and they shall serve
for buttons to his lips to keep his tongue from catching cold.

MARTINO   An excellent policy! And now, sirs, having   65
divided him, what shall the body do?

[FAUSTUS *rises.*]

BENVOLIO   Zounds, the devil's alive again.

FREDERICK   Give him his head, for God's sake.

FAUSTUS
Nay, keep it. Faustus will have heads and hands,
Ay, all your hearts, to recompense this deed.   70
Knew you not, traitors, I was limited
For four-and-twenty years to breathe on earth?
And had you cut my body with your swords,
Or hewed this flesh and bones as small as sand,
Yet in a minute had my spirit returned,   75
And I had breathed a man made free from harm.
But wherefore do I dally my revenge?
Asteroth, Belimoth, Mephistophilis!

Enter MEPHISTOPHILIS *and other* DEVILS.

Go, horse these traitors on your fiery backs,
And mount aloft with them as high as heaven;   80
Thence pitch them headlong to the lowest hell.
Yet stay. The world shall see their misery,
And hell shall after plague their treachery.
Go, Belimoth, and take this caitiff hence,
And hurl him in some lake of mud and dirt.   85
Take thou this other; drag him through the woods
Amongst the pricking thorns and sharpest briars,
Whilst with my gentle Mephistophilis
This traitor flies unto some steepy rock
That, rolling down, may break the villain's bones   90

    As he intended to dismember me.
    Fly hence. Dispatch my charge immediately.
FREDERICK   Pity us, gentle Faustus. Save our lives.
FAUSTUS   Away!
FREDERICK   He must needs go that the devil
    drives.   *Exeunt* SPIRITS *with the* KNIGHTS.

Enter the ambushed SOLDIERS.

FIRST SOLDIER
    Come, sirs, prepare yourselves in readiness.   95
    Make haste to help these noble gentlemen;
    I heard them parley with the conjurer.
SECOND SOLDIER
    See where he comes. Dispatch and kill the slave.
FAUSTUS
    What's here? An ambush to betray my life?
    Then, Faustus, try thy skill. Base peasants, stand,   100
    For lo, these trees remove at my command
    And stand as bulwarks 'twixt yourselves and me,
    To shield me from your hated treachery.
    Yet to encounter this your weak attempt,
    Behold an army comes incontinent.   105
            FAUSTUS *strikes the door, and enter a* DEVIL
                playing on a drum, after him another
                bearing an ensign, and divers with weapons,
                MEPHISTOPHILIS *with fireworks. They set*
                upon the SOLDIERS *and drive them out.* [*Exit*
                                                    FAUSTUS.]

Scene Four

Enter at several doors BENVOLIO, FREDERICK, *and*
MARTINO, *their heads and faces bloody and be-*
smeared with mud and dirt, all having horns on their
heads.

MARTINO   What ho, Benvolio!
BENVOLIO   Here! What, Frederick, ho!

FREDERICK   O, help me, gentle friend. Where is Mar-
   tino?
MARTINO   Dear Frederick, here,
   Half smothered in a lake of mud and dirt,   5
   Through which the Furies dragged me by the heels.
FREDERICK   Martino, see! Benvolio's horns again.
MARTINO   O misery! How now, Benvolio?
BENVOLIO   Defend me, heaven. Shall I be haunted
   still?
MARTINO   Nay, fear not man; we have not power to
   kill.   10
BENVOLIO
   My friends transformèd thus! O hellish spite!
   Your heads are all set with horns.
FREDERICK   You hit it right.
   It is your own you mean. Feel on your head.
BENVOLIO
   Zounds, horns again!
MARTINO
   Nay, chafe not man. We all are sped.   15
BENVOLIO
   What devil attends this damned magician,
   That, spite of spite, our wrongs are doublèd?
FREDERICK
   What may we do, that we may hide our shames?
BENVOLIO
   If we should follow him to work revenge,
   He'd join long asses' ears to these huge horns,   20
   And make us laughingstocks to all the world.
MARTINO
   What shall we then do, dear Benvolio?
BENVOLIO
   I have a castle joining near these woods,
   And thither we'll repair and live obscure
   Till time shall alter these our brutish shapes.   25
   Sith black disgrace hath thus eclipsed our fame,
   We'll rather die with grief than live with shame.

                                        Exeunt omnes.

Scene Five

Enter FAUSTUS *and* MEPHISTOPHILIS.

FAUSTUS
Now, Mephistophilis, the restless course
That time doth run with calm and silent foot,
Shortening my days and thread of vital life,
Calls for the payment of my latest years.
Therefore, sweet Mephistophilis, let us   5
Make haste to Wittenberg.
MEPHISTOPHILIS   What, will you go on horseback, or
on foot?
FAUSTUS   Nay, till I am past this fair and pleasant
green,
I'll walk on foot.   [*Exit* MEPHISTOPHILIS.]

Enter a HORSECORSER.

HORSECORSER   I have been all this day seeking one   10
Master Fustian. Mass, see where he is. God save
you, master doctor.
FAUSTUS   What, horsecorser! You are well met.
HORSECORSER   I beseech your worship, accept of
these forty dollars.   15
FAUSTUS   Friend, thou canst not buy so good a horse
for so small a price. I have no great need to sell him,
but if thou likest him for ten dollars more, take him,
because I see thou hast a good mind to him.
HORSECORSER   I beseech you, sir, accept of this. I am   20
a very poor man and have lost very much of late by
horse-flesh, and this bargain will set me up again.
FAUSTUS   Well, I will not stand with thee. Give me the
money. [*The* HORSECORSER *gives* FAUSTUS *money.*]
Now, sirrah, I must tell you that you may ride him   25
o'er hedge and ditch, and spare him not. But, do you
hear? In any case, ride him not into the water.
HORSECORSER   How, sir? Not into the water? Why,
will he not drink of all waters?
FAUSTUS   Yes, he will drink of all waters, but ride him   30
not into the water—o'er hedge and ditch, or where

thou wilt, but not into the water. Go, bid the hostler
deliver him unto you, and remember what I say.

HORSECORSER   I warrant you, sir. O joyful day! Now
am I a man made forever.   *Exit.*   35

FAUSTUS   What art thou, Faustus, but a man con-
demned to die?
Thy fatal time draws to a final end.
Despair doth drive distrust into my thoughts.
Confound these passions with a quiet sleep.   40
Tush! Christ did call the thief upon the cross;
Then rest thee, Faustus, quiet in conceit.
                        He sits to sleep [in his chair].

Enter the HORSECORSER, *wet.*

HORSECORSER   O, what a cozening doctor was this? I
riding my horse into the water, thinking some hidden
mystery had been in the horse, I had nothing under   45
me but a little straw and had much ado to escape
drowning. Well, I'll go rouse him and make him give
me my forty dollars again. Ho, sirrah doctor, you
cozening scab! Master doctor, awake and rise, and
give me my money again, for your horse is turned to   50
a bottle of hay. Master doctor!
                        He [tries to wake FAUSTUS, *and in doing so]*
                        pulls off his leg.
Alas, I am undone! What shall I do? I have pulled off
his leg.   [FAUSTUS *awakes.*]

FAUSTUS   O, help, help! The villain hath murdered
me.   55

HORSECORSER   Murder or not murder, now he has but
one leg, I'll outrun him and cast this leg into some
ditch or other.

FAUSTUS   Stop him, stop him, stop him! Ha, ha, ha,
Faustus hath his leg again, and the horsecorser a   60
bundle of hay for his forty dollars.

Enter WAGNER.

How now, Wagner, what news with thee?

WAGNER If it please you, the Duke of Anholt doth
earnestly entreat your company and hath sent some
of his men to attend you with provision fit for your   65
journey.
FAUSTUS The Duke of Anholt's an honorable gentleman, and one to whom I must be no niggard of my
cunning. Come away.   *Exeunt*.

                      Scene Six

Enter [ROBIN, *the*] *clown*, DICK, [*the*] HORSE-
CORSER, *and a* CARTER.

CARTER Come, my masters, I'll bring you to the best
beer in Europe. What ho, hostess! Where be these
whores?

Enter HOSTESS.

HOSTESS How now, what lack you? What, my old
guests, welcome.   5
ROBIN Sirrah, Dick, dost thou know why I stand so
mute?
DICK No, Robin; why is't?
ROBIN I am eighteen pence on the score. But say
nothing; see if she have forgotten me.   10
HOSTESS Who's this that stands so solemnly by him-
self? What, my old guest?
ROBIN O hostess, how do you? I hope my score
stands still.
HOSTESS Ay, there's no doubt of that, for methinks   15
you make no haste to wipe it out.
DICK Why, hostess, I say, fetch us some beer.
HOSTESS You shall presently. Look up into th' hall
there, ho!   *Exit*.
DICK Come, sirs, what shall we do now till mine   20
hostess come?
CARTER Marry, sir, I'll tell you the bravest tale how a
conjurer served me. You know Doctor Fauster?
HORSECORSER Ay, a plague take him. Here's some
on's have cause to know him. Did he conjure thee   25
too?

CARTER   I'll tell you how he served me. As I was going
to Wittenberg t'other day with a load of hay, he met
me and asked me what he should give me for as
much hay as he could eat. Now, sir, I thinking that a   30
little would serve his turn, bade him take as much as
he would for three farthings. So he presently gave me
my money and fell to eating; and as I am a cursen
man, he never left eating till he had eat up all my
load of hay.   35

ALL   O, monstrous! Eat a whole load of hay!

ROBIN   Yes, yes, that may be, for I have heard of one
that has eat a load of logs.

HORSECORSER   Now, sirs, you shall hear how vil-
lainously he served me. I went to him yesterday to   40
buy a horse of him, and he would by no means sell
him under forty dollars. So, sir, because I knew him
to be such a horse as would run over hedge and ditch
and never tire, I gave him his money. So when I had
my horse, Doctor Fauster bade me ride him night   45
and day and spare him no time; but, quoth he, in any
case ride him not into the water. Now, sir, I thinking
the horse had had some rare quality that he would
not have me know of, what did I but rid him into a
great river, and when I came just in the midst, my   50
horse vanished away, and I sat straddling upon a
bottle of hay.

ALL   O brave doctor!

HORSECORSER   But you shall hear how bravely I
served him for it. I went me home to his house, and   55
there I found him asleep. I kept a hallooing and
whooping in his ears, but all could not wake him. I
seeing that, took him by the leg and never rested
pulling till I had pulled me his leg quite off, and now
'tis at home in mine hostry.   60

ROBIN   And has the doctor but one leg then? That's
excellent, for one of his devils turned me into the
likeness of an ape's face.

CARTER   Some more drink, hostess.

ROBIN   Hark you, we'll into another room and drink a   65
while, and then we'll go seek out the doctor.

                                    Exeunt.

Scene Seven

Enter the DUKE OF ANHOLT, *his* DUCHESS, FAUSTUS, *and* MEPHISTOPHILIS, [SERVANTS *and* ATTENDANTS].

DUKE   Thanks, master doctor, for these pleasant sights. Nor know I how sufficiently to recompense your great deserts in erecting that enchanted castle in the air, the sight whereof so delighted me, as nothing in the world could please me more.   5
FAUSTUS   I do think myself, my good lord, highly recompensed in that it pleaseth Your Grace to think but well of that which Faustus hath performed. But, gracious lady, it may be that you have taken no pleasure in those sights. Therefore, I pray you, tell   10
me what is the thing you most desire to have; be it in the world, it shall be yours. I have heard that great-bellied women do long for things are rare and dainty.
DUCHESS   True, master doctor, and since I find you so kind, I will make known unto you what my heart   15
desires to have. And were it now summer, as it is January, a dead time of the winter, I would request no better meat than a dish of ripe grapes.
FAUSTUS   This is but a small matter. Go, Mephistophilis, away!   *Exit* MEPHISTOPHILIS.   20
Madam, I will do more than this for your content.

Enter MEPHISTOPHILIS *again with the grapes.*

Here; now taste ye these. They should be good, for they come from a far country, I can tell you.
DUKE   This makes me wonder more than all the rest, that at this time of year, when every tree is barren of   25
his fruit, from whence you had these ripe grapes.
FAUSTUS   Please it, Your Grace, the year is divided into two circles over the whole world, so that when it is winter with us, in the contrary circle it is likewise summer with them, as in India, Saba, and such   30
countries that lie far east, where they have fruit twice a year. From whence, by means of a swift

spirit that I have, I had these grapes brought, as you
see.

DUCHESS   And trust me, they are the sweetest grapes   35
that e'er I tasted.

    The CLOWN[S, ROBIN, DICK, *the* CARTER, *and the*
        HORSECORSER,] *bounce at the gate within.*

DUKE
What rude disturbers have we at the gate?
Go, pacify their fury. Set it ope,
And then demand of them what they would have.
                          [*Exit a* SERVANT.]

They knock again and call out to talk with FAUSTUS.

[*Enter* SERVANT *to them.*]

SERVANT
Why, how now, masters, what a coil is there?   40
What is the reason you disturb the duke.

DICK   We have no reason for it; therefore a fig for
him.

SERVANT   What, saucy varlets, dare you be so bold?

HORSECORSER   I hope, sir, we have wit enough to be   45
more bold than welcome.

SERVANT
It appears so. Pray be bold elsewhere,
And trouble not the duke.

DUKE   What would they have?

SERVANT   They all cry out to speak with Doctor
Faustus.   50

CARTER   Ay, and we will speak with him.

DUKE   Will you, sir? Commit the rascals.

DICK   Commit with us! He were as good commit with
his father as commit with us.

FAUSTUS
I do beseech Your Grace, let them come in;   55
They are good subject for a merriment.

DUKE   Do as thou wilt, Faustus. I give thee leave.

FAUSTUS   I thank Your Grace.

Enter ROBIN, DICK, CARTER, *and* HORSECORSER.

        Why, how now, my good friends?
Faith you are too outrageous, but come near;
I have procured your pardons. Welcome all!   60

ROBIN   Nay, sir, we will be welcome for our money,
and we will pay for what we take. What ho! Give's
half a dozen of beer here, and be hanged.

FAUSTUS   Nay, hark you; can you tell me where you
are?   65

CARTER   Ay, marry can I: we are under heaven.

SERVANT   Ay, but, sir sauce-box, know you in what
place?

HORSECORSER   Ay, ay, the house is good enough to
drink in. Zounds, fill us some beer, or we'll break all   70
the barrels in the house and dash out all your brains
with your bottles.

FAUSTUS

Be not so furious. Come, you shall have beer.
My lord, beseech you give me leave a while:
I'll gage my credit, 'twill content Your Grace.   75

DUKE

With all my heart, kind doctor. Please thyself;
Our servants and our court's at thy command.

FAUSTUS

I humbly thank Your Grace. Then fetch some beer.

HORSECORSER

Ay, marry, there spake a doctor indeed, and 'faith,
I'll drink a health to thy wooden leg for that word.   80

FAUSTUS   My wooden leg? What dost thou mean by
that?

CARTER   Ha, ha, ha! Dost hear him, Dick? He has
forgot his leg.

HORSECORSER   Ay, ay, he does not stand much upon   85
that.

FAUSTUS   No, faith; not much upon a wooden leg.

CARTER   Good lord, that flesh and blood should be so
frail with your worship! Do not you remember a
horsecorser you sold a horse to?   90

FAUSTUS   Yes, I remember I sold one a horse.

CARTER   And do you remember you bid he should not
ride into the water?

FAUSTUS   Yes, I do very well remember that.

CARTER   And do you remember nothing of your leg?   95

FAUSTUS   No, in good sooth.

CARTER   Then, I pray, remember your courtesy.

FAUSTUS   I thank you, sir.

CARTER   'Tis not so much worth. I pray you, tell me
one thing.   100

FAUSTUS   What's that?

CARTER   Be both your legs bedfellows every night
together?

FAUSTUS   Wouldst thou make a Colossus of me, that
thou askest me such questions?   105

CARTER   No, truly, sir. I would make nothing of you,
but I would fain know that.

Enter HOSTESS *with drink.*

FAUSTUS   Then, I assure thee, certainly they are.

CARTER   I thank you; I am fully satisfied.

FAUSTUS   But wherefore dost thou ask?   110

CARTER   For nothing, sir. But methinks you should
have a wooden bedfellow of one of 'em.

HORSECORSER   Why, do you hear, sir; did not I pull off
one of your legs when you were asleep?

FAUSTUS   But I have it again, now I am awake. Look   115
you here, sir.

ALL   O, horrible! Had the doctor three legs?

CARTER   Do you remember, sir, how you cozened me
and ate up my load of—

                      [FAUSTUS *charms him dumb.*]

DICK   Do you remember how you made me wear an   120
ape's—

                      [FAUSTUS *charms him dumb.*]

HORSECORSER   You whoreson conjuring scab, do you
remember how you cozened me with a ho—

                      [FAUSTUS *charms him dumb.*]

ROBIN   Ha' you forgotten me? You think to carry it
away with your *hey-pass* and *re-pass;* do you re-   125
member the dog's fa—

                      [FAUSTUS *charms him dumb.*]
                              Exeunt CLOWNS.

HOSTESS   Who pays for the ale? Hear you, master
doctor, now you have sent away my guests, I pray
who shall pay me for my a—

                      [FAUSTUS *charms her dumb.*]
                              Exit HOSTESS.

DUCHESS My lord,   130
  We are much beholding to this learnèd man.

DUKE
  So are we, madam, which we will recompense
  With all the love and kindness that we may.
  His artful sport drives all sad thoughts away.

                                  Exeunt.

ACT FIVE
Scene One

Thunder and Lightning. Enter DEVILS *with covered
dishes.* MEPHISTOPHILIS *leads them into* FAUSTUS'
study. Then enter WAGNER.

WAGNER
  I think my master means to die shortly.
  He has made his will and given me his wealth,
  His house, his goods, and store of golden plate,
  Besides two thousand ducats ready coined.
  I wonder what he means. If death were nigh,   5
  He would not frolic thus. He's now at supper
  With the scholars, where there's such belly-cheer
  As Wagner in his life ne'er saw the like.
  And see where they come; belike the feast is done.

                                         Exit.

Enter FAUSTUS, MEPHISTOPHILIS, *and two or three*
SCHOLARS.

FIRST SCHOLAR Master Doctor Faustus, since our   10
  conference about fair ladies, which was the beau-
  tifulest in all the world, we have determined with
  ourselves that Helen of Greece was the admirablest
  lady that ever lived. Therefore, master doctor, if you
  will do us so much favor as to let us see that peerless   15
  dame of Greece, whom all the world admires for
  majesty, we should think ourselves much beholding
  unto you.

FAUSTUS
  Gentlemen,
  For that I know your friendship is unfeigned,   20

And Faustus' custom is not to deny
The just requests of those that wish him well,
You shall behold that peerless dame of Greece,
No otherwise for pomp and majesty
Than when Sir Paris crossed the seas with her   25
And brought the spoils to rich Dardania.
Be silent then, for danger is in words.

Music sounds. MEPHISTOPHILIS *brings in* HELEN;
she passeth over the stage.

SECOND SCHOLAR
Was this fair Helen, whose admirèd worth
Made Greece with ten years war afflict poor Troy?
Too simple is my wit to tell her praise,   30
Whom all the world admires for majesty.
THIRD SCHOLAR
No marvel though the angry Greeks pursued
With ten years war the rape of such a queen,
Whose heavenly beauty passeth all compare.
FIRST SCHOLAR
Since we have seen the pride of nature's works   35
And only paragon of excellence,
We'll take our leaves, and for this blessèd sight
Happy and blest be Faustus evermore.
FAUSTUS
Gentlemen, farewell; the same wish I to you.

                                    Exeunt SCHOLARS.
Enter an OLD MAN.

OLD MAN
O gentle Faustus, leave this damnèd art,   40
This magic that will charm thy soul to hell
And quite bereave thee of salvation.
Though thou hast now offended like a man,
Do not persevere in it like a devil.
Yet, yet, thou hast an amiable soul,   45
If sin by custom grow not into nature.
Then, Faustus, will repentance come too late;
Then thou art banished from the sight of heaven.
No mortal can express the pains of hell.
It may be this my exhortation   50

Seems harsh and all unpleasant; let it not,
For, gentle son, I speak it not in wrath
Or envy of thee, but in tender love
And pity of thy future misery.
And so have hope that this my kind rebuke,   55
Checking thy body, may amend thy soul.

FAUSTUS

Where art thou, Faustus, Wretch, what hast thou
    done?
Damned art thou, Faustus, damned; despair and
    die!
Hell claims his right, and with a roaring voice
Says, "Faustus, come; thine hour is almost come";   60
And Faustus now will come to do thee right.
                MEPHISTOPHILIS *gives him a dagger.*

OLD MAN

O, stay, good Faustus, stay thy desperate steps.
I see an angel hovers o'er thy head,
And with a vial full of precious grace
Offers to pour the same into thy soul.   65
Then call for mercy and avoid despair.

FAUSTUS

Ah, my sweet friend, I feel thy words
To comfort my distressèd soul.
Leave me a while to ponder on my sins.

OLD MAN

Faustus, I leave thee, but with grief of heart,   70
Fearing the enemy of thy hapless soul.   *Exit.*

FAUSTUS

Accursèd Faustus, where is mercy now?
I do repent, and yet I do despair.
Hell strives with grace for conquest in my breast.
What shall I do to shun the snares of death?   75

MEPHISTOPHILIS

Thou traitor, Faustus, I arrest thy soul
For disobedience to my sovereign lord.
Revolt, or I'll in piecemeal tear thy flesh.

FAUSTUS

I do repent I e'er offended him.
Sweet Mephistophilis, entreat thy lord   80
To pardon my unjust presumption,
And with my blood again I will confirm
The former vow I made to Lucifer.

MEPHISTOPHILIS
   Do it then, Faustus, with unfeignèd heart,
   Lest greater dangers do attend thy drift.   85
           [FAUSTUS *stabs his arm and writes on a*
                      paper with his blood.]

FAUSTUS
   Torment, sweet friend, that base and agèd man
   That durst dissuade me from thy Lucifer,
   With greatest torment that our hell affords.

MEPHISTOPHILIS
   His faith is great; I cannot touch his soul,
   But what I may afflict his body with   90
   I will attempt, which is but little worth.

FAUSTUS
   One thing, good servant, let me crave of thee
   To glut the longing of my heart's desire—
   That I may have unto my paramour
   That heavenly Helen which I saw of late,   95
   Whose sweet embracings may extinguish clear
   Those thoughts that do dissuade me from my vow,
   And keep mine oath I made to Lucifer.

MEPHISTOPHILIS
   This, or what else my Faustus shall desire,
   Shall be performed in twinkling of an eye.   100

Enter HELEN *again, passing over* [*the stage*] *between two* CUPIDS.

FAUSTUS
   Was this the face that launched a thousand ships
   And burnt the topless towers of Ilium?
   Sweet Helen, make me immortal with a kiss.
                      [*She kisses him.*]
   Her lips suck forth my soul. See where it flies!
   Come, Helen, come, give me my soul again.   105
   Here will I dwell, for heaven is in these lips,
   And all is dross that is not Helena.

[*Enter the* OLD MAN.]

   I will be Paris, and for love of thee
   Instead of Troy shall Wittenberg be sacked;
   And I will combat with weak Menelaus   110

And wear thy colors on my plumèd crest.
Yea, I will wound Achilles in the heel
And then return to Helen for a kiss.
O, thou art fairer than the evening's air,
Clad in the beauty of a thousand stars.   115
Brighter art thou than flaming Jupiter
When he appeared to hapless Semele.
More lovely than the monarch of the sky
In wanton Arethusa's azured arms,
And none but thou shalt be my paramour.   120

Exeunt [all but the OLD MAN].

OLD MAN
Accursèd Faustus, miserable man,
That from thy soul exclud'st the grace of heaven
And fliest the throne of his tribunal seat!

Enter the DEVILS.

Satan begins to sift me with his pride.
As in this furnace God shall try my faith,   125
My faith, vile hell, shall triumph over thee.
Ambitious fiends, see how the heavens smiles
At your repulse and laughs your state to scorn.
Hence hell, for hence I fly unto my God.   *Exeunt.*

Scene Two

Thunder. Enter [above] LUCIFER, BEËLZEBUB, *and*
MEPHISTOPHILIS.

LUCIFER
Thus from infernal Dis do we ascend
To view the subjects of our monarchy,
Those souls which sin seals the black sons of hell,
'Mong which as chief, Faustus, we come to thee,
Bringing with us lasting damnation   5
To wait upon thy soul. The time is come
Which makes it forfeit.
MEPHISTOPHILIS   And this gloomy night,
Here in this room will wretched Faustus be.
BEËLZEBUB
And here we'll stay
To mark him how he doth demean himself.   10

MEPHISTOPHILIS
How should he, but in desperate lunacy?
Fond worldling, now his heart-blood dries with
 grief;
His conscience kills it, and his laboring brain
Begets a world of idle fantasies
To overreach the devil. But all in vain;   15
His store of pleasures must be sauced with pain.
He and his servant, Wagner, are at hand.
Both come from drawing Faustus' latest will.
See where they come.

Enter FAUSTUS *and* WAGNER.

FAUSTUS
Say, Wagner, thou hast perused my will;   20
How dost thou like it?
WAGNER   Sir, so wondrous well
As in all humble duty I do yield
My life and lasting service for your love.

Enter the SCHOLARS.

FAUSTUS   Gramercies, Wagner. Welcome, gentlemen.
                              [*Exit* WAGNER.]
FIRST SCHOLAR   Now, worthy Faustus, methinks your   25
 looks are changed.
FAUSTUS   Ah, gentlemen!
SECOND SCHOLAR   What ails Faustus?
FAUSTUS   Ah, my sweet chamber-fellow, had I lived
 with thee, then had I lived still, but now must die   30
 eternally. Look, sirs: comes he not? Comes he not?
FIRST SCHOLAR   O my dear Faustus, what imports
 this fear?
SECOND SCHOLAR   Is all our pleasure turned to melan-
 choly?   35
THIRD SCHOLAR   He is not well with being over-
 solitary.
SECOND SCHOLAR   If it be so, we'll have physicians,
 and Faustus shall be cured.
THIRD SCHOLAR   'Tis but a surfeit, sir; fear nothing.   40
FAUSTUS   A surfeit of deadly sin that hath damned
 both body and soul.

SECOND SCHOLAR   Yet, Faustus, look up to heaven,
and remember mercy is infinite.

FAUSTUS   But Faustus' offense can ne'er be pardoned.   45
The serpent that tempted Eve may be saved, but not
Faustus. Ah, gentlemen, hear me with patience and
tremble not at my speeches. Though my heart pants
and quivers to remember that I have been a student
here these thirty years. O, would I had never seen   50
Wittenberg, never read book. And what wonders I
have done, all Germany can witness—yea, all the
world—for which Faustus hath lost both Germany
and the world, yea heaven itself, heaven the seat of
God, the throne of the blessed, the kingdom of joy,   55
and must remain in hell forever. Hell, ah hell forever!
Sweet friends, what shall become of Faustus, being
in hell forever?

SECOND SCHOLAR   Yet, Faustus, call on God.

FAUSTUS   On God, whom Faustus hath abjured? On   60
God, whom Faustus hath blasphemed? Ah, my God,
I would weep, but the devil draws in my tears. Gush
forth blood instead of tears, yea life and soul. O, he
stays my tongue! I would lift up my hands, but see,
they hold 'em; they hold 'em.   65

ALL   Who, Faustus?

FAUSTUS   Why, Lucifer and Mephistophilis. Ah,
gentlemen, I gave them my soul for my cunning.

ALL   God forbid!

FAUSTUS   God forbade it indeed, but Faustus hath   70
done it. For the vain pleasure of four-and-twenty
years hath Faustus lost eternal joy and felicity. I writ
them a bill with mine own blood. The date is expired.
This is the time, and he will fetch me.

FIRST SCHOLAR   Why did not Faustus tell us of this   75
before, that divines might have prayed for thee?

FAUSTUS   Oft have I thought to have done so, but the
devil threatened to tear me in pieces if I named God,
to fetch me, body and soul, if I once gave ear to
divinity. And now 'tis too late. Gentlemen, away, lest   80
you perish with me.

SECOND SCHOLAR   O, what may we do to save
Faustus?

FAUSTUS   Talk not of me, but save yourselves and
depart.   85

THIRD SCHOLAR   God will strengthen me; I will stay
   with Faustus.

FIRST SCHOLAR   Tempt not God, sweet friend, but let
   us into the next room and there pray for him.

FAUSTUS   Ay, pray for me, pray for me; and what   90
   noise soever you hear, come not unto me, for nothing
   can rescue me.

SECOND SCHOLAR   Pray thou, and we will pray that
   God may have mercy upon thee.

FAUSTUS   Gentlemen, farewell. If I live till morning,   95
   I'll visit you; if not, Faustus is gone to hell.

ALL   Faustus, farewell.   *Exeunt* SCHOLARS.

MEPHISTOPHILIS [*Above*]
   Ay, Faustus, now thou hast no hope of heaven;
   Therefore despair. Think only upon hell,
   For that must be thy mansion, there to dwell.   100

FAUSTUS
   O thou bewitching fiend, 'twas thy temptation
   Hath robbed me of eternal happiness.

MEPHISTOPHILIS
   I do confess it, Faustus, and rejoice.
   'Twas I that, when thou wert i' the way to heaven,
   Damned up thy passage. When thou took'st the
      book   105
   To view the Scriptures, then I turned the leaves
   And led thine eye.
   What, weep'st thou? 'Tis too late. Despair!
      Farewell!
   Fools that will laugh on earth must weep in hell.

                                     Exit.

Enter the GOOD ANGEL *and the* BAD ANGEL *at several doors.*

GOOD ANGEL
   Ah, Faustus, if thou hadst given ear to me,   110
   Innumerable joys had followed thee;
   But thou didst love the world.

BAD ANGEL
                        Gave ear to me,
   And now must taste hell's pains perpetually.

GOOD ANGEL
   O, what will all thy riches, pleasures, pomps
   Avail thee now?

BAD ANGEL   Nothing but vex thee more,   115
To want in hell, that had on earth such store.
                    Music while the throne descends.

GOOD ANGEL
O, thou hast lost celestial happiness,
Pleasures unspeakable, bliss without end.
Hadst thou affected sweet divinity,
Hell or the devil had had no power on thee.   120
Hadst thou kept on that way, Faustus, behold
In what resplendent glory thou hadst sat
In yonder throne, like those bright shining saints,
And triumphed over hell. That hast thou lost,
And now, poor soul, must thy good angel leave thee.   125
                              [*The throne ascends.*]
The jaws of hell are open to receive thee.   *Exit.*
                              Hell is discovered.

BAD ANGEL
Now, Faustus, let thine eyes with horror stare
Into that vast perpetual torture-house.
There are the Furies tossing damnèd souls
On burning forks; their bodies boil in lead.   130
There are live quarters broiling on the coals,
That ne'er can die. This ever-burning chair
Is for o'er-tortured souls to rest them in.
These that are fed with sops of flaming fire
Were gluttons and loved only delicates   135
And laughed to see the poor starve at their gates.
But yet all these are nothing; thou shalt see
Ten thousand tortures that more horrid be.

FAUSTUS
O, I have seen enough to torture me.

BAD ANGEL
Nay, thou must feel them, taste the smart of all.   140
He that loves pleasure must for pleasure fall.
And so I leave thee, Faustus, till anon;
Then wilt thou tumble in confusion.   *Exit.*
            [*Hell disappears.*] *The clock strikes eleven.*

FAUSTUS
Ah, Faustus,
Now hast thou but one bare hour to live,   145
And then thou must be damned perpetually.
Stand still, you ever-moving spheres of heaven,

That time may cease and midnight never come.
Fair nature's eye, rise, rise again, and make
Perpetual day; or let this hour be but   150
A year, a month, a week, a natural day,
That Faustus may repent and save his soul.
O lente, lente currite noctis equi!
The stars move still; time runs; the clock will strike;
The devil will come, and Faustus must be damned,   155
O, I'll leap up to my God! Who pulls me down?
See, see, where Christ's blood streams in the
    firmament!
One drop would save my soul, half a drop! Ah, my
    Christ!
Rend not my heart for naming of my Christ!
Yet will I call on him. O, spare me, Lucifer!   160
Where is it now? 'Tis gone. And see where God
Stretcheth out his arm and bends his ireful brows.
Mountains and hills, come, come, and fall on me,
And hide me from the heavy wrath of God.
No, no!   165
Then will I headlong run into the earth.
Earth, gape! O, no, it will not harbor me!
You stars that reigned at my nativity,
Whose influence hath allotted death and hell,
Now draw up Faustus like a foggy mist   170
Into the entrails of yon laboring cloud,
That when you vomit forth into the air,
My limbs may issue from your smoky mouths,
So that my soul may but ascend to heaven.
                                    The watch strikes.
Ah, half the hour is past; 'twill all be past anon.   175
O God,
If thou wilt not have mercy on my soul,
Yet for Christ's sake, whose blood hath ransomed
    me,
Impose some end to my incessant pain.
Let Faustus live in hell a thousand years,   180
A hundred thousand, and at last be saved.
O, no end is limited to damnèd souls.
Why wert thou not a creature wanting soul?

153 O lente . . . equi O slowly, slowly run you horses of night

Or why is this immortal that thou hast?
Ah, Pythagoras' *metempsychosis*, were that true,   185
This soul should fly from me and I be changed
Into some brutish beast. All beasts are happy,
For, when they die
Their souls are soon dissolved in elements,
But mine must live still to be plagued in hell.   190
Cursed be the parents that engendered me!
No, Faustus, curse thyself, curse Lucifer
That hath deprived thee of the joys of heaven.
                              The clock strikes twelve.
O, it strikes, it strikes! Now, body, turn to air,
Or Lucifer will bear thee quick to hell.   195
O soul, be changed to little waterdrops,
And fall into the ocean, ne'er be found!
                    Thunder, and enter the DEVILS.
My God, my God, look not so fierce on me!
Adders and serpents, let me breathe a while!
Ugly hell, gape not! Come not, Lucifer!   200
I'll burn my books! Ah, Mephistophilis!
                    Exeunt [FAUSTUS *and* DEVILS].

                    Scene Three

Enter the SCHOLARS.

FIRST SCHOLAR
    Come, gentlemen, let us go visit Faustus,
    For such a dreadful night was never seen
    Since first the world's creation did begin.
    Such fearful shrieks and cries were never heard.
    Pray heaven the doctor have escaped the danger.   5
SECOND SCHOLAR
    O, help us, heaven! See, here are Faustus' limbs,
    All torn asunder by the hand of death.
THIRD SCHOLAR
    The devils whom Faustus served have torn him
        thus;
    For 'twixt the hours of twelve and one, methought

185 metempsychosis belief in the transmigration of souls

I heard him shriek and call aloud for help, 10
At which self time the house seemed all on fire
With dreadful horror of these damnèd fiends.

SECOND SCHOLAR

Well, gentlemen, though Faustus' end be such
As every Christian heart laments to think on,
Yet, for he was a scholar, once admired 15
For wondrous knowledge in our German schools,
We'll give his mangled limbs due burial;
And all the students, clothed in mourning black,
Shall wait upon his heavy funeral. *Exeunt.*

EPILOGUE

Enter CHORUS.

CHORUS

Cut is the branch that might have grown full
straight,
And burnèd is Apollo's laurel bough
That sometime grew within this learnèd man.
Faustus is gone. Regard his hellish fall,
Whose fiendful fortune may exhort the wise 5
Only to wonder at unlawful things,
Whose deepness doth entice such forward wits
To practice more than heavenly power permits.
[Exit.]
Terminat hora diem; terminat author opus.

KING LEAR

BY
William Shakespeare

EDITED BY
David Bevington

CHARACTERS

KING LEAR
GONERIL,
REGAN, } *Lear's daughters*
CORDELIA,
DUKE OF ALBANY, *Goneril's husband*
DUKE OF CORNWALL, *Regan's husband*
KING OF FRANCE, *Cordelia's suitor and husband*
DUKE OF BURGUNDY, *suitor to Cordelia*

EARL OF KENT, *later disguised as Caius*
EARL OF GLOUCESTER
EDGAR, *Gloucester's son and heir, later disguised as poor Tom*
EDMUND, *Gloucester's bastard son*

OSWALD, *Goneril's steward*
A KNIGHT *serving King Lear*
Lear's FOOL
CURAN, *in Gloucester's household*
GENTLEMEN
Three SERVANTS
OLD MAN, *a tenant of Gloucester*
Three MESSENGERS
DOCTOR *attending Cordelia*
Two CAPTAINS
HERALD

Knights, Gentlemen, Attendants, Servants, Officers, Soldiers, Trumpeters

SCENE: *Britain*

ACT ONE
Scene One
[KING LEAR'S PALACE.]

Enter KENT, GLOUCESTER, *and* EDMUND.

KENT   I thought the King had more affected the Duke   1
of Albany than Cornwall.   2

GLOUCESTER   It did always seem so to us; but now in
the division of the kingdom it appears not which of
the dukes he values most, for equalities are so   5
weighed that curiosity in neither can make choice of   6
either's moiety.   7

KENT   Is not this your son, my lord?

GLOUCESTER   His breeding, sir, hath been at my   9
charge. I have so often blushed to acknowledge him   10
that now I am brazed to 't.   11

KENT   I cannot conceive you.   12

GLOUCESTER   Sir, this young fellow's mother could;
whereupon she grew round-wombed and had indeed,
sir, a son for her cradle ere she had a husband for her
bed. Do you smell a fault?   16

KENT   I cannot wish the fault undone, the issue of it   17
being so proper.   18

GLOUCESTER   But I have a son, sir, by order of law,   19
some year elder than this, who yet is no dearer in my   20
account. Though this knave came something saucily   21

---

1 more affected better liked   **2 Albany** i.e., Scotland   **5–7 equalities
. . . moiety** the shares balance so equally that close scrutiny cannot find
advantage in either's portion   **9 breeding** raising, care **10 charge** expense   **11 brazed** hardened   **12 conceive** understand. (But Gloucester
puns in the sense of "become pregnant.")   **16 fault** (1) sin (2) loss of
scent by the hounds   **17 issue** (1) result (2) offspring   **18 proper** (1) excellent (2) handsome   **19 by order of law** legitimate   **20 some year**
about a year   **21 account** estimation.   **knave** young fellow (not said
disapprovingly, though the word is ironic).   **something** somewhat

to the world before he was sent for, yet was his
mother fair, there was good sport at his making, and
the whoreson must be acknowledged.—Do you   24
know this noble gentleman, Edmund?

EDMUND   No, my lord.

GLOUCESTER   My lord of Kent. Remember him hereafter as my honorable friend.

EDMUND   My services to your lordship.   29

KENT   I must love you, and sue to know you better.   30

EDMUND   Sir, I shall study deserving.   31

GLOUCESTER   He hath been out nine years, and   32
away he shall again. The King is coming.   33

*Sennet. Enter [one bearing a coronet, then] KING
LEAR, CORNWALL, ALBANY, GONERIL, REGAN, COR-
DELIA, and attendants.*

LEAR
Attend the lords of France and Burgundy,
  Gloucester.   34
GLOUCESTER   I shall, my liege.   *Exit*.
LEAR
Meantime we shall express our darker purpose.   36
Give me the map there. [*He takes a map.*] Know that
  we have divided
In three our kingdom; and 'tis our fast intent   38
To shake all cares and business from our age,
Conferring them on younger strengths while we
Unburdened crawl toward death. Our son of Cornwall,
And you, our no less loving son of Albany,
We have this hour a constant will to publish   43

---

24 whoreson low fellow; suggesting bastardy, but (like *knave* above) used
with affectionate condescension   **29 services** duty   **30 sue** petition,
beg   **31 study deserving** strive to be worthy (of your esteem)   **32 out**
i.e., abroad, absent   **33 s.d. Sennet** trumpet signal heralding a procession. **one . . . then** (This direction is from the quarto. The *coronet* is
perhaps intended for Cordelia or her betrothed. A coronet signifies
nobility below the rank of king.)   **34 Attend** i.e., wait on them cere-
monially, usher them into our presence   **36 we, our** (The royal plural;
also in ll. 37–44, etc.)   **darker purpose** undeclared intention   **38 fast**
firm   **43 constant . . . publish** firm resolve to proclaim

Our daughters' several dowers, that future strife   44
May be prevented now. The princes, France and
    Burgundy,   45
Great rivals in our youngest daughter's love,
Long in our court have made their amorous sojourn
And here are to be answered. Tell me, my daughters—
Since now we will divest us both of rule,
Interest of territory, cares of state—   50
Which of you shall we say doth love us most,
That we our largest bounty may extend
Where nature doth with merit challenge? Goneril,   53
Our eldest born, speak first.

GONERIL

Sir, I love you more than words can wield the matter,
Dearer than eyesight, space, and liberty,   56
Beyond what can be valued, rich or rare,   57
No less than life, with grace, health, beauty, honor;
As much as child e'er loved, or father found;   59
A love that makes breath poor and speech unable.   60
Beyond all manner of so much I love you.

CORDELIA [*Aside*]

What shall Cordelia speak? Love and be silent.

LEAR [*Indicating on map*]

Of all these bounds, even from this line to this,
With shadowy forests and with champains riched,   64
With plenteous rivers and wide-skirted meads,   65
We make thee lady. To thine and Albany's issue
Be this perpetual.—What says our second daughter,
Our dearest Regan, wife of Cornwall? Speak.

REGAN

I am made of that self mettle as my sister,   69

---

44 several individual   **45 prevented** forestalled   **50 Interest** possession   **53 Where . . . challenge** where both natural affection and merit
claim it as due   **56 space** freedom from confinement. **liberty** freedom
of action   **57 valued** estimated   **59 found** i.e., found himself to be loved
60 breath voice, speech. **unable** incompetent, inadequate   **64 shadowy**
shady. **champains riched** fertile plains   **65 wide-skirted meads** extensive,
spread out meadows   **69 self** same. **mettle** spirit, temperament. (But
with the meaning also of *metal*, substance, continued in the metaphor of
prize and *worth*, 1.1.70)

And prize me at her worth. In my true heart   70
I find she names my very deed of love;   71
Only she comes too short, that I profess   72
Myself an enemy to all other joys
Which the most precious square of sense
  possesses,   74
And find I am alone felicitate   75
In your dear Highness' love.

CORDELIA [*Aside*]   Then poor Cordelia!
  And yet not so, since I am sure my love's
  More ponderous than my tongue.   78

LEAR
To thee and thine hereditary ever
Remain this ample third of our fair kingdom,
No less in space, validity, and pleasure   81
Than that conferred on Goneril.—Now, our joy,
Although our last and least, to whose young love   83
The vines of France and milk of Burgundy   84
Strive to be interessed, what can you say to draw   85
A third more opulent than your sisters'? Speak.

CORDELIA   Nothing, my lord.

LEAR   Nothing?

CORDELIA   Nothing.

LEAR
Nothing will come of nothing. Speak again.

CORDELIA
Unhappy that I am, I cannot heave
My heart into my mouth. I love Your Majesty
According to my bond, no more nor less.   93

LEAR
How, how, Cordelia? Mend your speech a little,
Lest you may mar your fortunes.

---

70 prize . . . worth value myself as her equal (in love for you) (*Prize*
suggests "price.")   **71 names . . . love** describes my love in very
deed   **72 that** in that   **74 most . . . possesses** most delicate test of my
sensibility, most delicately sensitive part of my nature, can enjoy   **75 felicitate** made happy   **78 ponderous** weighty   **81 validity**
value. **pleasure** pleasing features   **83 least** youngest   **84 vines** vine-
yards. **milk** pastures (?)   **85 be interessed** be affiliated, establish a claim,
be admitted as to a privilege. **draw** win   **93 bond** filial obligation

CORDELIA   Good my lord,
  You have begot me, bred me, loved me. I
  Return those duties back as are right fit,   97
  Obey you, love you, and most honor you.
  Why have my sisters husbands if they say
  They love you all? Haply, when I shall wed,   100
  That lord whose hand must take my plight shall
    carry   101
  Half my love with him, half my care and duty.
  Sure I shall never marry like my sisters,
  To love my father all.

LEAR
  But goes thy heart with this?

CORDELIA   Ay, my good lord.

LEAR   So young, and so untender?

CORDELIA   So young, my lord, and true.

LEAR
  Let it be so! Thy truth then be thy dower!
  For, by the sacred radiance of the sun,
  The mysteries of Hecate and the night,   110
  By all the operation of the orbs   111
  From whom we do exist and cease to be,   112
  Here I disclaim all my paternal care,
  Propinquity, and property of blood,   114
  And as a stranger to my heart and me
  Hold thee from this forever. The barbarous
    Scythian,   116
  Or he that makes his generation messes   117
  To gorge his appetite, shall to my bosom
  Be as well neighbored, pitied, and relieved
  As thou my sometime daughter.

KENT   Good my liege—   120

---

97 right fit proper and fitting   **100 all** exclusively, and with all of themselves. **Haply** perhaps   **101 plight** troth-plight, pledge   **110 mysteries** secret rites. **Hecate** goddess of witchcraft and the moon   **111 operation** influence. **orbs** heavenly bodies   **112 From whom** under whose influence   **114 Propinquity . . . blood** intimacy and close kinship   **116 this** this time forth. **Scythian** Scythians were famous in antiquity for savagery.   **117 makes . . . messes** makes meals of his children or parents   **120 sometime** former

LEAR

    Peace, Kent!
    Come not between the dragon and his wrath.
    I loved her most, and thought to set my rest   123
    On her kind nursery. [*To* CORDELIA.] Hence, and
      avoid my sight!—   124
    So be my grave my peace, as here I give   125
    Her father's heart from her! Call France. Who stirs? 126
    Call Burgundy. [*Exit one*.] Cornwall and Albany,
    With my two daughters' dowers digest the third.   128
    Let pride, which she calls plainness, marry her.   129
    I do invest you jointly with my power,
    Preeminence, and all the large effects   131
    That troop with majesty. Ourself by monthly
      course,   132
    With reservation of an hundred knights   133
    By you to be sustained, shall our abode
    Make with you by due turns. Only we shall retain
    The name and all th' addition to a king.   136
    The sway, revenue, execution of the rest,
    Belovèd sons, be yours, which to confirm,
    This coronet part between you.

KENT   Royal Lear, 139

    Whom I have ever honored as my king,
    Loved as my father, as my master followed,
    As my great patron thought on in my prayers—

LEAR

    The bow is bent and drawn. Make from the shaft.   143

---

123 set my rest repose myself. (A phrase from a game of cards meaning
"to stake all.")   **124 nursery** nursing, care. **avoid** leave   **125 So . . .
peace, as** as I hope to rest peacefully in my grave   **126 Who stirs?** i.e.,
somebody do something; don't just stand there   **128 digest** assimilate,
incorporate   **129 Let . . . her** let her pride be her dowry and get her a
husband   **131 effects** outward shows   **132 troop with** accompany, serve.
Ourself (The royal "we.")   **133 With reservation of** reserving to myself
the right to be attended by   **136 addition** honors and prerogatives   **139 coronet** (Perhaps Lear gestures toward this coronet that
was to have symbolized Cordelia's dowry and marriage, or hands it to
his sons-in-law, or actually attempts to divide it.)   **143 Make from** get
out of the way of

KENT
Let it fall rather, though the fork invade   144
The region of my heart. Be Kent unmannerly   145
When Lear is mad. What wouldst thou do, old
   man?   146
Think'st thou that duty shall have dread to speak
When power to flattery bows?
To plainness honor's bound   149
When majesty falls to folly. Reserve thy state,   150
And in thy best consideration check   151
This hideous rashness. Answer my life my
   judgment,   152
Thy youngest daughter does not love thee least,
Nor are those emptyhearted whose low sounds
Reverb no hollowness.

LEAR   Kent, on thy life, no more.   155

KENT
My life I never held but as a pawn   156
To wage against thine enemies, nor fear to lose it,   157
Thy safety being motive.

LEAR   Out of my sight!   158

KENT
See better, Lear, and let me still remain   159
The true blank of thine eye.   160

LEAR   Now, by Apollo—

KENT
Now, by Apollo, King,
Thou swear'st thy gods in vain.

LEAR   O, vassal! Miscreant!   164

[Laying his hand on his sword.]

---

144 fall strike. **fork** barbed head of an arrow   **145–146 Be . . . mad** i.e., I must be unmannerly when you behave so madly   **149 To . . . bound** allegiance demands frankness   **150 Reserve thy state** retain your royal authority **151 in . . . consideration** with wise deliberation. **check** restrain, withhold   **152 Answer . . . judgment** I wager my life on my judgment that   **155 Reverb no hollowness** i.e., do not reverberate like a hollow drum, insincerely **156 held** regarded. **pawn** stake, chess piece   **157 wage** wager, hazard in warfare   **158 motive** that which prompts me to act   **159 still** always   **160 The true . . . eye** i.e., the means to enable you to see better. (*Blank* means the white center of the target, or, more probably, the true direct aim, as in "point-blank," traveling in a straight line.)   **164 vassal** i.e., wretch. **Miscreant** (Literally, infidel; hence, villain, rascal.)

ALBANY, CORNWALL   Dear sir, forbear.

KENT
Kill thy physician, and the fee bestow
Upon the foul disease. Revoke thy gift,
Or whilst I can vent clamor from my throat
I'll tell thee thou dost evil.

LEAR
Hear me, recreant, on thine allegiance hear me!   170
That thou hast sought to make us break our vows,   171
Which we durst never yet, and with strained pride   172
To come betwixt our sentence and our power,   173
Which nor our nature nor our place can bear,   174
Our potency made good, take thy reward.   175
Five days we do allot thee for provision
To shield thee from disasters of the world,   177
And on the sixth to turn thy hated back
Upon our kingdom. If on the tenth day following
Thy banished trunk be found in our dominions,   180
The moment is thy death. Away! By Jupiter,
This shall not be revoked.

KENT
Fare thee well, King. Sith thus thou wilt appear,   183
Freedom lives hence and banishment is here.
[To CORDELIA.] The gods to their dear shelter take
   thee, maid,
That justly think'st and hast most rightly said!
[To REGAN and GONERIL.] And your large speeches
   may your deeds approve,   187
That good effects may spring from words of love.
Thus Kent, O princes, bids you all adieu.
He'll shape his old course in a country new.   Exit.   190

---

170 recreant traitor   **171 That** in that, since   **172 strained** exces-
sive   **173 To . . . power** i.e., to block my power to give sentence   **174 Which . . . place** which neither my temperament nor my
office as king   **175 Our . . . good** my potency now being validated, to
show that I am not merely threatening   **177 disasters** misfortunes   **180 trunk** body   **183 Sith** since   **187 your . . . approve** may
your deeds confirm your speeches with their vast claims   **190 shape
. . . course** follow his traditional plainspoken ways

Flourish. Enter GLOUCESTER, *with* FRANCE *and* BUR-
GUNDY; *attendants.*

GLOUCESTER
Here's France and Burgundy, my noble lord.

LEAR
My lord of Burgundy,
We first address toward you, who with this king   193
Hath rivaled for our daughter. What in the least   194
Will you require in present dower with her
Or cease your quest of love?

BURGUNDY   Most royal Majesty,
I crave no more than hath Your Highness offered,
Nor will you tender less.

LEAR   Right noble Burgundy,   198
When she was dear to us we did hold her so,   199
But now her price is fallen. Sir, there she stands.
If aught within that little-seeming substance,   201
Or all of it, with our displeasure pieced,   202
And nothing more, may fitly like Your Grace,   203
She's there, and she is yours.

BURGUNDY   I know no answer.

LEAR
Will you, with those infirmities she owes,   205
Unfriended, new-adopted to our hate,
Dowered with our curse and strangered with our
   oath,   207
Take her, or leave her?

BURGUNDY   Pardon me, royal sir.
Election makes not up in such conditions.   209

LEAR
Then leave her, sir, for by the power that made me,
I tell you all her wealth. [*To* FRANCE.] For you, great
   King,   211

---

193 address address myself   **194 rivaled** competed   **198 tender** offer   **199 so** i.e., *dear*, beloved and valued at a high price   **201 little-
seeming substance** one who seems substantial but whose substance is in
fact little; or, one who refuses to flatter   **202 pieced** added,
joined   **203 like** please   **205 owes** owns   **207 strangered with** made a
stranger by   **209 Election . . . conditions** no choice is possible under
such conditions   **211 tell you** (1) inform you of (2) enumerate for you.
For as for

I would not from your love make such a stray   212
To match you where I hate; therefore beseech you   213
T' avert your liking a more worthier way   214
Than on a wretch whom Nature is ashamed
Almost t' acknowledge hers.

FRANCE   This is most strange,
That she whom even but now was your best object,   217
The argument of your praise, balm of your age,   218
The best, the dearest, should in this trice of time
Commit a thing so monstrous to dismantle   220
So many folds of favor. Sure her offense
Must be of such unnatural degree
That monsters it, or your forevouched affection   223
Fall into taint, which to believe of her   224
Must be a faith that reason without miracle
Should never plant in me.   226

CORDELIA   I yet beseech Your Majesty—
If for I want that glib and oily art   228
To speak and purpose not, since what I well intend   229
I'll do 't before I speak—that you make known
It is no vicious blot, murder, or foulness,
No unchaste action or dishonored step
That hath deprived me of your grace and favor,
But even for want of that for which I am richer: 234
A still-soliciting eye and such a tongue   235
That I am glad I have not, though not to have it
Hath lost me in your liking.

LEAR   Better thou
Hadst not been born than not t' have pleased me
    better.

---

212 **make such a stray** stray so far 213 **To** as to. **beseech** I beseech 214 **avert your liking** turn your affections 217 **whom** who. **best
object** main object of love 218 **argument** theme 220 **to** as
to 223 **monsters it** makes it monstrous 223–224 **or . . . taint** or else
the affection for her you have hitherto affirmed *(forevouched)* must fall
into suspicion *(taint);* or, before (ere, *or*) your hitherto-proclaimed affection could have fallen into decay 224 **which** i.e., that her offense is
monstrous 226 **Should** could 228 **for I want** because I lack 229 **purpose not** not intend to do what I say 234 **for which** for want of
which 235 **still-soliciting** ever-begging

FRANCE
  Is it but this? A tardiness in nature
  Which often leaves the history unspoke   240
  That it intends to do? My lord of Burgundy,
  What say you to the lady? Love's not love
  When it is mingled with regards that stands   243
  Aloof from th' entire point. Will you have her?   244
  She is herself a dowry.
BURGUNDY   Royal King,
  Give but that portion which yourself proposed,
  And here I take Cordelia by the hand,
  Duchess of Burgundy.
LEAR
  Nothing. I have sworn. I am firm.
BURGUNDY [*To* CORDELIA]
  I am sorry, then, you have so lost a father
  That you must lose a husband.
CORDELIA
                      Peace be with Burgundy!
  Since that respects of fortune are his love,   252
  I shall not be his wife.
FRANCE
  Fairest Cordelia, that art most rich being poor,
  Most choice, forsaken, and most loved, despised,
  Thee and thy virtues here I seize upon,
  Be it lawful I take up what's cast away.   257
                      [*He takes her hand.*]
  Gods, gods! 'Tis strange that from their cold'st
    neglect   258
  My love should kindle to inflamed respect.—   259
  Thy dowerless daughter, King, thrown to my
    chance,   260
  Is queen of us, of ours, and our fair France.

---

240 leaves . . . unspoke does not speak aloud the action   **243–244 regards . . . point** irrelevant considerations   **252 Since that** since. **respects of fortune** concern for wealth and position   **257 Be it lawful** if it be lawful that   **258 from . . . neglect** i.e., because the gods seem to have deserted Cordelia   **259 inflamed respect** ardent affection   **260 chance** lot

Not all the dukes of waterish Burgundy   262
Can buy this unprized precious maid of me.—   263
Bid them farewell, Cordelia, though unkind.   264
Thou losest here, a better where to find.   265

LEAR
Thou hast her, France. Let her be thine, for we
Have no such daughter, nor shall ever see
That face of hers again. Therefore begone   268
Without our grace, our love, our benison.   269
Come, noble Burgundy.

     Flourish. Exeunt [all but FRANCE, GONERIL,
          REGAN, *and* CORDELIA].

FRANCE Bid farewell to your sisters.

CORDELIA
The jewels of our father, with washed eyes   272
Cordelia leaves you. I know you what you are,
And like a sister am most loath to call   274
Your faults as they are named. Love well our father.   275
To your professèd bosoms I commit him.   276
But yet, alas, stood I within his grace,
I would prefer him to a better place.   278
So, farewell to you both.

REGAN
Prescribe not us our duty.

GONERIL   Let your study
Be to content your lord, who hath received you
At Fortune's alms. You have obedience scanted,   282
And well are worth the want that you have wanted.   283

---

262 **waterish** (1) well-watered with rivers (2) feeble, wa-
tery 263 **unprized** not appreciated (with perhaps a sense also of
"priceless") 264 **though unkind** though they have behaved un-
naturally 265 **here** this place. **where** place elsewhere 268–269 **Therefore . . . benison** (Said perhaps to Cordelia and to the King of France.)
benison blessing 272 **The** you, the. **washed** tear-washed 274 **like a
sister** i.e., because I am your sister 275 **as . . . named** by their true
names 276 **professèd bosoms** publicly avowed love 278 **prefer** advance, recommend 282 **At . . . alms** as a pittance or dole from Fortune.
scanted stinted 283 **well . . . wanted** well deserve the lack of affection
which you yourself have shown. (*Want* may also refer to her dowry.)

CORDELIA
   Time shall unfold what plighted cunning hides;   284
   Who covers faults, at last shame them derides.   285
   Well may you prosper!
FRANCE   Come, my fair Cordelia.
                          Exeunt FRANCE *and*
                                      CORDELIA.

GONERIL   Sister, it is not little I have to say of what
   most nearly appertains to us both. I think our father
   will hence tonight.
REGAN   That's most certain, and with you; next month
   with us.
GONERIL   You see how full of changes his age is; the
   observation we have made of it hath not been little.
   He always loved our sister most, and with what poor
   judgment he hath now cast her off appears too
   grossly.   296
REGAN   'Tis the infirmity of his age. Yet he hath ever
   but slenderly known himself.
GONERIL   The best and soundest of his time hath been   299
   but rash. Then must we look from his age to receive   300
   not alone the imperfections of long-ingraffed con-   301
   dition, but therewithal the unruly waywardness that   302
   infirm and choleric years bring with them.
REGAN   Such unconstant starts are we like to have   304
   from him as this of Kent's banishment.
GONERIL   There is further compliment of leave-tak-   306
   ing between France and him. Pray you, let us hit to-   307
   gether. If our father carry authority with such disposition as he bears, this last surrender of his will   309
   but offend us.   310

---

284 plighted pleated, enfolded   **285 Who . . . derides** i.e., time, who
may conceal faults for a while, at last exposes and derides them shame-
fully   **296 grossly** obviously   **299–300 The best . . . rash** i.e., even in
the prime of his life, he was stormy and unpredictable   **301–302 long-
ingraffed condition** long-implanted habit   **302 therewithal** added
thereto   **304 unconstant starts** impulsive acts.   **like** likely
306 compliment ceremony   **307 hit** agree   **309 last surrender** latest ab-
dication   **310 offend** harm, injure

REGAN We shall further think of it.
GONERIL We must do something, and i' the heat.   312
                                          Exeunt.

Scene Two
[THE EARL OF GLOUCESTER'S HOUSE.]

Enter Bastard [EDMUND, *with a letter*].

EDMUND
  Thou, Nature, art my goddess; to thy law   1
  My services are bound. Wherefore should I
  Stand in the plague of custom and permit   3
  The curiosity of nations to deprive me,   4
  For that I am some twelve or fourteen moonshines   5
  Lag of a brother? Why bastard? Wherefore base?   6
  When my dimensions are as well compact,   7
  My mind as generous, and my shape as true,   8
  As honest madam's issue? Why brand they us   9
  With base? With baseness? Bastardy? Base, base?
  Who in the lusty stealth of nature take   11
  More composition and fierce quality   12
  Than doth within a dull, stale, tirèd bed
  Go to th' creating a whole tribe of fops   14
  Got 'tween asleep and wake? Well then,   15

312 i' the heat i.e., while the iron is hot
1 Nature i.e., the material world, governed solely by mechanistic amoral forces **3 Stand . . . custom** submit to the vexatious injustice of convention **4 curiosity** fastidious distinctions. **nations** societies **5 For that** because. **moonshines** months **6 Lag of** younger than **7 compact** knit together, fitted **8 generous** noble, refined **9 honest** chaste **11–12 take . . . quality** acquire greater completeness and energetic force **14 fops** fools **15 Got** begotten

Legitimate Edgar, I must have your land.
Our father's love is to the bastard Edmund
As to th' legitimate. Fine word, "legitimate"!
Well, my legitimate, if this letter speed   19
And my invention thrive, Edmund the base   20
Shall top th' legitimate. I grow, I prosper.
Now, gods, stand up for bastards!

Enter GLOUCESTER.

GLOUCESTER
Kent banished thus? And France in choler parted?
And the King gone tonight? Prescribed his power,   24
Confined to exhibition? All this done   25
Upon the gad? Edmund, how now? What news?   26
EDMUND   So please your lordship, none.
                              [*Putting up the letter.*]
GLOUCESTER   Why so earnestly seek you to put up
that letter?
EDMUND   I know no news, my lord.
GLOUCESTER   What paper were you reading?
EDMUND   Nothing, my lord.
GLOUCESTER   No? What needed then that terrible dis-   33
patch of it into your pocket? The quality of nothing   34
hath not such need to hide itself. Let's see. Come, if
it be nothing I shall not need spectacles.
EDMUND   I beseech you, sir, pardon me. It is a letter
from my brother, that I have not all o'erread; and for
so much as I have perused, I find it not fit for your
o'erlooking.   40
GLOUCESTER   Give me the letter, sir.
EDMUND   I shall offend either to detain or give it. The
contents, as in part I understand them, are to blame.   43
GLOUCESTER   Let's see, let's see.

19 speed succeed, prosper **20 invention thrive** scheme prosper **24 tonight** last night. **Prescribed** limited **25 exhibition** an allowance, pension **26 Upon the gad** suddenly, as if pricked by a gad or
spur **33–34 terrible dispatch** fearful haste **40 o'erlooking** per-
usal **43 to blame** (The Folio reading, *too blame,* "too blameworthy to
be shown," may be correct.)

[EDMUND *gives the letter.*]

EDMUND I hope for my brother's justification he
wrote this but as an essay or taste of my virtue.   46

GLOUCESTER (*Reads*) "This policy and reverence of   47
age makes the world bitter to the best of our times,   48
keeps our fortunes from us till our oldness cannot
relish them. I begin to find an idle and fond bondage   50
in the oppression of aged tyranny, who sways not as   51
it hath power but as it is suffered. Come to me, that   52
of this I may speak more. If our father would sleep
till I waked him, you should enjoy half his revenue
forever and live the beloved of your brother, Edgar."
Hum! Conspiracy! "Sleep till I waked him, you
should enjoy half his revenue." My son Edgar! Had
he a hand to write this? A heart and brain to breed it
in? When came you to this? Who brought it?   59

EDMUND It was not brought me, my lord; there's the
cunning of it. I found it thrown in at the casement of   61
my closet.   62

GLOUCESTER You know the character to be your   63
brother's?

EDMUND If the matter were good, my lord, I drust   65
swear it were his; but in respect of that I would fain   66
think it were not.

GLOUCESTER It is his.

EDMUND It is his hand, my lord, but I hope his heart
is not in the contents.

GLOUCESTER Has he never before sounded you in
this business?

EDMUND Never, my lord. But I have heard him oft
maintain it to be fit that, sons at perfect age and   74

---

46 essay or taste i.e., assay, test   **47 policy and reverence of** i.e., policy of
reverencing   **48 the best . . . times** the best years of our lives, i.e., our
youth   **50 idle** useless. **fond** foolish   **51 who sways** which rules
52 suffered permitted (by the young, who could seize power if they
wished)   **59 to this** upon this (letter)   **61 casement** window   **62 closet**
private room   **63 character** handwriting   **65 matter** contents   **66 in
. . . that** considering what the contents are. **fain** gladly   **74 fit** fitting,
appropriate. **perfect age** full maturity

fathers declined, the father should be as ward to the 75
son, and the son manage his revenue.

GLOUCESTER   O villain, villain! His very opinion in 77
the letter! Abhorred villain! Unnatural, detested, 78
brutish villain! Worse than brutish! Go, sirrah, seek 79
him. I'll apprehend him. Abominable villain! Where
is he?

EDMUND   I do not well know, my lord. If it shall
please you to suspend your indignation against my
brother till you can derive from him better testimony
of his intent, you should run a certain course; where, 85
if you violently proceed against him, mistaking his
purpose, it would make a great gap in your own
honor and shake in pieces the heart of his obedience.
I dare pawn down my life for him that he hath writ 89
this to feel my affection to your honor, and to no 90
other pretense of danger. 91

GLOUCESTER   Think you so?

EDMUND   If your honor judge it meet, I will place you 93
where you shall hear us confer of this, and by an
auricular assurance have your satisfaction, and that
without any further delay than this very evening.

GLOUCESTER   He cannot be such a monster—

EDMUND   Nor is not, sure.

GLOUCESTER   To his father, that so tenderly and
entirely loves him. Heaven and earth! Edmund, seek
him out; wind me into him, I pray you. Frame the 101
business after your own wisdom. I would unstate 102
myself to be in a due resolution. 103

EDMUND   I will seek him, sir, presently, convey the 104

---

75 declined having become feeble   **77 villain** i.e., vile wretch, diabolical
schemer   **78 Abhorred** abhorrent. **detested** detestable   **79 sirrah** (form
of address used to inferiors or children.)   **85 run a certain course** proceed with safety and certainty. **where** whereas   **89 pawn down**
stake   **90 feel** feel out   **91 pretense of danger** dangerous purpose   **93 meet** fitting, proper   **101 wind me into him** insinuate yourself
into his confidence. (*Me* is used colloquially.) **Frame** arrange   **102 after
your own wisdom** as you think best   **102–103 unstate . . . resolution**
suffer loss of all to know the truth, have my doubts resolved   **104 presently** immediately. **convey** manage

business as I shall find means, and acquaint you
withal.   106
GLOUCESTER These late eclipses in the sun and moon   107
portend no good to us. Though the wisdom of nature   108
can reason it thus and thus, yet nature finds itself
scourged by the sequent effects. Love cools, friend-   110
ship falls off, brothers divide; in cities, mutinies; in
countries, discord; in palaces, treason; and the bond
cracked twixt son and father. This villain of mine
comes under the prediction; there's son against father. The King falls from bias of nature; there's fa-   115
ther against child. We have seen the best of our time.
Machinations, hollowness, treachery, and all
ruinous disorders follow us disquietly to our graves.
Find out this villain, Edmund; it shall lose thee
nothing. Do it carefully. And the noble and true-
hearted Kent banished! His offense, honesty! 'Tis
strange.   *Exit.*
EDMUND This is the excellent foppery of the world,   123
that when we are sick in fortune—often the surfeits
of our own behavior—we make guilty of our disasters the sun, the moon, and stars, as if we were
villains on necessity, fools by heavenly compulsion,   127
knaves, thieves, and treachers by spherical predomi-   128
nance, drunkards, liars, and adulterers by an en-   129
forced obedience of planetary influence, and all that
we are evil in, by a divine thrusting on. An admirable   131
evasion of whoremaster man, to lay his goatish dis-   132
position on the charge of a star! My father com-   133
pounded with my mother under the Dragon's tail and   134
my nativity was under Ursa Major, so that it follows   135
I am rough and lecherous. Fut, I should have been   136

---

106 withal therewith   **107 late** recent   **108 the wisdom of nature** natural
science   **110 sequent   effects** i.e., devastating consequences
115 bias of nature natural inclination   **123 foppery** foolishness   **127 on**
by   **128 treachers** traitors   **128–129 spherical predominance** astrological
determinism; because a certain planet was ascendant at the hour of our
birth   **131 divine** supernatural   **132 goatish** lecherous   **133–134 com-
pounded . . . Dragon's tail** had sex with my mother under the con-
stellation Draco   **135 Ursa Major** the big bear   **136 Fut** i.e., 'sfoot, by
Christ's foot

that I am, had the maidenliest star in the firmament 137
twinkled on my bastardizing. Edgar—

Enter EDGAR.

and pat he comes like the catastrophe of the old 139
comedy. My cue is villainous melancholy, with a sigh
like Tom o' Bedlam.—O, these eclipses do portend 141
these divisions! Fa, sol, la, mi.

EDGAR How now, brother Edmund, what serious
contemplation are you in?

EDMUND I am thinking, brother, of a prediction I
read this other day, what should follow these 146
eclipses.

EDGAR Do you busy yourself with that?

EDMUND I promise you, the effects he writes of suc- 149
ceed unhappily, as of unnaturalness between the 150
child and the parent, death, dearth, dissolutions of
ancient amities, divisions in state, menaces and
maledictions against king and nobles, needless diffi- 153
dences, banishment of friends, dissipation of co- 154
horts, nuptial breaches, and I know not what. 155

EDGAR How long have you been a sectary astronomi- 156
cal? 157

EDMUND Come, come, when saw you my father last?

EDGAR The night gone by.

EDMUND Spake you with him?

EDGAR Ay, two hours together.

EDMUND Parted you in good terms? Found you no
displeasure in him by word nor countenance? 163

EDGAR None at all.

EDMUND Bethink yourself wherein you may have offended him, and at my entreaty forbear his presence 166

---

137 that what **139 catastrophe** conclusion, resolution (of a
play) **141 Tom o' Bedlam** a lunatic patient of Bethlehem Hospital in
London turned out to beg for his bread **146 this other day** the other
day **149–150 succeed unhappily** follow unluckily **153–154 needless
diffidences** groundless distrust of others **154–155 dissipation of cohorts**
breaking up of military companies, large-scale desertions **156–157 sectary astronomical** believer in astrology **163 countenance** de-
meanor **166 forbear his presence** avoid meeting him

until some little time hath qualified the heat of his   167
displeasure, which at this instant so rageth in him
that with the mischief of your person it would   169
scarcely allay.   170

EDGAR Some villain hath done me wrong.

EDMUND That's my fear. I pray you, have a continent   172
forbearance till the speed of his rage goes slower;   173
and, as I say, retire with me to my lodging, from
whence I will fitly bring you to hear my lord speak.   175
Pray ye, go! There's my key. [*He gives a key.*] If you
do stir abroad, go armed.

EDGAR Armed, brother?

EDMUND Brother, I advise you to the best. I am no
honest man if there be any good meaning toward   180
you. I have told you what I have seen and heard, but
faintly, nothing like the image and horror of it. Pray   182
you, away.

EDGAR Shall I hear from you anon?

EDMUND
I do serve you in this business.   *Exit* [EDGAR].
A credulous father and a brother noble,
Whose nature is so far from doing harms
That he suspects none; on whose foolish honesty
My practices ride easy. I see the business.   189
Let me, if not by birth, have lands by wit.   190
All with me's meet that I can fashion fit.   *Exit.* 191

---

167 qualified moderated   **169 with . . . person** with the harmful effect of
your presence; or, even if there were injury done to you   **170 allay** be
allayed   **172–173 have . . . forbearance** keep a wary distance   **175 fitly**
at a fit time   **180 meaning** intention   **182 image and horror** horrid reality   **189 practices** plots. **the business** i.e., how my plots should proceed   **190 wit** intelligence   **191 meet** justifiable. **fit** i.e., to my purpose

Scene Three
[THE DUKE OF ALBANY'S PALACE.]

Enter GONERIL, *and* [OSWALD, *her*] *steward.*

GONERIL   Did my father strike my gentleman for chid-
ing of his fool?
OSWALD   Ay, madam.
GONERIL
By day and night he wrongs me! Every hour
He flashes into one gross crime or other   5
That sets us all at odds. I'll not endure it.
His knights grow riotous, and himself upbraids us
On every trifle. When he returns from hunting
I will not speak with him. Say I am sick.
If you come slack of former services   ·   10
You shall do well; the fault of it I'll answer.
                          [*Horns within.*]
OSWALD   He's coming, madam. I hear him.
GONERIL
Put on what weary negligence you please,
You and your fellows. I'd have it come to question.   14
If he distaste it, let him to my sister,   15
Whose mind and mine, I know, in that are one,
Not to be overruled. Idle old man,   17
That still would manage those authorities   18
That he hath given away! Now, by my life,
Old fools are babes again, and must be used
With checks as flatteries, when they are seen
    abused.   21
Remember what I have said.
OSWALD   Well, madam.
GONERIL
And let his knights have colder looks among you.
What grows of it, no matter. Advise your fellows so.

5 **crime** offense   10 **come slack** fall short   14 **come to question** be made
an issue   15 **distaste** dislike   17 **Idle** foolish   18 **manage those authorities** i.e., assert those prerogatives   21 **With . . . abused** with re-
bukes instead of flattery, when they (old men) act unselfknowingly (as
Lear does)

I would breed from hence occasions, and I shall,   26
That I may speak. I'll write straight to my sister   27
To hold my very course. Prepare for dinner.

Exeunt.

Scene Four
[THE DUKE OF ALBANY'S PALACE STILL.
THE SENSE OF TIME IS VIRTUALLY CONTINUOUS.]

Enter KENT [*disguised*].

KENT
If but as well I other accents borrow   1
That can my speech diffuse, my good intent   2
May carry through itself to that full issue   3
For which I rased my likeness. Now, banished
    Kent,   4
If thou canst serve where thou dost stand
    condemned,
So may it come thy master, whom thou lov'st,   6
Shall find thee full of labors.

Horns within. Enter LEAR, [KNIGHTS,] *and attendants.*

LEAR   Let me not stay a jot for dinner. Go get it ready.   8
[*Exit an attendant.*] How now, what art thou?   9
KENT   A man, sir.
LEAR   What dost thou profess? What wouldst thou   11
with us?

26–27 **I would . . . speak** I wish to create from these incidents the
opportunity to speak out   27 **straight** immediately.
1 **as well** i.e., as well as I have disguised myself by means of costume   2 **diffuse** i.e., disguise   3 **carry . . . issue** succeed to that perfect
result   4 **rased my likeness** erased my outward appearance (perhaps
with a sense also of having *razed* or scraped off his beard)   6 **come**
come to pass that   8 **stay** wait   9 **s.d. attendant** (This attendant may be
a knight; certainly the one who speaks at 1.4.50 is a knight.)   11 **What
. . . profess** what is your special calling. (But Kent puns in his answer on
profess meaning to "claim.")

KENT I do profess to be no less than I seem: to serve
him truly that will put me in trust, to love him that is
honest, to converse with him that is wise and   15
says little, to fear judgment, to fight when I   16
cannot choose, and to eat no fish.   17

LEAR What art thou?

KENT A very honest-hearted fellow, and as poor as
the King.

LEAR If thou be'st as poor for a subject as he's for a
king, thou'rt poor enough. What wouldst thou?

KENT Service.

LEAR Who wouldst thou serve?

KENT You.

LEAR Dost thou know me, fellow?

KENT No, sir, but you have that in your countenance   27
which I would fain call master.

LEAR What's that?

KENT Authority.

LEAR What services canst thou do?

KENT I can keep honest counsel, ride, run, mar a   32
curious tale in telling it, and deliver a plain message 33
bluntly. That which ordinary men are fit for I am
qualified in, and the best of me is diligence.

LEAR How old art thou?

KENT Not so young, sir, to love a woman for singing, 37
nor so old to dote on her for anything. I have years
on my back forty-eight.

LEAR Follow me; thou shalt serve me. If I like thee no
worse after dinner, I will not part from thee yet.
Dinner, ho, dinner! Where's my knave, my fool? Go
you and call my fool hither.   [*Exit one*.]

Enter steward [OSWALD].

You! You, sirrah, where's my daughter?

OSWALD So please you—   *Exit.*

---

15 honest honorable. **converse** associate **16 judgment** i.e., God's judgment **17 choose** i.e., choose but to fight. **eat no fish** i.e., eat a manly
diet (?), be a good Protestant (?) **27 countenance** face and bearing **32 keep honest counsel** respect confidences **33 curious** ornate,
elaborate **37 to love** as to love

LEAR   What says the fellow there? Call the clodpoll   46
back. [*Exit a* KNIGHT.] Where's my fool, ho? I think
the world's asleep.

Enter KNIGHT.

How now? Where's that mongrel?

KNIGHT   He says, my lord, your daughter is not well.

LEAR   Why came not the slave back to me when I
called him?

KNIGHT   Sir, he answered me in the roundest manner,   53
he would not.

LEAR   He would not?

KNIGHT   My lord, I know not what the matter is, but
to my judgment Your Highness is not entertained   57
with that ceremonious affection as you were wont.
There's a great abatement of kindness appears as
well in the general dependents as in the Duke himself also and your daughter.

LEAR   Ha? Sayst thou so?

KNIGHT   I beseech you, pardon me, my lord, if I be
mistaken, for my duty cannot be silent when I think
Your Highness wronged.

LEAR   Thou but rememberest me of mine own con-   66
ception. I have perceived a most faint neglect of late,   67
which I have rather blamed as mine own jealous   68
curiosity than as a very pretense and purpose of   69
unkindness. I will look further into 't. But where's
my fool? I have not seen him this two days.   71

KNIGHT   Since my young lady's going into France, sir,
the Fool hath much pined away.

LEAR   No more of that. I have noted it well. Go you
and tell my daughter I would speak with her.
                                              [*Exit one.*]
Go you call hither my fool.   [*Exit one.*]

Enter steward [OSWALD].

---

46 clodpoll blockhead   **53 roundest** bluntest   **57 entertained** treated
66 rememberest remind   **66–67 conception** idea, thought   **67 faint**
halfhearted   **68–69 jealous curiosity** overscrupulous regard for matters
of etiquette   **69 very pretense** true intention   **71 this** these

O, you, sir, you, come you hither, sir. Who am I, sir?

OSWALD My lady's father.

LEAR "My lady's father"? My lord's knave! You whoreson dog, you slave, you cur!

OSWALD I am none of these, my lord, I beseech your pardon.

LEAR Do you bandy looks with me, you rascal? 83
[*He strikes* OSWALD.]

OSWALD I'll not be strucken, my lord. 84

KENT Nor tripped neither, you base football player. 85
[*He trips up* OSWALD's *heels.*]

LEAR I thank thee, fellow. Thou serv'st me, and I'll love thee.

KENT Come, sir, arise, away! I'll teach you dif- 88
ferences. Away, away! If you will measure your lub- 89
ber's length again, tarry; but away! Go to. Have you 90
wisdom? So. [*He pushes* OSWALD *out.*] 91

LEAR Now, my friendly knave, I thank thee. There's
earnest of thy service. [*He gives* KENT *money.*] 93

Enter FOOL.

FOOL Let me hire him too. Here's my coxcomb. 94
[*Offering* KENT *his cap.*]

LEAR How now, my pretty knave, how dost thou?

FOOL [*To* KENT] Sirrah, you were best take my cox- 96
comb.

KENT Why, Fool?

FOOL Why? For taking one's part that's out of favor.
Nay, an thou canst not smile as the wind sits, thou'lt 100
catch cold shortly. There, take my coxcomb. Why, 101
this fellow has banished two on 's daughters and did 102

---

83 bandy volley, exchange (as in tennis) **84 strucken** struck
85 football (A raucous street game played by the lower classes.)
88–89 differences distinctions in rank **89–90 If . . . again** i.e., if you
want to be laid out flat again, you clumsy ox **90–91 Have you wisdom**
i.e., are you smart enough to make a quick retreat **93 earnest** partial
advance payment **94 coxcomb** fool's cap, crested with a red
comb **96 you were best** you had better **100 an . . . sits** i.e., if you can't
play along with those in power **101 catch cold** i.e., find yourself out in
the cold **102 banished** (i.e., paradoxically, by giving Goneril and Regan
his kingdom, Lear has lost them, given them power over him). **on 's** of
his

the third a blessing against his will. If thou follow   103
him, thou must needs wear my coxcomb.—How
now, nuncle? Would I had two coxcombs and two   105
daughters.

LEAR   Why, my boy?

FOOL   If I gave them all my living, I'd keep my cox-   108
combs myself. There's mine; beg another of thy
daughters.

LEAR   Take heed, sirrah—the whip.

FOOL   Truth's a dog must to kennel. He must be
whipped out, when the Lady Brach may stand by   113
the fire and stink.

LEAR   A pestilent gall to me!   115

FOOL   Sirrah, I'll teach thee a speech.

LEAR   Do.

FOOL   Mark it, nuncle:
Have more than thou showest,
Speak less than thou knowest,
Lend less than thou owest,   121
Ride more than thou goest,   122
Learn more than thou trowest,   123
Set less than thou throwest;   124
Leave thy drink and thy whore,
And keep in-a-door,   126
And thou shalt have more   127
Than two tens to a score.   128

KENT   This is nothing, Fool.

FOOL   Then 'tis like the breath of an unfee'd lawyer;   130
you gave me nothing for 't. Can you make no use of
nothing, nuncle?

---

103 blessing i.e., bestowing Cordelia on France   **105 nuncle** (Contraction of "mine uncle," the Fool's way of addressing Lear.)   **108 living** property   **113 Brach** hound bitch (here suggesting flattery)
115 gall irritation   **121 owest** own   **122 goest** i.e., on foot. (Travel prudently on horseback, not afoot.)   **123 Learn** i.e., listen to. **trowest** believe   **124 Set . . . throwest** stake less at dice than you have a chance to
throw, i.e., don't bet all you can   **126 in-a-door** indoors, at home   **127–
128 shalt . . . score** i.e., will do better than break even (since a *score*
equals two tens, or 20)   **130 breath** speech, counsel

LEAR Why, no, boy. Nothing can be made out of nothing.

FOOL [*To* KENT] Prithee, tell him; so much the rent of 135
his land comes to. He will not believe a fool.

LEAR A bitter fool! 137

FOOL Dost thou know the difference, my boy, between a bitter fool and a sweet one?

LEAR No, lad. Teach me.

FOOL
That lord that counseled thee
  To give away thy land,
Come place him here by me;
  Do thou for him stand. 144
The sweet and bitter fool
  Will presently appear: 146
The one in motley here, 147
  The other found out there. 148

LEAR Dost thou call me fool, boy?

FOOL All thy other titles thou hast given away; that thou wast born with.

KENT This is not altogether fool, my lord.

FOOL No, faith, lords and great men will not let me; if 153
I had a monopoly out, they would have part on 't. 154
And ladies too, they will not let me have all the fool
to myself; they'll be snatching. Nuncle, give me an 156
egg and I'll give thee two crowns.

LEAR What two crowns shall they be?

FOOL Why, after I have cut the egg i' the middle and
eat up the meat, the two crowns of the egg. When 160
thou clovest thy crown i' the middle and gav'st away

---

135 rent (Lear has no land, hence no rent.) **137 bitter** satirical **144 for him stand** impersonate him **146 presently** immediately **147 motley** the particolored dress of the professional fool. (The Fool identifies himself as the sweet fool, Lear as the bitter fool who counseled himself to give away his kingdom.) **148 there** (The Fool points at Lear.) **153 No . . . let me** i.e., great persons at court will not let me monopolize folly; I am not *altogether fool* in the sense of being "all the fool there is" **154 a monopoly out** a corner on the market. (The granting of monopolies was a common abuse under King James and Queen Elizabeth.) **on 't** of it **156 snatching** i.e., at the Fool's phallic bauble **160 eat** eaten, **the meat** the edible part

both parts, thou bor'st thine ass on thy back o'er the   162
dirt. Thou hadst little wit in thy bald crown when   163
thou gav'st thy golden one away. If I speak like   164
myself in this, let him be whipped that first finds it   165
so.   166
[*Sings*] "Fools had ne'er less grace in a year,   167
   For wise men are grown foppish   168
 And know not how their wits to wear,   169
   Their manners are so apish."

LEAR When were you wont to be so full of songs,
sirrah?

FOOL I have used it, nuncle, e'er since thou mad'st   173
thy daughters thy mothers; for when thou gav'st
them the rod and putt'st down thine own breeches,
[*Sings*] "Then they for sudden joy did weep,
   And I for sorrow sung,
   That such a king should play bo-peep   178
   And go the fools among."
Prithee, nuncle, keep a schoolmaster that can teach
thy fool to lie. I would fain learn to lie.

LEAR An you lie, sirrah, we'll have you whipped.   182

FOOL I marvel what kin thou and thy daughters are.
They'll have me whipped for speaking true, thou'lt
have me whipped for lying, and sometimes I am
whipped for holding my peace. I had rather be any
kind o' thing than a fool. And yet I would not be
thee, nuncle. Thou hast pared thy wit o' both sides
and left nothing i' the middle. Here comes one o' the
parings.

Enter GONERIL.

LEAR
How now, daughter? What makes that frontlet on?   191
You are too much of late i' the frown.

162–163 bor'st . . . dirt i.e., bore the ass instead of letting the ass bear
you   164–165 like myself i.e., like a fool   165 whipped i.e., as a fool
165–166 finds it so discovers from his experience that it is true (as Lear is
now discovering)   167 Fools . . . year fools have never enjoyed less
favor; i.e., they are made obsolete by the folly of supposed wise
men   168 foppish foolish, vain   169 wear use   173 used practiced   178 bo-peep a child's game   182 An if   191 frontlet a band worn
on the forehead; here, frown

FOOL Thou wast a pretty fellow when thou hadst no
   need to care for her frowning; now thou art an O   193
   without a figure. I am better than thou art now; I am   194
   a fool, thou art nothing. [*To* GONERIL.] Yes, forsooth,
   I will hold my tongue; so your face bids me, though
   you say nothing.
      Mum, mum,
      He that keeps nor crust nor crumb,   199
      Weary of all, shall want some.   200
   [*Pointing to* LEAR.] That's a shelled peascod.   201
GONERIL
   Not only, sir, this your all-licensed fool,   202
   But other of your insolent retinue
   Do hourly carp and quarrel, breaking forth   204
   In rank and not-to-be-endurèd riots. Sir,   205
   I had thought by making this well known unto you
   To have found a safe redress, but now grow fearful,   207
   By what yourself too late have spoke and done,   208
   That you protect this course and put it on   209
   By your allowance; which if you should, the fault   210
   Would not scape censure, nor the redresses sleep   211
   Which in the tender of a wholesome weal   212
   Might in their working do you that offense,
   Which else were shame, that then necessity   214
   Will call discreet proceeding.   215

193–194 **O without a figure** cipher of no value unless preceded by a
digit 199–200 **He . . . some** i.e., that person who gives away all his
possessions, having wearied of them, will find himself in need of part of
what is gone. **nor . . . nor** neither . . . nor 200 **want** lack 201 **shelled
peascod** shelled pea pod, i.e., nothing, empty 202 **all-licensed** autho-
rized to speak or act freely 204 **carp** find fault 205 **rank** gross, exces-
sive 207 **safe** certain 208 **too late** all too recently 209 **put it on**
encourage it 210 **allowance** approval 211 **redresses sleep** punishments
(for the riotous conduct of Lear's attendants) lie dormant 212 **tender
. . . weal** care for preservation of the peace of the state 214 **else were** in
other circumstances would be regarded as. **then necessity** the necessity
of the times 215 **discreet** prudent

FOOL   For you know, nuncle,
           "The hedge sparrow fed the cuckoo so long   217
           That it had its head bit off by its young."   218
       So, out went the candle, and we were left darkling.   219

LEAR   Are you our daughter?

GONERIL
   I would you would make use of your good wisdom,
   Whereof I know you are fraught, and put away   222
   These dispositions which of late transport you   223
   From what you rightly are.

FOOL   May not an ass know when the cart draws the   225
       horse? Whoop, Jug! I love thee.   226

LEAR
   Does any here know me? This is not Lear.
   Does Lear walk thus, speak thus? Where are his
       eyes?
   Either his notion weakens, his discernings   229
   Are lethargied—Ha! Waking? 'Tis not so.   230
   Who is it that can tell me who I am?

FOOL   Lear's shadow.

LEAR
   I would learn that; for, by the marks of sovereignty,   233
   Knowledge, and reason, I should be false persuaded   234
   I had daughters.   235

FOOL   Which they will make an obedient father.   236

LEAR   Your name, fair gentlewoman?

GONERIL
   This admiration, sir, is much o' the savor   238

---

217 cuckoo a bird that lays its eggs in other birds' nests   **218 its young**
i.e., the young cuckoo   **219 darkling** in the dark   **222 fraught**
freighted, laden   **223 dispositions** states of mind, moods   **225–226 May
. . . horse** i.e., may not even a fool see that matters are backwards when
a daughter lectures her father   **226 Jug** i.e., Joan. (The origin of this
phrase is uncertain.)   **229 notion** intellectual power   **229–230 discernings Are lethargied** faculties are asleep   **230 Waking** i.e., am I really
awake   **233 that** i.e., who I am.   **marks of sovereignty** outward and
visible evidence of being king   **234–235 I should . . . daughters** i.e., all
these outward signs of sanity and status would seem to suggest (falsely)
that I am the king who had obedient daughters   **236 Which**
whom   **238 admiration** (guise of) wonderment

Of other your new pranks. I do beseech you   239
To understand my purposes aright.
As you are old and reverend, should be wise.   241
Here do you keep a hundred knights and squires,
Men so disordered, so debauched and bold,   243
That this our court, infected with their manners,
Shows like a riotous inn. Epicurism and lust   245
Makes it more like a tavern or a brothel
Than a graced palace. The shame itself doth speak   247
For instant remedy. Be then desired,   248
By her that else will take the thing she begs,
A little to disquantity your train,   250
And the remainders that shall still depend   251
To be such men as may besort your age,   252
Which know themselves and you.

LEAR   Darkness and devils!
Saddle my horses! Call my train together!

                                [Exit one.]
Degenerate bastard, I'll not trouble thee.
Yet have I left a daughter.

GONERIL
You strike my people, and your disordered rabble
Make servants of their betters.

Enter ALBANY.

LEAR
Woe, that too late repents!—O, sir, are you come?   259
Is it your will? Speak, sir.—Prepare my horses.

                                [Exit one.]
Ingratitude, thou marble-hearted fiend,
More hideous when thou show'st thee in a child
Than the sea monster!

---

239 other other of   **241 should** i.e., you should   **241 disordered** disorderly   **245 Shows** appears. **Epicurism** luxury   **247 graced** honorable   **248 desired** requested   **250 disquantity your train** diminish the number of your attendants   **251 the remainders . . . depend** those who remain to attend you   **252 besort** befit   **259 Woe, that** woe to the person who

ALBANY   Pray, sir, be patient.

LEAR [*To* GONERIL]   Detested kite, thou liest!   265
  My train are men of choice and rarest parts,   266
  That all particulars of duty know
  And in the most exact regard support   268
  The worships of their name. O most small fault,   269
  How ugly didst thou in Cordelia show!
  Which, like an engine, wrenched my frame of
    nature   271
  From the fixed place, drew from my heart all love,
  And added to the gall. O Lear, Lear, Lear!
  Beat at this gate [*Striking his head*] that let thy folly
    in
  And thy dear judgment out! Go, go, my people.   275
                                   [*Exeunt some.*]

ALBANY
  My lord, I am guiltless as I am ignorant
  Of what hath moved you.

LEAR   It may be so, my lord.
  Hear, Nature, hear! Dear goddess, hear!
  Suspend thy purpose if thou didst intend
  To make this creature fruitful!
  Into her womb convey sterility;
  Dry up in her the organs of increase,
  And from her derogate body never spring   283
  A babe to honor her! If she must teem,   284
  Create her child of spleen, that it may live   285
  And be a thwart disnatured torment to her!   286
  Let it stamp wrinkles in her brow of youth,
  With cadent tears fret channels in her cheeks,   288
  Turn all her mother's pains and benefits   289
  To laughter and contempt, that she may feel

---

265 kite bird of prey   **266 parts** qualities   **268 in . . . regard** with extreme care **269 worships** honors, reputations   **271 engine** powerful mechanical contrivance, able to wrench Lear's *frame of nature* or natural self from his *fixed place* or foundation like a building being torn from its foundation   **275 dear** precious   **283 derogate** debased   **284 teem** increase the species   **285 of spleen** consisting only of malice   **286 thwart disnatured** obstinate, perverse, and unnatural, unfilial   **288 cadent** falling.   **fret** wear   **289 mother's** motherly.   **benefits** kind offerings

How sharper than a serpent's tooth it is
To have a thankless child! Away, away!

               Exit [with KENT *and the rest*
                 of LEAR's *followers].*

ALBANY

  Now, gods that we adore, whereof comes this?

GONERIL

  Never afflict yourself to know more of it,
  But let his disposition have that scope   295
  As dotage gives it.   296

Enter LEAR.

LEAR

  What, fifty of my followers at a clap?
  Within a fortnight?

ALBANY   What's the matter, sir?

LEAR

  I'll tell thee. [*To* GONERIL.] Life and death! I am
    ashamed
  That thou hast power to shake my manhood thus,
  That these hot tears, which break from me
    perforce,
  Should make thee worth them. Blasts and fogs
    upon thee!
  Th' untented woundings of a father's curse   303
  Pierce every sense about thee! Old fond eyes,   304
  Beweep this cause again, I'll pluck ye out   305
  And cast you, with the waters that you loose,   306
  To temper clay. Yea, is 't come to this?   307
  Ha! Let it be so. I have another daughter,
  Who, I am sure, is kind and comfortable.   309
  When she shall hear this of thee, with her nails
  She'll flay thy wolvish visage. Thou shalt find
  That I'll resume the shape which thou dost think
  I have cast off forever.   *Exit.*

GONERIL   Do you mark that?

---

295 disposition humor, mood   **296 As** which   **303 untented** too deep to
be probed and cleansed   **304 fond** foolish   **305 Beweep** if you weep
for   **306 loose** let loose   **307 temper** soften   **309 comfortable** willing to
comfort

ALBANY
  I cannot be so partial, Goneril,
  To the great love I bear you—   315

GONERIL
  Pray you, content.—What, Oswald, ho!
  [*To the* FOOL.] You, sir, more knave than fool, after
    your master.

FOOL   Nuncle Lear, nuncle Lear! Tarry, take the Fool   318
  with thee.   319
      A fox, when one has caught her,
      And such a daughter
      Should sure to the slaughter,   322
      If my cap would buy a halter.
      So the Fool follows after.   *Exit.*

GONERIL
  This man hath had good counsel. A hundred
    knights?
  'Tis politic and safe to let him keep   326
  At point a hundred knights—yes, that on every
    dream,   327
  Each buzz, each fancy, each complaint, dislike,   328
  He may enguard his dotage with their powers
  And hold our lives in mercy.—Oswald, I say!   330

ALBANY   Well, you may fear too far.   331

GONERIL
  Safer than trust too far.
  Let me still take away the harms I fear,   333
  Not fear still to be taken. I know his heart.   334
  What he hath uttered I have writ my sister.
  If she sustain him and his hundred knights
  When I have showed th' unfitness—

Enter steward [OSWALD].
                      How now, Oswald?
  What, have you writ that letter to my sister?

315 To because of   **318–319 take . . . thee** (1) take me with you (2) take
the name "fool" with you. (A stock phrase of taunting farewell.)
322 Should sure should certainly be sent **326 politic** prudent. (Said
ironically.) **327 At point** under arms **328 buzz** idle rumor **330 in
mercy** at his mercy **331 fear too far** overestimate the danger **333 take
away** remove **333, 334 still** always **334 taken** overtaken (by the
harms)

OSWALD Ay, madam.

GONERIL
Take you some company and away to horse.
Inform her full of my particular fear,
And thereto add such reasons of your own
As may compact it more. Get you gone,   343
And hasten your return. [*Exit* OSWALD.] No, no, my
    lord,
This milky gentleness and course of yours   345
Though I condemn not, yet, under pardon,   346
You're much more attasked for want of wisdom   347
Than praised for harmful mildness.   348

ALBANY
How far your eyes may pierce I cannot tell.   349
Striving to better, oft we mar what's well.

GONERIL Nay, then—

ALBANY Well, well, th' event.   *Exeunt.* 352

Scene Five
[BEFORE ALBANY'S PALACE.]

Enter LEAR, KENT [*disguised as* CAIUS], *and* FOOL.

LEAR [*Giving a letter to* KENT] Go you before to
    Gloucester with these letters. Acquaint my daughter   2
    no further with anything you know than comes from
    her demand out of the letter. If your diligence be not 4
    speedy, I shall be there afore you.

KENT I will not sleep, my lord, till I have delivered
    your letter.   *Exit.*

FOOL If a man's brains were in 's heels, were 't not in
    danger of kibes?   9

343 **compact** confirm   345 **milky . . . course** humane and gentle
way   346 **under pardon** if you'll excuse my saying so   347 **attasked**
taken to task for, blamed   348 **harmful mildness** mildness that causes
harm   349 **pierce** i.e., see into matters   352 **th' event** i.e., time will
show
2 **Gloucester** i.e., the place in Gloucestershire. **these letters** this
letter   4 **demand** inquiry. **out of** prompted by   9 **kibes** chilblains

LEAR   Ay, boy.

FOOL   Then, I prithee, be merry. Thy wit shall not go
slipshod.   12

LEAR   Ha, ha, ha!

FOOL   Shalt see thy other daughter will use thee   14
kindly, for though she's as like this as a crab's like an   15
apple, yet I can tell what I can tell.

LEAR   What canst tell, boy?

FOOL   She will taste as like this as a crab does to a
crab. Thou canst tell why one's nose stands i' the
middle on 's face?   20

LEAR   No.

FOOL   Why, to keep one's eyes of either side 's nose,   22
that what a man cannot smell out he may spy into.

LEAR   I did her wrong.   24

FOOL   Canst tell how an oyster makes his shell?

LEAR   No.

FOOL   Nor I neither. But I can tell why a snail has a
house.

LEAR   Why?

FOOL   Why, to put 's head in, not to give it away to his
daughters and leave his horns without a case.   31

LEAR   I will forget my nature. So kind a father!—Be   32
my horses ready?

FOOL   Thy asses are gone about 'em. The reason why   34
the seven stars are no more than seven is a pretty   35
reason.

LEAR   Because they are not eight.

FOOL   Yes, indeed. Thou wouldst make a good fool.

---

12 slipshod in slippers, worn because of chilblains. (There are no brains,
thinks the Fool, in Lear's heels when they are on their way to visit
Regan.) **14 Shalt** thou shalt **15 kindly** (1) according to filial nature.
(Said ironically.) (2) according to her own nature **15 crab** crab apple **20 on 's** of his **22 of either side's** on either side of his **24 her** i.e.,
Cordelia **31 horns** (Suggests cuckold's horns, as though Lear were
figuratively not the father of Goneril and Regan.) **32 forget my nature**
(Compare 1.4.231: "Who is it that can tell me who I am?" Lear can no
longer recognize the kind, beloved father he thought himself to be.)
34 Thy . . . 'em i.e., your servants (who labor like asses) have gone
about readying the horses **35 seven stars** Pleiades

LEAR To take 't again perforce! Monster ingratitude! 39
FOOL If thou wert my fool, nuncle, I'd have thee beaten for being old before thy time.
LEAR How's that?
FOOL Thou shouldst not have been old till thou hadst been wise.

LEAR
O, let me not be mad, not mad, sweet heaven!
Keep me in temper; I would not be mad!

[*Enter* GENTLEMAN.]

How now, are the horses ready?
GENTLEMAN Ready, my lord.
LEAR Come, boy.   [*Exeunt all except the* FOOL.]
FOOL
She that's a maid now, and laughs at my departure,
Shall not be a maid long, unless things be cut
  shorter.   *Exit.* 51

ACT TWO
Scene One
[THE EARL OF GLOUCESTER'S HOUSE.]

Enter Bastard [EDMUND] *and* CURAN, *severally.*

EDMUND Save thee, Curan.   1
CURAN And you, sir. I have been with your father and given him notice that the Duke of Cornwall and Regan his duchess will be here with him this night.
EDMUND How comes that?
CURAN Nay, I know not. You have heard of the news abroad—I mean the whispered ones, for they are yet 7
but ear-kissing arguments?   8

39 **To take . . . perforce** i.e., to think that Goneril would forcibly take back again the privileges guaranteed to me. (Some editors suggest, less persuasively, that Lear is meditating an armed restoration of his monarchy.) **51 things** i.e., penises. **cut shorter** (A bawdy joke addressed to the audience.)
s.d. severally separately **1 Save** God save **7 ones** i.e., the news, regarded as plural **8 ear-kissing arguments** lightly whispered topics

EDMUND   Not I. Pray you, what are they?

CURAN   Have you heard of no likely wars toward   10
twixt the Dukes of Cornwall and Albany?

EDMUND   Not a word.

CURAN   You may do, then, in time. Fare you well, sir.

Exit.

EDMUND
The Duke be here tonight? The better! Best!   14
This weaves itself perforce into my business.
My father hath set guard to take my brother,
And I have one thing, of a queasy question,   17
Which I must act. Briefness and fortune, work!—   18
Brother, a word. Descend. Brother, I say!

Enter EDGAR.

My father watches. O sir, fly this place!
Intelligence is given where you are hid.
You have now the good advantage of the night.
Have you not spoken 'gainst the Duke of Cornwall?
He's coming hither, now, i' the night, i' the haste,   24
And Regan with him. Have you nothing said
Upon his party 'gainst the Duke of Albany?   26
Advise yourself.

EDGAR   I am sure on 't, not a word.   27

EDMUND
I hear my father coming. Pardon me;
In cunning I must draw my sword upon you.
Draw. Seem to defend yourself. Now, quit you
well.—   30

[*They draw.*]

Yield! Come before my father!—Light, ho, here!—   31
Fly, brother.—Torches, torches!—So, farewell.   32

Exit EDGAR.

10 toward impending   14 The better! Best so much the better; in fact, the
best that could happen   17 queasy question hazardous or ticklish
nature   18 Briefness and fortune expeditious dispatch and good
luck   24 i' the haste in great haste   26 Upon his party 'gainst i.e., on
Cornwall's side, reflecting on his feud with   27 Advise yourself think
it over carefully. on 't of it   30 quit you defend, acquit yourself
31–32 Yield . . . farewell (Edmund speaks loudly as though trying to
arrest Edgar, calls for others to help, and privately bids Edgar to flee.)

Some blood drawn on me would beget opinion   33
Of my more fierce endeavor. I have seen drunkards   34
Do more than this in sport. [*He wounds himself in
the arm.*] Father, Father!
Stop, stop! No help?

Enter GLOUCESTER, *and servants with torches.*

GLOUCESTER   Now, Edmund, where's the villain?
EDMUND
Here stood he in the dark, his sharp sword out,
Mumbling of wicked charms, conjuring the moon
To stand 's auspicious mistress.
GLOUCESTER   But where is he?   39
EDMUND
Look, sir, I bleed.
GLOUCESTER   Where is the villain, Edmund?
EDMUND
Fled this way, sir. When by no means he could—
GLOUCESTER
Pursue him, ho! Go after. [*Exeunt some servants.*]
By no means what?
EDMUND
Persuade me to the murder of your lordship,
But that I told him the revenging gods   44
'Gainst parricides did all the thunder bend,   45
Spoke with how manifold and strong a bond
The child was bound to the father; sir, in fine,   47
Seeing how loathly opposite I stood   48
To his unnatural purpose, in fell motion   49
With his preparèd sword he charges home   50
My unprovided body, latched mine arm;   51
And when he saw my best alarumed spirits,   52

33–34 beget . . . endeavor create an impression of my having fought
fiercely **39 stand 's** stand his, act as his **44 that** when **45 bend**
aim **47 in fine** in conclusion **48 loathly opposite** loathingly opposed **49 fell motion** deadly thrust **50 preparèd** unsheathed and
ready. **home** to the very heart **51 unprovided** unprotected. **latched**
nicked, lanced **52 best alarumed** thoroughly aroused to action as by a
trumpet

Bold in the quarrel's right, roused to th' encounter,   53
Or whether gasted by the noise I made,   54
Full suddenly he fled.
GLOUCESTER   Let him fly far.   55
Not in this land shall he remain uncaught;
And found—dispatch. The noble Duke my master,   57
My worthy arch and patron, comes tonight.   58
By his authority I will proclaim it.
That he which finds him shall deserve our thanks,
Bringing the murderous coward to the stake;   61
He that conceals him, death.
EDMUND
When I dissuaded him from his intent
And found him pight to do it, with curst speech   64
I threatened to discover him. He replied,   65
"Thou unpossessing bastard, dost thou think,   66
If I would stand against thee, would the reposal   67
Of any trust, virtue, or worth in thee
Make thy words faithed? No. What I should deny—   69
As this I would, ay, though thou didst produce
My very character—I'd turn it all   71
To thy suggestion, plot, and damnèd practice;   72
And thou must make a dullard of the world   73
If they not thought the profits of my death   74
Were very pregnant and potential spirits   75
To make thee seek it."
GLOUCESTER   O strange and fastened villain! 76
Would he deny his letter, said he?
I never got him.   *Tucket within.*   78

---

53 quarrel's right justice of the cause   **54 gasted** frightened   **55 Let him fly far** i.e., any fleeing, no matter how far, will be in vain   **57 dispatch** i.e., that will be the end for him   **58 arch and patron** chief patron   **61 to the stake** i.e., to reckoning   **64 pight** determined. **curst** angry   **65 discover** expose   **66 unpossessing** unable to inherit, beggarly   **67 reposal** placing   **69 faithed** believed   **71 character** written testimony, handwriting   **72 suggestion** instigation.   **practice** plot   **73 make . . . world** think everyone idiotic   **74 not thought** did not think. **of my death** i.e., that Edmund would gain through Edgar's death   **75 pregnant . . . spirits** fertile and potent tempters   **76 strange** unnatural. **fastened** hardened   **78 got** begot   **s.d. Tucket** series of notes on the trumpet, here indicating Cornwall's arrival

Hark, the Duke's trumpets! I know not why he
  comes.
All ports I'll bar; the villain shall not scape.   80
The Duke must grant me that. Besides, his picture
I will send far and near, that all the kingdom
May have due note of him; and of my land,
Loyal and natural boy, I'll work the means   84
To make thee capable.   85

Enter CORNWALL, REGAN, *and attendants.*

CORNWALL
How now, my noble friend? Since I came hither,
Which I can call but now, I have heard strange
  news.
REGAN
If it be true, all vengeance comes too short
Which can pursue th' offender. How dost, my lord?
GLOUCESTER
O madam, my old heart is cracked, it's cracked!
REGAN
What, did my father's godson seek your life?
He whom my father named? Your Edgar?
GLOUCESTER
O, lady, lady, shame would have it hid!
REGAN
Was he not companion with the riotous knights
That tended upon my father?
GLOUCESTER
I know not, madam. 'Tis too bad, too bad.
EDMUND
Yes, madam, he was of that consort.   97
REGAN
No marvel, then, though he were ill affected.   98
'Tis they have put him on the old man's death,   99

---

80 ports seaports, or gateways   **84 natural** (1) prompted by natural
feelings of loyalty and affection (2) bastard   **85 capable** legally able to
become the inheritor   **97 consort** set, company   **98 though** if. **ill affected** ill disposed, disloyal   **99 put him on** incited him to

To have th' expense and waste of his revenues.   100
I have this present evening from my sister
Been well informed of them, and with such
    cautions
That if they come to sojourn at my house
I'll not be there.
CORNWALL   Nor I, assure thee, Regan.
    Edmund, I hear that you have shown your father
    A childlike office.
EDMUND   It was my duty, sir.   106
GLOUCESTER [To CORNWALL]
    He did bewray his practice, and received   107
    This hurt you see striving to apprehend him.   108
CORNWALL   Is he pursued?
GLOUCESTER   Ay, my good lord.
CORNWALL
    If he be taken, he shall never more
    Be feared of doing harm. Make your own purpose,   112
    How in my strength you please. For you, Edmund,   113
    Whose virtue and obedience doth this instant
    So much commend itself, you shall be ours.
    Natures of such deep trust we shall much need;
    You we first seize on.
EDMUND   I shall serve you, sir,
    Truly, however else.   118
GLOUCESTER   For him I thank Your Grace.
CORNWALL
    You know not why we came to visit you—
REGAN
    —Thus out of season, threading dark-eyed night:
    Occasions, noble Gloucester, of some prize,   122
    Wherein we must have use of your advice.
    Our father he hath writ, so hath our sister,
    Of differences, which I best thought it fit   125

---

100 expense and waste squandering   **106 childlike** filial   **107 bewray his
practice** expose his (Edgar's) plot   **108 apprehend** arrest   **112–113
Make . . . please** form your plans, making free use of my authority and
resources   **113 For** as for   **118 however else** i.e., whether capably or
not   **122 prize** significance   **125 differences** quarrels.   **which** i.e.,
Lear's and Goneril's letters

To answer from our home; the several messengers   126
From hence attend dispatch. Our good old friend,   127
Lay comforts to your bosom, and bestow
Your needful counsel to our businesses,   129
Which craves the instant use.

GLOUCESTER   I serve you, madam.   130
Your Graces are right welcome.

                            Flourish. Exeunt.

                          Scene Two
                  [BEFORE GLOUCESTER'S HOUSE.]

Enter KENT [*disguised as* CAIUS] *and steward* [OS-
WALD], *severally.*

OSWALD   Good dawning to thee, friend. Art of this   1
   house?
KENT   Ay.
OSWALD   Where may we set our horses?
KENT   I' the mire.
OSWALD   Prithee, if thou lov'st me, tell me.   6
KENT   I love thee not.
OSWALD   Why then, I care not for thee.   8
KENT   If I had thee in Lipsbury pinfold, I would make   9
   thee care for me.   10
OSWALD   Why dost thou use me thus? I know thee   11
   not.   12
KENT   Fellow, I know thee.   13

126 **from** away from   127 **attend dispatch** wait to be dispatched   129
needful necessary   130 **the instant use** immediate attention
s.d. severally at separate doors   1 **dawning** (It is not yet day.)   6 **if thou
lov'st me** i.e., if you bear good will toward me. (But Kent deliberately
takes the phrase in its literal, not courtly, sense.)   8–10 **care not for . . .
care for** do not like . . . have an anxious regard for   9 **Lipsbury pinfold**
i.e., within the pinfold of the lips, between my teeth. (A *pinfold* is a
pound for stray animals.)   11–13 **know thee not . . . know thee** am
unacquainted with you . . . can see through you

OSWALD   What dost thou know me for?

KENT   A knave, a rascal, an eater of broken meats; a 15
base, proud, shallow, beggarly, three-suited, hun- 16
dred-pound, filthy worsted-stocking knave; a lily- 17
livered, action-taking, whoreson, glass-gazing, su- 18
perserviceable, finical rogue; one-trunk-inheriting 19
slave; one that wouldst be a bawd in way of good 20
service, and art nothing but the composition of a 21
knave, beggar, coward, pander, and the son and heir
of a mongrel bitch; one whom I will beat into clamorous whining if thou deny'st the least syllable of thy
addition. 25

OSWALD   Why, what a monstrous fellow art thou thus
to rail on one that is neither known of thee nor
knows thee!

KENT   What a brazen-faced varlet art thou to deny
thou knowest me! Is it two days since I tripped up
thy heels and beat thee before the King? Draw, you
rogue, for though it be night, yet the moon shines. I'll
make a sop o' the moonshine of you, you whoreson 33
cullionly barbermonger. Draw! 34

                [*He brandishes his sword.*]

OSWALD   Away! I have nothing to do with thee.

KENT   Draw, you rascal! You come with letters
against the King, and take Vanity the puppet's part 37

---

15 broken meats scraps of food (such as were passed out to the most
lowly)   **16 three-suited** (Three suits a year were allowed to servants.)   **16–17 hundred-pound** (Possible allusion to the minimum property qualification for the status of gentleman.)   **17 worsted-stocking** i.e.,
too poor and menial to wear silk stockings   **17–18 lily-livered** cowardly
(the liver being pale through lack of blood)   **18 action-taking** settling
quarrels by resort to law instead of arms, cowardly. **glass-gazing** fond of
looking in the mirror   **18–19 superserviceable** officious   **19 finical** foppish, fastidious. **one-trunk-inheriting** possessing effects sufficient for
one trunk only   **20–21 bawd . . . service** i.e., pimp or pander as a way of
providing good service   **21 composition** compound   **25 addition** titles   **33 sop o' the moonshine** something so perforated that it will soak
up moonshine as a sop (floating piece of toast) soaks up liquor
34 cullionly barbermonger base frequenter of barber shops, fop. (*Cullion*
originally meant "testicle.")   **37 Vanity . . . part** i.e., the part of Goneril
(here personified as a character in a morality play)

against the royalty of her father. Draw, you rogue, or
I'll so carbonado your shanks—draw, you rascal!　　39
Come your ways.　　40

OSWALD　Help, ho! Murder! Help!

KENT　Strike, you slave! Stand, rogue, stand, you neat　　42
slave, strike!　　　　　　　　　　　　[*He beats him.*]

OSWALD　Help, ho! Murder! Murder!

Enter Bastard [EDMUND, *with his rapier drawn*],
CORNWALL, REGAN, GLOUCESTER, *servants.*

EDMUND　How now, what's the matter? Part!　　45

KENT　With you, goodman boy, an you please! Come,　　46
I'll flesh ye. Come on, young master.　　47

GLOUCESTER　Weapons? Arms? What's the matter
here?

CORNWALL　Keep peace, upon your lives! [KENT *and*
OSWALD *are parted.*] He dies that strikes again.
What is the matter?

REGAN　The messengers from our sister and the King.

CORNWALL　What's your difference? Speak.　　54

OSWALD　I am scarce in breath, my lord.

KENT　No marvel, you have so bestirred your valor.
You cowardly rascal, nature disclaims in thee. A　　57
tailor made thee.

CORNWALL　Thou art a strange fellow. A tailor make a
man?

KENT　A tailor, sir. A stonecutter or a painter could
not have made him so ill, though they had been but
two years o' the trade.

CORNWALL　Speak yet, how grew your quarrel?

OSWALD　This ancient ruffian, sir, whose life I have
spared at suit of his gray beard—

---

39 carbonado cut crosswise like meat for broiling　**40 Come your ways**
come on　**42 neat** (1) foppish (2) calflike. (*Neat* means "horned cattle.")　**45 matter** i.e., trouble. (But Kent takes the meaning "cause for
quarrel.")　**46 With you** I'll fight with you; my quarrel is with you.
goodman boy (A contemptuous epithet, a title of mock respect, addressed seemingly to Edmund.) **an** if　**47 flesh** initiate into combat　**54**
difference quarrel　**57 disclaims in** disowns

KENT Thou whoreson zed! Thou unnecessary let-   67
ter!—My lord, if you'll give me leave, I will tread this
unbolted villain into mortar and daub the wall of a   69
jakes with him.—Spare my gray beard, you wagtail?   70
CORNWALL Peace, sirrah!
You beastly knave, know you no reverence?
KENT
Yes, sir, but anger hath a privilege.
CORNWALL Why art thou angry?
KENT
That such a slave as this should wear a sword,
Who wears no honesty. Such smiling rogues as
    these,
Like rats, oft bite the holy cords atwain   77
Which are t' intrinse t' unloose; smooth every
    passion   78
That in the natures of their lords rebel,
Bring oil to fire, snow to their colder moods,   80
Renege, affirm, and turn their halcyon beaks   81
With every gale and vary of their masters,   82
Knowing naught, like dogs, but following.—
A plague upon your epileptic visage!   84
Smile you my speeches, as I were a fool?   85
Goose, an I had you upon Sarum plain,   86
I'd drive ye cackling home to Camelot.   87
CORNWALL What, art thou mad, old fellow?

67 zed the letter *z* regarded as unnecessary and often not included in
dictionaries of the time **69 unbolted** unsifted; hence, coarse. **daub**
plaster **70 jakes** privy. **wagtail** i.e., bird wagging its tail feathers in
pert obsequiousness **77 holy cords** sacred bonds of affection and
order **78. t' intrinse** too intrinsicate, tightly knotted. **smooth** flatter,
humor **80 Bring oil to fire** i.e., flattering servants fuel the flame of their
masters' angry passions **81 Renege** deny. **halcyon beaks** (The halcyon or
kingfisher, if hung up, would supposedly turn its beak against the
wind.) **82 gale and vary** variation in the wind **84 epileptic** i.e., trembling and pale with fright and distorted with a grin **85 Smile you** do you
smile at. **as** as if **86–87 Goose . . . Camelot** (The reference is obscure,
but the general sense is that Kent scorns Oswald as a cackling goose.) **an**
if. **Sarum** Salisbury. **Camelot** legendary seat of King Arthur and his
Round Table, said to have been at Cadbury and at Winchester and hence
in the general vicinity of Salisbury and Gloucester

GLOUCESTER How fell you out? Say that.

KENT
No contraries hold more antipathy
Than I and such a knave.

CORNWALL
Why dost thou call him knave? What is his fault?

KENT His countenance likes me not. 93

CORNWALL
No more, perchance, does mine, nor his, nor hers.

KENT
Sir, 'tis my occupation to be plain:
I have seen better faces in my time
Than stands on any shoulder that I see
Before me at this instant.

CORNWALL This is some fellow
Who, having been praised for bluntness, doth affect
A saucy roughness, and constrains the garb 100
Quite from his nature. He cannot flatter, he; 101
An honest mind and plain, he must speak truth!
An they will take 't, so; if not, he's plain. 103
These kind of knaves I know, which in this
  plainness
Harbor more craft and more corrupter ends
Than twenty silly-ducking observants 106
That stretch their duties nicely. 107

KENT
Sir, in good faith, in sincere verity, 108
Under th' allowance of your great aspect, 109
Whose influence, like the wreath of radiant fire 110
On flickering Phoebus' front—

CORNWALL What mean'st by this? 111

KENT To go out of my dialect, which you discom-

---

93 likes pleases **100–101 constrains . . . nature** i.e., distorts plainness
to the point of caricature, away from its true purpose **103 An . . . plain**
if people will take his rudeness, fine; if not, his excuse is that he speaks
plain truth **106 silly-ducking observants** foolishly bowing, obsequious
attendants **107 stretch . . . nicely** exert themselves in their courtly
duties punctiliously **108 Sir, in good faith,** etc. (Kent assumes the
wordy mannerisms of courtly flattery.) **109 allowance** approval. **aspect**
(1) countenance (2) astrological position **110 influence** astrological
might **111 Phoebus' front** i.e., the sun's forehead

mend so much. I know, sir, I am no flatterer. He that   113
beguiled you in a plain accent was a plain knave,   114
which for my part I will not be, though I should win   115
your displeasure to entreat me to 't.   116

CORNWALL [To OSWALD] What was th' offense you
gave him?

OSWALD   I never gave him any.
It pleased the King his master very late   120
To strike at me, upon his misconstruction;   121
When he, compact, and flattering his displeasure,   122
Tripped me behind; being down, insulted, railed,   123
And put upon him such a deal of man   124
That worthied him, got praises of the King   125
For him attempting who was self-subdued;   126
And, in the fleshment of this dread exploit,   127
Drew on me here again.

KENT   None of these rogues and cowards   129
But Ajax is their fool.

CORNWALL   Fetch forth the stocks!   130
You stubborn ancient knave, you reverend braggart,   131
We'll teach you.

KENT   Sir, I am too old to learn.
Call not your stocks for me. I serve the King,

113–114 He . . . accent i.e., the man who used plain speech to you
craftily (see 2.2.104.107) and thereby taught you to suspect plain speak-
ers of deceit   115–116 which . . . me to 't i.e., I will no longer use plain
speech, despite the incentive of incurring your displeasure by doing so.
(Kent prefers to displease Cornwall, since Cornwall is pleased only by
flatterers, and Kent has assumed until now that plain speech was the
best way to offend; but he now argues mockingly that he can no longer
speak plainly, since his honest utterance will be interpreted as du-
plicity.)   120 late recently   121 upon his misconstruction as a result of
the King's misunderstanding (me)   122 he i.e., Kent. compact joined,
united with the King. flattering his displeasure gratifying the King's
anger (at me)   123 being down, insulted i.e., when I was down, he
exulted over me   124 put . . . man acted like such a hero
125 worthied won reputation for   126 For . . . self-subdued for assailing
one (i.e., myself) who chose not to resist   127 fleshment excitement resulting from a first success. dread exploit (Said ironically.)
129–130 None . . . fool i.e., you never find any rogues and cowards of
this sort who do not outdo the blustering Ajax in their boasting
131 reverend (because old)

On whose employment I was sent to you.
You shall do small respect, show too bold malice
Against the grace and person of my master,   136
Stocking his messenger.

CORNWALL
Fetch forth the stocks! As I have life and honor,
There shall he sit till noon.

REGAN
Till noon? Till night, my lord, and all night too.

KENT
Why, madam, if I were your father's dog
You should not use me so.   142

REGAN   Sir, being his knave, I will.   143

CORNWALL
This is a fellow of the selfsame color   144
Our sister speaks of.—Come, bring away the
    stocks!   145

                              Stocks brought out.

GLOUCESTER
Let me beseech Your Grace not to do so.
His fault is much, and the good King his master
Will check him for 't. Your purposed low correction   148
Is such as basest and contemned'st wretches   149
For pilferings and most common trespasses
Are punished with. The King must take it ill
That he, so slightly valued in his messenger,
Should have him thus restrained.

CORNWALL   I'll answer that.   153

REGAN
My sister may receive it much more worse
To have her gentleman abused, assaulted,
For following her affairs. Put in his legs.

                        [KENT *is put in the stocks.*]

Come, my good lord, away.

                Exeunt [*all but* GLOUCESTER *and* KENT].

---

136 grace sovereignty   **142 should** would   **143 being** since you are   **144 color** complexion, character   **145 away** along   **148 check** rebuke, correct   **149 contemned'st** most despised   **153 answer** be answerable for

GLOUCESTER
  I am sorry for thee, friend. 'Tis the Duke's pleasure,
  Whose disposition, all the world well knows,
  Will not be rubbed nor stopped. I'll entreat for thee.   160

KENT
  Pray, do not, sir. I have watched and traveled hard.   161
  Some time I shall sleep out; the rest I'll whistle.
  A good man's fortune may grow out at heels.   163
  Give you good morrow!   164

GLOUCESTER
  The Duke's to blame in this. 'Twill be ill taken.

                                                   Exit.

KENT
  Good King, that must approve the common saw,   166
  Thou out of heaven's benediction com'st
  To the warm sun!   [*He takes out a letter.*]
  Approach, thou beacon to this under globe,   169
  That by thy comfortable beams I may   170
  Peruse this letter. Nothing almost sees miracles   171
  But misery. I know 'tis from Cordelia,   172
  Who hath most fortunately been informed
  Of my obscurèd course, and shall find time   174
  From this enormous state, seeking to give   175
  Losses their remedies. All weary and o'erwatched,   176

---

160 rubbed hindered, obstructed. (A term from bowls.)   **161 watched**
gone sleepless   **163 A . . . heels** i.e., even good men suffer decline in
fortune at times   **164 Give you** i.e., God give you   **166 approve** prove
true. **saw** proverb (i.e., "To run out of God's blessing into the warm
sun," meaning "to go from better to worse")   **169 beacon . . . globe** i.e.,
the sun (?) (Some editors believe that Kent means the moon, since it is
night at ll. 32 and 179, but he probably is saying that he hopes for
daylight soon in order that he can read the letter from Cordelia.)
170 comfortable useful, aiding   **171–172 Nothing . . . misery** i.e.,
scarcely anything can make one appreciate miracles like being in a state
of misery; miracles are most often experienced by those who suffer
misfortune   **174 obscurèd** disguised. **shall** she shall   **174–176 and . . .
remedies** (This seemingly incoherent passage may be textually corrupt
or may be meant to represent fragments from the letter Kent is reading.)
175 From i.e., to provide relief from (?) **enormous state** monstrous state
of affairs, enormity   **176 Losses** reversals of fortune. **o'erwatched** exhausted with staying awake

Take vantage, heavy eyes, not to behold 177
This shameful lodging. 178
Fortune, good night. Smile once more; turn thy
  wheel! [*He sleeps.*] 179

Scene Three
[SCENE CONTINUES. KENT IS DOZING IN THE STOCKS.]

Enter EDGAR.

EDGAR I heard myself proclaimed,
  And by the happy hollow of a tree 2
  Escaped the hunt. No port is free, no place 3
  That guard and most unusual vigilance 4
  Does not attend my taking. Whiles I may scape 5
  I will preserve myself, and am bethought 6
  To take the basest and most poorest shape
  That ever penury, in contempt of man, 8
  Brought near to beast. My face I'll grime with filth,
  Blanket my loins, elf all my hairs in knots, 10
  And with presented nakedness outface 11
  The winds and persecutions of the sky.
  The country gives me proof and precedent 13
  Of Bedlam beggars who with roaring voices 14
  Strike in their numbed and mortified arms 15
  Pins, wooden pricks, nails, sprigs of rosemary; 16
  And with this horrible object, from low farms, 17
  Poor pelting villages, sheepcotes, and mills, 18

177 vantage advantage (of sleep) **178 lodging** i.e., the stocks **179 wheel** (Since Kent is at the bottom of Fortune's wheel, any turning will improve his situation.)
2 happy luckily found **3 port** (See 2.1.80 and note.) **4 That** in which **5 attend** watch, wait for **6 bethought** resolved **8 in . . . man** in order to show how contemptible humankind is **10 elf** tangle into elflocks **11 presented** exposed to view, displayed **13 proof** example **14 Bedlam** (See note to 1.2.141.) **15 Strike** stick. **mortified** deadened **16 wooden pricks** skewers **17 object** spectacle. **low** lowly **18 pelting** paltry

Sometimes with lunatic bans, sometimes with
  prayers,   19
Enforce their charity. Poor Turlygod! Poor Tom!   20
That's something yet. Edgar I nothing am.   *Exit*.   21

Scene Four
[SCENE CONTINUES BEFORE GLOUCESTER'S HOUSE.
KENT STILL DOZING IN THE STOCKS.]

Enter LEAR, FOOL, *and* GENTLEMAN.

LEAR
  'Tis strange that they should so depart from home
  And not send back my messenger.
GENTLEMAN   As I learned,
  The night before there was no purpose in them
  Of this remove.
KENT   Hail to thee, noble master!   4
LEAR   Ha?
  Mak'st thou this shame thy pastime?
KENT   No, my lord.
FOOL   Ha, ha, he wears cruel garters. Horses are tied   7
  by the heads, dogs and bears by the neck, monkeys
  by the loins, and men by the legs. When a man's
  overlusty at legs, then he wears wooden nether-   10
  stocks.   11
LEAR
  What's he that hath so much thy place mistook
  To set thee here?
KENT

                                It is both he and she: 13
  Your son and daughter.
LEAR   No.
KENT   Yes.

19 bans curses   **20 Poor . . . Tom** (Edgar practices the begging role he is
about to adopt. Beggars were known as poor Toms.) **Turlygod** (Meaning
unknown.)   **21 That's something yet** there's some kind of existence still
for me as poor Tom. **Edgar** i.e., as Edgar
4 remove change of residence   **7 cruel** (In the quarto: *crewell*, a double
meaning [1] unkind [2] crewel, a thin yarn of which garters were
made.)   **overlusty at legs** given to running away   **11 netherstocks** stockings   **13 To** as to

LEAR   No, I say.

KENT   I say yea.

LEAR   No, no, they would not.

KENT   Yes, they have.

LEAR   By Jupiter, I swear no.

KENT   By Juno, I swear ay.

LEAR   They durst not do 't!
   They could not, would not do 't. 'Tis worse than
    murder
To do upon respect such violent outrage.   24
Resolve me with all modest haste which way   25
Thou mightst deserve, or they impose, this usage,
Coming from us.

KENT   My lord, when at their home   27
I did commend Your Highness' letters to them,   28
Ere I was risen from the place that showed   29
My duty kneeling, came there a reeking post,   30
Stewed in his haste, half breathless, panting forth   31
From Goneril his mistress salutations;
Delivered letters, spite of intermission,   33
Which presently they read; on whose contents   34
They summoned up their meiny, straight took
   horse,   35
Commanded me to follow and attend
The leisure of their answer, gave me cold looks;
And meeting here the other messenger,
Whose welcome, I perceived, had poisoned mine—
Being the very fellow which of late
Displayed so saucily against Your Highness—   41
Having more man than wit about me, drew.   42
He raised the house with loud and coward cries.

---

24 upon respect i.e., against my delegates (who deserve respect) **25 Resolve** enlighten. **modest** moderate **27 their home** (Kent and Oswald went first to Cornwall's palace after leaving Albany's palace.) **28 commend** deliver **29–30 from . . . kneeling** from the kneeling posture that showed my duty **30 reeking** steaming (with heat of travel) **31 Stewed** i.e., thoroughly heated, soaked **33 spite of intermission** in disregard of interrupting me; or, in spite of the interruptions caused by his being out of breath **34 presently** instantly. **on** on the basis of **35 meiny** retinue of servants, household **41 Displayed so saucily** behaved so insolently **42 man** manhood, courage. **wit** discretion, sense

Your son and daughter found this trespass worth
The shame which here it suffers.

FOOL   Winter's not gone yet if the wild geese fly that   46
way.   47
    Fathers that wear rags
      Do make their children blind,   49
    But fathers that bear bags   50
      Shall see their children kind.
    Fortune, that arrant whore,
      Ne'er turns the key to the poor.   53
But, for all this, thou shalt have as many dolors for   54
thy daughters as thou canst tell in a year.   55

LEAR
O, how this mother swells up toward my heart!   56
Hysterica passio, down, thou climbing sorrow!   57
Thy element's below.—Where is this daughter?   58

KENT   With the Earl, sir, here within.

LEAR   Follow me not. Stay here.   *Exit.*

GENTLEMAN
Made you no more offense but what you speak of?

KENT   None.
How chance the King comes with so small a   63
number?

FOOL   An thou hadst been set i' the stocks for that   64
question, thou'dst well deserved it.

KENT   Why, Fool?

FOOL   We'll set thee to school to an ant to teach thee   67
there's no laboring i' the winter. All that follow their   68

46–47 Winter's . . . way i.e., the signs still point to continued and
worsening fortune; the wild geese are still flying south
49 blind i.e., indifferent to their father's needs   **50 bags** i.e., of gold
53 turns the key opens the door   **54 dolors** griefs (with pun on *dollars,*
English word for an Austrian or Spanish coin). **for** on account of
55 tell (1) relate (2) count   **56, 57 mother, Hysterica passio** i.e., hysteria,
giving the sensation of choking or suffocating   **58 element's** proper
place is. (Hysteria was thought to be produced by vapors ascending
from the abdomen.)   **63 chance** chances it   **64 An** if   **67–68 We'll . . .
winter** i.e., just as the ant knows not to labor in the winter, the wise man
knows not to labor for one whose fortunes are fallen   **68–71 All . . .
stinking** i.e., one who is out of favor can be easily detected (he smells of
misfortune), and so is easily avoided by timeservers

noses are led by their eyes but blind men, and there's 69
not a nose among twenty but can smell him that's 70
stinking. Let go thy hold when a great wheel runs 71
down a hill lest it break thy neck with following; but
the great one that goes upward, let him draw thee
after. When a wise man gives thee better counsel,
give me mine again. I would have none but knaves
follow it, since a fool gives it.

That sir which serves and seeks for gain,
    And follows but for form,
Will pack when it begins to rain 79
    And leave thee in the storm.
But I will tarry; the fool will stay,
    And let the wise man fly.
The knave turns fool that runs away; 83
    The fool no knave, pardie. 84

Enter LEAR *and* GLOUCESTER.

KENT   Where learned you this, Fool?
FOOL   Not i' the stocks, fool.
LEAR
Deny to speak with me? They are sick? They are
    weary?
They have traveled all the night? Mere fetches, 88
The images of revolt and flying off. 89
Fetch me a better answer.
GLOUCESTER   My dear lord,
You know the fiery quality of the Duke,
How unremovable and fixed he is
In his own course.
LEAR
Vengeance! Plague! Death! Confusion! 94
Fiery? What quality? Why, Gloucester, Gloucester,
I'd speak with the Duke of Cornwall and his wife.

---

79 pack be off   **83 The knave . . . away** i.e., deserting one's master is the
greatest folly   **84 pardie** *par Dieu* (French), by God   **88 fetches** pre-
texts, dodges   **89 images** signs. **flying off** desertion   **94 Confusion** destruction

GLOUCESTER

  Well, my good lord, I have informed them so.

LEAR

  Informed them? Dost thou understand me, man?

GLOUCESTER Ay, my good lord.

LEAR

  The King would speak with Cornwall. The dear
    father
  Would with his daughter speak, commands, tends,
    service.   101
  Are they informed of this? My breath and blood!
  Fiery? The fiery Duke? Tell the hot Duke that—
  No, but not yet. Maybe he is not well.
  Infirmity doth still neglect all office   105
  Whereto our health is bound; we are not ourselves   106
  When nature, being oppressed, commands the mind
  To suffer with the body. I'll forbear,
  And am fallen out with my more headier will,   109
  To take the indisposed and sickly fit   110
  For the sound man. [*Looking at* KENT.] Death on
    my state! Wherefore   111
  Should he sit here? This act persuades me
  That this remotion of the Duke and her   113
  Is practice only. Give me my servant forth.   114
  Go tell the Duke and 's wife I'd speak with them,
  Now, presently. Bid them come forth and hear me,   116
  Or at their chamber door I'll beat the drum
  Till it cry sleep to death.   118

GLOUCESTER I would have all well betwixt you. *Exit*.

LEAR

  O me, my heart, my rising heart! But down!

FOOL Cry to it, nuncle, as the cockney did to the eels   121
  when she put 'em i' the paste alive. She knapped 'em   122

---

101 tends attends, waits for **105 still** always **105–106 all . . . bound**
duties which in good health we are bound to perform **109–110 am . . .
take** now disapprove of my more impetuous will in having rashly
taken **111 Death on my state** may death come to my royal authority. (An
oath with ironic appropriateness.) **113 remotion** removal, inac-
cessibility **114 practice** deception. **forth** out of the stocks **116 presently** at once **118 cry sleep to death** i.e., put an end to sleep by the
noise **121 cockney** i.e., a Londoner, ignorant of ways of cooking
eels **122 paste** pastry pie. **knapped** rapped

o' the coxcombs with a stick and cried, "Down,   123
wantons, down!" 'Twas her brother that, in pure   124
kindness to his horse, buttered his hay.   125

Enter CORNWALL, REGAN, GLOUCESTER, [*and*] *servants.*

LEAR   Good morrow to you both.
CORNWALL   Hail to Your Grace!
                              KENT *here set at liberty.*
REGAN   I am glad to see Your Highness.
LEAR
Regan, I think you are. I know what reason
I have to think so. If thou shouldst not be glad,
I would divorce me from thy mother's tomb,   131
Sepulch'ring an adult'ress. [*To* KENT.] O, are you
   free?   132
Some other time for that.—Belovèd Regan,
Thy sister's naught. O Regan, she hath tied   134
Sharp-toothed unkindness, like a vulture, here.
              [*He lays his hand on his heart.*]
I can scarce speak to thee. Thou'lt not believe
With how depraved a quality—O Regan!   137
REGAN
I pray you, sir, take patience. I have hope   138
You less know how to value her desert   139
Than she to scant her duty.
LEAR   Say? How is that?   140
REGAN
I cannot think my sister in the least
Would fail her obligation. If, sir, perchance
She have restrained the riots of your followers,

---

123 coxcombs heads   **124 wantons** playful creatures, promiscuous things   **124–125 'Twas . . . hay** (Another city ignorance; the act is well-intended, but horses do not like greasy hay. As with Lear, good intentions are not enough.) **brother** i.e., fellow creature, foolishly tenderhearted in the same way   **131 divorce me from** i.e., refuse to be buried beside   **132 Sepulch'ring** i.e., since it would surely contain the dead body of   **134 naught** wicked   **137 quality** disposition   **138–140 I have . . . duty** i.e., I trust this is more a matter of your undervaluing her merit than of her falling slack in her duty to you

'Tis on such ground and to such wholesome end
As clears her from all blame.

LEAR   My curses on her!

REGAN
O, sir, you are old;
Nature in you stands on the very verge   148
Of his confine. You should be ruled and led   149
By some discretion that discerns your state   150
Better than you yourself. Therefore, I pray you,
That to our sister you do make return.
Say you have wronged her.

LEAR   Ask her forgiveness?
Do you but mark how this becomes the house: 154
                         [*He kneels.*]
   "Dear daughter, I confess that I am old;
   Age is unnecessary. On my knees I beg   156
   That you'll vouchsafe me raiment, bed, and food."

REGAN
Good sir, no more. These are unsightly tricks.
Return you to my sister.

LEAR [*Rising*]   Never, Regan.
She hath abated me of half my train,   160
Looked black upon me, struck me with her tongue
Most serpentlike upon the very heart.
All the stored vengeances of heaven fall
On her ingrateful top! Strike her young bones,   164
You taking airs, with lameness!

CORNWALL   Fie, sir, fie!   165

LEAR
You nimble lightnings, dart your blinding flames
Into her scornful eyes! Infect her beauty,

148–149 **Nature . . . confine** i.e., your life has almost completed its
allotted scope   150 **discretion** discreet person. **discerns your state** understands your dependent situation and aged condition   154 **becomes the
house** suits domestic decorum, is suited to the family or household and its dutiful relationships   156 **Age is unnecessary** old
people are useless   160 **abated** deprived   164 **ingrateful top** ungrateful
head. **her young bones** i.e., of her not-yet-born progeny (?)
165 **taking** infectious

You fen-sucked fogs drawn by the powerful sun 168
To fall and blister! 169

REGAN

O the blest gods! So will you wish on me
When the rash mood is on.

LEAR

No, Regan, thou shalt never have my curse.
Thy tender-hafted nature shall not give 173
Thee o'er to harshness. Her eyes are fierce, but
   thine
Do comfort and not burn. 'Tis not in thee
To grudge my pleasures, to cut off my train,
To bandy hasty words, to scant my sizes, 177
And, in conclusion, to oppose the bolt 178
Against my coming in. Thou better know'st
The offices of nature, bond of childhood, 180
Effects of courtesy, dues of gratitude. 181
Thy half o' the kingdom hast thou not forgot,
Wherein I thee endowed.

REGAN   Good sir, to the purpose. 183

LEAR

Who put my man i' the stocks?   *Tucket within.*

CORNWALL   What trumpet's that?

REGAN

I know 't—my sister's. This approves her letter, 185
That she would soon be here.

Enter steward [OSWALD].

                      Is your lady come?

LEAR

This is a slave, whose easy-borrowed pride 187

---

168 fen-sucked (It was supposed that the sun sucked up poisons from fens or marshes.) **169 To fall and blister** to fall upon her and blister her beauty **173 tender-hafted** set in a tender *haft*, i.e., handle or frame; moved by a tender feeling, gently disposed **177 bandy** volley, exchange. **scant my sizes** diminish my allowances **178 oppose the bolt** lock the door **180 offices of nature** natural duties. **bond of childhood** filial obligations due to parents **181 Effects** actions, manifestations **183 purpose** point **185 approves** confirms **187 easy-borrowed** i.e., acquired with little effort at deserving and with weak commitment

Dwells in the fickle grace of her he follows.   188
Out, varlet, from my sight!

CORNWALL   What means Your Grace?   189

LEAR

Who stocked my servant? Regan, I have good hope
Thou didst not know on 't.

Enter GONERIL.

                          Who comes here? O heavens,
If you do love old men, if your sweet sway
Allow obedience, if you yourselves are old,   193
Make it your cause; send down, and take my part!
[*To Goneril.*] Art not ashamed to look upon this
    beard?   [GONERIL *and* REGAN *join hands.*]
O Reagan, will you take her by the hand?

GONERIL

Why not by the hand, sir? How have I offended?
All's not offense that indiscretion finds   198
And dotage terms so.

LEAR

                    O sides, you are too tough!   199
Will you yet hold?—How came my man i' the
    stocks?

CORNWALL

I set him there, sir; but his own disorders
Deserved much less advancement.

LEAR   You? Did you?   202

REGAN

I pray you, Father, being weak, seem so.   203
If till the expiration of your month
You will return and sojourn with my sister,
Dismissing half your train, come then to me.
I am now from home, and out of that provision
Which shall be needful for your entertainment.   208

---

188 grace favor **189 varlet** worthless fellow **193 Allow** approve, sanction **198 indiscretion finds** poor judgment deems to be so **199 sides** i.e., sides of the chest (stretched by the swelling heart) **202 much less advancement** far less honor, i.e., far worse treatment **203 seem so** i.e., don't act as if you were strong **208 entertainment** proper reception V

LEAR
  Return to her? And fifty men dismissed?
  No! Rather I abjure all roofs, and choose
  To wage against the enmity o' th' air,   211
  To be a comrade with the wolf and owl—
  Necessity's sharp pinch. Return with her?
  Why, the hot-blooded France, that dowerless took   214
  Our youngest born—I could as well be brought
  To knee his throne and, squirelike, pension beg   216
  To keep base life afoot. Return with her?
  Persuade me rather to be slave and sumpter   218
  To this detested groom.   *[He points to* OSWALD.]
GONERIL   At your choice, sir.
LEAR
  I prithee, daughter, do not make me mad.
  I will not trouble thee, my child. Farewell.
  We'll no more meet, no more see one another.
  But yet thou art my flesh, my blood, my daughter—
  Or rather a disease that's in my flesh,
  Which I must needs call mine. Thou art a boil,
  A plague-sore, or embossèd carbuncle   226
  In my corrupted blood. But I'll not chide thee;
  Let shame come when it will, I do not call it.   228
  I do not bid the thunder-bearer shoot,   229
  Nor tell tales of thee to high-judging Jove.   230
  Mend when thou canst; be better at thy leisure.
  I can be patient. I can stay with Regan,
  I and my hundred knights.
REGAN
  Not altogether so.
  I looked not for you yet, nor am provided   235
  For your fit welcome. Give ear, sir, to my sister;
  For those that mingle reason with your passion   237
  Must be content to think you old, and so—
  But she knows what she does.

---

211 wage wage war   **214 hot-blooded** choleric. (Cf. 1.2.23.)   **216 knee** fall on my knees before   **218 sumpter** packhorse; hence, drudge   **226 embossèd** swollen, tumid   **228 call** summon   **229 the thunder-bearer** i.e., Jove   **230 high-judging** judging from on high   **235 looked not for** did not expect   **237 mingle . . . passion** consider your passionate behavior reasonably

LEAR   Is this well spoken?
REGAN
  I dare avouch it, sir. What, fifty followers?   240
  Is it not well? What should you need of more?
  Yea, or so many, sith that both charge and danger   242
  Speak 'gainst so great a number? How in one house
  Should many people under two commands
  Hold amity? 'Tis hard, almost impossible.
GONERIL
  Why might not you, my lord, receive attendance
  From those that she calls servants, or from mine?
REGAN
  Why not, my lord? If then they chanced to slack ye,   248
  We could control them. If you will come to me—   249
  For now I spy a danger—I entreat you
  To bring but five-and-twenty. To no more
  Will I give place or notice.   252
LEAR
  I gave you all—
REGAN   And in good time you gave it.
LEAR
  Made you my guardians, my depositaries,   254
  But kept a reservation to be followed   255
  With such a number. What, must I come to you
  With five-and-twenty? Regan, said you so?
REGAN
  And speak 't again, my lord. No more with me.
LEAR
  Those wicked creatures yet do look well-favored   259
  When others are more wicked; not being the worst
  Stands in some rank of praise. [To GONERIL.] I'll go
    with thee.   261
  The fifty yet doth double five-and-twenty,
  And thou art twice her love.
GONERIL   Hear me, my lord:
  What need you five-and-twenty, ten, or five,

---

240 avouch vouch for   **242 sith that** since. **charge** expense   **248 slack**
neglect   **249 control** correct   **252 notice** recognition, acknowledg-
ment   **254 depositaries** trustees   **255 kept a reservation** reserved a
right   **259 well-favored** attractive, fair of feature   **261 Stands . . . praise**
achieves, by necessity, some relative deserving of praise

To follow in a house where twice so many 265
Have a command to tend you?

REGAN   What need one?

LEAR

O, reason not the need! Our basest beggars 267
Are in the poorest thing superfluous. 268
Allow not nature more than nature needs, 269
Man's life is cheap as beast's. Thou art a lady;
If only to go warm were gorgeous, 271
Why, nature needs not what thou gorgeous wear'st, 272
Which scarcely keeps thee warm. But, for true
need— 273
You heavens, give me that patience, patience I
need!
You see me here, you gods, a poor old man,
As full of grief as age, wretched in both.
If it be you that stirs these daughters' hearts
Against their father, fool me not so much 278
To bear it tamely; touch me with noble anger, 279
And let not women's weapons, water drops,
Stain my man's cheeks! No, you unnatural hags,
I will have such revenges on you both
That all the world shall—I will do such things—
What they are yet I know not, but they shall be
The terrors of the earth. You think I'll weep;
No, I'll not weep.   *Storm and tempest.*
I have full cause of weeping; but this heart
Shall break into a hundred thousand flaws 288
Or ere I'll weep. O Fool, I shall go mad! 289

Exeunt [LEAR, GLOUCESTER, KENT, *and*
FOOL].

---

265 follow be your attendants   **267 reason not** do not dispassionately analyze. **Our basest** even our most wretched   **268 Are . . . superfluous** have some wretched possession they can dispense with   **269 Allow not** if you do not allow. **needs** i.e., to survive   **271–273 If . . . warm** i.e., if fashions in clothes were determined only by the need for warmth, this natural standard wouldn't justify the rich robes you wear to be gorgeous—which don't serve well for warmth in any case   **273 for** as for   **278–279 fool . . . To** do not make me so foolish as to   **288 flaws** fragments   **289 Or ere** before

CORNWALL
  Let us withdraw. 'Twill be a storm.
REGAN
  This house is little. The old man and 's people
  Cannot be well bestowed.   292
GONERIL
  'Tis his own blame hath put himself from rest,   293
  And must needs taste his folly.   294
REGAN
  For his particular, I'll receive him gladly,   295
  But not one follower.
GONERIL
  So am I purposed. Where is my lord of Gloucester?
CORNWALL
  Followed the old man forth.

Enter GLOUCESTER.

                                    He is returned.
GLOUCESTER
  The King is in high rage.
CORNWALL   Whither is he going?
GLOUCESTER
  He calls to horse, but will I know not whither.
CORNWALL
  'Tis best to give him way. He leads himself.   301
GONERIL
  My lord, entreat him by no means to stay.
GLOUCESTER
  Alack, the night comes on, and the bleak winds
  Do sorely ruffle. For many miles about   304
  There's scarce a bush.
REGAN   O, sir, to willful men
  The injuries that they themselves procure
  Must be their schoolmasters. Shut up your doors.

---

292 bestowed lodged   **293 blame** fault. **hath** that he has, or, that has.
from rest i.e., out of the house; also, lacking peace of mind   **294 taste**
experience   **295 For his particular** as for him individually   **301 give . . .**
himself give him his own way. He is guided only by his own
willfulness   **304 ruffle** bluster

He is attended with a desperate train,
And what they may incense him to, being apt   309
To have his ear abused, wisdom bids fear.   310

CORNWALL
  Shut up your doors, my lord; 'tis a wild night.
  My Regan counsels well. Come out o' the storm.

                                              Exeunt.

ACT THREE
Scene One
[AN OPEN PLACE IN GLOUCESTERSHIRE.]

Storm still. Enter KENT [*disguised as* CAIUS] *and a*
GENTLEMAN, *severally.*

KENT   Who's there, besides foul weather?
GENTLEMAN
  One minded like the weather, most unquietly.
KENT   I know you. Where's the King?
GENTLEMAN
  Contending with the fretful elements;
  Bids the wind blow the earth into the sea
  Or swell the curlèd waters 'bove the main,   6
  That things might change or cease; tears his white
      hair,
  Which the impetuous blasts with eyeless rage
  Catch in their fury and make nothing of;   9
  Strives in his little world of man to outstorm   10
  The to-and-fro-conflicting wind and rain.
  This night, wherein the cub-drawn bear would
      couch,   12
  The lion and the belly-pinchèd wolf
  Keep their fur dry, unbonneted he runs
  And bids what will take all.

309–310 being . . . abused (he) being inclined to hearken to wild counsel
s.d. severally at separate doors   **6 main** mainland   **9 make nothing of**
treat disrespectfully   **10 little world of man** i.e., the microcosm, which
is an epitome of the macrocosm or universe   **12 cub-drawn** famished,
with udders sucked dry (and hence ravenous). **couch** lie close in its
den   **15 take all** (A cry of desperate defiance, said by a gambler in
staking his last.)

KENT   But who is with him?   15
GENTLEMAN
None but the Fool, who labors to outjest   16
His heart-struck injuries.
KENT   Sir, I do know you,
And dare upon the warrant of my note   18
Commend a dear thing to you. There is division,   19
Although as yet the face of it is covered
With mutual cunning, twixt Albany and Cornwall;
Who have—as who have not, that their great stars   22
Throned and set high?—servants, who seem no
     less,   23
Which are to France the spies and speculations   24
Intelligent of our state. What hath been seen,   25
Either in snuffs and packings of the Dukes,   26
Or the hard rein which both of them hath borne
Against the old kind King, or something deeper,
Whereof perchance these are but furnishings—   29
But true it is, from France there comes a power   30
Into this scattered kingdom, who already, ·   31
Wise in our negligence, have secret feet   32
In some of our best ports and are at point   33
To show their open banner. Now to you:
If on my credit you dare build so far   35
To make your speed to Dover, you shall find
Some that will thank you, making just report   37
Of how unnatural and bemadding sorrow
The King hath cause to plain.   39
I am a gentleman of blood and breeding,
And from some knowledge and assurance offer
This office to you.   42

16 **outjest** exorcise or relieve by jesting   18 **upon . . . note** on the strength of what I know (about you)   19 **Commend . . . thing** entrust a precious undertaking   22 **that** whom. **stars** destinies   23 **no less** i.e., no other than servants   24 **speculations** scouts, spies   25 **Intelligent of** supplying intelligence pertinent to   26 **snuffs** quarrels. **packings** intrigues   29 **furnishings** outward shows   30 **power** army   31 **scattered** divided   32 **Wise in** taking advantage of. **feet** i.e., foothold   33 **at point** ready   35 **credit** trustworthiness. **so far** so far as   37 **making just report** for making an accurate report   39 **plain** complain   42 **office** assignment

GENTLEMAN
  I will talk further with you.
KENT   No, do not.
  For confirmation that I am much more
  Than my outwall, open this purse and take   45
  What it contains. [*He gives a purse and a ring.*] If
    you shall see Cordelia—
  As fear not but you shall—show her this ring,
  And she will tell you who that fellow is   48
  That yet you do not know. Fie on this storm!
  I will go seek the King.
GENTLEMAN
  Give me your hand. Have you no more to say?
KENT
  Few words, but, to effect, more than all yet: 52
  That when we have found the King—in which your
    pain   53
  That way, I'll this—he that first lights on him   54
  Holla the other.   *Exeunt* [*separately*].

                        Scene Two
              [AN OPEN PLACE, AS BEFORE.]

  Storm still. Enter LEAR *and* FOOL.

LEAR
  Blow, winds, and crack your cheeks! Rage, blow!
  You cataracts and hurricanoes, spout   2
  Till you have drenched our steeples, drowned the
    cocks!   3
  You sulfurous and thought-executing fires,   4
  Vaunt-couriers of oak-cleaving thunderbolts,   5
  Singe my white head! And thou, all-shaking
    thunder,

---

45 outwall exterior appearance **48 fellow** i.e., Kent **52 to effect** in
their consequences **53–54 in which . . . this** in which task, you search
in that direction while I go this way
2 hurricanoes waterspouts **3 drenched** drowned. **cocks** weather-
cocks **4 thought-executing** acting with the quickness of thought. **fires**
i.e., lightning **5 Vaunt-couriers** forerunners

Strike flat the thick rotundity o' the world!
Crack nature's molds, all germens spill at once   8
That makes ingrateful man!

FOOL   O nuncle, court holy water in a dry house is   10
better than this rainwater out o' door. Good nuncle,
in, ask thy daughters' blessing. Here's a night pities   12
neither wise men nor fools.

LEAR

Rumble thy bellyful! Spit, fire! Spout, rain!
Nor rain, wind, thunder, fire, are my daughters.
I tax not you, you elements, with unkindness;   16
I never gave you kingdom, called you children.
You owe me no subscription. Then let fall   18
Your horrible pleasure. Here I stand your slave,
A poor, infirm, weak, and despised old man.
But yet I call you servile ministers,   21
That will with two pernicious daughters join
Your high-engendered battles 'gainst a head   23
So old and white as this. O, ho! 'Tis foul!

FOOL   He that has a house to put 's head in has a good
    headpiece.   26
      The codpiece that will house   27
        Before the head has any,   28
      The head and he shall louse;   29
        So beggars marry many.   30
      The man that makes his toe   31
        What he his heart should make   32
      Shall of a corn cry woe,   33
        And turn his sleep to wake.   34

---

8 nature's molds the molds in which nature makes men. **germens** germs,
seeds. **spill** destroy   **10 court holy water** flattery   **12 ask . . . blessing**
(For Lear to do so would be to acknowledge their authority.)   **16 tax**
accuse. **with** of   **18 subscription** allegiance   **21 ministers** agents
23 high-engendered battles battalions engendered in the heavens   **26 headpiece** (1) helmetlike covering for the head (2) head for
common sense   **27–34 The codpiece . . . wake** i.e., a man who houses
his genitals in a sexual embrace before he provides a roof for his head
can expect lice-infested penury; and one who elevates what is base
above what is noble (as Lear has done with his daughters) can expect
misery and wakeful tossing also. If he values the toe more than the
heart, his reward will be that the toe will cause him suffering. **codpiece**
covering for the genitals worn by men with their close-fitting hose; here
representing the genitals themselves

For there was never yet fair woman but she made   35
mouths in a glass.   36

LEAR
No, I will be the pattern of all patience;
I will say nothing.

Enter KENT, [*disguised as* CAIUS].

KENT   Who's there?
FOOL   Marry, here's grace and a codpiece; that's a   40
wise man and a fool.
KENT
Alas, sir, are you here? Things that love night
Love not such nights as these. The wrathful skies
Gallow the very wanderers of the dark   44
And make them keep their caves. Since I was man,   45
Such sheets of fire, such bursts of horrid thunder,
Such groans of roaring wind and rain I never
Remember to have heard. Man's nature cannot
carry   48
Th' affliction nor the fear.
LEAR   Let the great gods,   49
That keep this dreadful pother o'er our heads,   50
Find out their enemies now. Tremble, thou wretch,   51
That hast within thee undivulgèd crimes
Unwhipped of justice! Hide thee, thou bloody
hand,   53
Thou perjured, and thou simular of virtue   54
That art incestuous! Caitiff, to pieces shake,   55
That under covert and convenient seeming   56
Has practiced on man's life! Close pent-up guilts,   57

35–36 made . . . glass practiced making attractive faces in a mirror   **40 Marry** (An oath, originally "by the Virgin Mary.") **grace** royal grace. **codpiece** (Often prominent in the Fool's costume.)   **44 Gallow** i.e., gally, frighten. **wanderers of the dark** wild beasts   **45 keep** occupy, remain inside   **48 carry** endure   **49 affliction** physical affliction   **50 pother** hubbub, turmoil   **51 Find . . . now** i.e., expose criminals (by their display of fear)   **53 of** by   **54 perjured** perjurer. **simular** pretender   **55 Caitiff** wretch   **56 seeming** hypocrisy   **57 practiced on** plotted against. **Close** secret

Rive your concealing continents and cry   58
These dreadful summoners grace! I am a man   59
More sinned against than sinning.
KENT   Alack, bareheaded?
  Gracious my lord, hard by here is a hovel;
  Some friendship will it lend you 'gainst the tempest.
  Repose you there while I to this hard house—
  More harder than the stones whereof 'tis raised,
  Which even but now, demanding after you,   65
  Denied me to come in—return and force
  Their scanted courtesy.
LEAR   My wits begin to turn.   67
  Come on, my boy. How dost, my boy? Art cold?
  I am cold myself.—Where is this straw, my fellow?
  The art of our necessities is strange,
  And can make vile things precious. Come, your
        hovel.—
  Poor fool and knave, I have one part in my heart
  That's sorry yet for thee.
FOOL [Sings]
      "He that has and a little tiny wit,   74
          With heigh-ho, the wind and the rain,
      Must make content with his fortunes fit,
          Though the rain it raineth every day."   77
LEAR
  True, boy.—Come, bring us to this hovel.
                                        Exit [with KENT].
FOOL   This is a brave night to cool a courtesan. I'll   79
  speak a prophecy ere I go:

  When priests are more in word than matter;   81
  When brewers mar their malt with water;   82

---

58 Rive split. **continents** covering, containers   **58–59 cry . . . grace** pray
for mercy at the hands of the officers of divine justice. (A *summoner* was
the police officer of an ecclesiastical court.)   **65 Which** i.e., the occu-
pants of the house. **demanding** inquiring   **67 scanted** stinted   **74–
77** (Derived from the popular song that Feste sings in *Twelfth
Night*)   **79 This . . . courtesan** i.e., this wretched night might at least
damp the fires of lust(?) **brave** fine   **81 more . . . matter** better in speech
than in substance or Gospel truth. (This and the next three lines satirize
the present state of affairs.)   **82 mar** adulterate

When nobles are their tailors' tutors, 83
No heretics burned but wenches' suitors, 84
Then shall the realm of Albion 85
Come to great confusion.

When every case in law is right, 87
No squire in debt, nor no poor knight;
When slanders do not live in tongues,
Nor cutpurses come not to throngs;
When usurers tell their gold i' the field, 91
And bawds and whores do churches build,
Then comes the time, who lives to see 't,
That going shall be used with feet. 94

This prophecy Merlin shall make, for I live before his 95
time. *Exit*.

Scene Three
[GLOUCESTER'S HOUSE.]

Enter GLOUCESTER *and* EDMUND [*with lights*].

GLOUCESTER Alack, alack, Edmund, I like not this
unnatural dealing. When I desired their leave that I
might pity him, they took from me the use of mine 3
own house, charged me on pain of perpetual displeasure neither to speak of him, entreat for him, or
any way sustain him.
EDMUND Most savage and unnatural!
GLOUCESTER Go to; say you nothing. There is division between the Dukes, and a worse matter than

83 are . . . tutors i.e., know more than their tailors about fashion 84 No . . . suitors i.e., when heresy is a matter not of religious faith
but of perjured lovers (whose burning is not at the stake but in catching
venereal disease) 85 realm of Albion kingdom of England. (The Fool is
parodying a pseudo-Chaucerian prophetic verse.) 87 right just. (This
and the next five lines offer a utopian vision of justice and charity that
will never be realized in this corrupted world.) 91 tell count. i' the field
i.e., openly, without fear 94 going . . . feet walking will be done on
foot 95 Merlin (A great wizard of the court of King Arthur, who came
after Lear.)
3 pity be merciful to, relieve

that. I have received a letter this night; 'tis dangerous
to be spoken; I have locked the letter in my closet.   11
These injuries the King now bears will be revenged
home; there is part of a power already footed. We   13
must incline to the King. I will look him and privily   14
relieve him. Go you and maintain talk with the Duke,
that my charity be not of him perceived. If he ask for   16
me, I am ill and gone to bed. If I die for 't, as no less
is threatened me, the King my old master must be
relieved. There is strange things toward, Edmund.   19
Pray you, be careful.   *Exit.*

EDMUND
This courtesy forbid thee shall the Duke   21
Instantly know, and of that letter too.
This seems a fair deserving, and must draw me   23
That which my father loses—no less than all.
The younger rises when the old doth fall.   *Exit.*

Scene Four
[AN OPEN PLACE. BEFORE A HOVEL.]

Enter LEAR, KENT [*disguised as* CAIUS], *and* FOOL.

KENT
Here is the place, my lord. Good my lord, enter.
The tyranny of the open night's too rough
For nature to endure.   *Storm still.*
LEAR   Let me alone.
KENT
Good my lord, enter here.
LEAR   Wilt break my heart?   4
KENT
I had rather break mine own. Good my lord, enter.

11 **closet** private chamber   13 **home** thoroughly.   **power** armed force.
footed landed   14 **incline to** side with.   **look** look for   16 **of** by   19 **to-**
ward impending   21 **courtesy forbid thee** kindness (to Lear) which you
were forbidden to show   23 **fair deserving** meritorious action
4 **break my heart** i.e., cause me anguish by relieving my physical wants
and thus forcing me to confront again my *greater malady* (3.4.8)

LEAR
Thou think'st 'tis much that this contentious storm
Invades us to the skin. So 'tis to thee,
But where the greater malady is fixed   8
The lesser is scarce felt. Thou'dst shun a bear,
But if thy flight lay toward the roaring sea
Thou'dst meet the bear i' the mouth. When the
   mind's free,   11
The body's delicate. This tempest in my mind   12
Doth from my senses take all feeling else
Save what beats there. Filial ingratitude!
Is it not as this mouth should tear this hand   15
For lifting food to 't? But I will punish home.   16
No, I will weep no more. In such a night
To shut me out? Pour on; I will endure.
In such a night as this? O Regan, Goneril,
Your old kind father, whose frank heart gave all—   20
O, that way madness lies; let me shun that!
No more of that.

KENT   Good my lord, enter here.

LEAR
Prithee, go in thyself; seek thine own ease.
This tempest will not give me leave to ponder   24
On things would hurt me more. But I'll go in.   25
[*To the* FOOL.] In, boy; go first. You houseless
   poverty—
Nay, get thee in. I'll pray, and then I'll sleep.
                     Exit [FOOL *into the hovel*].
Poor naked wretches, wheresoe'er you are,
That bide the pelting of this pitiless storm,   29
How shall your houseless heads and unfed sides,
Your looped and windowed raggedness, defend you   31
From seasons such as these? O, I have ta'en

---

8 fixed lodged, implanted   **11 i' the mouth** i.e., head-on. **free** free of anxiety   **12 The body's delicate** i.e., the body's importunate needs can assert themselves   **15 as** as if   **16 home** fully   **20 frank** liberal   **24 will . . . leave** i.e., keeps me too preoccupied   **25 things would** things (such as filial ingratitude) that would   **29 bide** endure   **31 looped and windowed** full of openings like windows and loopholes

Too little care of this! Take physic, pomp;   33
Expose thyself to feel what wretches feel,
That thou mayst shake the superflux to them   35
And show the heavens more just.

EDGAR [*Within*] Fathom and half, fathom and half!   37
Poor Tom!

Enter FOOL [*from the hovel*].

FOOL   Come not in here, nuncle; here's a spirit. Help
me, help me!

KENT   Give me thy hand. Who's there?

FOOL   A spirit, a spirit! He says his name's poor Tom.

KENT
What art thou that dost grumble there i' the straw?
Come forth.

Enter EDGAR [*disguised as a madman*].

EDGAR   Away! The foul fiend follows me! Through the   45
sharp hawthorn blows the cold wind. Hum! Go to   46
thy bed and warm thee.

LEAR   Didst thou give all to thy daughters? And art
thou come to this?

EDGAR   Who gives anything to poor Tom? Whom the
foul fiend hath led through fire and through flame,
through ford and whirlpool, o'er bog and quagmire;
that hath laid knives under his pillow and halters in   53
his pew, set ratsbane by his porridge, made him   54
proud of heart, to ride on a bay trotting horse over   55
four-inched bridges to course his own shadow for a   56
traitor. Bless thy five wits! Tom's a-cold. O, do de,   57

---

33 **Take physic, pomp** cure yourself, O distempered great ones   35 **superflux** superfluity (with suggestion of *flux*, "bodily discharge," intro-
duced by *physic*, "purgative," in 3.4.33)   37 **Fathom and half** (A sailor's
cry while taking soundings, hence appropriate to a deluge.)   45 **Away**
keep away   45–46 **Through . . . wind** (Possibly a line from a ballad.)   53–54 **knives, halters, ratsbane** (Tempting means to commit sui-
cide and hence be damned.)   54 **pew** gallery, place (?)   **porridge** soup
55–56 **over four-inched bridges** i.e., taking mad risks on narrow bridges
with the devil's assistance   56 **course** chase. **for** as   57 **five wits** either
the five senses, or common wit, imagination, fantasy, estimation, and
memory

do de, do de. Bless thee from whirlwinds, star-blast- 58
ing, and taking! Do poor Tom some charity, whom 59
the foul fiend vexes. There could I have him now— 60
and there—and there again—and there. *Storm still.*

LEAR
Has his daughters brought him to this pass? 62
Couldst thou save nothing? Wouldst thou give 'em
all?

FOOL   Nay, he reserved a blanket, else we had been all 64
shamed.

LEAR
Now, all the plagues that in the pendulous air 66
Hang fated o'er men's faults light on thy daughters! 67

KENT   He hath no daughters, sir.

LEAR
Death, traitor! Nothing could have subdued nature
To such a lowness but his unkind daughters.
Is it the fashion that discarded fathers
Should have thus little mercy on their flesh? 72
Judicious punishment! 'Twas this flesh begot 73
Those pelican daughters. 74

EDGAR   Pillicock sat on Pillicock Hill. Alow, alow, loo, 75
loo!

FOOL   This cold night will turn us all to fools and
madmen.

EDGAR   Take heed o' the foul fiend. Obey thy parents;
keep thy word's justice; swear not; commit not with 80
man's sworn spouse; set not thy sweet heart on
proud array. Tom's a-cold.

58–59 star-blasting being blighted by influence of the stars   **59 taking**
pestilence; or witchcraft   **60 There** (Perhaps he slaps at lice and other
vermin as if they were devils.)   **62 pass** miserable plight   **64 reserved a
blanket** kept a wrap (for his nakedness)   **66 pendulous** suspended, overhanging   **67 fated** having the power of fate   **72 have . . . flesh** i.e.,
punish themselves, as Edgar has done (probably with pins and thorns
stuck in his flesh)   **73 Judicious** appropriate to the crime   **74 pelican**
greedy. (Young pelicans supposedly smote their parents and fed on the
blood of their mothers' breasts.)   **75 Pillicock** (From an old rhyme, suggested by the sound of *pelican. Pillicock* in nursery rhyme seems to
have been a euphemism for penis, *Pillicock Hill* for the Mount of
Venus.)   **80 justice** integrity. **commit not** i.e., do not commit adultery.
(Edgar's mad catechism contains fragments of the Ten Command-
ments.)

LEAR   What hast thou been?

EDGAR   A servingman, proud in heart and mind, that   84
curled my hair, wore gloves in my cap, served the   85
lust of my mistress' heart, and did the act of
darkness with her; swore as many oaths as I spake
words, and broke them in the sweet face of heaven.
One that slept in the contriving of lust and waked to
do it. Wine loved I deeply, dice dearly, and in woman
out-paramoured the Turk. False of heart, light of ear,   91
bloody of hand; hog in sloth, fox in stealth, wolf in
greediness, dog in madness, lion in prey. Let not the   93
creaking of shoes nor the rustling of silks betray thy
poor heart to woman. Keep thy foot out of brothels,
thy hand out of plackets, thy pen from lenders'   96
books, and defy the foul fiend. Still through the   97
hawthorn blows the cold wind; says suum, mun,   98
nonny. Dolphin my boy, boy, sessa! Let him trot by.   99
                                        Storm still.

LEAR   Thou wert better in a grave than to answer with
thy uncovered body this extremity of the skies. Is
man no more than this? Consider him well. Thou
ow'st the worm no silk, the beast no hide, the sheep   103
no wool, the cat no perfume. Ha! Here's three on 's   104
are sophisticated. Thou art the thing itself; unaccom-   105
modated man is no more but such a poor, bare,   106
forked animal as thou art. Off, off, you lendings!
Come, unbutton here.   [*Tearing off his clothes.*]

---

84 servingman either a "servant" in the language of courtly love or an
ambitious servant in a household   **85 gloves** i.e., my mistress's
favors   **91 out-paramoured the Turk** outdid the Sultan in keeping mis-
tresses.   **light of ear** foolishly credulous; frivolous   **93 prey** prey-
ing   **96 plackets** slits in skirts or petticoats   **96–97 thy pen . . . books**
i.e., do not sign a contract for a loan   **98–99 suum . . . nonny** (Imitative
of the wind?)   **99 Dolphin my boy** (A slang phrase, or bit of song?)   **sessa**
i.e., away, cease (?)   **103 ow'st** have borrowed from   **104 cat** civet
cat   **105 sophisticated** clad in the trappings of civilized life; adulter-
ated   **105–106 unaccommodated** unfurnished with the trappings of civilization

FOOL Prithee, nuncle, be contented; 'tis a naughty   109
night to swim in. Now a little fire in a wild field were   110
like an old lecher's heart—a small spark, all the rest
on 's body cold.   112

Enter GLOUCESTER, *with a torch.*

Look, here comes a walking fire.
EDGAR This is the foul fiend Flibbertigibbet! He be-   114
gins at curfew and walks till the first cock; he gives   115
the web and the pin, squinnies the eye and makes the   116
harelip, mildews the white wheat, and hurts the poor   117
creature of earth.
　　Swithold footed thrice the 'old;   119
　　He met the nightmare and her ninefold;   120
　　　Bid her alight,
　　　And her troth plight,
　　And aroint thee, witch, aroint thee!   123
KENT How fares Your Grace?
LEAR What's he?
KENT Who's there? What is 't you seek?
GLOUCESTER What are you there? Your names?
EDGAR Poor Tom, that eats the swimming frog, the
toad, the tadpole, the wall newt and the water; that in   129
the fury of his heart, when the foul fiend rages, eats
cow dung for salads, swallows the old rat and the
ditch-dog, drinks the green mantle of the standing   132

109 naughty bad　**110 wild** barren, uncultivated　**112 on 's** of his
114 Flibbertigibbet (A devil from Elizabethan folklore whose name appears in Samuel Harsnett's *Declaration* of 1603 and elsewhere.)
115 first cock midnight　**116 web and the pin** cataract of the
eye.　**squinnies** causes to squint　**117 white** ripening　**119 Swithold**
Saint Withold, a famous Anglo-Saxon exorcist, who here provides defense against the *nightmare,* or demon thought to afflict sleepers, by
commanding the nightmare to *alight,* i.e., stop riding over the sleeper,
and *plight* her *troth,* i.e., vow true faith, promise to do no harm. **footed
. . . 'old** thrice traversed the wold (tract of hilly upland)　**120 ninefold**
nine offspring (with possible pun on *fold, foal*).　**123 aroint thee** begone　**129 water** i.e., water newt　**132 ditch-dog** i.e., dead dog in a
ditch. **mantle** scum. **standing** stagnant

pool; who is whipped from tithing to tithing and   133
stock-punished and imprisoned; who hath had three   134
suits to his back, six shirts to his body,   135
    Horse to ride, and weapon to wear;
    But mice and rats and such small deer   137
    Have been Tom's food for seven long year.
Beware my follower. Peace, Smulkin! Peace, thou
fiend!   139

GLOUCESTER
What, hath Your Grace no better company?

EDGAR   The Prince of Darkness is a gentleman. Modo   141
he's called, and Mahu.   142

GLOUCESTER
Our flesh and blood, my lord, is grown so vile
That it doth hate what gets it.   144

EDGAR   Poor Tom's a-cold.

GLOUCESTER
Go in with me. My duty cannot suffer   146
T' obey in all your daughters' hard commands.
Though their injunction be to bar my doors
And let this tyrannous night take hold upon you,
Yet have I ventured to come seek you out
And bring you where both fire and food is ready.

LEAR
First let me talk with this philosopher.
[*To* EDGAR.] What is the cause of thunder?

KENT   Good my lord,
Take his offer. Go into the house.

LEAR
I'll talk a word with this same learnèd Theban.   155
[*To* EDGAR.] What is your study?   156

EDGAR   How to prevent the fiend, and to kill vermin.   157

---

133 **tithing to tithing** i.e., one ward or parish to another   134 **stock-punished** placed in the stocks   134–135 **three suits** (Like the menial servant at 2.2.16.)   137 **deer** animals   139 **follower** familiar, attendant devil   139, 141–142 **Smulkin, Modo, Mahu** (Shakespeare found these Elizabethan devils in Samuel Harsnett's *Declaration*.)   144 **gets** begets   146 **suffer** permit me   155 **Theban** i.e., one deeply versed in "philosophy" or natural science   156 **study** special competence   157 **prevent** thwart

LEAR   Let me ask you one word in private.
                              [LEAR *and* EDGAR *talk apart.*]
KENT [*To* GLOUCESTER]
   Importune him once more to go, my lord.
   His wits begin t' unsettle.
GLOUCESTER   Canst thou blame him?
                                          Storm still.
   His daughters seek his death. Ah, that good Kent!
   He said it would be thus, poor banished man.
   Thou sayest the King grows mad; I'll tell thee,
      friend,
   I am almost mad myself. I had a son,
   Now outlawed from my blood; he sought my life   165
   But lately, very late. I loved him, friend,
   No father his son dearer. True to tell thee,
   The grief hath crazed my wits. What a night's
      this!—
   I do beseech Your Grace—
LEAR   O, cry you mercy, sir.   170
   [*To* EDGAR.] Noble philosopher, your company.
EDGAR   Tom's a-cold.
GLOUCESTER [*To Edgar*]   In, fellow, there, into the
   hovel. Keep thee warm.
LEAR [*Starting toward the hovel*]
   Come, let's in all.
KENT   This way, my lord.
LEAR   With him!
   I will keep still with my philosopher.
KENT [*To* GLOUCESTER]
   Good my lord, soothe him. Let him take the fellow.   177
GLOUCESTER [*To* KENT]   Take him you on.   178
KENT [*To* EDGAR]
   Sirrah, come on. Go along with us.
LEAR   Come, good Athenian.   180
GLOUCESTER   No words, no words! Hush.

---

165 outlawed . . . blood exiled from kinship with me and legally outlawed   **170 cry you mercy** I beg your pardon   **177 soothe** humor
178 Take . . . on i.e., take Edgar along with you   **180 Athenian** i.e.,
philosopher

EDGAR
    Child Rowland to the dark tower came;   182
    His word was still, "Fie, foh, and fum,   183
      I smell the blood of a British man."   *Exeunt.*   184

Scene Five
[GLOUCESTER'S HOUSE.]

Enter CORNWALL *and* EDMUND [*with a letter*].

CORNWALL   I will have my revenge ere I depart his
house.

EDMUND   How, my lord, I may be censured, that   3
nature thus gives way to loyalty, something fears me   4
to think of.

CORNWALL   I now perceive it was not altogether your
brother's evil disposition made him seek his death,   7
but a provoking merit set awork by a reprovable   8
badness in himself.   9

EDMUND   How malicious is my fortune that I must
repent to be just! This is the letter he spoke of, which   11
approves him an intelligent party to the advantages   12
of France. O heavens! That this treason were not, or
not I the detector!

CORNWALL   Go with me to the Duchess.

EDMUND   If the matter of this paper be certain, you
have mighty business in hand.

CORNWALL   True or false, it hath made thee Earl of
Gloucester. Seek out where thy father is, that he
may be ready for our apprehension.   20

---

182 Child Rowland, etc. (Probably a fragment of a ballad about the hero
of the Charlemagne legends. A *child* is a candidate for
knighthood.)   **183 word** watchword. **still** always   **183–184 Fie . . . man**
(This is essentially what the Giant says in "Jack, the Giant Killer.")
3 censured judged   **4 something fears** somewhat frightens   **7 his** i.e.,
his father's   **8–9 a provoking . . . himself** i.e., the badness of Gloucester
which deserved punishment, set awork by an evil propensity in Edgar
himself   **11 to be just** that I am righteous in my duty (to Cornwall)   **12 approves** proves. **an intelligent . . . advantages** a spy in the
service   **20 apprehension** arrest

EDMUND [*Aside*]   If I find him comforting the King, it   21
   will stuff his suspicion more fully.—I will persevere   22
   in my course of loyalty, though the conflict be sore
   between that and my blood.   24
CORNWALL   I will lay trust upon thee, and thou shalt
   find a dearer father in my love.   *Exeunt*.

Scene Six
[WITHIN A BUILDING ON GLOUCESTER'S ESTATE, NEAR OR
ADJOINING HIS HOUSE; OR PART OF THE HOUSE ITSELF. SEE
3.4.146–154. CUSHIONS ARE PROVIDED, AND STOOLS.]

Enter KENT [*disguised as* CAIUS] *and* GLOUCESTER.

GLOUCESTER   Here is better than the open air; take it
   thankfully. I will piece out the comfort with what   2
   addition I can. I will not be long from you.
KENT   All the power of his wits have given way to his
   impatience. The gods reward your kindness!   5
                                    Exit [GLOUCESTER].

Enter LEAR, EDGAR [*as poor Tom*], *and* FOOL.

EDGAR   Frateretto calls me, and tells me Nero is an   6
   angler in the lake of darkness. Pray, innocent, and   7
   beware the foul fiend.
FOOL   Prithee, nuncle, tell me whether a madman be a
   gentleman or a yeoman?
LEAR   A king, a king!
FOOL   No, he's a yeoman that has a gentleman to his
   son; for he's a mad yeoman that sees his son a
   gentleman before him.

---

21 him i.e., Gloucester. **comforting** offering aid and comfort to, helping   **22 his** i.e., Cornwall's or, *his suspicion* may mean "suspicion of
him, Gloucester"   **24 blood** family loyalty, filial instincts
2 piece eke   **5 impatience** rage, inability to endure more   **6 Frateretto**
(Another of the fiends from Harsnett.)   **6–7 Nero is an angler** (See
Chaucer's "Monk's Tale," ll. 485–486; in Rabelais, 2.30, Nero is de-
scribed as a fiddler and Trajan an angler in the underworld.)   **7 innocent**
simpleton, fool (i.e., the Fool)

LEAR
  To have a thousand with red burning spits
  Come hizzing in upon 'em—   16
EDGAR   The foul fiend bites my back.
FOOL   He's mad that trusts in the tameness of a wolf, a
  horse's health, a boy's love, or a whore's oath.

LEAR
  It shall be done; I will arraign them straight.
  [*To* EDGAR.] Come, sit thou here, most learnèd
      justicer.   21
  [*To the* FOOL.] Thou, sapient sir, sit here. Now, you
      she-foxes!
EDGAR   Look where he stands and glares! Want'st   23
  thou eyes at trial, madam?   24
  [*Sings.*] "Come o'er the burn, Bessy, to me—"   25
FOOL [*Sings.*]
          Her boat hath a leak,
          And she must not speak
      Why she dares not come over to thee.
EDGAR   The foul fiend haunts poor Tom in the voice of
  a nightingale. Hoppedance cries in Tom's belly for   30
  two white herring. Croak not, black angel; I have no   31
  food for thee.
KENT
  How do you, sir? Stand you not so amazed.   33
  Will you lie down and rest upon the cushions?
LEAR
  I'll see their trial first. Bring in their evidence.   35
  [*To* EDGAR.] Thou robèd man of justice, take thy
      place;   36

---

16 hizzing hissing   **21 justicer** judge, justice   **23 he** (Probably one of
Edgar's devils; or Lear.)   **23–24 Want'st . . . trial** do you lack spectators at your trial, or do you want to have them   **25 Come . . . me** (First
line of a ballad by William Birche, 1558. A *burn* is a brook. The Fool
makes a ribald reply, in which the *leaky boat* suggests her easy virtue or
perhaps her menstrual period.)   **30 Hoppedance** (Harsnett mentions
"Hoberdidance.")   **31 white** unsmoked (contrasted with *black angel*).
Croak (Refers to the rumbling in Edgar's stomach denoting hunger.)   **33 amazed** bewildered   **35 their evidence** the witnesses against
them   **36 robèd man** i.e., Edgar, with his blanket

[*To the* FOOL.] And thou, his yokefellow of equity,   37
Bench by his side. [*To* KENT.] You are o' the
commission;   38
Sit you too.   [*They sit.*]

EDGAR   Let us deal justly.   [*He sings.*]
Sleepest or wakest thou, jolly shepherd?
Thy sheep be in the corn;   42
And for one blast of thy minikin mouth,   43
Thy sheep shall take no harm.   44
Purr the cat is gray.   45

LEAR   Arraign her first; 'tis Goneril, I here take my
oath before this honorable assembly, kicked the poor   47
King her father.

FOOL   Come hither, mistress. Is your name Goneril?

LEAR   She cannot deny it.

FOOL   Cry you mercy, I took you for a joint stool.   51

LEAR
And here's another, whose warped looks proclaim
What store her heart is made on. Stop her there!   53
Arms, arms, sword, fire! Corruption in the place!   54
False justicer, why hast thou let her scape?

EDGAR   Bless thy five wits!

KENT
O, pity! Sir, where is the patience now
That you so oft have boasted to retain?

EDGAR [*Aside*]
My tears begin to take his part so much
They mar my counterfeiting.

---

37 yokefellow of equity partner in the law   **38 Bench** take your place on
the bench. **o' the commission** one commissioned to be a justice   **42 corn**
grain field   **43–44 And . . . harm** (This may mean that if the shepherd
recalls his sheep by piping to them before they consume the grainfield,
they will not be put in the pound.)   **43 minikin** dainty, pretty   **45 Purr
the cat** (A devil or familiar from Harsnett; see 3.4.114, note. *Purr* may be
the sound the familiar makes.)   **47 kicked** who kicked   **51 joint stool**
low stool made by a joiner, or maker of furniture with joined parts.
(Proverbially the phrase "I took . . . stool" meant "I beg your pardon
for failing to notice you." The reference is also presumably to a real
stool onstage.)   **53 store** material. **on** of   **54 Corruption in the place** i.e.,
there is iniquity or bribery in this court

LEAR   The little dogs and all,
   Tray, Blanch, and Sweetheart, see, they bark at me.
EDGAR   Tom will throw his head at them. Avaunt, you   63
   curs!
      Be thy mouth or black or white,
      Tooth that poisons if it bite,
      Mastiff, greyhound, mongrel grim,
      Hound or spaniel, brach or lym,   68
      Or bobtail tike or trundle-tail,   69
      Tom will make him weep and wail;
      For, with throwing thus my head,
      Dogs leapt the hatch, and all are fled.   72
   Do de, de, de. Sessa! Come, march to wakes and   73
   fairs and market towns. Poor Tom, thy horn is dry.   74
LEAR   Then let them anatomize Regan; see what   75
   breeds about her heart. Is there any cause in nature
   that make these hard hearts? [*To* EDGAR.] You, sir, I
   entertain for one of my hundred; only I do not like   78
   the fashion of your garments. You will say they are
   Persian; but let them be changed.   80
KENT
   Now, good my lord, lie here and rest awhile.
LEAR   [*Lying on cushions*] Make no noise, make no
   noise. Draw the curtains. So, so. We'll go to supper i' 83
   the morning.   [*He sleeps.*]
   FOOL   And I'll go to bed at noon.

   Enter GLOUCESTER.

GLOUCESTER
   Come hither, friend. Where is the King my master?
KENT
   Here, sir, but trouble him not. His wits are gone.

63 throw his head at i.e., threaten   **68 brach** hound bitch. **lym** blood-
hound   **69 bobtail** short-tailed small dog, cur. **trundle-tail** long-tailed
dog   **72 hatch** lower half of a divided door   **73 Sessa** i.e., away, cease
(?) **wakes** (Here, parish festivals.)   **74 horn** i.e., horn bottle used by
beggars to beg for drinks   **75 anatomize** dissect   **78 entertain** take into
my service   **80 Persian** i.e., gorgeous intricate attire   **83 curtains** bed-
curtains. (They presumably exist only in Lear's mad imagination.)

GLOUCESTER
　Good friend, I prithee, take him in thy arms.
　I have o'erheard a plot of death upon him.　　　　　89
　There is a litter ready; lay him in 't
　And drive toward Dover, friend, where thou shalt
　　meet
　Both welcome and protection. Take up thy master.
　If thou shouldst dally half an hour, his life,
　With thine and all that offer to defend him,
　Stand in assurèd loss. Take up, take up,　　　　　95
　And follow me, that will to some provision　　　　96
　Give thee quick conduct.

KENT　　　　　　　　　　Oppressèd nature sleeps.　97
　This rest might yet have balmed thy broken sinews,　98
　Which, if convenience will not allow,　　　　　99
　Stand in hard cure. [*To the* FOOL.] Come, help to
　　bear thy master.　　　　　　　　　　100
　Thou must not stay behind.　　[*They pick up* LEAR.]

GLOUCESTER　　　　　　　　Come, come, away!
　　　　　　　　Exeunt [*all but* EDGAR].

EDGAR
　When we our betters see bearing our woes,　　　　102
　We scarcely think our miseries our foes.　　　　103
　Who alone suffers suffers most i' the mind,　　　104
　Leaving free things and happy shows behind;　　　105
　But then the mind much sufferance doth o'erskip　106
　When grief hath mates, and bearing fellowship.　107
　How light and portable my pain seems now,　　　108
　When that which makes me bend makes the King
　　bow—
　He childed as I fathered. Tom, away!　　　　　110

89 upon against **95 Stand . . . loss** will assuredly be lost　**96 provision** supplies; or, means of providing for safety　**97 conduct** guidance　**98 balmed** cured, healed. **sinews** nerves　**99 convenience** fortunate circumstances　**100 Stand . . . cure** will be hard to cure　**102 our woes** woes like ours　**103 our foes** i.e., hostile toward us alone (since we see how human suffering afflicts even the great)　**104 Who . . . mind** i.e., he who suffers alone suffers mental agonies greater than those who perceive they have companions in misery　**105 free** carefree. **shows** scenes　**106 sufferance** suffering　**107 bearing fellowship** tribulation (has) company　**108 portable** bearable, endurable　**110 He . . . fathered** i.e., he suffering cruelty from his children as I from my father

Mark the high noises, and thyself bewray   111
When false opinion, whose wrong thoughts defile
    thee,
In thy just proof repeals and reconciles thee.   113
What will hap more tonight, safe scape the King! 114
Lurk, lurk.   [*Exit.*]

Scene Seven
[GLOUCESTER'S HOUSE.]

Enter CORNWALL, REGAN, GONERIL, *Bastard* [ED-
MUND], *and* SERVANTS.

CORNWALL [*To* GONERIL]   Post speedily to my lord   1
    your husband; show him this letter. [*He gives a
    letter.*] The army of France is landed.—Seek out the
    traitor Gloucester.   [*Exeunt some* SERVANTS.]
REGAN   Hang him instantly.
GONERIL   Pluck out his eyes.
CORNWALL   Leave him to my displeasure. Edmund,
    keep you our sister company. The revenges we are   8
    bound to take upon your traitorous father are not fit 9
    for your beholding. Advise the Duke, where you are   10
    going, to a most festinate preparation; we are bound 11
    to the like. Our posts shall be swift and intelligent 12
    betwixt us. Farewell, dear sister; farewell, my lord of 13
    Gloucester.   14

Enter steward [OSWALD].

---

111 Mark . . . noises i.e., observe what is being said about those in high
places, or about great events. bewray reveal   113 In . . . thee upon your
being proved innocent recalls you and restores you to favor   114 What
. . . King whatever else happens tonight, may the King escape safely
1 Post speedily hurry   8 sister i.e., sister-in-law, Goneril   9 bound
intending; obliged   10 the Duke i.e., Albany   11 festinate hasty. are
bound intend, are committed   12 posts messengers. intelligent serviceable in bearing information, knowledgeable   13–14 my . . . Gloucester
i.e., Edmund, the recipient now of his father's forfeited estate and title.
(Two lines later, Oswald uses the same title to refer to Edmund's father.)

How now? Where's the King?
OSWALD
My lord of Gloucester hath conveyed him hence.
Some five- or six-and-thirty of his knights,   17
Hot questrists after him, met him at gate,   18
Who, with some other of the lord's dependents,   19
Are gone with him toward Dover, where they boast
To have well-armèd friends.
CORNWALL   Get horses for your mistress.
                                        [*Exit* OSWALD.]
GONERIL   Farewell, sweet lord, and sister.
CORNWALL
Edmund, farewell.   *Exeunt* [GONERIL *and* EDMUND].
                    Go seek the traitor Gloucester.
Pinion him like a thief; bring him before us.
                                        [*Exeunt* SERVANTS.]
Though well we may not pass upon his life   26
Without the form of justice, yet our power
Shall do a court'sy to our wrath, which men   28
May blame but not control.

Enter GLOUCESTER, *and* SERVANTS [*leading him*].

                            Who's there? The traitor?
REGAN   Ingrateful fox! 'Tis he.
CORNWALL   Bind fast his corky arms.   31
GLOUCESTER
What means Your Graces? Good my friends, consider
You are my guests. Do me no foul play, friends.
CORNWALL
Bind him, I say.   [SERVANTS *bind him*.]
REGAN   Hard, hard. O filthy traitor!
GLOUCESTER
Unmerciful lady as you are, I'm none.

17–18 his, him i.e., Lear's, Lear   **18 questrists** searchers   **19 the lord's** i.e., Gloucester's   **26 pass upon his life** pass the death sentence upon him   **28 do a court'sy** i.e., bow before, yield precedence   **31 corky** withered with age

CORNWALL
    To this chair bind him.—Villain, thou shalt find—
                    [REGAN *plucks* GLOUCESTER's *beard*.]
GLOUCESTER
    By the kind gods, 'tis most ignobly done
    To pluck me by the beard.
REGAN
    So white, and such a traitor?
GLOUCESTER   Naughty lady,   39
    These hairs which thou dost ravish from my chin
    Will quicken and accuse thee. I am your host.   41
    With robbers' hands my hospitable favors   42
    You should not ruffle thus. What will you do?   43
CORNWALL
    Come, sir, what letters had you late from France?   44
REGAN
    Be simple-answered, for we know the truth.   45
CORNWALL
    And what confederacy have you with the traitors
    Late footed in the kingdom?
REGAN   To whose hands   47
    You have sent the lunatic King. Speak.
GLOUCESTER
    I have a letter guessingly set down,   49
    Which came from one that's of a neutral heart,
    And not from one opposed.
CORNWALL   Cunning.
REGAN   And false.
CORNWALL   Where hast thou sent the King?
GLOUCESTER   To Dover.
REGAN
    Wherefore to Dover? Wast thou not charged at
        peril—   56
CORNWALL
    Wherefore to Dover? Let him answer that.

---

39 white i.e., white-haired, venerable. **Naughty** wicked   **41 quicken**
come to life   **42 my hospitable favors** the features of me, your
host   **43 ruffle** tear or snatch at, treat with such violence   **44 late**
lately   **45 simple-answered** straightforward in your answers   **47 footed**
landed   **49 guessingly set down** which was tentatively stated
56 charged at peril commanded on peril of your life

GLOUCESTER
I am tied to the stake, and I must stand the course. 58
REGAN   Wherefore to Dover?
GLOUCESTER
Because I would not see thy cruel nails
Pluck out his poor old eyes, nor thy fierce sister
In his anointed flesh rash boarish fangs. 62
The sea, with such a storm as his bare head
In hell-black night endured, would have buoyed up 64
And quenched the stellèd fires; 65
Yet, poor old heart, he holp the heavens to rain. 66
If wolves had at thy gate howled that dern time, 67
Thou shouldst have said, "Good porter, turn the
key." 68
All cruels else subscribe. But I shall see 69
The wingèd Vengeance overtake such children. 70

CORNWALL
See 't shalt thou never. Fellows, hold the chair.
Upon these eyes of thine I'll set my foot.

GLOUCESTER
He that will think to live till he be old, 73
Give me some help!
        [SERVANTS *hold the chair as* CORNWALL *grinds
        out one of* GLOUCESTER'*s eyes with his boot*.]
                              O cruel! O you gods!

REGAN
One side will mock another. Th' other too.

CORNWALL
If you see Vengeance—
FIRST SERVANT   Hold your hand, my lord!
I have served you ever since I was a child;
But better service have I never done you
Than now to bid you hold.

---

58 tied to the stake i.e., like a bear to be baited with dogs. **the course** the dogs' attack   **62 anointed** consecrated with holy oil. **rash** slash sideways   **64–65 would . . . fires** i.e., would have swelled high enough to quench the stars. (The storm was monstrous in its scope and in its assault on order.) **buoyed** lifted itself. **stellèd fires** stars **66 holp** helped   **67 dern** dire, dread   **68 turn the key** i.e., let them in   **69 All . . . subscribe** all other cruel creatures would show forgiveness except you; this cruelty is unparalleled   **70 The wingèd Vengeance** the swift vengeance of the avenging angel of divine wrath   **73 will think** hopes

REGAN   How now, you dog?
FIRST SERVANT [*To* REGAN]
    If you did wear a beard upon your chin,
    I'd shake it on this quarrel.—What do you mean?   81
CORNWALL   My villain?   [*He draws his sword.*]   82
FIRST SERVANT [*Drawing*]
    Nay, then, come on, and take the chance of anger.   83
            [*They fight.* CORNWALL *is wounded.*]
REGAN [*To another* SERVANT]
    Give me thy sword. A peasant stand up thus?   84
      [*She takes a sword and runs at him behind.*]
FIRST SERVANT
    O, I am slain! My lord, you have one eye left
    To see some mischief on him. O!   [*He dies.*]   86
CORNWALL
    Lest it see more, prevent it. Out, vile jelly!
        [*He puts out* GLOUCESTER's *other eye.*]
    Where is thy luster now?
GLOUCESTER
    All dark and comfortless. Where's my son Edmund?
    Edmund, enkindle all the sparks of nature   90
    To quit this horrid act.
REGAN   Out, treacherous villain!   91
    Thou call'st on him that hates thee. It was he
    That made the overture of thy treasons to us,   93
    Who is too good to pity thee.
GLOUCESTER
    O my follies! Then Edgar was abused.   95
    Kind gods, forgive me that, and prosper him!

---

81 I'd . . . quarrel i.e., I'd pull your beard in vehement defiance in this cause. **What do you mean** i.e., what are you thinking of, what do you think you're doing. (Said perhaps to Cornwall.) **82 villain** servant, bondman. (Cornwall's question implies, "How dare you do such a thing?") **83 the chance of anger** the risks of an angry encounter **84 s.d. She . . . behind** (This stage direction appears in the quarto.) **86 mischief** injury **90 nature** i.e., filial love **91 quit** requite. **Out** (An exclamation of anger or impatience.) **93 overture** disclosure **95 abused** wronged

REGAN
    Go thrust him out at gates and let him smell
    His way to Dover.
                    Exit [a SERVANT] *with* GLOUCESTER.
                        How is 't, my lord? How look you?   98

CORNWALL
    I have received a hurt. Follow me, lady.—
    Turn out that eyeless villain. Throw this slave
    Upon the dunghill.—Regan, I bleed apace.
    Untimely comes this hurt. Give me your arm.
                    *Exit [*CORNWALL, *supported by* REGAN].

SECOND SERVANT
    I'll never care what wickedness I do,
    If this man come to good.

THIRD SERVANT   If she live long,
    And in the end meet the old course of death,   105
    Women will all turn monsters.

SECOND SERVANT
    Let's follow the old Earl, and get the Bedlam
    To lead him where he would. His roguish madness   108
    Allows itself to anything.   109

THIRD SERVANT
    Go thou. I'll fetch some flax and whites of eggs
    To apply to his bleeding face. Now, heaven help
        him!   111
                    Exeunt [separately].

98 How look you how is it with you   **105 old** customary, natural   **108–109 His . . . anything** i.e., his being a madman and derelict allows him to do anything   **111 s.d. Exeunt** (At some point after ll. 100–101 the body of the slain First Servant must be removed.)

ACT FOUR
Scene One
[AN OPEN PLACE.]

Enter EDGAR [*as Poor Tom*].

EDGAR
Yet better thus, and known to be contemned,   1
Than still contemned and flattered. To be worst,   2
The lowest and most dejected thing of fortune,   3
Stands still in esperance, lives not in fear.   4
The lamentable change is from the best;   5
The worst returns to laughter. Welcome, then,   6
Thou unsubstantial air that I embrace!
The wretch that thou hast blown unto the worst
Owes nothing to thy blasts.

Enter GLOUCESTER, *and an* OLD MAN [*leading him*].

                              But who comes here?   9
My father, poorly led? World, world, O world!
But that thy strange mutations make us hate thee,   11
Life would not yield to age.   12

OLD MAN
O, my good lord, I have been your tenant
And your father's tenant these fourscore years.

GLOUCESTER
Away, get thee away! Good friend, begone.
Thy comforts can do me no good at all;   16
Thee they may hurt.

OLD MAN   You cannot see your way.

---

1 Yet better thus i.e., it is better to be a beggar. **known** know what it is. **contemned** despised **2 contemned and flattered** despised behind your back and flattered to your face **3 dejected . . . of** debased or humbled by **4 esperance** hope. **fear** i.e., of something worse happening **5–6 The lamentable . . . laughter** i.e., any change from the best is grievous, just as any change from the worst is bound to be for the better **9 Owes nothing** can pay no more, is free of obligation **11–12 But . . . age** i.e., if it were not for your hateful inconstancy, we would never be reconciled to old age and death **16 comforts** kindnesses

GLOUCESTER
   I have no way and therefore want no eyes;
   I stumbled when I saw. Full oft 'tis seen
   Our means secure us, and our mere defects   20
   Prove our commodities. O dear son Edgar,   21
   The food of thy abusèd father's wrath!   22
   Might I but live to see thee in my touch,   23
   I'd say I had eyes again!
OLD MAN   How now? Who's there?
EDGAR [*Aside*]
   O gods! Who is 't can say, "I am at the worst"?
   I am worse than e'er I was.
OLD MAN   'Tis poor mad Tom.
EDGAR [*Aside*]
   And worse I may be yet. The worst is not   27
   So long as we can say, "This is the worst."   28
OLD MAN
   Fellow, where goest?
GLOUCESTER   Is it a beggar-man?
OLD MAN   Madman and beggar too.
GLOUCESTER
   He has some reason, else he could not beg.   31
   I' the last night's storm I such a fellow saw,
   Which made me think a man a worm. My son
   Came then into my mind, and yet my mind
   Was then scarce friends with him. I have heard
      more since.
   As flies to wanton boys are we to the gods;   36
   They kill us for their sport.
EDGAR [*Aside*]   How should this be?   37
   Bad is the trade that must play fool to sorrow,   38
   Ang'ring itself and others.—Bless thee, master!   39

---

20 Our means secure us our prosperity makes us overconfident. **mere defects** sheer afflictions   **21 commodities** benefits   **22 The . . . wrath** on whom thy deceived father's wrath fed, the object of his anger   **23 in** i.e., by means of   **27–28 The worst . . . worst** so long as we can speak and act and delude ourselves with false hopes, our fortunes can in fact grow worse   **31 reason** power of reason   **36 wanton** playful   **37 How . . . be** i.e., how can he have suffered so much, changed so much   **38 Bad . . . sorrow** i.e., it's a bad business to have to play the fool to my sorrowing father   **39 Ang'ring** offending, distressing

GLOUCESTER
  Is that the naked fellow?
OLD MAN   Ay, my lord.
GLOUCESTER
  Then, prithee, get thee gone. If for my sake
  Thou wilt o'ertake us hence a mile or twain   42
  I' the way toward Dover, do it for ancient love,   43
  And bring some covering for this naked soul,
  Which I'll entreat to lead me.
OLD MAN   Alack, sir, he is mad.
GLOUCESTER
  'Tis the times' plague, when madmen lead the blind.   46
  Do as I bid thee, or rather do thy pleasure;
  Above the rest, begone.   48
OLD MAN
  I'll bring him the best 'parel that I have,
  Come on 't what will.   *Exit*.
GLOUCESTER   Sirrah, naked fellow—   50
EDGAR
  Poor Tom's a-cold. [*Aside*.] I cannot daub it further.   51
GLOUCESTER Come hither, fellow.
EDGAR [*Aside*]
  And yet I must.—Bless thy sweet eyes, they bleed.
GLOUCESTER Know'st thou the way to Dover?
EDGAR Both stile and gate, horseway and footpath.
  Poor Tom hath been scared out of his good wits.
  Bless thee, good man's son, from the foul fiend! Five
  fiends have been in poor Tom at once: of lust, as
  Obidicut; Hobbididance, prince of dumbness;   59
  Mahu, of stealing; Modo, of murder; Flibbertigibbet,   60
  of mopping and mowing, who since possesses cham-   61
  bermaids and waiting-women. So, bless thee, master!

---

42 o'ertake us catch up to us (after you have found clothing for Tom o'
Bedlam) **43 ancient love** i.e., the mutually trusting relationship of master
and tenant that Gloucester and the Old Man have long enjoyed   **46 'Tis
the times' plague** i.e., it well expresses the spreading sickness of our
present state   **48 the rest** all   **50 on 't** of it   **51 daub it further** i.e., keep
up this pretense   **59–60 Obidicut . . . Flibbertigibbet** (Fiends borrowed,
as before in 3.4.139–142, from Harsnett.)   **61 mopping and mowing**
making grimaces and mouths.   **since** since that time

GLOUCESTER [*Giving a purse*]
  Here, take this purse, thou whom the heavens'
    plagues
  Have humbled to all strokes. That I am wretched   64
  Makes thee the happier. Heavens, deal so still!
  Let the superfluous and lust-dieted man,   66
  That slaves your ordinance, that will not see   67
  Because he does not feel, feel your pow'r quickly!   68
  So distribution should undo excess
  And each man have enough. Dost thou know
    Dover?
EDGAR   Ay, master.
GLOUCESTER
  There is a cliff, whose high and bending head   72
  Looks fearfully in the confinèd deep.   73
  Bring me but to the very brim of it
  And I'll repair the misery thou dost bear
  With something rich about me. From that place
  I shall no leading need.
EDGAR   Give me thy arm.
  Poor Tom shall lead thee.   *Exeunt.*

                        Scene Two
              [BEFORE THE DUKE OF ALBANY'S PALACE.]

        Enter GONERIL [*and*] *Bastard* [EDMUND].

GONERIL
  Welcome, my lord. I marvel our mild husband   1
  Not met us on the way.

        [*Enter*] *Steward* [OSWALD].

                        Now, where's your master?   2

64 Have . . . strokes have brought so low as to be prepared to accept
every blow of Fortune **66 superfluous** having a superfluity. **lust-dieted**
feeding luxuriously **67 slaves your ordinance** i.e., makes the laws of
heaven his slaves **68 feel** feel sympathy or fellow feeling; suffer   **72 bending** overhanging **73 in . . . deep** i.e., into the sea below,
which is confined by its shores
1 Welcome (Goneril, who has just arrived home from Gloucestershire
escorted by Edmund, bids him brief welcome before he must return.)
2 Not met has not met

OSWALD
Madam, within, but never man so changed.
I told him of the army that was landed;
He smiled at it. I told him you were coming;
His answer was "The worse." Of Gloucester's
   treachery
And of the loyal service of his son
When I informed him, then he called me sot   8
And told me I had turned the wrong side out.
What most he should dislike seems pleasant to him;
What like, offensive.
GONERIL [*To* EDMUND]   Then shall you go no further.
It is the cowish terror of his spirit,   12
That dares not undertake. He'll not feel wrongs   13
Which tie him to an answer. Our wishes on the way   14
May prove effects. Back, Edmund, to my brother;   15
Hasten his musters and conduct his powers.   16
I must change names at home and give the distaff   17
Into my husband's hands. This trusty servant
Shall pass between us. Ere long you are like to
   hear,   19
If you dare venture in your own behalf,
A mistress's command. Wear this; spare speech.   21
                       [*She gives him a favor.*]
Decline your head. [*She kisses him.*] This kiss, if it
   durst speak,
Would stretch thy spirits up into the air.
Conceive, and fare thee well.   24

---

8 sot fool   **12 cowish** cowardly   **13 undertake** venture   **13–14 He'll
. . . answer** he will ignore insults that, if he took notice, would oblige
him to respond, to fight   **14–15 Our . . . effects** i.e., the hopes we
discussed on our journey here (presumably concerning the supplanting
of Albany by Edmund) may come to pass   **15 brother** i.e., brother-in-
law, Cornwall   **16 musters** assembling of troops. **powers** armed
forces   **17 change names** i.e., exchange the roles of master and mistress
of the household, and exchange the insignia of man and woman: the
sword and the *distaff*. **distaff** spinning staff, symbolizing the wife's
role   **19 like** likely   **21 mistress's** (with sexual double meaning)
24 Conceive understand, take my meaning (with sexual double entendre,
continuing from *stretch thy spirits* in the previous line and continued in
death, 4.2.25

EDMUND
  Yours in the ranks of death.   *Exit*.
GONERIL
                            My most dear
  Gloucester!
  O, the difference of man and man!
  To thee a woman's services are due;
  My fool usurps my body.   28
OSWALD   Madam, here comes my lord.   [*Exit*.]   29

  Enter ALBANY.

GONERIL
  I have been worth the whistling.
ALBANY   O Goneril,   30
  You are not worth the dust which the rude wind
  Blows in your face. I fear your disposition;   32
  That nature which contemns its origin   33
  Cannot be bordered certain in itself.   34
  She that herself will sliver and disbranch   35
  From her material sap perforce must wither   36
  And come to deadly use.   37
GONERIL   No more. The text is foolish.   38
ALBANY
  Wisdom and goodness to the vile seem vile;
  Filths savor but themselves. What have you done?   40
  Tigers, not daughters, what have you performed?
  A father, and a gracious agèd man,
  Whose reverence even the head-lugged bear would
    lick,   •   43

28 **My fool . . . body** i.e., my husband claims possession of me but is
unfitted to do so   29 s.d. **Exit** (Oswald could exit later with Goneril, at
4.2.88.)   30 **worth the whistling** i.e., worth the attentions of men. (Al-
ludes to the proverb, "It is a poor dog that is not worth the whistling.")   32 **fear your disposition** mistrust your nature   33 **contemns**
despises   34 **bordered certain** safely restrained, kept within
bounds   35 **sliver** tear off   36 **material sap** nourishing substance, the
stock from which she grew   37 **to deadly use** to destruction, like fire-
wood   38 **The text** i.e., on which you have been preaching   40 **savor but
themselves** i.e., hunger only for that which is filthy   43 **head-lugged**
dragged by the head (or by the ring in its nose) and infuriated

Most barbarous, most degenerate, have you
    madded.   44
Could my good brother suffer you to do it?   45
A man, a prince, by him so benefited?
If that the heavens do not their visible spirits   47
Send quickly down to tame these vile offenses,
It will come,
Humanity must perforce prey on itself,
Like monsters of the deep.
GONERIL   Milk-livered man,   51
That bear'st a cheek for blows, a head for wrongs,
Who hast not in thy brows an eye discerning   53
Thine honor from thy suffering, that not know'st   54
Fools do those villains pity who are punished   55
Ere they have done their mischief. Where's thy
    drum?   56
France spreads his banners in our noiseless land,   57
With plumèd helm thy state begins to threat,   58
Whilst thou, a moral fool, sits still and cries,   59
"Alack, why does he so?"
ALBANY   See thyself, devil!   60
Proper deformity shows not in the fiend   61
So horrid as in woman.
GONERIL   O vain fool!
ALBANY
Thou changèd and self-covered thing, for shame,   63

44 **madded** driven mad   45 **brother** brother-in-law (Cornwall)
47 **visible** made visible   51 **Milk-livered** white-livered, cowardly   53–
54 **discerning . . . suffering** able to tell the difference between an insult
to your honor and something you should tolerate   55 **Fools** i.e., only
fools. (Goneril goes on to say that only fools are so tenderhearted as to
worry about injustices to potential troublemakers, like Lear and
Gloucester, instead of applauding measures taken to insure order.)
56 **thy drum** i.e., your military preparations   57 **noiseless** peaceful, having none of the bustle of war   58 **thy state** . . . **threat** i.e., France begins
to threaten your kingdom   59 **moral** moralizing   60 **why does he so** i.e.,
why does the King of France invade England   61 **Proper deformity** i.e.,
the deformity appropriate to the fiend. (Such deformity seems even
uglier in a woman's features than in a fiend's, since it is appropriate in a
fiend's.)   63 **changèd** transformed. **self-covered** having the true nature
concealed

Bemonster not thy feature. Were 't my fitness 64
To let these hands obey my blood, 65
They are apt enough to dislocate and tear 66
Thy flesh and bones. Howe'er thou art a fiend, 67
A woman's shape doth shield thee. 68
GONERIL   Marry, your manhood! Mew! 69

Enter a MESSENGER.

ALBANY   What news?
MESSENGER
O, my good lord, the Duke of Cornwall's dead,
Slain by his servant, going to put out
The other eye of Gloucester.
ALBANY   Gloucester's eyes!
MESSENGER
A servant that he bred, thrilled with remorse, 74
Opposed against the act, bending his sword 75
To his great master, who, thereat enraged, 76
Flew on him and amongst them felled him dead, 77
But not without that harmful stroke which since
Hath plucked him after.
ALBANY   This shows you are above, 79
You justicers, that these our nether crimes 80
So speedily can venge! But, O poor Gloucester!
Lost he his other eye?
MESSENGER   Both, both, my lord.—
This letter, madam, craves a speedy answer;
'Tis from your sister.   [*He gives her a letter.*]
GONERIL [*Aside*]   One way I like this well; 84
But being widow, and my Gloucester with her,

64 Bemonster . . . feature i.e., do not, however evil you are, take on the outward form of a monster or fiend. **my fitness** suitable for me   **65 blood** passion   **66 apt** ready   **67 Howe'er . . . fiend** however much you may be a fiend in reality   **68 shield** (Since I, as a gentleman, cannot lay violent hands on a lady.)   **69 Mew** (An exclamation of disgust, a derisive catcall: You speak of manhood in shielding me as a woman. Some manhood!)   **74 bred** kept in his household. **thrilled with remorse** deeply moved with pity   **75 Opposed** opposed himself   **75–76 bending . . . To** directing his sword against   **77 amongst them** together with the others (?) in their midst (?) out of their number (?)   **79 after** along (to death)   **80 justicers** (heavenly judges. **nether** i.e., committed here below, on earth   **84 One way** i.e., because Edmund is now Duke of Gloucester, and Cornwall, a dangerous rival for the throne, is dead

May all the building in my fancy pluck   86
Upon my hateful life. Another way   87
The news is not so tart.—I'll read, and answer.   88

                                                [*Exit.*]

ALBANY
Where was his son when they did take his eyes?
MESSENGER
Come with my lady hither.
ALBANY   He is not here.
MESSENGER
No, my good lord. I met him back again.   91
ALBANY   Knows he the wickedness?
MESSENGER
Ay, my good lord. 'Twas he informed against him,
And quit the house on purpose that their
   punishment
Might have the freer course.
ALBANY   Gloucester, I live
To thank thee for the love thou show'dst the King
And to revenge thine eyes.—Come hither, friend.
Tell me what more thou know'st.   *Exeunt.*

Scene Three
[THE FRENCH CAMP NEAR DOVER.]

Enter KENT *and a* GENTLEMAN.

KENT   Why the King of France is so suddenly gone
   back know you no reason?
GENTLEMAN   Something he left imperfect in the state,   3
   which since his coming forth is thought of, which
   imports to the kingdom so much fear and danger that 5
   his personal return was most required and necessary.
KENT
Who hath he left behind him general?

86–87 **May . . . life** i.e., may pull down my imagined happiness (of
possessing the entire kingdom with Edmund) and make hateful my
life **88 tart** bitter, sour **91 back** going back
3 imperfect in the state unsettled in state affairs **5 imports** portends

GENTLEMAN
  The Marshal of France, Monsieur La Far.
KENT   Did your letters pierce the Queen to any dem-
  onstration of grief?
GENTLEMAN
  Ay, sir. She took them, read them in my presence,
  And now and then an ample tear trilled down   12
  Her delicate cheek. It seemed she was a queen
  Over her passion, who, most rebel-like,   14
  Sought to be king o'er her.
KENT   O, then it moved her?
GENTLEMAN
  Not to a rage. Patience and sorrow strove
  Who should express her goodliest. You have seen   17
  Sunshine and rain at once. Her smiles and tears
  Were like a better way; those happy smilets   19
  That played on her ripe lip seemed not to know
  What guests were in her eyes, which parted thence   21
  As pearls from diamonds dropped. In brief,
  Sorrow would be a rarity most beloved   23
  If all could so become it.   24
KENT   Made she no verbal question?   25
GENTLEMAN
  Faith, once or twice she heaved the name of
    "father"   26
  Pantingly forth, as if it pressed her heart;
  Cried, "Sisters, sisters! Shame of ladies, sisters!
  Kent! Father! Sisters! What, i' the storm, i' the
    night?
  Let pity not be believed!" There she shook   30
  The holy water from her heavenly eyes,
  And, clamor-moistened, then away she started   32
  To deal with grief alone.

---

12 trilled trickled   **14 passion, who** emotion, which   **17 Who . . . good-liest** which of the two could make her appear more lovely   **19 like a better way** better than that, though similar   **21 which** i.e., the *guests* or tears   **23 a rarity** i.e., a precious thing, like a jewel   **24 If . . . it** i.e., if all persons were as attractive in sorrow as she   **25 verbal** i.e., as distinguished from her tears and looks   **26 heaved** breathed out with difficulty   **30 believed** i.e., believed to be extant   **32 clamor-moistened** i.e., her outcry of grief assuaged by tears. **started** i.e., went

KENT   It is the stars,
  The stars above us, govern our conditions,   34
  Else one self mate and make could not beget   35
  Such different issues. You spoke not with her
    since?   36

GENTLEMAN   No.

KENT
  Was this before the King returned?

GENTLEMAN   No, since.   38

KENT
  Well, sir, the poor distressèd Lear's i' the town,
  Who sometimes in his better tune remembers   40
  What we are come about, and by no means
  Will yield to see his daughter.

GENTLEMAN   Why, good sir?

KENT
  A sovereign shame so elbows him—his own
    unkindness   43
  That stripped her from his benediction, turned her   44
  To foreign casualties, gave her dear rights   45
  To his dog-hearted daughters—these things sting
  His mind so venomously that burning shame
  Detains him from Cordelia.

GENTLEMAN   Alack, poor gentleman!

KENT
  Of Albany's and Cornwall's powers you heard not?   50

GENTLEMAN   'Tis so. They are afoot.   51

KENT
  Well, sir, I'll bring you to our master Lear
  And leave you to attend him. Some dear cause   53
  Will in concealment wrap me up awhile.
  When I am known aright, you shall not grieve   55
  Lending me this acquaintance. I pray you, go   56
  Along with me.   *Exeunt.*

---

34 conditions characters   **35 Else . . . make** otherwise, one couple (husband and wife)   **36 issues** offspring   **38 the King** the King of
France   **40 better tune** more composed state   **43 sovereign** overruling.
elbows him i.e., prods his memory, jostles him, thrusts him
back   **44 turned her** turned her out   **45 foreign casualties** chances of
fortune abroad   **50 powers** troops, armies   **51 afoot** on the
march   **53 dear cause** important purpose   **55–56 grieve . . . acquaintance** regret having made my acquaintance

Scene Four
[THE FRENCH CAMP.]

Enter, with drum and colors, CORDELIA, DOCTOR, *and soldiers.*

CORDELIA

Alack, 'tis he! Why, he was met even now
As mad as the vexed sea, singing aloud,
Crowned with rank fumiter and furrow weeds, 3
With hardocks, hemlock, nettles, cuckooflowers, 4
Darnel, and all the idle weeds that grow 5
In our sustaining corn. A century send forth! 6
Search every acre in the high-grown field
And bring him to our eye. [*Exit a soldier or soldiers.*]
    What can man's wisdom 8
In the restoring his bereavèd sense?
He that helps him take all my outward worth. 10

DOCTOR

There is means, madam.
Our foster nurse of nature is repose,
The which he lacks. That to provoke in him 13
Are many simples operative, whose power 14
Will close the eye of anguish.

CORDELIA   All blest secrets,
All you unpublished virtues of the earth, 16
Spring with my tears! Be aidant and remediate 17
In the good man's distress! Seek, seek for him,
Lest his ungoverned rage dissolve the life 19
That wants the means to lead it.

Enter MESSENGER.

---

3 fumiter i.e., fumitory, a weed or herb   **4 hardocks** i.e., burdocks or hoardocks, white-leaved (?) (Identity uncertain.)   **5 Darnel** (A weed of the grass kind.) **idle** worthless   **6 sustaining** giving sustenance. **corn** grain. **century** troop of 100 men   **8 What . . . wisdom** i.e., what can medical knowledge accomplish   **10 outward** material   **13 That to provoke** to induce that   **14 simples** medicinal plants. **operative** effective   **16 unpublished virtues** little-known benign herbs   **17 Spring** grow. **aidant and remediate** helpful and remedial   **19 rage** frenzy
20 wants lacks. **means** i.e., his reason

MESSENGER   News, madam.   20
  The British powers are marching hitherward.   21

CORDELIA
  'Tis known before. Our preparation stands
  In expectation of them. O dear Father,
  It is thy business that I go about;
  Therefore great France
  My mourning and importuned tears hath pitied.   26
  No blown ambition doth our arms incite,   27
  But love, dear love, and our aged father's right.
  Soon may I hear and see him!   *Exeunt.*

Scene Five
[GLOUCESTER'S HOUSE.]

Enter REGAN *and Steward* [OSWALD].

REGAN   But are my brother's powers set forth?   1
OSWALD   Ay, madam.
REGAN   Himself in person there?
OSWALD   Madam, with much ado.   4
  Your sister is the better soldier.

REGAN
  Lord Edmund spake not with your lord at home?
OSWALD   No, madam.

REGAN
  What might import my sister's letter to him?   8
OSWALD   I know not, lady.

REGAN
  Faith, he is posted hence on serious matter.   10
  It was great ignorance, Gloucester's eyes being out,   11
  To let him live. Where he arrives he moves
  All hearts against us. Edmund, I think, is gone,
  In pity of his misery, to dispatch
  His nighted life; moreover to descry   15
  The strength o' th' enemy.

---

21 powers armies   **26 importuned** importunate   **27 blown** puffed up
with pride
1 my brother's powers i.e., Albany's forces   **4 with much ado** after much
fuss and persuasion   **8 import** bear as its purport, express   **10 is posted**
has hurried   **11 ignorance** error, folly   **15 nighted** benighted, blinded

OSWALD
  I must needs after him, madam, with my letter.
REGAN
  Our troops set forth tomorrow. Stay with us;
  The ways are dangerous.
OSWALD   I may not, madam.
  My lady charged my duty in this business.   20
REGAN
  Why should she write to Edmund? Might not you
  Transport her purposes by word? Belike   22
  Something—I know not what. I'll love thee much;
  Let me unseal the letter.
OSWALD   Madam, I had rather—
REGAN
  I know your lady does not love her husband,
  I am sure of that; and at her late being here   26
  She gave strange oeillades and most speaking looks   27
  To noble Edmund. I know you are of her bosom.   28
OSWALD I, madam?
REGAN
  I speak in understanding; y' are, I know 't.   30
  Therefore I do advise you, take this note: 31
  My lord is dead; Edmund and I have talked,   32
  And more convenient is he for my hand   33
  Than for your lady's. You may gather more.   34
  If you do find him, pray you, give him this;   35
  And when your mistress hears thus much from you,   36
  I pray, desire her call her wisdom to her.   37
  So, fare you well.
  If you do chance to hear of that blind traitor,
  Preferment falls on him that cuts him off.   40

20 charged ordered strictly **22 Belike** it may be **26 late** recently **27 oeillades** amorous glances **28 of her bosom** in her confidence **30 y' are** you are **31 take this note** i.e., mark this advice **32 have talked** have come to an understanding **33 convenient** fitting **34 gather more** i.e., infer what I am trying to suggest **35 this** i.e., this information, or possibly a letter (though only one letter, Goneril's, is found on his dead body at 4.6.262) **36 thus much** what I have told you **37 call . . . to her** recall her to her senses **40 Preferment** advancement

OSWALD
  Would I could meet him, madam! I should show
  What party I do follow.
REGAN   Fare thee well.
                          Exeunt [separately].

Scene Six
[OPEN PLACE NEAR DOVER.]

Enter GLOUCESTER, *and* EDGAR [*in peasant's
clothes, leading his father*].

GLOUCESTER
  When shall I come to the top of that same hill?   1
EDGAR
  You do climb up it now. Look how we labor.
GLOUCESTER
  Methinks the ground is even.
EDGAR   Horrible steep.
  Hark, do you hear the sea?
GLOUCESTER   No, truly.
EDGAR
  Why, then, your other senses grow imperfect
  By your eyes' anguish.
GLOUCESTER   So may it be, indeed.
  Methinks thy voice is altered, and thou speak'st
  In better phrase and matter than thou didst.
EDGAR
  You're much deceived. In nothing am I changed
  But in my garments.
GLOUCESTER   Methinks you're better spoken.
EDGAR
  Come on, sir, here's the place. Stand still. How
    fearful
  And dizzy 'tis to cast one's eyes so low!
  The crows and choughs that wing the midway air   13
  Show scarce so gross as beetles. Halfway down   14

1 that same hill i.e., the cliff we talked about (4.1.72–74)   13 choughs
jackdaws. midway halfway down   14 gross large

Hangs one that gathers samphire—dreadful trade!   15
Methinks he seems no bigger than his head.
The fishermen that walk upon the beach
Appear like mice, and yond tall anchoring bark
Diminished to her cock; her cock, a buoy   19
Almost too small for sight. The murmuring surge,
That on th' unnumbered idle pebble chafes,   21
Cannot be heard so high. I'll look no more,
Lest my brain turn, and the deficient sight   23
Topple down headlong.

GLOUCESTER   Set me where you stand.   24

EDGAR
Give me your hand. You are now within a foot
Of th' extreme verge. For all beneath the moon
Would I not leap upright.

GLOUCESTER   Let go my hand.   27
Here, friend, 's another purse; in it a jewel
Well worth a poor man's taking. [*He gives a purse.*]
  Fairies and gods   29
Prosper it with thee! Go thou further off.   30
Bid me farewell, and let me hear thee going.

EDGAR [*Moving away*]
Now fare ye well, good sir.

GLOUCESTER   With all my heart.

EDGAR [*Aside*]
Why I do trifle thus with his despair
Is done to cure it.

GLOUCESTER [*Kneeling*]   O you mighty gods!
This world I do renounce, and in your sights
Shake patiently my great affliction off.
If I could bear it longer, and not fall
To quarrel with your great opposeless wills,   38
My snuff and loathèd part of nature should   39

15 **samphire** (An herb used in pickling.) 19 **Diminished . . . cock** reduced to the size of her cockboat, small ship's boat 21 **unnumbered** innumerable. **idle** randomly shifting. **pebble** pebbles 23–24 **the deficient sight Topple** my failing sight topple me 27 **upright** i.e., up and down, much less forward 29–30 **Fairies . . . thee** i.e., may the fairies and gods who guard hidden treasure cause this to multiply in your possession 38 **To quarrel with** into rebellion against. **opposeless** irresistible 39 **snuff** i.e., useless residue. (Literally, the smoking wick of a candle.) **of nature** i.e., of my life

Burn itself out. If Edgar live, O, bless him!
Now, fellow, fare thee well.   [*He falls forward.*]

EDGAR   Gone, sir. Farewell.—
And yet I know not how conceit may rob   42
The treasury of life, when life itself
Yields to the theft. Had he been where he thought,   44
By this had thought been past. Alive or dead?—
Ho, you, sir! Friend! Hear you, sir! Speak!—
Thus might he pass indeed; yet he revives.—   47
What are you, sir?

GLOUCESTER   Away, and let me die.   48

EDGAR
Hadst thou been aught but gossamer, feathers, air,
So many fathom down precipitating,
Thou'dst shivered like an egg; but thou dost
    breathe,
Hast heavy substance, bleed'st not, speak'st, art
    sound.   52
Ten masts at each make not the altitude   53
Which thou hast perpendicularly fell.
Thy life's a miracle. Speak yet again.

GLOUCESTER   But have I fallen or no?

EDGAR
From the dread summit of this chalky bourn.   57
Look up aheight; the shrill-gorged lark so far   58
Cannot be seen or heard. Do but look up.

GLOUCESTER   Alack, I have no eyes.
Is wretchedness deprived that benefit
To end itself by death? 'Twas yet some comfort
When misery could beguile the tyrant's rage   63
And frustrate his proud will.

EDGAR   Give me your arm.
                              [*He lifts him up.*]
Up—so. How is 't? Feel you your legs? You stand.

---

42 conceit imagination   **44 Yields** consents   **47 pass** die   **48 What**
who. (Edgar now speaks in a new voice, differing from that of "poor
Tom" and also from the "altered" voice he used at the start of this
scene; see 4.6.7-10.)   **52 heavy substance** the substance of the flesh
53 at each end to end   **57 bourn** limit, boundary (i.e., the edge of the
sea)   **58 aheight** on high. **shrill-gorged** shrill-throated   **63 beguile** out-
wit

GLOUCESTER
Too well, too well.
EDGAR   This is above all strangeness.
Upon the crown o' the cliff what thing was that
Which parted from you?
GLOUCESTER   A poor unfortunate beggar.
EDGAR
As I stood here below, methought his eyes
Were two full moons; he had a thousand noses,
Horns whelked and waved like the enridgèd sea.   71
It was some fiend. Therefore, thou happy father,   72
Think that the clearest gods, who make them
    honors   73
Of men's impossibilities, have preserved thee.   74
GLOUCESTER
I do remember now. Henceforth I'll bear
Affliction till it do cry out itself.   76
"Enough, enough," and die. That thing you speak
    of,   77
I took it for a man; often 'twould say
"The fiend, the fiend." He led me to that place.
EDGAR
Bear free and patient thoughts.

Enter LEAR [*mad, fantastically dressed with wild flowers*].
                       But who comes here?   80
The safer sense will ne'er accommodate   81
His master thus.   82
LEAR   No, they cannot touch me for coining. I am the   83
King himself.

---

71 whelked twisted, convoluted. **enridgèd** furrowed (by the wind)   **72 happy father** lucky old man   **73 clearest** purest, most righteous   **73–74 who . . . impossibilities** who win our awe and reverence by doing things impossible to men   **76–77 till . . . die** i.e., until affliction itself has had enough, or until I die   **80 free** i.e., free from despair **81–82 The safer . . . thus** i.e., a person in his right senses would never dress himself in such a fashion. **His master** the owner of the *safer sense* or sane mind. (*His* means "its.")   **83 touch** arrest, prosecute. **coining** minting coins. (A royal prerogative; the King wants money for his imaginary soldiers, 4.6.86–87.)

EDGAR   O thou side-piercing sight!   85

LEAR   Nature's above art in that respect. There's your   86
press money. That fellow handles his bow like a   87
crowkeeper. Draw me a clothier's yard. Look, look,   88
a mouse! Peace, peace; this piece of toasted cheese
will do 't. There's my gauntlet; I'll prove it on a giant.   90
Bring up the brown bills. O, well flown, bird! I' the   91
clout, i' the clout—hewgh! Give the word.   92

EDGAR   Sweet marjoram.   93

LEAR   Pass.

GLOUCESTER   I know that voice.

LEAR   Ha! Goneril with a white beard? They flattered
me like a dog and told me I had white hairs in my   97
beard ere the black ones were there. To say ay and   98
no to everything that I said ay and no to was no good   99
divinity. When the rain came to wet me once and the   100
wind to make me chatter, when the thunder would
not peace at my bidding, there I found 'em, there I   102
smelt 'em out. Go to, they are not men o' their   103
words. They told me I was everything. 'Tis a lie; I am
not ague-proof.

GLOUCESTER
The trick of that voice I do well remember.   106
Is 't not the King?

---

85 side-piercing heartrending (with a suggestion also of Christ's suffering
on the cross)   **86 Nature's . . . respect** i.e., a born king is proof against
any counterfeiting; his coinage is superior to that of the counter-
feiter (?)   **87 press money** enlistment bonus **88 crowkeeper** laborer hired
to scare away the crows.   **me** for me. **clothier's yard** arrow the length of a
cloth yard   **90 do 't** i.e., capture the mouse, an imagined enemy. **gauntlet** armored glove thrown down as a challenge. **prove it on** maintain it
against   **91 brown bills** soldiers carrying pikes (painted brown), or the
pikes themselves. **well flown, bird** (Lear uses the language of hawking to
describe the flight of an arrow.) **92 clout** target, bull's-eye.   **hewgh** (The
arrow's noise.) **word** password **93 Sweet marjoram** (An herb used to
cure madness.)   **97 like a dog** i.e., as a dog fawns   **97–98 had . . . beard**
i.e., had wisdom   **98–99 To . . . no to** i.e., to agree flatteringly
with   **99–100 no good divinity** not good theology, contrary to biblical
teaching. (See 2 Cor. 1:18 and James 5:12.) **102 found 'em** found them
out   **103 Go to** (An expression of impatience.)   **106 trick** peculiar
characteristic

LEAR   Ay, every inch a king.
When I do stare, see how the subject quakes.
I pardon that man's life. What was thy cause?   109
Adultery?
Thou shalt not die. Die for adultery? No.
The wren goes to 't, and the small gilded fly
Does lecher in my sight.
Let copulation thrive; for Gloucester's bastard son
Was kinder to his father than my daughters
Got 'tween the lawful sheets.
To 't, luxury, pell-mell, for I lack soldiers.   117
Behold yond simpering dame,
Whose face between her forks presages snow,   119
That minces virtue and does shake the head   120
To hear of pleasure's name;   121
The fitchew nor the soilèd horse goes to 't   122
With a more riotous appetite.
Down from the waist they are centaurs,   124
Though women all above.
But to the girdle do the gods inherit;   126
Beneath is all the fiends'.
There's hell, there's darkness, there is the sulfurous
    pit,
burning, scalding, stench, consumption. Fie, fie, fie!
Pah, pah! Give me an ounce of civet, good
    apothecary,   130
sweeten my imagination. There's money for thee.
GLOUCESTER   O, let me kiss that hand!
LEAR   Let me wipe it first; it smells of mortality.
GLOUCESTER
O ruined piece of nature! This great world   134
Shall so wear out to naught. Dost thou know me?   135

109 cause offense   **117 luxury** lechery   **119 Whose . . . snow** whose
frosty countenance seems to suggest frigidity between her
legs   **120 minces** affects, mimics   **121 pleasure's name** i.e., any talk of
sexual pleasure   **122 fitchew** polecat. **soilèd horse** horse turned out to
grass, well-fed and hence wanton   **124 centaurs** incontinent monsters,
half man, half horse   **126 But** only. **girdle** waist. **inherit** possess   **130 civet** musk perfume   **134 piece** masterpiece. **This great world**
i.e., the macrocosm, of which man, the masterpiece of nature, is the
microcosm   **135 so** similarly

LEAR   I remember thine eyes well enough. Dost thou
squinny at me? No, do thy worst, blind Cupid; I'll   137
not love. Read thou this challenge. Mark but the
penning of it.

GLOUCESTER
Were all thy letters suns, I could not see.

EDGAR [*Aside*]
I would not take this from report. It is,   141
And my heart breaks at it.

LEAR   Read.

GLOUCESTER   What, with the case of eyes?   144

LEAR   Oho, are you there with me? No eyes in your   145
head, nor no money in your purse? Your eyes are in a
heavy case, your purse in a light, yet you see how   147
this world goes.

GLOUCESTER   I see it feelingly.   149

LEAR   What, art mad? A man may see how this world
goes with no eyes. Look with thine ears. See how
yond justice rails upon yond simple thief. Hark in   152
thine ear: change places and, handy-dandy, which is   153
the justice, which is the thief? Thou hast seen a
farmer's dog bark at a beggar?

GLOUCESTER   Ay, sir.

LEAR   And the creature run from the cur? There thou   157
mightst behold the great image of authority: a dog's   158
obeyed in office.   159
Thou rascal beadle, hold thy bloody hand!   160
Why dost thou lash that whore? Strip thine own
   back;
Thou hotly lusts to use her in that kind   162
For which thou whipp'st her. The usurer hangs the
   cozener.   163

---

137 squinny squint   **141 take** believe, credit. **It is** it is taking place,
incredibly enough   **144 case** mere sockets   **145 are . . . me** is that your
meaning, the point you are making, or your situation   **147 heavy case**
sad plight (with pun on *case* in l. 144)   **149 feelingly** (1) by touch (2)
keenly, painfully   **152 simple** of humble station   **153 handy-dandy** take
your choice of hands (as in a well-known child's game)   **157 creature**
poor fellow   **158–159 a dog's . . . office** i.e., even currish power commands submission   **160 beadle** parish officer, responsible for giving
whippings   **162 kind** way   **163 The usurer** i.e., a judge guilty of lending
money at usurious rates. **cozener** petty cheater

Through tattered clothes small vices do appear;
Robes and furred gowns hide all. Plate sin with
    gold, 165
And the strong lance of justice hurtless breaks; 166
Arm it in rags, a pygmy's straw does pierce it.
None does offend, none, I say, none. I'll able 'em. 168
Take that of me, my friend, who have the power 169
To seal th' accuser's lips. Get thee glass eyes, 170
And like a scurvy politician seem
To see the things thou dost not. Now, now, now,
    now!
Pull off my boots. Harder, harder! So.

EDGAR [*Aside*]
O, matter and impertinency mixed, 174
Reason in madness!

LEAR
If thou wilt weep my fortunes, take my eyes.
I know thee well enough; thy name is Gloucester.
Thou must be patient. We came crying hither.
Thou know'st the first time that we smell the air
We wawl and cry. I will preach to thee. Mark.

GLOUCESTER   Alack, alack the day!

LEAR
When we are born, we cry that we are come
To this great stage of fools.—This' a good block. 183
It were a delicate stratagem to shoe 184
A troop of horse with felt. I'll put 't in proof, 185
And when I have stolen upon these son-in-laws,
Then, kill, kill, kill, kill, kill, kill!

Enter a GENTLEMAN [*with attendants*].

---

165 Plate arm in plate armor **166 hurtless breaks** splinters harmlessly **168 able** give warrant to **169 that** i.e., a guarantee of immunity **170 glass eyes** (With glass eyes, possibly spectacles, Gloucester could pretend to see or understand what he does not comprehend, like a vile *politician* governing through opportunism and trickery, hiding his blindness behind his glass eyes.) **174 matter and impertinency** sense and nonsense **183 This'** this is. **block** felt hat (?) (Lear may refer to the weeds strewn in his hair, which he removes as though doffing a hat before preaching a sermon.) **184 delicate** subtle **185 in proof** to the test

GENTLEMAN
  O, here he is. Lay hand upon him.—Sir,
  Your most dear daughter—
LEAR
  No rescue? What, a prisoner? I am even
  The natural fool of fortune. Use me well;   191
  You shall have ransom. Let me have surgeons;
  I am cut to the brains.
GENTLEMAN   You shall have anything.   193
LEAR   No seconds? All myself?   194
  Why, this would make a man a man of salt   195
  To use his eyes for garden waterpots,
  Ay, and laying autumn's dust.
  I will die bravely, like a smug bridegroom. What?   198
  I will be jovial. Come, come, I am a king,
  Masters, know you that?
GENTLEMAN
  You are a royal one, and we obey you.
LEAR   Then there's life in 't. Come, an you get it, you   202
  shall get it by running. Sa, sa, sa, sa.   203
                  Exit [running, followed by attendants].
GENTLEMAN
  A sight most pitiful in the meanest wretch,
  Past speaking of in a king! Thou hast one daughter
  Who redeems nature from the general curse   206
  Which twain have brought her to.
EDGAR   Hail, gentle sir.   208
GENTLEMAN   Sir, speed you. What's your will?   209
EDGAR
  Do you hear aught, sir, of a battle toward?   210
GENTLEMAN
  Most sure and vulgar. Everyone hears that   211
  Which can distinguish sound.

---

191 natural fool born plaything   **193 cut** wounded   **194 seconds** sup-
porters   **195 of salt** of salt tears   **198 bravely** (1) courageously (2) splen-
didly attired. **smug** trimly dressed. (*Bridegroom* continues the punning
sexual suggestion of *die bravely,* have sex successfully.)   **202 life** i.e.,
hope still. **an if**   **203 Sa . . . sa** (A hunting cry.)   **206 general curse**
universal damnation   **208 gentle** noble   **209 speed** God speed
210 toward imminent   **211 vulgar** in everyone's mouth, generally
known   **212 Which** who

EDGAR   But, by your favor,   212
   How near's the other army?

GENTLEMAN
   Near and on speedy foot. The main descry   214
   Stands on the hourly thought.   215

EDGAR   I thank you, sir; that's all.

GENTLEMAN
   Though that the Queen on special cause is here,   217
   Her army is moved on.

EDGAR   I thank you, sir.
                    Exit [GENTLEMAN].

GLOUCESTER
   You ever-gentle gods, take my breath from me;
   Let not my worser spirit tempt me again   220
   To die before you please!

EDGAR   Well pray you, father.

GLOUCESTER   Now, good sir, what are you?   223

EDGAR
   A most poor man, made tame to fortune's blows,   224
   Who, by the art of known and feeling sorrows,   225
   Am pregnant to good pity. Give me your hand.   226
   I'll lead you to some biding.   [*He offers his arm.*]

GLOUCESTER   Hearty thanks.   227
   The bounty and the benison of heaven   228
   To boot, and boot!

Enter Steward [OSWALD].

OSWALD   A proclaimed prize! Most happy!   229
                   [*He draws his sword.*]
   That eyeless head of thine was first framed flesh   230

214–215 The main . . . thought the full view of the main body is expected every hour   **217 on special cause** for a special reason, i.e., to minister to Lear   **220 worser spirit** bad angel, or ill thoughts   **223 what** who. (Again, Edgar alters his voice to personate a new stranger assisting Gloucester. See l. 48, above, and note.)   **224 tame** submissive **225 known** personally experienced. **feeling** heartfelt, deep   **226 pregnant** prone   **227 biding** abiding place   **228–229 The bounty . . . and boot** i.e., in addition to my thanks, I wish you the bounty and blessings of heaven   **229 proclaimed prize** one with a price on his head. **happy** fortunate   **230 framed flesh** born

To raise my fortunes. Thou old unhappy traitor,
Briefly thyself remember. The sword is out   232
That must destroy thee.
GLOUCESTER   Now let thy friendly hand   233
Put strength enough to 't.   [EDGAR *intervenes*.]
OSWALD   Wherefore, bold peasant,
Durst thou support a published traitor? Hence,   235
Lest that th' infection of his fortune take   236
Like hold on thee. Let go his arm.   237
EDGAR   'Chill not let go, zir, without vurther 'cagion.   238
OSWALD   Let go, slave, or thou diest!
EDGAR   Good gentleman, go your gait, and let poor   240
volk pass. An 'chud ha' bin zwaggered out of my life,   241
'twould not ha' bin zo long as 'tis by a vortnight.
Nay, come not near th' old man; keep out, 'che vor   243
ye, or Ise try whether your costard or my ballow be   244
the harder. 'Chill be plain with you.
OSWALD   Out, dunghill!
EDGAR   'Chill pick your teeth, zir. Come, no matter
vor your foins.   248
        [*They fight.* EDGAR *fells him with his cudgel.*]
OSWALD
Slave, thou hast slain me. Villain, take my purse.   249
If ever thou wilt thrive, bury my body
And give the letters which thou find'st about me   251
To Edmund, Earl of Gloucester. Seek him out
Upon the English party. O, untimely death!   253
Death!   [*He dies.*]
EDGAR
I know thee well: a serviceable villain,   255
As duteous to the vices of thy mistress
As badness would desire.

---

232 thyself remember i.e., confess your sins   **233 friendly** i.e., welcome,
since I desire death   **235 published** proclaimed   **236 Lest that**
lest   **237 Like** similar   **238 'Chill** I will. (Literally, a contraction of *Ich
will.* Edgar adopts Somerset dialect, a stage convention regularly used
for peasants.)   **vurther 'cagion** further occasion   **240 go your gait** go your
own way   **241 An 'chud** if I could.   **zwaggered** swaggered, bluffed   **243–
244 'che vor ye** I warrant you   **244 Ise** I shall.   **costard** head. (Literally, an
apple.)   **ballow** cudgel   **248 foins** thrusts   **249 Villain** serf   **251 letters** letter.   **about me** upon my person   **253 Upon** on.   **party** side   **255 serviceable** officious

GLOUCESTER   What, is he dead?
EDGAR   Sit you down, father. Rest you.

                              [GLOUCESTER *sits.*]
Let's see these pockets; the letters that he speaks
   of
May be my friends. He's dead; I am only sorry
He had no other deathsman. Let us see.   262
                  [*He finds a letter, and opens it.*]
Leave, gentle wax, and, manners, blame us not.   263
To know our enemies' minds we rip their hearts;
Their papers is more lawful.   (*Reads the letter.*)
   "Let our reciprocal vows be remembered. You
have many opportunities to cut him off; if your will
want not, time and place will be fruitfully offered.   268
There is nothing done if he return the conqueror.   269
Then am I the prisoner, and his bed my jail, from the
loathed warmth whereof deliver me and supply the
place for your labor.   272
   Your—wife, so I would say—
                  Affectionate servant,   Goneril."
O indistinguished space of woman's will!   275
A plot upon her virtuous husband's life,
And the exchange my brother! Here in the sands
Thee I'll rake up, the post unsanctified   278
Of murderous lechers; and in the mature time   279
With this ungracious paper strike the sight   280
Of the death-practiced Duke. For him 'tis well   281
That of thy death and business I can tell.

GLOUCESTER
The King is mad. How stiff is my vile sense,   283
That I stand up and have ingenious feeling   284

---

262 deathsman executioner   **263 Leave** by your leave. **wax** wax seal on
the letter   **268 want not** is not lacking.   **fruitfully** plentifully and with
results   **269 There is nothing done** i.e., we will have accomplished
nothing   **272 for your labor** (1) as recompense for your efforts (2) as a
place for your amorous labors   **275 indistinguished . . . will** limitless
and incalculable range of woman's appetite   **278 rake up** cover up. **post
unsanctified** unholy messenger   **279 in . . . time** when the time is
ripe   **280 ungracious** wicked. **strike** blast   **281 death-practiced** whose
death is plotted   **283 stiff** obstinate. **sense** consciousness, sane mental
powers   **284 ingenious** conscious. (Gloucester laments that he remains
sane and hence fully conscious of his troubles, unlike Lear.)

Of my huge sorrows! Better I were distract;   285
So should my thoughts be severed from my griefs,
And woes by wrong imaginations lose   287
The knowledge of themselves.   *Drum afar off.*

EDGAR   Give me your hand.
Far off, methinks, I hear the beaten drum.
Come, father, I'll bestow you with a friend. *Exeunt.*   290

Scene Seven
[THE FRENCH CAMP.]

Enter CORDELIA, KENT [*dressed still in his disguise
costume, and* DOCTOR].

CORDELIA
O thou good Kent, how shall I live and work
To match thy goodness? My life will be too short,
And every measure fail me.   3

KENT
To be acknowledged, madam, is o'erpaid.
All my reports go with the modest truth,   5
Nor more nor clipped, but so.

CORDELIA   Be better suited.   6
These weeds are memories of those worser hours;   7
I prithee, put them off.

KENT   Pardon, dear madam;
Yet to be known shortens my made intent.   9
My boon I make it that you know me not   10
Till time and I think meet.   11

285 distract distracted, crazy 287 wrong imaginations delusions
290 bestow lodge. (At the scene's end, Edgar leads off Gloucester;
presumably he also disposes of Oswald's body, which must be removed
from the stage or somehow concealed.)
3 every . . . me i.e., every attempt to match your goodness will fall
short 5 All my reports go i.e., let all reports (of my service as Caius to
Lear) conform 6 Nor . . . clipped i.e., neither more nor less. suited
dressed 7 weeds garments. memories remembrances 9 Yet . . . intent
i.e., to reveal my true identity now would alter my carefully made
plan 10 My . . . it the reward I seek is. know acknowledge 11 meet
appropriate

CORDELIA
Then be 't so, my good lord. [*To the* DOCTOR.] How
  does the King?
DOCTOR   Madam, sleeps still.
CORDELIA   O you kind gods,
  Cure this great breach in his abusèd nature!
  Th' untuned and jarring senses, O, wind up   16
  Of this child-changèd father!   17
DOCTOR   So please Your Majesty
  That we may wake the King? He hath slept long.
CORDELIA
  Be governed by your knowledge, and proceed
  I' the sway of your own will.—Is he arrayed?   21

Enter LEAR *in a chair carried by servants,* [*attended
by a* GENTLEMAN].

GENTLEMAN
  Ay, madam. In the heaviness of sleep
  We put fresh garments on him.
DOCTOR
  Be by, good madam, when we do awake him.
  I doubt not of his temperance.
CORDELIA   Very well.   [*Music.*]   25
DOCTOR
  Please you, draw near.—Louder the music there!
CORDELIA [*Kissing him*]
  O my dear Father! Restoration hang
  Thy medicine on my lips, and let this kiss
  Repair those violent harms that my two sisters
  Have in thy reverence made!
KENT   Kind and dear
    princess!
CORDELIA
  Had you not been their father, these white flakes   31
  Did challenge pity of them. Was this a face   32

16 **wind up** tune (as by winding the slackened string of an instru-
ment)   17 **child-changèd** changed (in mind) by children's cruelty   21 **I'
the sway** under the direction   25 **temperance** self-control, calm behavior   31 **Had you** even if you had. **flakes** locks of hair   32 **Did challenge** would have demanded

To be opposed against the warring winds?
To stand against the deep dread-bolted thunder   34
In the most terrible and nimble stroke
Of quick cross lightning? To watch—poor perdu!—   36
With this thin helm? Mine enemy's dog,   37
Though he had bit me, should have stood that night
Against my fire; and wast thou fain, poor Father,   39
To hovel thee with swine and rogues forlorn   40
In short and musty straw? Alack, alack!   41
'Tis wonder that thy life and wits at once
Had not concluded all.—He wakes! Speak to him.   43

DOCTOR   Madam, do you; 'tis fittest.

CORDELIA
How does my royal lord? How fares Your Majesty?

LEAR
You do me wrong to take me out o' the grave.
Thou art a soul in bliss; but I am bound
Upon a wheel of fire, that mine own tears   48
Do scald like molten lead.

CORDELIA   Sir, do you know me?

LEAR
You are a spirit, I know. When did you die?

CORDELIA   Still, still, far wide!   51

DOCTOR
He's scarce awake. Let him alone awhile.

LEAR
Where have I been? Where am I? Fair daylight?
I am mightily abused. I should ev'n die with pity   54
To see another thus. I know not what to say.   55
I will not swear these are my hands. Let's see;
I feel this pinprick. Would I were assured
Of my condition!

---

34 deep bass-voiced. **dread-bolted** furnished with the dreadful thunderstone **36 cross** zigzag. **watch** stay awake (like a sentry on duty).
perdu soldier placed in a position of peculiar danger **37 helm** helmet, i.e., his scanty hair **39 Against** before, in front of. **fain** glad, constrained **40 rogues forlorn** abandoned vagabonds **41 short** broken up and hence uncomfortable **43 concluded all** come to an end altogether **48 wheel of fire** (A hellish torment for the eternally damned.) **that** so that **51 wide** wide of the mark, wandering **54 abused** confused, deluded **55 thus** i.e., thus confused, bewildered

CORDELIA   O, look upon me, sir,
And hold your hand in benediction o'er me.
                              [*He attempts to kneel.*]
No, sir, you must not kneel.
LEAR   Pray, do not mock me.
I am a very foolish fond old man,   61
Fourscore and upward, not an hour more nor less;
And, to deal plainly,
I fear I am not in my perfect mind.
Methinks I should know you, and know this man,
Yet I am doubtful; for I am mainly ignorant   66
What place this is, and all the skill I have
Remembers not these garments, nor I know not
Where I did lodge last night. Do not laugh at me,
For, as I am a man, I think this lady
To be my child Cordelia.
CORDELIA [*Weeping*] And so I am, I am.
LEAR
Be your tears wet? Yes, faith. I pray, weep not.
If you have poison for me I will drink it.
I know you do not love me, for your sisters
Have, as I do remember, done me wrong.
You have some cause, they have not.
CORDELIA   No cause, no cause.
LEAR   Am I in France?
KENT   In your own kingdom, sir.
LEAR   Do not abuse me.   81
DOCTOR
Be comforted, good madam. The great rage,   82
You see, is killed in him, and yet it is danger
To make him even o'er the time he has lost.   84
Desire him to go in. Trouble him no more
Till further settling.   86
CORDELIA   Will 't please Your Highness walk?   87
LEAR   You must bear with me.
Pray you now, forget and forgive.
I am old and foolish.

---

61 fond foolish   **66 mainly** perfectly   **81 abuse** deceive   **82 rage**
frenzy   **84 even o'er** fill in, go over in his mind   **86 settling** composing
of his mind   **87 walk** withdraw

Exeunt [all but KENT *and* GENTLEMAN].

GENTLEMAN   Holds it true, sir, that the Duke of Corn-   91
wall was so slain?

KENT   Most certain, sir.

GENTLEMAN   Who is conductor of his people?   94

KENT   As 'tis said, the bastard son of Gloucester.

GENTLEMAN   They say Edgar, his banished son, is
with the Earl of Kent in Germany.

KENT   Report is changeable. 'Tis time to look about;   98
the powers of the kingdom approach apace.   99

GENTLEMAN   The arbitrament is like to be bloody.   100
Fare you well, sir.   *Exit.*

KENT
My point and period will be throughly wrought,   102
Or well or ill, as this day's battle's fought.   *Exit.*   103

ACT FIVE
Scene One
[THE BRITISH CAMP NEAR DOVER.]

Enter, with drum and colors, EDMUND, REGAN,
GENTLEMEN, *and soldiers.*

EDMUND [*To a* GENTLEMAN]
Know of the Duke if his last purpose hold,   1
Or whether since he is advised by aught   2
To change the course. He's full of alteration   3
And self-reproving. Bring his constant pleasure.   4
                              [*Exit* GENTLEMAN.]

91 Holds it true is it still held to be true   **94 conductor** leader, general   **98 look about** i.e., be wary   **99 powers of the kingdom** British
armies (marching against the French invaders)   **100 arbitrament** decision by arms, decisive encounter   **102 My . . . wrought** i.e., the conclusion of my destiny (literally, the full stop at the end of my life's
sentence) will be thoroughly brought about   **103 Or** either. **as** according
as

I Know inquire. **last purpose hold** most recent intention (to fight) remain
firm   **2 since** since then. **advised by aught** persuaded by any consideration   **3 alteration** vacillation   **4 constant pleasure** settled decision

REGAN
  Our sister's man is certainly miscarried.   5
EDMUND
  'Tis to be doubted, madam.
REGAN   Now, sweet lord,   6
  You know the goodness I intend upon you.   7
  Tell me, but truly—but then speak the truth—
  Do you not love my sister?
EDMUND   In honored love.   9
REGAN
  But have you never found my brother's way
  To the forfended place?   11
EDMUND   That thought abuses you.   12
REGAN
  I am doubtful that you have been conjunct   13
  And bosomed with her, as far as we call hers.   14
EDMUND   No, by mine honor, madam.
REGAN
  I never shall endure her. Dear my lord,
  Be not familiar with her.   17
EDMUND
  Fear me not.—She and the Duke her husband!   18

  Enter, with drum and colors, ALBANY, GONERIL,
  [*and*] *soldiers.*

GONERIL [*Aside*]
  I had rather lose the battle than that sister
  Should loosen him and me.
ALBANY
  Our very loving sister, well bemet.   21
  Sir, this I heard: the King is come to his daughter,
  With others whom the rigor of our state   23
  Forced to cry out. Where I could not be honest,   24

5 **man** i.e., Oswald. **miscarried** lost, perished   6 **doubted** feared   7 **intend**
intend to confer   9 **honored** honorable   11 **forfended** forbidden (by the
commandment against adultery)   12 **abuses** degrades, wrongs   13–14
I am . . . hers I suspect that you have been coupled and intimate with
her in the fullest manner   17 **familiar** intimate   18 **Fear me not** don't
worry about me on that score   21 **bemet** met   23 **rigor of our state**
harshness of our rule   24 **Where** in a case where. **honest** honorable

I never yet was valiant. For this business,   25
It touches us as France invades our land,   26
Not bolds the King, with others whom, I fear,   27
Most just and heavy causes make oppose.   28
EDMUND   Sir, you speak nobly.
REGAN   Why is this reasoned?   30
GONERIL
Combine together 'gainst the enemy;
For these domestic and particular broils   32
Are not the question here.
ALBANY   Let's then determine
With th' ancient of war on our proceeding.   34
EDMUND
I shall attend you presently at your tent.   35
REGAN   Sister, you'll go with us?
GONERIL   No.
REGAN
'Tis most convenient. Pray, go with us.   38
GONERIL [*Aside*]
Oho, I know the riddle.—I will go.   39

[*As they are going out,*] enter EDGAR [*disguised*].

EDGAR [*To* ALBANY]
If e'er Your Grace had speech with man so poor,
Hear me one word.
ALBANY [*To the others*]   I'll overtake you.
                          Exeunt both the armies.
                                      Speak.
EDGAR [*Giving a letter*]
Before you fight the battle, ope this letter.
If you have victory, let the trumpet sound   43

25 For as for **26 touches us as** concerns us insofar as **27–28 Not . . .
oppose** not because France encourages the King and others who, I fear,
are driven into opposition by just and weighty grievances. **bolds** embold-
ens by offering encouragement and support **30 reasoned** argued (i.e.,
why are we arguing about reasons for fighting, instead of fighting)
32 particular broils private quarrels **34 ancient of war** veteran officers
35 presently at once **38 convenient** proper, befitting **39 know the riddle**
i.e., understand Regan's enigmatic demand that Goneril accompany her,
which is that Regan wants to keep Goneril from Edmund **43 sound**
sound a summons

For him that brought it. Wretched though I seem,
I can produce a champion that will prove   45
What is avouchèd there. If you miscarry,   46
Your business of the world hath so an end,
And machination ceases. Fortune love you!   48

ALBANY   Stay till I have read the letter.

EDGAR
I was forbid it.
When time shall serve, let but the herald cry
And I'll appear again.   *Exit* [EDGAR].

ALBANY
Why, fare thee well. I will o'erlook thy paper.   53

Enter EDMUND.

EDMUND
The enemy's in view. Draw up your powers.
                    [*He offers* ALBANY *a paper.*]
Here is the guess of their true strength and forces   55
By diligent discovery, but your haste   56
Is now urged on you.

ALBANY   We will greet the time.   *Exit*.   57

EDMUND
To both these sisters have I sworn my love,
Each jealous of the other, as the stung   59
Are of the adder. Which of them shall I take?
Both? One? Or neither? Neither can be enjoyed
If both remain alive. To take the widow
Exasperates, makes mad her sister Goneril,
And hardly shall I carry out my side,   64
Her husband being alive. Now then, we'll use
His countenance for the battle, which being done,   66
Let her who would be rid of him devise
His speedy taking off. As for the mercy   68

---

45 prove i.e., in trial by combat   **46 avouchèd** maintained. **miscarry**
perish, come to destruction   **48 machination** plotting (against your
life)   **53 o'erlook** peruse   **55 guess** estimate   **56 discovery** reconnoiter-
ing   **57 greet the time** meet the occasion   **59 jealous** suspicious   **64 carry out my side** fulfill my ambition, and satisfy her
(Goneril)   **66 countenance** backing, authority of his name   **68 taking off**
killing

Which he intends to Lear and to Cordelia,
The battle done and they within our power,
Shall never see his pardon, for my state   71
Stands on me to defend, not to debate.   *Exit.*   72

Scene Two
[THE BATTLEFIELD.]

Alarum within. Enter, with drum and colors, LEAR,
CORDELIA, *and soldiers, over the stage; and exeunt.*

Enter EDGAR *and* GLOUCESTER.

EDGAR
Here, father, take the shadow of this tree
For your good host. Pray that the right may thrive.   2
If ever I return to you again,
I'll bring you comfort.
GLOUCESTER   Grace go with you, sir!   4
                                Exit [EDGAR].

Alarum and retreat within. Enter EDGAR.

EDGAR
Away, old man! Give me thy hand, away!
King Lear hath lost, he and his daughter ta'en.
Give me thy hand. Come on.
GLOUCESTER
No further, sir. A man may rot even here.
EDGAR
What, in ill thoughts again? Men must endure
Their going hence, even as their coming hither;
Ripeness is all. Come on.
GLOUCESTER   And that's true too.   11
                                Exeunt.

---

71 Shall they shall **71–72 my state . . . debate** my position depends
upon maintenance by force, not by talk
s.d. Alarum trumpet call to arms **2 host** shelterer **4 s.d. retreat**
trumpet signal for withdrawal **11 Ripeness** i.e., fulfillment of one's allotted years and readiness for death when it comes

Scene Three
[THE BRITISH CAMP.]

Enter, in conquest, with drum and colors, EDMUND;
LEAR *and* CORDELIA, *as prisoners; soldiers.* CAP-
TAIN.

EDMUND
  Some officers take them away. Good guard,   1
  Until their greater pleasures first be known   2
  That are to censure them.
CORDELIA [*To* LEAR]   We are not the first   3
  Who with best meaning have incurred the worst.   4
  For thee, oppressèd King, I am cast down;
  Myself could else outfrown false Fortune's frown.
  Shall we not see these daughters and these sisters?   7
LEAR
  No, no, no, no! Come, let's away to prison.
  We two alone will sing like birds i' the cage.
  When thou dost ask me blessing, I'll kneel down
  And ask of thee forgiveness. So we'll live,
  And pray, and sing, and tell old tales, and laugh
  At gilded butterflies, and hear poor rogues   13
  Talk of court news; and we'll talk with them too—
  Who loses and who wins; who's in, who's out—
  And take upon 's the mystery of things,   16
  As if we were God's spies; and we'll wear out,   17
  In a walled prison, packs and sects of great ones,   18
  That ebb and flow by the moon.
EDMUND   Take them away.   19

---

1 Good guard guard them well   **2 their greater pleasures** i.e., the wishes
of those in command   **3 censure** judge   **4 meaning** intentions   **7 Shall
. . . sisters** i.e., aren't we even allowed to speak to Goneril and Regan
before they order to prison their own father and sister   **13 gilded butterflies** i.e., gaily dressed courtiers and other ephemeral types, or perhaps actual butterflies   **16 take upon 's** assume the burden of, or profess
to understand   **17 God's spies** i.e., detached observers surveying the
deeds of mankind from an eternal vantage point. **wear out** outlast **18–
19 packs . . . moon** i.e., followers and cliques attached to persons of
high station, whose fortunes change erratically and constantly

LEAR
  Upon such sacrifices, my Cordelia,
  The gods themselves throw incense. Have I caught
    thee?   21
  He that parts us shall bring a brand from heaven   22
  And fire us hence like foxes. Wipe thine eyes;   23
  The goodyears shall devour them, flesh and fell,   24
  Ere they shall make us weep. We'll see 'em starved
    first.
  Come.   *Exit [with* CORDELIA, *guarded].*

EDMUND
  Come hither, Captain. Hark.
  Take thou this note [*Giving a paper*]; go follow
    them to prison.
  One step I have advanced thee; if thou dost
  As this instructs thee, thou dost make thy way
  To noble fortunes. Know thou this: that men
  Are as the time is. To be tender-minded
  Does not become a sword. Thy great employment   33
  Will not bear question; either say thou'lt do 't   34
  Or thrive by other means.
CAPTAIN   I'll do 't, my lord.
EDMUND
  About it, and write "happy" when th' hast done.   36
  Mark, I say, instantly, and carry it so   37
  As I have set it down.
CAPTAIN
  I cannot draw a cart, nor eat dried oats;
  If it be man's work, I'll do 't.   *Exit* CAPTAIN.

  Flourish. Enter ALBANY, GONERIL, REGAN, [*another*
  CAPTAIN, *and*] *soldiers.*

---

21 throw incense participate as celebrants   **22–23 He . . . foxes** i.e.,
anyone seeking to part us will have to employ a heavenly firebrand to
drive us out of our prison refuge as foxes are driven out of their holes by
fire and smoke. (Suggests that only death will part them.)   **24 goodyears**
(Apparently a word connoting evil or conceivably the passage of time.)
flesh and fell flesh and skin, completely   **33 become a sword** i.e., suit a
warrior   **34 bear question** admit of discussion   **36 write "happy"** call
yourself fortunate. **th'** thou   **37 carry it** arrange it

ALBANY
 Sir, you have showed today your valiant strain,
 And fortune led you well. You have the captives
 Who were the opposites of this day's strife;   43
 I do require them of you, so to use them
 As we shall find their merits and our safety
 May equally determine.

EDMUND
                     Sir, I thought it fit
 To send the old and miserable King
 To some retention and appointed guard,   49
 Whose age had charms in it, whose title more,   50
 To pluck the common bosom on his side   51
 And turn our impressed lances in our eyes   52
 Which do command them. With him I sent the
   Queen,   53
 My reason all the same; and they are ready
 Tomorrow, or at further space, t' appear   55
 Where you shall hold your session. At this time
 We sweat and bleed; the friend hath lost his friend,
 And the best quarrels in the heat are cursed   58
 By those that feel their sharpness.   59
 The question of Cordelia and her father
 Requires a fitter place.

ALBANY   Sir, by your patience,
 I hold you but a subject of this war,   62
 Not as a brother.

REGAN   That's as we list to grace him.   63
 Methinks our pleasure might have been demanded   64
 Ere you had spoke so far. He led our powers,
 Bore the commission of my place and person,

---

43 opposites enemies   **49 retention** confinement   **50 Whose** i.e., the
King's   **51 common bosom** affection of the multitude   **52 turn . . . eyes**
i.e., turn against us the weapons of those very troops whom we impressed into service   **53 Which** we who   **55 space** interval of time   **58–
59 And . . . sharpness** i.e., and even the best of causes, at this moment
when the passions of battle have not cooled, are viewed with hatred by
those who have suffered the painful consequences. (Edmund pretends to
worry that Lear and Cordelia would not receive a fair trial.) **quarrels**
causes. **sharpness** keenness, painful consequences   **62 subject of** subor-
dinate in   **63 list** please   **64 pleasure** wish. **demanded** asked about

The which immediacy may well stand up   67
And call itself your brother.

GONERIL   Not so hot!
In his own grace he doth exalt himself
More than in your addition.

REGAN   In my rights,   70
By me invested, he compeers the best.   71

GONERIL
That were the most if he should husband you.   72

REGAN
Jesters do oft prove prophets.

GONERIL   Holla, holla!   73
That eye that told you so looked but asquint.   74

REGAN
Lady, I am not well, else I should answer
From a full-flowing stomach. [*To* EDMUND.]
    General,   76
Take thou my soldiers, prisoners, patrimony;   77
Dispose of them, of me; the walls is thine.   78
Witness the world that I create thee here
My lord and master.

GONERIL   Mean you to enjoy him?

ALBANY
The let-alone lies not in your good will.   81

EDMUND
Nor in thine, lord.

ALBANY   Half-blooded fellow, yes.   82

REGAN [*To* EDMUND]
Let the drum strike and prove my title thine.   83

ALBANY
Stay yet; hear reason. Edmund, I arrest thee

---

67 immediacy nearness of connection   **70 your addition** the titles you
confer   **71 compeers** is equal with   **72 That . . . most** that investiture
would be most complete   **73 prove** turn out to be   **74 asquint** (Jealousy
proverbially makes the eye look *asquint,* furtively, suspiciously.)   **76 full-flowing stomach** full tide of angry re-
joinder   **77 patrimony** inheritance   **78 the walls is thine** i.e., the citadel
of my heart and body surrenders completely to you   **81 let-alone** pre-
venting, denying   **82 Half-blooded** only partly of noble blood, bastard   **83 Let . . . strike** i.e., let there be a public announcement (?) a
battle (?)

On capital treason; and, in thy attaint   85
                    [Pointing to GONERIL]
This gilded serpent. For your claim, fair sister,
I bar it in the interest of my wife;
'Tis she is subcontracted to this lord,
And I, her husband, contradict your banns.   89
If you will marry, make your loves to me;
My lady is bespoke.

GONERIL   An interlude!   91

ALBANY
Thou art armed, Gloucester. Let the trumpet sound.
If none appear to prove upon thy person
Thy heinous, manifest, and many treasons,
There is my pledge. [*He throws down a glove.*] I'll
   make it on thy heart,   95
Ere I taste bread, thou art in nothing less   96
Than I have here proclaimed thee.

REGAN   Sick, O, sick!

GONERIL [*Aside*]   If not, I'll ne'er trust medicine.   99

EDMUND [*Throwing down a glove*]
There's my exchange. What in the world he is   100
That names me traitor, villain-like he lies.
Call by the trumpet. He that dares approach,
On him, on you—who not?—I will maintain
My truth and honor firmly.

ALBANY
A herald, ho!

EDMUND   A herald, ho, a herald!

Enter a HERALD.

ALBANY
Trust to thy single virtue; for thy soldiers,   106
All levied in my name, have in my name
Took their discharge.

REGAN   My sickness grows upon me.

---

85 in thy attaint i.e., as partner in your corruption and as one who has (unwittingly) provided that *attaint* or impeachment against you   **89 banns** public announcement of a proposed marriage   **91 An interlude** a play; i.e., you are being melodramatic; or, what a farce this is   **95 make** prove   **96 in nothing less** in no respect less guilty   **99 medicine** i.e., poison   **100 What** whoever   **106 single virtue** unaided prowess

ALBANY
    She is not well. Convey her to my tent.
                        [*Exit* REGAN, *supported.*]
    Come hither, herald. Let the trumpet sound,
    And read out this.   [*He gives a paper.*]
CAPTAIN Sound, trumpet!   *A trumpet sounds.*
HERALD *(Reads)* "If any man of quality or degree   113
    within the lists of the army will maintain upon Ed-
    mund, supposed Earl of Gloucester, that he is a
    manifold traitor, let him appear by the third sound of
    the trumpet. He is bold in his defense."
EDMUND   Sound!   *First trumpet.*
HERALD   Again!   *Second trumpet.*
HERALD   Again!   .   *Third trumpet.*
                  Trumpet answers within.

Enter EDGAR, *armed,* [*with a trumpeter before him*].

ALBANY
    Ask him his purposes, why he appears
    Upon this call o' the trumpet.
HERALD   What are you?   122
    Your name, your quality, and why you answer
    This present summons?
EDGAR   Know my name is lost,
    By treason's tooth bare-gnawn and canker-bit.   125
    Yet am I noble as the adversary
    I come to cope.
ALBANY   Which is that adversary?   127
EDGAR
    What's he that speaks for Edmund, Earl of
      Gloucester?
EDMUND
    Himself. What sayst thou to him?
EDGAR   Draw thy sword,
    That, if my speech offend a noble heart,
    Thy arm may do thee justice. Here is mine.
                [*He draws his sword.*]

113 **degree** rank   122 **What** who   125 **canker-bit** eaten as by the cater-
pillar 127 **cope** encounter

Behold, it is the privilege of mine honors,   132
My oath, and my profession. I protest,   133
Maugre thy strength, place, youth, and eminence,   134
Despite thy victor sword and fire-new fortune,   135
Thy valor, and thy heart, thou art a traitor—   136
False to thy gods, thy brother, and thy father,
Conspirant 'gainst this high-illustrious prince,
And from th' extremest upward of thy head   139
To the descent and dust below thy foot   140
A most toad-spotted traitor. Say thou no,   141
This sword, this arm, and my best spirits are bent   142
To prove upon thy heart, whereto I speak,
Thou liest.

EDMUND   In wisdom I should ask thy name.   144
But since thy outside looks so fair and warlike,
And that thy tongue some say of breeding breathes,   146
What safe and nicely I might well delay   147
By rule of knighthood, I disdain and spurn.   148
Back do I toss these treasons to thy head,   149
With the hell-hated lie o'erwhelm thy heart,   150
Which—for they yet glance by and scarcely
    bruise—   151
This sword of mine shall give them instant way,   152
Where they shall rest forever. Trumpets, speak!   153
    [*He draws.*] *Alarums. Fight.* [EDMUND *falls.*]

---

132 of mine honors i.e., of my knighthood **133 profession** i.e.,
knighthood **134 Maugre** in spite of **135 victor** victorious. **fire-new**
newly minted **136 heart** courage **139 upward** top **140 descent** lowest
extreme **141 toad-spotted** venomous, or having spots of infamy. **Say
thou** if you say **142 bent** prepared **144 wisdom** prudence **146 say**
smack, taste, indication **147 safe and nicely** prudently and punctiliously **148 I . . . spurn** i.e., I disdain to insist on my right to refuse
combat with one of lower rank **149 treasons . . . head** i.e., accusations
of treason in your teeth **150 hell-hated** hated as hell is
hated **151 Which . . . bruise** i.e., which charges of treason—since they
merely glance off your armor and do no harm. **for** since. **yet** as yet
152 give . . . way i.e., provide them an immediate pathway to your
heart **153 Where . . . forever** i.e., my victory in trial by combat will
prove forever that the charges of treason apply to you

ALBANY [*To* EDGAR]
  Save him, save him!
GONERIL   This is practice, Gloucester.   154
  By th' law of war thou wast not bound to answer
  An unknown opposite. Thou art not vanquished,
  But cozened and beguiled.
ALBANY   Shut your mouth, dame,   157
  Or with this paper shall I stopple it.—Hold, sir.—   158
  [*To* GONERIL.] Thou worse than any name, read
      thine own evil.   [*He shows her the letter.*]
  No tearing, lady; I perceive you know it.
GONERIL
  Say if I do, the laws are mine, not thine.
  Who can arraign me for 't?
ALBANY   Most monstrous! O!
  Know'st thou this paper?
GONERIL   Ask me not what I know.
                                  Exit.

ALBANY
  Go after her. She's desperate; govern her.   164
                          [*Exit a* SOLDIER.]
EDMUND
  What you have charged me with, that have I done,
  And more, much more. The time will bring it out.
  'Tis past, and so am I. But what art thou
  That hast this fortune on me? If thou'rt noble,   168
  I do forgive thee.
EDGAR   Let's exchange charity.   169
  I am no less in blood than thou art, Edmund;
  If more, the more th' hast wronged me.   171
  My name is Edgar, and thy father's son.
  The gods are just, and of our pleasant vices   173
  Make instruments to plague us.
  The dark and vicious place where thee he got   175
  Cost him his eyes.

154 Save spare. (Albany wishes to spare Edmund's life so that he may confess and be found guilty.) practice trickery; or (said sardonically) astute management 157 cozened tricked 158 stopple stop up. Hold, sir (Perhaps addressed to Edgar; see 5.3.154 and note.) 164 govern restrain 168 fortune on victory over 169 charity forgiveness (for Edmund's wickedness toward Edgar and Edgar's having slain Edmund) 171 th' thou 173 pleasant pleasurable 175 got begot

EDMUND   Th' hast spoken right. 'Tis true.
  The wheel is come full circle; I am here.   177
ALBANY [*To* EDGAR]
  Methought thy very gait did prophesy
  A royal nobleness. I must embrace thee.
                          [*They embrace.*]
  Let sorrow split my heart if ever I
  Did hate thee or thy father!
EDGAR   Worthy prince, I know 't.
ALBANY   Where have you hid yourself?
  How have you known the miseries of your father?
EDGAR
  By nursing them, my lord. List a brief tale,
  And when 'tis told, O, that my heart would burst!
  The bloody proclamation to escape   187
  That followed me so near—O, our lives' sweetness,
  That we the pain of death would hourly die
  Rather than die at once!—taught me to shift
  Into a madman's rags, t' assume a semblance
  That very dogs disdained; and in this habit
  Met I my father with his bleeding rings,   193
  Their precious stones new lost; became his guide,
  Led him, begged for him, saved him from despair;
  Never—O fault!—revealed myself unto him   196
  Until some half hour past, when I was armed.
  Not sure, though hoping, of this good success,   198
  I asked his blessing, and from first to last
  Told him our pilgrimage. But his flawed heart—   200
  Alack, too weak the conflict to support—
  Twixt two extremes of passion, joy and grief,
  Burst smilingly.
EDMUND   This speech of yours hath moved me,
  And shall perchance do good. But speak you on;
  You look as you had something more to say.
ALBANY
  If there be more, more woeful, hold it in,
  For I am almost ready to dissolve,   207
  Hearing of this.

---

177 wheel i.e., wheel of fortune. **here** i.e., at its bottom   **187 The . . .
escape** in order to escape the death-threatening proclamation   **193 rings**
sockets   **196 fault** mistake   **198 success** outcome   **200 flawed**
cracked   **207 dissolve** i.e., in tears

EDGAR   This would have seemed a period   208
To such as love not sorrow; but another,   209
To amplify too much, would make much more   210
And top extremity. Whilst I   211
Was big in clamor, came there in a man   212
Who, having seen me in my worst estate,
Shunned my abhorred society; but then, finding
Who 'twas that so endured, with his strong arms
He fastened on my neck and bellowed out
As he'd burst heaven, threw him on my father,   217
Told the most piteous tale of Lear and him
That ever ear received, which in recounting
His grief grew puissant, and the strings of life   220
Began to crack. Twice then the trumpets sounded,
And there I left him tranced.
ALBANY   But who was this?   222
EDGAR
Kent, sir, the banished Kent, who in disguise
Followed his enemy king and did him service   224
Improper for a slave.

Enter a GENTLEMAN [*with a bloody knife*].

GENTLEMAN
Help, help, O, help!
EDGAR   What kind of help?
ALBANY   Speak, man.
EDGAR
What means this bloody knife?
GENTLEMAN   'Tis hot, it smokes.   227
It came even from the heart of—O, she's dead!
ALBANY   Who dead? Speak, man.

208 a period the limit   209 love not are not in love with 209–211 but . . .
extremity i.e., another sorrowful circumstance, adding to what is already
too much, would increase it and exceed the limit 212 big in clamor loud
in my lamenting 217 As as if. threw . . . father threw himself on my
father's body   220 His i.e., Kent's. puissant powerful. strings of life
heartstrings   222 tranced entranced, senseless 224 his enemy king i.e.,
the king who had rejected and banished him   227 smokes steams

GENTLEMAN
  Your lady, sir, your lady! And her sister
  By her is poisoned; she confesses it.
EDMUND
  I was contracted to them both. All three
  Now marry in an instant.
EDGAR   Here comes Kent.

  Enter KENT.

ALBANY
  Produce the bodies, be they alive or dead.
                          [*Exit* GENTLEMAN.]
  This judgment of the heavens, that makes us
     tremble,
  Touches us not with pity.—O, is this he?
  [*To* KENT.] The time will not allow the compliment   237
  Which very manners urges.
KENT   I am come   238
  To bid my king and master aye good night.   239
  Is he not here?
ALBANY   Great thing of us forgot!
  Speak, Edmund, where's the King? And where's
     Cordelia?

  GONERIL's *and* REGAN's *bodies* [*are*] *brought out.*

  Seest thou this object, Kent?   242
KENT Alack, why thus?
EDMUND Yet Edmund was beloved.   244
  The one the other poisoned for my sake
  And after slew herself.   246
ALBANY Even so. Cover their faces.
EDMUND
  I pant for life. Some good I mean to do,
  Despite of mine own nature. Quickly send—

---

237 compliment ceremony **238 very manners urges** mere decency requires **239 aye good night** farewell forever. (Kent believes he himself is
near death, his heartstrings having begun to crack.) **242 object**
sight **244 Yet** despite everything **246 after** afterwards

Be brief in it—to the castle, for my writ
Is on the life of Lear and on Cordelia.
Nay, send in time.

ALBANY   Run, run, O, run!

EDGAR
To who, my lord? Who has the office? Send   253
Thy token of reprieve.

EDMUND   Well thought on. Take my sword.
Give it the Captain.

EDGAR   Haste thee, for thy life.
                    [*Exit one with* EDMUND'*s sword.*]

EDMUND
He hath commission from thy wife and me
To hang Cordelia in the prison and
To lay the blame upon her own despair,
That she fordid herself.   260

ALBANY
The gods defend her! Bear him hence awhile.
                    [EDMUND *is borne off.*]

Enter LEAR, *with* CORDELIA *in his arms;* [CAPTAIN].

LEAR
Howl, howl, howl! O, you are men of stones!
Had I your tongues and eyes, I'd use them so
That heaven's vault should crack. She's gone
    forever.
I know when one is dead and when one lives;
She's dead as earth. Lend me a looking glass;
If that her breath will mist or stain the stone, 267
Why, then she lives.

KENT   Is this the promised end? 268

EDGAR
Or image of that horror?

ALBANY   Fall and cease!   269

253 office commission   **260 fordid** destroyed   **267 stone** crystal or pol-
ished stone of which the mirror is made   **268 promised end** i.e., Last
Judgment   **269 image** representation. **Fall and cease** i.e., let heavens fall
and all things cease

LEAR
This feather stirs; she lives! If it be so,
It is a chance which does redeem all sorrows
That ever I have felt.
KENT [*Kneeling*]
O my good master!
LEAR
Prithee, away.
EDGAR
'Tis noble Kent, your friend.
LEAR
A plague upon you, murderers, traitors all!
I might have saved her; now she's gone forever!
Cordelia, Cordelia! Stay a little. Ha?
What is 't thou sayst? Her voice was ever soft,
Gentle, and low, an excellent thing in woman.
I killed the slave that was a-hanging thee.
CAPTAIN
'Tis true, my lords, he did.
LEAR
Did I not, fellow?
I have seen the day, with my good biting falchion   281
I would have made them skip. I am old now,
And these same crosses spoil me.—Who are you?   283
Mine eyes are not o' the best; I'll tell you straight.   284
KENT
If Fortune brag of two she loved and hated,   285
One of them we behold.
LEAR
This is a dull sight. Are you not Kent?
KENT
The same,   287
Your servant Kent. Where is your servant Caius?   288

281 falchion light sword   **283 crosses spoil me** adversities take away my strength   **284 I'll . . . straight** I'll recognize you in a moment   **285 two** i.e., Lear, and a hypothetical individual whose misfortunes are without parallel. **loved and hated** i.e., first raised and then lowered   **287 This . . . sight** i.e., my vision is clouding; or, this is a dismal spectacle   **288 Caius** (Kent's disguise name)

LEAR
  He's a good fellow, I can tell you that;
  He'll strike, and quickly too. He's dead and rotten.
KENT
  No, my good lord, I am the very man—
LEAR I'll see that straight.   292
KENT
  That from your first of difference and decay   293
  Have followed your sad steps—
LEAR
                         You are welcome
  hither.
KENT
  Nor no man else. All's cheerless, dark, and deadly.   295
  Your eldest daughters have fordone themselves,   296
  And desperately are dead.
LEAR   Ay, so I think.   297
ALBANY
  He knows not what he says, and vain is it
  That we present us to him.
EDGAR   Very bootless.   299

    Enter a MESSENGER.

MESSENGER Edmund is dead, my lord.
ALBANY
  That's but a trifle here.
  You lords and noble friends, know our intent:
  What comfort to this great decay may come   303
  Shall be applied. For us, we will resign,
  During the life of this old majesty,
  To him our absolute power; [*To* EDGAR *and* KENT]
    you, to your rights,
  With boot and such addition as your honors   307
  Have more than merited. All friends shall taste

---

292 see that straight attend to that in a moment; or, comprehend that
soon **293 first of difference** beginning of your change for the
worse **295 Nor . . . else** no, not I nor anyone else; or, I am *the very man*
(l. 291), him and no one else. **deadly** deathlike **296 fordone** destroyed **297 desperately** in despair **299 bootless** in vain **303 What
. . . come** i.e., whatever means of comforting this ruined king may
present themselves **307 boot** advantage, good measure. **addition** titles,
further distinctions

The wages of their virtue, and all foes
The cup of their deservings.—O, see, see!

LEAR

And my poor fool is hanged! No, no, no life? 311
Why should a dog, a horse, a rat, have life,
And thou no breath at all? Thou'lt come no more,
Never, never, never, never, never!
Pray you, undo this button. Thank you, sir.
Do you see this? Look on her, look, her lips,
Look there, look there! *He dies.*

EDGAR   He faints. My lord, my lord!

KENT

Break, heart, I prithee, break!

EDGAR   Look up, my lord.

KENT

Vex not his ghost. O, let him pass! He hates him 319
That would upon the rack of this tough world 320
Stretch him out longer.

EDGAR   He is gone indeed.

KENT

The wonder is he hath endured so long.
He but usurped his life.

ALBANY

Bear them from hence. Our present business
Is general woe. [*To* KENT *and* EDGAR.] Friends of
    my soul, you twain
Rule in this realm, and the gored state sustain.

KENT

I have a journey, sir, shortly to go. 327
My master calls me; I must not say no.

EDGAR

The weight of this sad time we must obey;
Speak what we feel, not what we ought to say.
The oldest hath borne most; we that are young
Shall never see so much nor live so long. 332

               Exeunt, with a dead march.

---

311 poor fool i.e., Cordelia. (*Fool* is here a term of endearment.) **319 ghost** departing spirit **320 rack** torture rack (with suggestion, in the Folio and quarto spelling *wracke,* of shipwreck, disaster) **327 journey** i.e., to another world **332 s.d. Exeunt** (Presumably the dead bodies are borne out in procession.)

HEDDA GABLER

BY
Henrik Ibsen

ADAPTATION BY Aloha Brown,

BASED ON A TRANSLATION BY
William Archer
and Edmund Gosse

CHARACTERS

MISS JULIANA TESMAN, *George's aunt*

BERTA, *the maid*

GEORGE[1] TESMAN, *research scholar in the history of culture*

HEDDA GABLER TESMAN, *his wife*

THEA[2] RYSING ELVSTED

JUDGE[3] BRACK

EILERT LÖVBORG

The action takes place in the Tesmans' villa in a fashionable suburb of Christiana, Norway, in the late 1800s.

---

[1] Name in the original is "Jörgen," but in English translation it is pronounced "George"
[2] Pronounced Tay' uh
[3] In the original, "Assessor"

ACT ONE

A spacious, handsome, and tastefully furnished drawing room, decorated in dark colors. In the back wall, a wide doorway with curtains open, leading into a smaller room decorated in the same style as the drawing room. In the right-hand wall of the front room, a folding door leading out to the hall. In the opposite wall, on the left, a glass door (or french windows), also with curtains drawn back. Through the glass can be seen part of a veranda and trees in autumn foliage. Standing well downstage left are an oval table, covered, and chairs. By the right wall, downstage of the folding door, is a wide stove of dark porcelain. Also, on stage right near the stove is an armchair with a cushioned footrest. Nearby are two footstools. Upstage right in an alcove is a settee or small sofa with a small round table in front of it. In front, stage left, a little away from the wall, is another sofa. Upstage of glass door (or windows), a piano. On either side of door to inner room are whatnot shelves with ornaments of terra-cotta and majolica. Against the back wall of the inner room a sofa, a table, and one or two chairs. On the wall above the sofa hangs the portrait of a handsome elderly man in a general's uniform. Over the table hangs a lamp with an opal glass shade. Bouquets of flowers are in vases and glasses. Others lie on tables. Floors in both rooms are thickly carpeted. Morning light. The sun shines through the glass.

MISS JULIANA TESMAN, wearing a hat and carrying a parasol, enters from the hall, followed by BERTA, who is carrying flowers wrapped in paper. MISS TESMAN is about sixty-five and of a pleasant appearance. She is simply dressed in gray tailored clothes. BERTA is past middle age and rustic.

MISS TESMAN [*Stops just inside the door, listens, and says softly*] Good gracious! I believe they're still asleep!

BERTA [*Also in hushed tones*] What did I tell you, Miss? Remember how late the boat got in last night. And, then, when they got home! Good lord, what a lot of unpacking the young mistress had me do before she'd go to bed!

MISS TESMAN Ah, well, let them enjoy a good rest. But when they do get up, let's have some fresh air waiting for them. [*Goes to the glass door and opens it wide.*]

BERTA [*By the table, perplexed, with the flowers in her hand*] I declare, there is not a bit of space left. I'll just put them here, Miss. [*Puts flowers on piano.*]

MISS TESMAN So now you have a new mistress, Berta. Heaven knows parting with you was not easy for me.

BERTA [*On the verge of tears*] And you think it wasn't hard for me, too, Miss? After all the blessed years I've been with you and Miss Rina.[1]

MISS TESMAN We must make the best of it, Berta. There's really nothing else to do. George needs you now, here in this house. He does. You know that. You've looked after him since he was a little boy.

BERTA That's true. But, Miss Juliana, I can't help thinking about Miss Rina, lying there in bed so helpless. And that new maid! She'll never learn how to take care of an invalid. Not that one!

MISS TESMAN Oh, I shall manage to train her. I'll do most of the work myself, you know, so don't you worry about my poor sister, Berta dear.

BERTA There's something else, too, Miss. I'm afraid I won't be able to please the young mistress.

MISS TESMAN Oh, well, there may be one or two things at first because—

BERTA Because she's a fine lady and very particular.

MISS TESMAN You can't wonder at that—just think, General Gabler's daughter! What a life she had in the general's day! You can't blame her if she was spoiled by him. Do you remember how we would see her galloping by with her father? And the long black riding outfit with a feather in her cap? How smart she looked!

BERTA Indeed I do, Miss Juliana. But heavens, I never

[1] Pronounced "Reena"

dreamed then that she and Master George would make a match of it!

MISS TESMAN   Neither did I. By the way, Berta—before I forget—you mustn't say Master George anymore—it's Dr. Tesman.

BERTA   Yes, the young mistress said that last night—the moment they set foot in the house. Is it true, then, Miss?

MISS TESMAN   Yes, it is! Just imagine, Berta, some foreign university has made him a doctor while he was abroad. It was a surprise to me, too, until he told me on the pier.

BERTA   Well, he's clever enough for anything, he is! But I never thought he'd go in for doctoring people.

MISS TESMAN   No, he's not that kind of doctor. [*Nods impressively.*] But, later on, you may have to call him something even grander!

BERTA   You don't say! What can that be, Miss?

MISS TESMAN   [*Smiles*] Hmm—wouldn't you like to know? [*Moved.*] Oh, dear God, if only my poor brother could look down and see what a great man his little boy has become! [*Looks around.*] But, what's this, Berta? Why have you taken the chintz covers off the furniture?

BERTA   The mistress told me to. She can't stand covers on chairs, she said.

MISS TESMAN   Are they going to make this their everyday sitting room?

BERTA   It seems so—with her. Master George—the doctor—didn't say anything.

GEORGE TESMAN *enters from the inner room humming to himself and carrying an empty open piece of luggage. He is average height, thirty-three, and stoutish. He has a round, cheerful face with blond hair and beard. He wears spectacles and is dressed in comfortable, old indoor clothes.*

MISS TESMAN   Good morning! Good morning, George!

TESMAN   [*In the doorway between the rooms*] Auntie JuJu! Dear Auntie JuJu! [*Comes forward and shakes her hand affectionately.*] You've come all the way out here! And so early, eh?

MISS TESMAN   I had to come and see how you were getting on.

TESMAN   You haven't had a proper night's sleep.

MISS TESMAN My dear boy, as if that mattered to me!

TESMAN You did get home all right from the pier, eh?

MISS TESMAN Why, of course I did, thank you. Judge Brack was good enough to see me right to my door.

TESMAN We were very sorry we couldn't give you a lift. But you saw for yourself. Hedda had so much luggage—and she insisted on having it all with her.

MISS TESMAN Yes, she did seem to have quite a bit!

BERTA Shall I ask the mistress if there is anything I can do for her?

TESMAN Er—thank you, Berta, you needn't bother. She said she'd ring if she needed anything.

BERTA Oh. [*Starts right.*] Very good, sir.

TESMAN But, Berta, take this bag, will you?

BERTA [*Takes luggage*] I'll put it in the attic. [*Exits into hall.*]

TESMAN Just fancy, Auntie JuJu—I filled that whole bag with notes. It's unbelievable what I managed to find in all the archives I examined, marvelous old documents that no one knew existed—

MISS TESMAN Yes, you don't seem to have wasted a single moment of your wedding trip, George dear!

TESMAN I certainly haven't. But, Auntie, do take off your hat. Here—let me untie it for you, eh?

MISS TESMAN [*While he does so*] How sweet! This is like the old days when you were living at home with us.

TESMAN What a splendid hat!

MISS TESMAN I bought it for Hedda's sake.

TESMAN For Hedda's sake? Eh?

MISS TESMAN Yes, I didn't want Hedda to feel ashamed of her old aunt—in case we go out together.

TESMAN [*Pats her cheek*] You think of everything, Auntie JuJu. [*Puts the hat on a chair by the table.*] Come, let's sit on the sofa and have a little chat until Hedda comes. [*They sit. She puts her parasol in a corner of the sofa.*]

MISS TESMAN [*Clasps both his hands and gazes at him*] What a joy to have you home again, George. Before my eyes! Dear Jochum's own boy!

TESMAN And how glad I am to see you, too. You've been a father and a mother to me.

MISS TESMAN Oh yes, I know you will always keep a place in your heart for your old aunts.

TESMAN But Auntie Rina—how is she? Any better, eh?

MISS TESMAN   Oh no—we can hardly expect that she'll ever be better. She lies there, just as she has all these years. May God let me keep her a little while longer! I don't know what I'd do with my life. Especially now that I don't have you to look after.

TESMAN   [*Pats her on the back*] There, there, there!

MISS TESMAN   [*Suddenly changes her tone and mood*] But, George, imagine! You're a married man now! And it was *you* who carried off Hedda Gabler! The beautiful Hedda Gabler! Surrounded by admirers!

TESMAN   Yes, I think there are quite a few men around town who would like to be in my shoes, eh?

MISS TESMAN   And then to have such a wonderful wedding trip! Five—almost six months!

TESMAN   Well, remember, I used it for research as well. All those libraries and archives I've been through! And the many books I've read!

MISS TESMAN   Yes, dear, of course, I can well believe it! [*Lowers her voice confidentially.*] But, tell me, George, haven't you something—something *special* to tell me?

TESMAN   From our trip?

MISS TESMAN   Yes.

TESMAN   No, I can't think of anything that I didn't write in my letters. My doctor's degree—but I told you that last night.

MISS TESMAN   Yes, yes, you told me about that. But, what I mean is—haven't you any—well—any "expectations"?

TESMAN   Expectations?

MISS TESMAN   My goodness, George. Surely you can talk frankly to your old aunt?

TESMAN   Why, actually, yes, I am expecting something.

MISS TESMAN   Ah!

TESMAN   I expect to become a professor before very long.

MISS TESMAN   A professor?

TESMAN   I think I may say the matter has been decided. But, Auntie, you know about that.

MISS TESMAN [*Chuckling*] Of course I do, dear. You're quite right. [*Changing the subject.*] Now, we were talking about your trip. It must have cost a great amount of money, George?

TESMAN   Well, that research scholarship was pretty ample—that went a long way.

MISS TESMAN   Still, I don't see how it could have been ample enough for two, especially traveling with a lady—they say that makes it ever so much more expensive.

TESMAN   Yes, it makes it a bit more expensive—but Hedda had to have that trip—she *had* to. It was the fashionable thing to do. Anything less grand wouldn't have suited her.

MISS TESMAN   No, no, I suppose not. A wedding trip abroad is the fashion nowadays. Tell me, have you had time to look around the house?

TESMAN   I have indeed! I've been up since daybreak.

MISS TESMAN   What do you think of it all?

TESMAN   It's splendid! Absolutely splendid! Only I don't know what we'll do with the two rooms between this back parlor and Hedda's bedroom.

MISS TESMAN   [*Laughs*] Oh, my dear George, I daresay you'll find some use for them—a little later on.

TESMAN   Yes, of course, Auntie JuJu, as I get more and more books, eh?

MISS TESMAN   [*Continues smiling*] Quite so, George dear. It was your library I was thinking of.

TESMAN   You know, I'm so pleased for Hedda's sake. She had her heart set on this house—it belonged to Secretary Falk—even before we were engaged she said it was the one place she'd like to live.

MISS TESMAN   And then to have it come on the market just after you'd sailed.

TESMAN   We've certainly had all the luck with us, eh?

MISS TESMAN   But the expense, my dear George! It will be very expensive!

TESMAN   Hmm, I suppose it will, won't it?

MISS TESMAN   Oh, George, really!

TESMAN   How much do you think it will cost? In round figures, I mean.

MISS TESMAN   It's impossible to say until we've seen the bills.

TESMAN   Fortunately, Judge Brack got most favorable terms. That's what he wrote Hedda.

MISS TESMAN   Don't you worry, George dear. I've given security for the furniture and all the carpets.

TESMAN   Security? You? Auntie JuJu, what security could you give?

MISS TESMAN   I've arranged a mortgage on our annuity.

TESMAN   [*Jumps up*] What! On Auntie Rina's and your annuity!

MISS TESMAN   I didn't know what else to do.

TESMAN   [*Stands in front of her*] Auntie, have you gone out of your senses? That annuity—it's all Auntie Rina and you have to live on!

MISS TESMAN   Now, now, don't get so excited about it. It's only a matter of form, Judge Brack says. He was kind enough to arrange it all for me. "Only a matter of form"— those were his exact words.

TESMAN   That's all very well, but still—

MISS TESMAN   You'll have a salary of your own now. And even if we should have to help out a little—just at first—it would be the greatest pleasure to us.

TESMAN   Isn't that just like you and Auntie Rina! Always making sacrifices for me.

MISS TESMAN   [*Rises and places her hands on his shoulders*] Have we any other happiness in the world except to smooth your way for you, my dear boy? You've had neither mother nor father to turn to. And we've reached our goal, George! We've been through some bad times, I admit—but, thank heaven, now we have nothing to fear.

TESMAN   Yes, it is really remarkable how everything has turned out for the best.

MISS TESMAN   And there's no one to stand in your way— even your most dangerous rival has fallen. Well, he made his bed—let him lie on it, poor misguided creature.

TESMAN   Have you heard news of Eilert? Since I went away, I mean.

MISS TESMAN   They say he's supposed to have published a new book.

TESMAN   Eilert Lövborg? A new book? Recently, eh?

MISS TESMAN   So they say. Heaven knows whether it can be worth anything! Ah, but when *your* new book appears— that will be another story, George! What's it to be about?

TESMAN   The domestic industries of Brabant during the Middle Ages.

MISS TESMAN   Just imagine—that *you* can write about things like that!

TESMAN   Mind you, it may be some time before I actually

write the book. I've made these very extensive notes, and
I have to file and index them first.

MISS TESMAN   Ah, yes! Making notes, filing, and indexing—
you've always been extraordinary in that. Just like your
dear father.

TESMAN   I can't wait to begin! Especially now that I have
my own comfortable home to work in.

MISS TESMAN   And most of all, now that you have the girl
you set your heart on, George dear.

TESMAN   Oh yes, Auntie JuJu, yes! Hedda—she's the love-
liest part of it all! [*Looks toward the inner room's doorway.*] I think I hear her coming, eh?

HEDDA *enters from the left through the inner room. She is
a woman of twenty-nine. Her face and figure show breeding and distinction. Her complexion is pale and opaque.
Her steel-gray eyes express a cold, unruffled calm. Her
hair is an agreeable medium-brown but not particularly
abundant. She wears a tasteful, loose-fitting morning
gown.*

MISS TESMAN   [*Goes to greet her*] Good morning, Hedda
dear, and welcome home!

HEDDA [*Holds out her hand*] Good morning, dear Miss
Tesman. Calling so early? That is kind of you.

MISS TESMAN   [*Slightly embarrassed*] Well—has the bride
slept well in her new home?

HEDDA   Thank you—yes. Fairly well.

TESMAN   Fairly well! I like that! You were sleeping like a
stone when I got up.

HEDDA   Yes. Fortunately. You know, Miss Tesman, one has
to adapt oneself to new surroundings—little by little.
[*Looks left.*] Oh! That maid has opened the veranda door
and let in a whole flood of sunlight.

MISS TESMAN   [*Goes toward the door*] Well, then we will
shut it.

HEDDA   No, no, not that! Tesman, dear, please draw the
curtains. That will give a softer light.

TESMAN   [*At the veranda door*] All right—all right. There
now, Hedda, you have both shade and fresh air.

HEDDA   Yes, we could do with some fresh air—all these
stacks of flowers! But—won't you sit down, Miss Tesman?

MISS TESMAN No, thank you. Now that I have seen that everything's right here, I must be getting home again to my poor sister.

TESMAN Do give her my very best love, Auntie, and say I shall look in and see her later in the day.

MISS TESMAN Yes, yes, dear, I'll do that. Oh! I'd almost forgotten— [*Feels in the pocket of her dress.*] I have something here for you.

TESMAN What is it, eh?

MISS TESMAN [*Produces a flat parcel wrapped in newspaper and hands it to him*] Look, my dear boy.

TESMAN [*Opens the parcel*] Oh, Auntie JuJu! You really kept them for me! Isn't that touching, Hedda, eh?

HEDDA [*Beside the whatnot shelves on the right*] What is it?

TESMAN My slippers, Hedda! My old bedroom slippers!

HEDDA Oh yes. I remember how often you spoke of them during the trip.

TESMAN I missed them dreadfully. Do have a look at them, Hedda—

HEDDA [*Goes toward stove*] I'm really not very interested.

TESMAN [*Follows her*] Imagine. Sick as she was, Auntie Rina embroidered these for me. They have such memories for me—

HEDDA Scarcely for me.

MISS TESMAN Of course not for Hedda, George.

TESMAN Yes, but I thought since she's one of the family now—

HEDDA [*Interrupts*] Tesman, we're never going to get on with this maid.

MISS TESMAN Not get on with Berta?

TESMAN Hedda, dear, why do you say that, eh?

HEDDA [*Points*] Look! She's left her old hat lying about.

TESMAN [*Shocked, drops the slippers*] But, Hedda—

HEDDA Suppose someone came in and saw it!

TESMAN But, Hedda! That's Auntie JuJu's hat!

HEDDA Oh?

MISS TESMAN [*Picks up hat*] Yes, indeed it is! And, what's more, it is not old, Madam Hedda.

HEDDA I did not look at it very closely, Miss Tesman.

MISS TESMAN [*Puts on the hat*] Let me tell you it's the very first time I've worn it. The very first time.

TESMAN   And it's lovely, too. Most attractive!

MISS TESMAN   Oh, it's hardly all that, George. [*Looks about.*] My parasol? Ah, here. [*Takes it.*] That is mine, too. [*Murmurs.*] Not Berta's.

TESMAN   A new hat and a new parasol! Just think, Hedda!

HEDDA   Quite charming, really.

TESMAN   Yes, isn't it, eh? But, Auntie JuJu, take a look at Hedda before you go. See how lovely *she* is!

MISS TESMAN   Hedda was always lovely, my dear boy. That's nothing new. [*Nods and goes right.*]

TESMAN   [*Follows her*] Yes, but have you noticed how healthy she looks? How she has filled out on the trip?

HEDDA   [*Crosses the room*] Oh, do be quiet—!

MISS TESMAN   [*Stops and turns*] Filled out?

TESMAN   Of course you can't see it in that loose gown—but I, who can see—

HEDDA   [*At the glass door impatiently*] Oh, you can't see anything.

TESMAN   It must have been the mountain air in the Tyrol—

HEDDA   [*Curtly interrupts him*] I'm exactly as I was when I left!

TESMAN   So you insist. But I'm quite certain you are not. What do you think, Auntie?

MISS TESMAN   [*Has folded her hands and is gazing at her*] Hedda is lovely—lovely—lovely. [*Goes to her, takes her head between both hands, draws it downward, and kisses her hair.*] God bless and keep you, Hedda Tesman—for George's sake.

HEDDA   [*Frees herself politely*] Oh! Let me go, please.

MISS TESMAN   [*Quietly, emotionally*] I shall not let a day pass without coming to see you.

TESMAN   Yes, Auntie JuJu, please do, eh?

MISS TESMAN   Good-bye—good-bye!

She exits by the hall door. TESMAN *sees her out. The door remains open.* TESMAN *is heard sending his love to* AUN-TIE RINA *and thanking her for his bedroom slippers. Meanwhile,* HEDDA *paces about the room, raising her arms and clenching her fists as if in desperation. She flings back the curtains of the glass door and stands looking out. A moment later,* TESMAN *returns, closing the door behind him.*

TESMAN [*Picks up the slippers from the floor*] What are you looking at, Hedda?

HEDDA [*Calm and controlled again*] I'm just looking at the leaves. They're so yellow—so withered.

TESMAN [*Wraps up the slippers and lays them on the table*] Yes, we're well into September.

HEDDA [*Again restless*] I know. September—September already!

TESMAN Wasn't Auntie JuJu a little strange? Almost a little—almost formal. What do you suppose was the matter with her, eh?

HEDDA I scarcely know her. Isn't she always like that?

TESMAN No, not as she was today.

HEDDA [*Leaves the glass door*] Perhaps she was annoyed about the hat.

TESMAN Oh, not especially. Perhaps—just for a moment.

HEDDA But, what an idea—leaving your hat about in a drawing room. People don't do such things.

TESMAN You may be sure Auntie JuJu doesn't do it very often.

HEDDA I shall manage to make my peace with her.

TESMAN Yes, my dear, good Hedda, if only you would!

HEDDA When you see them this afternoon you might invite her to spend the evening here.

TESMAN Yes, I will. And there's one other thing you could do that would delight her.

HEDDA What is it?

TESMAN If you could call her Auntie JuJu. For my sake, Hedda, eh?

HEDDA No, no, don't ask me to do that. I've told you so once before. I shall try to call her "Aunt." You must be satisfied with that.

TESMAN I only thought—well, now that you belong to the family, you—

HEDDA I can't in the least see why— [*Goes toward the opening to the inner room.*]

TESMAN [*After a moment*] Is something the matter, Hedda, eh?

HEDDA I'm looking at my old piano. It doesn't go well with the other things.

TESMAN The first time I draw my salary, we'll see about exchanging it.

HEDDA Why exchange it? I don't want to part with it.
Suppose we put it there in the inner room and get a new
one for here? That is, when we can afford it.

TESMAN [*Slightly taken aback*] Yes—of course we could do
that.

HEDDA [*Takes up the bouquet from the piano*] These
flowers were not here last night when we arrived.

TESMAN Auntie JuJu must have brought them for you.

HEDDA [*Examines the bouquet*] Here's a card. [*Takes a
card from the bouquet and reads.*] "Shall return later in
the day." Can you guess whose card it is?

TESMAN No. Whose, eh?

HEDDA The name is "Mrs. Elvsted."

TESMAN Really? Sheriff Elvsted's wife? The former Miss
Rysing?

HEDDA Exactly. The girl with that irritating hair that she
was always showing off. An old flame of yours, I heard.

TESMAN [*Laughs*] Oh, that didn't last long and it was
before I met you, Hedda. Fancy her being in town!

HEDDA It's odd that she should call on us. I haven't seen
her since we left school.

TESMAN I haven't seen her either for—heaven knows how
long. I wonder how she can endure living in such an out-of-
the-way place, eh?

HEDDA I wonder! [*After a moment, says suddenly.*] Tell
me, Tesman, doesn't Eilert Lövborg live somewhere near
there?

TESMAN Yes, that's right. So he does. Somewhere in that
neighborhood.

BERTA [*Enters by hall door*] That lady, ma'am, who left
some flowers a while ago, is here again. [*Points.*] The
flowers you have in your hand, ma'am.

HEDDA Ah, is she? Very well, please show her in.

BERTA *opens the door for* MRS. ELVSTED *and exits.* MRS.
ELVSTED *is a soft, fragile woman with pretty features. Her
eyes are light blue, large, round, and somewhat prominent
with a startled, questioning expression. Her hair is extremely fair, almost flaxen, and extremely thick and wavy.
She is a couple of years younger than* HEDDA. *She wears a
dark visiting dress, in good taste but not in the latest
fashion.*

HEDDA [*Receives her warmly*] How do you do, my dear Mrs. Elvsted? How delightful to see you again after all these years.

MRS. ELVSTED [*Nervously tries to control herself*] Yes, it's a very long time since we met.

TESMAN [*Gives her his hand*] Or since *we* met, eh?

HEDDA Thank you for your lovely flowers.

MRS. ELVSTED Oh, not at all—I wanted to come yesterday afternoon. But I heard that you were away.

TESMAN Have you just come to town, eh?

MRS. ELVSTED I arrived yesterday before noon. Oh, I became almost desperate when I heard that you were away—

HEDDA Desperate! But why?

TESMAN My dear Mrs. Rysing—I mean Mrs. Elvsted—

HEDDA I hope that you're not in any trouble.

MRS. ELVSTED Well, yes, I am, and I don't know another living creature I can turn to.

HEDDA [*Puts the bouquet on the table*] Come—let us sit here on the sofa.

MRS. ELVSTED Oh, I'm really too restless to sit down.

HEDDA Of course you're not. Come along now. [*Draws MRS. ELVSTED down to the sofa and sits beside her.*]

TESMAN Well? What is it, Mrs. Elvsted?

HEDDA Has anything gone wrong at home?

MRS. ELVSTED Yes—that is, yes and no. I do want so much that you don't misunderstand me.

HEDDA Then you better tell us the whole story, Mrs. Elvsted.

TESMAN That's why you've come, eh?

MRS. ELVSTED Yes—yes, it is. Well, then, first of all—but perhaps you've already heard—Eilert Lövborg is in town, too.

HEDDA Lövborg!

TESMAN What! Eilert Lövborg back! Do you hear that, Hedda?

HEDDA Good heavens, yes, I hear it.

MRS. ELVSTED He's been here for a week. Imagine—a whole week. In this town, alone! With so many temptations on all sides.

HEDDA But, my dear Mrs. Elvsted, what concern is he of yours?

MRS. ELVSTED   [*Gives her a startled look and says quickly*]
He is the children's tutor.

HEDDA   Your children?

MRS. ELVSTED   My husband's. I have none.

HEDDA   Oh, your stepchildren, then.

MRS. ELVSTED   Yes.

TESMAN   [*Gropingly*] But was he—I don't know quite how
to put it—sufficiently regular in his habits to be fit for the
post, eh?

MRS. ELVSTED   For the last two years, his conduct has been
irreproachable.

TESMAN   Has it indeed? Think of that, Hedda!

HEDDA   Yes, yes, yes. I heard.

MRS. ELVSTED   Perfectly irreproachable, I assure you! In
every respect. All the same—in this big city—with money
in his pockets—I'm dreadfully frightened for him.

TESMAN   Why didn't he stay where he was? With you and
your husband, eh?

MRS. ELVSTED   After his book was published, he was too
restless to remain with us.

TESMAN   Yes, Auntie JuJu said he'd brought out a new
book.

MRS. ELVSTED   A big book—a wonderful book. A sort of
outline of civilization. It came out a fortnight ago. Everyone's been buying it and reading it—it's created a tremen-
dous stir—

TESMAN   Has it really? It must be something he wrote
during his better days.

MRS. ELVSTED   Long ago, you mean?

TESMAN   Yes.

MRS. ELVSTED   No, he's written it all since he has been with
us—within the last year.

TESMAN   Isn't that splendid news, Hedda? Think of that!

MRS. ELVSTED   Oh yes, if only he can go on like this!

HEDDA   Have you seen him here in town?

MRS. ELVSTED   No, not yet. I had such difficulty in finding
his address, but this morning I discovered it at last.

HEDDA   [*Looks searchingly at her*] I must say it seems a
little odd of your husband to—

MRS. ELVSTED   [*With a nervous start*] Of my husband—
what?

HEDDA   That he should send you all the way to town on

such an errand. Why didn't he come himself to look after his friend?

MRS. ELVSTED Oh no—no—my husband has no time. Besides—I—er—wanted to do some shopping here.

HEDDA [*Smiles slightly*] Oh, I see! That is a different matter.

MRS. ELVSTED [*Rises quickly and uneasily*] Please, Mr. Tesman—I implore you—receive Eilert Lövborg kindly if he should come to see you. I'm sure he will. You were great friends in the old days, and after all you are both studying the same subject, as far as I can understand. You're in the same field, aren't you?

TESMAN We used to be, at any rate.

MRS. ELVSTED That is why I beg so earnestly that you—you will keep a sharp eye on him. Oh, Mr. Tesman, do promise me that you will.

TESMAN With the greatest of pleasure, Mrs. Rysing—

HEDDA Elvsted.

TESMAN I'd be delighted to do anything in my power to help Eilert. You may rely on me.

MRS. ELVSTED Oh, how very, very kind of you! [*Presses his hands.*] Thank you, thank you, thank you— [*Frightened.*] You see, my husband is so very fond of him.

HEDDA Yes—I see. You ought to write to him, Tesman. He may not come to you of his own accord.

TESMAN Yes, that probably would be best, Hedda, eh?

HEDDA Yes. The sooner the better. Why not at once?

MRS. ELVSTED Oh yes, please do!

TESMAN I'll write him this very moment. Have you his address, Mrs. Ry—Mrs. Elvsted?

MRS. ELVSTED [*Takes a slip of paper from her pocket and hands it to him*] Here it is.

TESMAN Good, good. Well, I'll go inside—[*Looks around*] where are my slippers? Ah! Here they are. [*Takes the parcel and starts to go.*]

HEDDA Be sure you write him a cordial, friendly letter. And a good long one, too.

TESMAN I most certainly will.

MRS. ELVSTED Please don't say a word that I suggested it.

TESMAN Good heavens, no, of course not, eh? [*Exits through inner door and then to the right.*]

HEDDA [*Goes to* MRS. ELVSTED, *smiles, and says softly*] There! We've killed two birds with one stone.

MRS. ELVSTED   What do you mean?

HEDDA   Didn't you see that I wanted him out of the room?

MRS. ELVSTED   Yes, to write the letter.

HEDDA   So that I could talk to you alone.

MRS. ELVSTED   [*Confused*] About the same thing?

HEDDA   Precisely.

MRS. ELVSTED   [*Apprehensively*] But there's nothing more, Mrs. Tesman! Absolutely nothing!

HEDDA   Oh yes, but there is. There's a great deal more. I can see that. Come along, sit here. We'll have a cozy chat. [*Forces* MRS. ELVSTED *down into the chair by the stove and seats herself on one of the footstools.*]

MRS. ELVSTED   [*Anxiously glances at her watch*] But, my dear Mrs. Tesman, I was planning to leave.

HEDDA   Oh, you can't be in such a hurry. Now! Tell me about how things are going at home.

MRS. ELVSTED   I prefer not to speak about that.

HEDDA   But, to me, dear! After all, we were at school together.

MRS. ELVSTED   Yes, but you were in the class ahead of me. Oh, I was terribly afraid of you then.

HEDDA   Afraid of me!

MRS. ELVSTED   Yes, dreadfully. When we met on the stairs, you always used to pull my hair.

HEDDA   Did I really!

MRS. ELVSTED   Yes, and once you said you were going to burn it all off.

HEDDA   Oh, that was just foolish talk, of course.

MRS. ELVSTED   I was so silly in those days—and afterward we drifted so far apart. I mean, we moved in different circles.

HEDDA   Well, then, we must drift together again. At school we always called each other by our first names—

MRS. ELVSTED   No, I'm sure you are mistaken.

HEDDA   No, not at all! I remember quite clearly. Now, we're going to be great friends again. [*Draws her stool closer to* MRS. ELVSTED.] There now. [*Kisses her cheek.*] You must call me Hedda.

MRS. ELVSTED   [*Squeezes her hands and pats them*] You're so kind. I'm not used to kindness.

HEDDA   There, there, there. And I shall call you my dear Thora.

MRS. ELVSTED   My name is Thea.

HEDDA   Of course. I meant Thea. [*Looks at her compassionately.*] So you're not used to kindness, Thea? Not in your own home?

MRS. ELVSTED   Oh, if only I had a home! But I haven't. I've never had one.

HEDDA   [*Looks at her for a moment*] I almost suspected as much.

MRS. ELVSTED   [*Gazes helplessly into space*] Yes—yes—yes.

HEDDA   I can't quite remember now—but didn't you first go to Mr. Elvsted as a housekeeper?

MRS. ELVSTED   I really went as a governess. But his wife—his late wife—was an invalid and rarely left her room. So I had to take charge of the house as well.

HEDDA   And eventually you became mistress of the house.

MRS. ELVSTED   [*Sadly*] Yes, I did.

HEDDA   Let me see—how long ago was that?

MRS. ELVSTED   That I married him?

HEDDA   Yes.

MRS. ELVSTED   Five years ago.

HEDDA   Yes, that's right.

MRS. ELVSTED   Oh, those five years! Especially the last two or three. Oh, Mrs. Tesman, if you only knew—!

HEDDA   [*Slaps her hand gently*] Mrs. Tesman? Thea!

MRS. ELVSTED   I'm sorry—I'll try to remember.

HEDDA   [*Casually*] Eilert Lövborg has been in your neighborhood about three years, hasn't he?

MRS. ELVSTED   [*Looks at her doubtfully*] Eilert Lövborg? Why, yes—he has.

HEDDA   Did you know him before? When you were here?

MRS. ELVSTED   No, not really. I mean—I knew him by name of course.

HEDDA   But you saw a great deal of him in the country?

MRS. ELVSTED   Yes, he came to see us every day. He was tutoring the children, you know. I had so much to do. I couldn't manage that, as well.

HEDDA   I'm sure you couldn't. And your husband? I suppose he often has to be away?

MRS. ELVSTED   Yes. You see, Mrs.—you see, Hedda, he has to cover the whole district.

HEDDA   [*Leans against the arm of the chair*] Thea, my poor pretty little Thea! You must tell me everything—exactly as it is.

MRS. ELVSTED   Well, then, you must question me.

HEDDA   What sort of man is your husband, Thea? I mean, as a person. Is he kind to you?

MRS. ELVSTED   [*Evasively*] I am sure he means well in everything.

HEDDA   But, isn't he much too old for you, dear? There must be at least twenty years between you.

MRS. ELVSTED   [*Irritably*] Yes, there's that, too. Oh, there are so many things! We're different in every way. We have nothing in common. Nothing whatever.

HEDDA   But, he loves you surely? In his way?

MRS. ELVSTED   Oh, I don't know. I think he regards me as a useful property. And I don't cost much to keep. I am not expensive.

HEDDA   That is stupid of you.

MRS. ELVSTED   [*Shakes her head*] It cannot be otherwise— not with him. I don't think he cares for anyone but himself—and perhaps a little for the children.

HEDDA   And for Eilert Lövborg, Thea.

MRS. ELVSTED   [*Looks at her*] Eilert Lövborg? Why do you say that?

HEDDA   Well, my dear, when he sends you all the way to town to look for him— [*Smiles imperceptibly*] Besides, you said so yourself to Tesman.

MRS. ELVSTED   [*With a nervous twitch*] Did I? Oh yes, I suppose I did. [*Vehemently, but not loudly.*] No—oh—I might as well tell you the truth. It will come out sooner or later.

HEDDA   Why, my dear Thea—

MRS. ELVSTED   Well, then—my husband did not know I was coming here.

HEDDA   What! Your husband didn't know!

MRS. ELVSTED   No, of course not. As a matter of fact, he wasn't even there. I couldn't stand it, Hedda. I simply couldn't. I would have been so alone up there now.

HEDDA   And then?

MRS. ELVSTED   So, I packed a few things—just those I needed most—I didn't say a word to anyone. And then I left the house.

HEDDA   Just like that!

MRS. ELVSTED   Yes, and took the train straight to town.

HEDDA   Why, my dear, good Thea—that you could dare to
do such a thing!

MRS. ELVSTED   [*Rises and moves about the room*] What else
could I possibly do?

HEDDA   But what will your husband say when you go home
again?

MRS. ELVSTED   [*At the table, looks at her*] Back to him?

HEDDA   Of course.

MRS. ELVSTED   I shall never go back to him.

HEDDA   [*Rises and moves toward her*] You mean you've
actually left your home for good?

MRS. ELVSTED   Yes. I didn't see what else I could do.

HEDDA   But, to leave like that, so openly—

MRS. ELVSTED   Oh, you can't keep a thing like that a secret.

HEDDA   What will people say about you, Thea?

MRS. ELVSTED   They say what they like. I don't care. [*Sits
wearily and sadly on the sofa.*] I did what I had to do.

HEDDA   What are your plans now? How are you going to
live?

MRS. ELVSTED   I don't know. I only know that I must live
wherever Eilert Lövborg is—if I am to live at all.

HEDDA   [*Takes a chair from the table, seats herself beside
MRS. ELVSTED, and strokes her hands*] My dear Thea—
how did this—this friendship—between you and Eilert
Lövborg happen?

MRS. ELVSTED   It grew gradually. I gained a sort of power
over him.

HEDDA   Really?

MRS. ELVSTED   Yes. After a while he gave up his old habits.
Not because I asked him to—I never would have dared do
that. But he saw how repulsive they were to me, and so he
dropped them.

HEDDA   [*Conceals a scornful smile*] Then you have reformed him—as the saying goes—my clever little Thea!

MRS. ELVSTED   Well, *he* says so, at any rate, and in return he
has made a real human being of me. Taught me to think
and to understand so many things.

HEDDA   Did he give you lessons, too, then?

MRS. ELVSTED   Not exactly lessons. But he talked to me.

Explained—oh, you've no idea—so many things! And then came the most wonderful time of all—when I began to share in his work—when he allowed me to help him!

HEDDA   He allowed you to help him!

MRS. ELVSTED   Yes! Whenever he wrote anything, we'd always work on it together.

HEDDA   Like two true companions—comrades—friends!

MRS. ELVSTED   Yes, that's what *he* says! I ought to be perfectly happy, but I'm not because I don't know how long it will last.

HEDDA   You don't seem very sure of him.

MRS. ELVSTED   [*Gloomily*] There's a woman's shadow between Eilert Lövborg and me.

HEDDA   Who can that be?

MRS. ELVSTED   I don't know. Someone from his past. Someone he's never been able to forget.

HEDDA   What has he told you—about her?

MRS. ELVSTED   He spoke of her once—quite vaguely.

HEDDA   What did he say?

MRS. ELVSTED   He said that when they parted she threatened to shoot him with a pistol.

HEDDA   What nonsense! No one does that sort of thing here!

MRS. ELVSTED   No, and that's why I think it must have been that red-haired singer that at one time he—

HEDDA   Ah, yes, very likely.

MRS. ELVSTED   I remember that they used to say of her that she carried loaded firearms.

HEDDA   Then, of course, she is the one.

MRS. ELVSTED   [*Wrings her hands*] And now, Hedda—I heard that this singer—that she's in town again! I'm so worried I don't know what to do!

HEDDA   [*Glances toward inner room*] Sh! Here comes Tesman. [*Rises and whispers.*] Thea—not a word to him—all this is between us.

MRS. ELVSTED   Yes—yes!

GEORGE TESMAN *enters from the right through the inner room. He has a letter in his hand.*

TESMAN   There now—the letter is signed and sealed.

HEDDA   Very good. Mrs. Elvsted was just leaving. Wait a
minute. I'll go with you to the garden gate.

TESMAN   Do you think Berta could post this letter for me?

HEDDA   [*Takes the letter*] I will tell her to.

BERTA   [*Enters from the hall*] Judge Brack wishes to know
if Mrs. Tesman will receive him.

HEDDA   Yes. Show him in. And post this letter, will you?

BERTA   [*Takes the letter*] Yes, ma'am.

She opens the door for JUDGE BRACK *and exits herself.*
BRACK *is forty-five, rather short but well built, and elastic
in his movements. He has a round face and an aristocratic
profile. His hair is short, still almost black, and carefully
dressed. His eyes are bright and sparkling; his eyebrows,
thick. His moustache is also thick with short-cut ends. He
wears an eyeglass, which he lets drop now and then.*

BRACK   [*Hat in hand, bows*] May one venture to call so
early in the day?

HEDDA   Of course one may.

TESMAN   [*Shakes hands with him*] You are welcome at any
time. [*Introduces him.*] Judge Brack––Miss Rysing—

HEDDA   Oh!

BRACK   [*Bows*] Ah—delighted—

HEDDA   [*Looks at him and laughs*] What fun to see you by
daylight, Judge!

BRACK   Do you find me—altered?

HEDDA   Yes, a little younger, I think.

BRACK   [*Laughs*] I thank you, most heartily.

TESMAN   But, what do you think of Hedda, eh? Doesn't she
look flourishing? She's positively—

HEDDA   For heaven's sake, leave me out of it. You ought to
thank Judge Brack for all the trouble he has taken.

BRACK   Nonsense. It is a pleasure, I assure you.

HEDDA   You are a friend indeed. But here stands Thea,
impatient to be off—so au revoir, Judge. I shall be back
directly. [*Mutual good-byes.* MRS. ELVSTED *and* HEDDA
exit by the hall door.]

BRACK   So, is your wife fairly satisfied, then?

TESMAN   Yes, we can't thank you enough. Of course, she
talks of rearranging here and there, and one or two things
are still wanting.

BRACK   Oh?

TESMAN   But, we won't trouble you. Hedda will see to that herself. Why don't we sit down, eh?

BRACK   Thanks, for the moment. [*Sits by the table.*] There's something I want to speak with you about, my dear Tesman.

TESMAN   Ah, I understand! [*Sits.*] The expenses, eh?

BRACK   That's not so pressing, although perhaps I wish we had managed things a bit more economically.

TESMAN   That would have been out of the question. Think of Hedda, dear fellow! You, who know her so well—she's used to a certain standard of living!

BRACK   No, no, that's the trouble, exactly.

TESMAN   Fortunately, it can't be long before I receive my appointment.

BRACK   Um—such things often hang fire for some time.

TESMAN   Have you heard anything definite, eh?

BRACK   Nothing definite. [*Interrupts himself.*] By the way, I have one piece of news for you.

TESMAN   Well?

BRACK   Your old friend Eilert Lövborg is back in town.

TESMAN   I know that already.

BRACK   Really? How did you hear?

TESMAN   That lady who left with Hedda.

BRACK   Oh yes, what was her name? I didn't quite catch it.

TESMAN   Mrs. Elvsted.

BRACK   Aha—Sheriff Elvsted's wife? Of course. Lövborg's been living up near them, hasn't he?

TESMAN   I'm delighted to hear that he's quite a reformed character.

BRACK   Yes, so they say.

TESMAN   And he's published a new book, eh?

BRACK   Indeed he has.

TESMAN   And it has caused some sensation!

BRACK   Quite an unusual sensation.

TESMAN   Isn't that good news? A man of such extraordinary talents. I was sorry to think he had gone to ruin.

BRACK   That was what everyone thought.

TESMAN   I can't imagine what he'll do now. How in the world will he make his living, eh?

As he speaks his last words, HEDDA *enters from the hall.*

HEDDA [*To* BRACK *with a scornful laugh*] Tesman is forever worrying about how people are to make a living.

TESMAN We were talking about poor Eilert Lövborg, Hedda dear.

HEDDA [*Glances at him quickly*] Oh? [*Seats herself in the armchair by the stove and asks casually.*] What is the matter with him?

TESMAN Well—he must have run through his inheritance long ago. And he can't write a new book every year, eh? So why shouldn't I worry what's to become of him?

BRACK Perhaps I can give some information on that point:

TESMAN Indeed!

BRACK You must remember that his relatives have a good deal of influence.

TESMAN But they washed their hands of him altogether.

BRACK At one time they called him the hope of the family.

TESMAN At one time, yes! But he soon put an end to that.

HEDDA Who knows? [*With a slight smile.*] I hear they have reformed him up at the Elvsteds'.

BRACK And then there's his new book—

TESMAN Well, I hope they find something for him. I have just written to him. I asked him to come and see us this evening, Hedda dear.

BRACK But, my dear fellow, you're coming to my stag party this evening. You promised me last night down on the pier.

HEDDA Had you forgotten, Tesman?

BRACK For that matter, you can rest assured that he won't come.

TESMAN What makes you say that, eh?

BRACK [*Hesitates, rises, and leans on the back of the chair*] My dear Tesman—and you, too, Mrs. Tesman—there's something I think you ought to know.

TESMAN Something that concerns Eilert, eh?

BRACK Both you and him.

TESMAN Well, my dear Judge—out with it!

BRACK You must be prepared to find your appointment deferred longer than you desired or expected.

TESMAN [*Jumps up quickly*] Is there some hitch about it, eh?

BRACK The nomination may depend on the result of a competition—

TESMAN Competition! Think of that, Hedda!

HEDDA [*Leans back farther in her chair*] Ah! How interesting!

TESMAN With whom? Surely you can't mean—

BRACK Yes. Precisely. Eilert Lövborg.

TESMAN No, no! It's quite inconceivable! Quite impossible, eh?

BRACK Hm, well, it may come to that all the same.

TESMAN But, Judge Brack, this would be incredibly unfair to me. [*Waves his arms.*] I'm a married man! We married on the strength of these prospects, Hedda and I. We've run into debt and borrowed money from my aunts, too. Why, they practically promised me the appointment, eh?

BRACK [*Calming*] Now, now. You'll probably get the appointment, only now you'll compete for it.

HEDDA [*Sits motionless in the armchair*] Just think, Tesman, it will have quite a sporting interest.

TESMAN Dearest Hedda, how can you be so indifferent about it?

HEDDA Indifferent! I am not at all indifferent. I am most eager to see who wins.

BRACK In any case, I thought it best you should know how things stand. I mean—before you buy any "additional trifles."

HEDDA This could not possibly make any difference, my dear Judge.

BRACK Indeed! Then I have no more to say. Good-bye! [*To* TESMAN.] I'll call for you later on my way back from my afternoon walk.

TESMAN Oh yes, yes—your news has quite upset me.

HEDDA [*Still reclining, holds out her hand*] Good-bye, Judge, and call in the afternoon.

BRACK Thank you. Good-bye, good-bye!

TESMAN [*Sees him to the hall door*] Good-bye, my dear Judge—you really must excuse me— [BRACK *exits by the hall door.*]

TESMAN [*Paces the room*] Oh, Hedda, one should never rush into adventures, eh?

HEDDA [*Looks at him and smiles*] Do *you* do *that*?

TESMAN There's no denying it—it was a big adventure to marry and set up house on mere expectations.

HEDDA You may be right.

TESMAN   Well, at least we have our lovely home, Hedda, eh? The home we both dreamt of. And set our hearts on.

HEDDA   [*Rises slowly and wearily*] It was part of our agreement to entertain often. We were to keep open house.

TESMAN   Yes, good heavens, I was looking forward to it all so much! To see you playing hostess to a select circle of society. Ah well, for the time being we shall have to be happy with each other's company, Hedda. We can always invite Auntie JuJu in now and then. But I wanted it to be so different for you, Hedda dear. So very different.

HEDDA   I suppose this means I cannot have a butler at the present time.

TESMAN   Yes, I'm afraid a butler is quite out of the question!

HEDDA   And the fine saddle horse I was to have?

TESMAN   [*Appalled*] The saddle horse!

HEDDA   I suppose that's out of the question, too?

TESMAN   Good heavens, yes! That's obvious.

HEDDA   Well, at least I have one thing to amuse myself.

TESMAN   Oh, thank heaven for that! What is it, Hedda, eh?

HEDDA   [*At the center opening, looks at him with suppressed scorn*] My pistols.

TESMAN   [*Alarmed*] Your pistols!

HEDDA   [*With cold eyes*] General Gabler's pistols. [*Exits through the inner room.*]

TESMAN   [*Rushes to the center opening and calls after her*] No, for heaven's sake, Hedda darling, don't touch those dangerous things! For my sake, Hedda, eh?

ACT TWO

The rooms at the TESMANS' *as in the first act, except the piano has been removed and replaced by an elegant writing table with bookshelves. A smaller table has been placed by the sofa left. Most of the bouquets have been removed.* MRS. ELVSTED's *bouquet stands on the large table downstage. It is afternoon.*

HEDDA, *dressed to receive callers, is alone in the room. She stands by the open glass door, loading a pistol. The matching pistol lies in an open pistol case on the writing table.*

HEDDA   [*Looks down into the garden and calls*] Welcome back, Judge!

BRACK   [*In the distance*] Thank you, Mrs. Tesman!

HEDDA   [*Raises the pistol and aims*] Now, I'm going to shoot you, Judge!

BRACK   [*Calling, unseen still*] No, no, no! Don't aim at me like that!

HEDDA   That's what comes of sneaking in the back way. [*She fires.*]

BRACK   [*Nearer*] Are you out of your mind!

HEDDA   Oh, dear! Did I happen to hit you?

BRACK   [*Still from outside*] I wish you'd stop all this nonsense.

HEDDA   All right, come on in, Judge.

JUDGE BRACK, *dressed for a men's party, enters by the glass door. He carries a light overcoat over his arm.*

BRACK   For God's sake? Are you still fooling with those pistols? What are you shooting at?

HEDDA   Oh, I'm only firing in the air.

BRACK   [*Gently taking the pistol out of her hand*] Allow me. Ah—I know this pistol well! [*Looks around.*] Where is the case? Ah, here it is. [*Lays the pistol in the case and shuts it.*] That game is finished for today.

HEDDA   What on earth *am* I to do?

BRACK   Had you no visitors?

HEDDA   Not one. I suppose all our friends are still out of town.

BRACK   Tesman isn't home either?

HEDDA   [*At the writing table, puts pistol case in a drawer and shuts it*] No, he rushed off to his aunts directly after lunch. He didn't expect you so early.

BRACK   Hmm, how stupid of me not to have thought of that!

HEDDA   [*Turns her head and looks at him*] Stupid?

BRACK   Because in that case I would have come a little— earlier.

HEDDA [*Crossing the room*] Then you would have found no one to receive you, for I have been in my room dressing ever since lunch.

BRACK But is there a crack in the door through which we might converse?

HEDDA You forgot to arrange one.

BRACK Another stupidity.

HEDDA Well, we'll just have to settle down here—and wait. Tesman may not be back for some time.

BRACK Never mind. I can be patient.

HEDDA *sits in a corner of the sofa.* BRACK *lays his overcoat over the back of the nearest chair and sits, but keeps his hat in his hand. A short silent pause. They look at each other.*

HEDDA Well?

BRACK [*In the same tone*] Well?

HEDDA I spoke first.

BRACK [*Leans forward slightly*] Come, let us have a nice, cozy little chat, Mrs. Hedda.

HEDDA [*Leans farther back on the sofa*] It seems ages since our last one, doesn't it, Judge? Oh, a few words last night and this morning, but they don't count.

BRACK You mean a *real* talk—just the two of us?

HEDDA Well, yes—that's roughly what I meant.

BRACK There wasn't a day that I didn't wish you were home again.

HEDDA So did I.

BRACK You? Really, Mrs. Hedda? And I imagined you were enjoying the trip tremendously!

HEDDA Oh yes, imagine!

BRACK Tesman's letters led me to think so.

HEDDA Tesman! You know Tesman, my dear Judge! His idea of happiness is grubbing about in libraries and dusty archives and making endless copies of old parchments— or whatever you call them.

BRACK [*With a touch of malice*] Well, that is his vocation— or a large part of it.

HEDDA Yes, of course. Then, it's all right for him! But for me! Oh, my dear Judge, I can't tell you how bored I was.

BRACK [*Sympathetically*] Do you mean that? Seriously?

HEDDA   Yes. Surely you can understand? To go for six whole months without meeting a soul who was one of our circle or who could talk about our kind of things.

BRACK   Ah, yes, that would bother me, too.

HEDDA   But the most intolerable of all was—

BRACK   What?

HEDDA   To be everlastingly with one and the same person.

BRACK   [*With a nod of agreement*] Morning, noon, and night—at all possible times and seasons.

HEDDA   I said "everlastingly."

BRACK   Right. But with our excellent Tesman, I would have thought—

HEDDA   Tesman is—a specialist, my dear Judge.

BRACK   Undeniably.

HEDDA   And specialists are not amusing traveling companions—not for long, at any rate.

BRACK   Not even the specialist one happens to love?

HEDDA   Ugh! Don't use that sickening, revolting word!

BRACK   [*Startled*] What? What's that, Mrs. Hedda?

HEDDA   Just try it, Judge! To hear nothing but the history of civilization morning, noon, and night—

BRACK   Everlastingly.

HEDDA   And then all this business about the domestic industries of Brabant during the Middle Ages! That's the most maddening part of all!

BRACK   But, tell me—if you feel like this, why on earth did you—uh—

HEDDA   Why on earth did I marry George Tesman, you mean?

BRACK   If you like to put it that way.

HEDDA   Do you think it so very strange?

BRACK   Well, yes and no, Mrs. Hedda.

HEDDA   I had danced myself tired, my dear Judge—and I wasn't getting any younger. [*With a slight shudder.*] But I won't talk about that. I won't even think about it.

BRACK   You certainly have no reason to.

HEDDA   Ah, reasons— [*Watching him carefully.*] And George Tesman—you would agree—is a very proper man, an acceptable choice.

BRACK   Proper, acceptable, and dependable—a most worthy man.

HEDDA And I don't see anything especially ridiculous about him. Do you?

BRACK Ridiculous? No-o-o—I wouldn't say that.

HEDDA Hmm. Anyway, he works incredibly hard on his research! Who knows? He may still make a name for himself.

BRACK [*Looks at her uncertainly*] I thought that you believed like everyone else that he was going to be quite famous some day.

HEDDA [*Wearily*] Yes, so I did. Then since he was so bent on supporting me, I really didn't see why I shouldn't accept his offer.

BRACK No, if you look at it like that—

HEDDA It was more than my other admirers were prepared to do, my dear Judge.

BRACK [*Laughs*] Well, I can't answer for the others—for myself, I've always had a considerable respect for the institution of marriage—as an institution.

HEDDA [*Jokingly*] Oh, I never had any hopes for *you*.

BRACK All I want is to have a warm circle of intimate friends, whom I can trust, where I can be of use, with the freedom to come and go as—as a trusted friend—

HEDDA Of the—master of the house, you mean?

BRACK [*Bows*] To be frank, preferably of the mistress. But of the master, too, of course! I find such a triangular friendship—if I may call it so—a great convenience to all concerned.

HEDDA Yes, God knows a third person would have been welcome on our trip. Oh, those infernal tête-à-têtes—in railway compartments!

BRACK Fortunately your wedding trip is over now.

HEDDA Not by a long—long way. I've only come to one stop on the line.

BRACK Why not jump out and stretch yourself a bit, Mrs. Hedda?

HEDDA I never jump out.

BRACK Why not?

HEDDA There's always someone around waiting to—

BRACK [*Laughs*] Stare at your legs, is that it?

HEDDA Precisely.

BRACK Well, but after all—

HEDDA [*With a gesture of disgust*] I won't have it. I'd rather keep my seat and continue the tête-à-tête.

BRACK But suppose a third person were to jump *in* and join the couple.

HEDDA Ah! That would be different!

BRACK A trusted friend, who understands—

HEDDA And was lively and entertaining in a variety of ways—

BRACK And not a bit of a specialist.

HEDDA [*With an audible sigh*] Yes, that would be a relief.

BRACK [*Hears the front door and glances in that direction*] The triangle is completed.

HEDDA [*Half aloud*] And on goes the train.

GEORGE TESMAN, *in a gray walking suit and a soft felt hat, enters from the hall. He has a great number of paper-bound books under his arms and in his pockets.*

TESMAN [*Goes up to the table beside the corner sofa*] Phew! It's hot work carrying all these books around, Hedda. [*Sets the books down.*] I'm positively perspiring. [HEDDA *makes a hardly audible "How charming!"*] Why, hullo, what's this—you're here already, Judge, eh? Berta didn't tell me.

BRACK I came in through the garden.

HEDDA What are all those books?

TESMAN [*Stands looking through them*] Oh, some new books on my special subject. I had to have them.

HEDDA Your special subject?

BRACK On his special subject, Mrs. Tesman. [*He and* HEDDA *exchange a confidential smile.*]

HEDDA Do you still need more books on your special subject?

TESMAN Yes, my dear Hedda, one can never have too many. One must keep abreast of the latest publications.

HEDDA Yes, I suppose one must.

TESMAN [*Searching among his books*] And look, I bought Eilert Lövborg's new book, too. [*Offers it to her.*] Perhaps you would care to have a look at it, Hedda, eh?

HEDDA No, thank you—well, perhaps later.

TESMAN I glanced through it on my way home.

BRACK   What do you think of it—as a specialist?

TESMAN   I think it's remarkable how sound and balanced it is. He never wrote like that before. [*Gathers the books together.*] I'll just take these into my study. I can hardly wait to cut the pages! And then I must change my clothes. [*To* BRACK.] We don't have to rush off yet, eh?

BRACK   Oh no. There's not the slightest hurry.

TESMAN   Then I'll take my time. [*Starts to go out with the books but stops at the center opening.*] By the way, Hedda, Auntie JuJu cannot come to see you this evening.

HEDDA   Not coming? Is she still annoyed about the hat?

TESMAN   Good heavens, no. How could you think such a thing? You see, Auntie Rina is very ill.

HEDDA   She always is.

TESMAN   Yes, but today she is worse than ever, poor dear.

HEDDA   Then it is only right for her sister to stay with her. I shall have to try to bear it.

TESMAN   You can't imagine, dear, how delighted Auntie JuJu was to see you looking so flourishing—and so filled out!

HEDDA   [*Rises, under her breath*] Oh, those everlasting aunts!

TESMAN   What?

HEDDA   [*Goes to glass door*] Nothing.

TESMAN   Oh, all right. [*He goes through the inner room, out to the right.*]

BRACK   What did you say about a hat?

HEDDA   Oh, something that happened this morning. Miss Tesman had removed her hat and laid it down [*Looks at him and smiles*] and I pretended it was the servant's.

BRACK   Why, my dear Mrs. Hedda, how could you do such a thing? Hurt that fine old lady?

HEDDA   [*Walks nervously about the room*] Well, you see— these impulses come over me suddenly—and I can't resist them. [*Flings herself down in the armchair by the stove.*] I don't know how to explain it myself.

BRACK   [*Behind the armchair*] You're not really happy. That's the heart of it.

HEDDA   [*Stares straight ahead*] Why on earth should I be happy? Can you give me a reason?

BRACK   For one thing, here you are in the house where you always longed to live.

HEDDA [*Looks at him and laughs*] You really believe that
  story?

BRACK Wasn't it true, then?

HEDDA Oh yes, it's partly true.

BRACK Well?

HEDDA There's truth in it that I made use of Tesman to see
  me home from parties last summer.

BRACK Unfortunately, my way lay in a different direction.

HEDDA Oh yes, you were going in a different direction last
  summer, weren't you, Judge?

BRACK [*Laughs*] How naughty of you, Mrs. Hedda! Back to
  you and Tesman—

HEDDA Well, one evening we walked by this house. And
  Tesman, poor thing, was turning and twisting to find something to talk about. And I felt sorry for a man of such
  learning—

BRACK [*Smiles skeptically*] You felt sorry? You! Hmm.

HEDDA Yes, I sincerely did. So, just to make conversation
  and help him out of his misery, I foolishly said what a
  charming house this was and how I should love to live in it.

BRACK No more than that?

HEDDA Not *that* evening.

BRACK But afterward?

HEDDA Yes, my foolishness had its consequences, my dear
  Judge.

BRACK Unfortunately, that happens all too often, Mrs.
  Hedda.

HEDDA Thanks! So, you see it was this fictitious enthusi-
  asm for Secretary Falk's villa that really brought Tesman
  and me together. From that came our engagement and our
  marriage, our wedding journey, and all the rest of it. Ah,
  well, Judge, as they say, as you make your bed so you must
  lie in it.

BRACK This is priceless! I suppose you didn't care a rap
  about the house?

HEDDA No, God knows, I didn't.

BRACK But even now? That we've made it so attractive and
  comfortable for you?

HEDDA Ugh! All the rooms smell of lavender and dried
  rose leaves. But maybe that scent was brought in by "Auntie JuJu."

BRACK [*Laughs*] No, that's probably a legacy from the late Mrs. Falk.

HEDDA Yes, there is the odor of mortality about it like a corsage—the day after the ball. [*Clasps her hands behind her head, leans back in her chair, and looks at him.*] Oh, my dear Judge—you can't imagine how incredibly I shall bore myself here!

BRACK Shouldn't you find some vocation, Mrs. Hedda?

HEDDA A vocation—that would attract me?

BRACK Preferably, yes.

HEDDA God only knows what that could be. I often wonder whether— [*Breaks off.*] No, that wouldn't do, either.

BRACK Who knows? Tell me.

HEDDA I was thinking perhaps I might persuade Tesman to go into politics.

BRACK [*Laughs*] Tesman? No, I can promise you, politics is not his line. In fact, the last thing in the world for him.

HEDDA Perhaps not, but I could try and get him into it all the same.

BRACK Why? What satisfaction could you find in that? If he can't succeed? Why should you want to drive him into it?

HEDDA Because I'm *bored*, I tell you! [*After a pause.*] Then, you think it's out of the question that he could ever be a cabinet minister?

BRACK Hmm—you see, Mrs. Hedda, to get into the ministry he would have to be a fairly rich man.

HEDDA [*Rises impatiently*] Yes, there you have it! Money! Always money! [*Crosses the room.*] It's this genteel poverty I've stumbled into that makes life so pitiful—so utterly ludicrous—for that's what it is!

BRACK Now, *I* should say the fault lies elsewhere.

HEDDA Where, then?

BRACK Nothing really exciting has ever happened to you. Nothing has ever really stirred you.

HEDDA Nothing serious, you mean?

BRACK Call it that if you like. But now perhaps it may come.

HEDDA [*Tosses her head*] Oh, you're thinking about the competition for that ridiculous professorship. That's Tesman's problem. I assure you I shall not waste a thought on it!

BRACK   I daresay. But suppose you should find yourself
faced with—what people would call—a grave responsibility—[*Smiles*] a *new* responsibility, Mrs. Hedda?

HEDDA   [*Angrily*] Be quiet! Nothing of that sort will ever
happen to me!

BRACK   [*Cautiously*] We'll talk of this a year from now, if not
before.

HEDDA   I have no talent for that sort of thing, Judge. And it
doesn't appeal to me. No responsibilities for me!

BRACK   What makes you think you're less fitted than other
women? It's a natural inclination for women to assume the
duty—

HEDDA   [*At the glass door*] Be quiet, I tell you! I often think
I have only one talent in life.

BRACK   [*Moves closer*] And what, may I ask, is that?

HEDDA   [*Looks out*] To bore myself to death! Now you
know it. [*Turns and looks toward the inner room.*] See
what I mean! Here comes the professor!

BRACK   [*Softly, in a tone of warning*] Now, now, Mrs.
Hedda!

GEORGE TESMAN, *dressed for the party, with gloves and
hat in his hand, enters from the right through the inner
room.*

TESMAN   Hedda, has there been a message from Eilert Lövborg, eh?

HEDDA   No.

TESMAN   Then, you'll see, he'll be here presently.

BRACK   Do you really think he will come?

TESMAN   I'm almost sure he will. What you told us this
morning was probably just a rumor, mere gossip.

BRACK   Oh?

TESMAN   Yes. Auntie JuJu said she didn't believe he'd dare
to stand in my way again. Think of that!

BRACK   Well, then, there's nothing to worry about.

TESMAN   [*Puts his hat and gloves on a chair, right*] You
must let me wait for him as long as possible, though.

BRACK   We've plenty of time yet. My guests won't arrive
before seven or half past.

TESMAN   Ah, then we can keep Hedda company and see
what happens, eh?

HEDDA [*Takes* BRACK*'s coat and hat to the settee*] And if the worst comes to the worst, Mr. Lövborg can sit and talk with me.

BRACK [*Offers to take his things*] Oh, allow me, Mrs. Tesman! What do you mean by "the worst"?

HEDDA If he refuses to go with you and Tesman.

TESMAN [*Looks at her dubiously*] But, Hedda, dear—do you think it would be quite right for him to stay here with you, eh? Remember Auntie JuJu can't come.

HEDDA No, but Mrs. Elvsted is coming. We three can have a cup of tea together.

TESMAN Oh yes, that would be *quite* all right.

BRACK [*Smiles*] It's perhaps the safest plan for him.

HEDDA Why so?

BRACK Well, you know, Mrs. Tesman, how rude you always were about my stag parties. You said they should be attended only by men of the strictest principles.

HEDDA I'm sure Mr. Lövborg is a man of principle now. After all—a reformed sinner—

BERTA *appears at the hall door.*

BERTA There's a gentleman asking to see you, ma'am.

HEDDA Oh yes. Show him in.

TESMAN [*Softly*] It must be Eilert! By Jove! Think of that!

EILERT LÖVBORG *enters from the hall. He is slim and lean. The same age as* TESMAN, *he looks older as though worn-out by life. Hair and beard are dark brown; his face, long and pale but with patches of color on the cheekbones. He wears a well-cut black visiting suit, quite new. He carries dark gloves and a silk hat. He stands near the door and makes a rapid bow, slightly embarrassed.*

TESMAN [*Goes to him and shakes his hand warmly*] Welcome, my dear Eilert! So at last we meet again!

LÖVBORG [*Speaks in a hushed voice*] It was good of you to write, George. [*Goes nearer to* HEDDA.] May I shake hands with you, too, Mrs. Tesman?

HEDDA [*Takes his hand*] I'm delighted to see you, Mr. Lövborg. [*With a motion of her hand.*] I don't know if you two gentlemen—

LÖVBORG [*Bows slightly*] Judge Brack, I believe.

BRACK [*Also bows slightly*] Of course. It's been some years—

TESMAN [*To* LÖVBORG *with his hands on his shoulders*] And, now, Eilert, make yourself at home. Right, Hedda? I hear you're going to settle in town again, eh?

LÖVBORG Yes, I plan to.

TESMAN That makes sense. I just got your new book, Eilert, but I haven't had time to read it.

LÖVBORG I wouldn't bother if I were you.

TESMAN Why? What do you mean?

LÖVBORG There's nothing much in it.

TESMAN By Jove! You can say that!

BRACK It's been enormously praised, I hear.

LÖVBORG That was what I wanted. So I put nothing in it that anyone could not agree with.

BRACK Very wise of you.

TESMAN But, my dear Eilert—

LÖVBORG You see, I want to make a fresh start, to build up my position again.

TESMAN [*Slightly embarrassed*] Oh, that's what you plan to do, eh?

LÖVBORG [*Smiles, puts down his hat, and takes a parcel wrapped in paper from his coat pocket*] But, when this one appears, George Tesman, you will have to read it, for this is a real book. My true self is here—in this.

TESMAN Indeed? And what is it?

LÖVBORG It's the sequel.

TESMAN Sequel? Of what?

LÖVBORG Of the other book.

TESMAN You mean the new one?

LÖVBORG Of course.

TESMAN Yes but, my dear Eilert—surely that comes down to our own time!

LÖVBORG Yes, but, this deals with the future.

TESMAN The future! But, good heavens, we know nothing about the future!

LÖVBORG True. Still, there's a thing or two that needs to be said about it all the same. [*Opens the packet.*] Look here—

TESMAN That's not your handwriting.

LÖVBORG I dictated it. [*Thumbs through the pages.*] It's in two sections. The first deals with the forces shaping the civilization of the future, and the second part [*Runs through pages to the end*] forecasts the probable lines of development it's likely to take.

TESMAN   How extraordinary! It would never occur to me to write about anything like that.

HEDDA   [*At the glass door, drumming on the pane*] No, I daresay not.

LÖVBORG   [*Puts the manuscript back in its wrapping and lays it on the table*] I brought it with me because I thought I might read you a bit of it this evening.

TESMAN   That was kind of you, Eilert, but this evening— [*Glances at* BRACK.] I don't see how we can manage it—

LÖVBORG   Well, then, some other time. There's no hurry.

BRACK   The truth is, Mr. Lövborg, I'm giving a little party this evening to honor Tesman, mainly.

LÖVBORG   [*Looks for his hat*] Oh—then I mustn't detain you.

BRACK   No, listen—won't you give me the pleasure of your company, also.

LÖVBORG   [*Curtly and decisively*] No, I can't. Thank you very much.

BRACK   Oh, nonsense! Do come. We shall be a select little circle and I can assure you we shall have a "jolly time," as Mrs. Hed—as Mrs. Tesman says.

LÖVBORG   I don't doubt it. Nevertheless—

BRACK   You could bring your manuscript and read it to Tesman at my house. I could give you a room to yourselves.

TESMAN   Yes, think of that, Eilert—why shouldn't you, eh?

HEDDA   [*Interrupts*] But, Tesman, if Mr. Lövborg would rather not! I'm sure he would prefer to stay here and have supper with me.

LÖVBORG   [*Looks at her*] With you, Mrs. Tesman?

HEDDA   And with Mrs. Elvsted.

LÖVBORG   Oh—[*Casually*] I saw her for a moment today.

HEDDA   Did you? Well, she's coming here this evening. So, you're almost obliged to stay, Mr. Lövborg. Otherwise, Mrs. Elvsted will have no one to see her home.

LÖVBORG   That's true. Many thanks, Mrs. Tesman, I will stay.

HEDDA   Splendid! I'll just tell the maid—

She goes to the hall door and rings. BERTA *enters.* HEDDA *talks to her in a whisper and points to the inner room.* BERTA *nods and exits.*

TESMAN [*At the same time*] Tell me, Eilert, is it this new subject, the future, that you're going to lecture about?

LÖVBORG Yes.

TESMAN They told me at the bookseller's that you're to deliver a series of lectures this autumn.

LÖVBORG Yes, I am. I hope you've no objection, George.

TESMAN No, not in the least! But—

LÖVBORG I can quite understand that it might interfere with your plans.

TESMAN [*Depressed*] I can't very well expect you, out of consideration for *me,* to—

LÖVBORG But, of course, I'll wait until you receive your appointment.

TESMAN What! You'll wait! But—but—aren't you going to compete with me for the post, eh?

LÖVBORG No, I only want people to realize that I *could* have—a moral victory, if you like.

TESMAN Why, bless me—then Auntie JuJu was right after all! Oh, I knew it! Hear that, Hedda? Just fancy—Eilert Lövborg is not going to stand in our way!

HEDDA Our way! Pray leave me out of it!

BERTA *enters. She goes toward the inner room and arranges a tray with decanters and glasses on the table.* HEDDA *joins her.* HEDDA *nods approval and comes forward again.* BERTA *exits.*

TESMAN [*At the same time*] What do you say to this, Judge, eh?

BRACK I say a moral victory—hmm—may be all very fine, but—

TESMAN Yes, of course. But still—

HEDDA [*Looks at* TESMAN *with a cold smile*] You stand there looking absolutely thunderstruck, Tesman.

TESMAN You know, I think I am.

BRACK A thunderstorm has just passed over us, Mrs. Tesman.

HEDDA   And now, gentlemen, won't you have a glass of cold punch before you go?

BRACK   [*Looks at his watch*] A stirrup cup? That's not such a bad idea.

TESMAN   A capital idea, Hedda. Just the thing! Now that the weight has been lifted from my mind—

HEDDA   You'll join them, Mr. Lövborg?

LÖVBORG   [*With a gesture of refusal*] No, thank you. Nothing for me.

BRACK   Good Lord, cold punch—it isn't poison, you know.

LÖVBORG   Perhaps not for everyone.

HEDDA   You two go ahead. I'll keep Mr. Lövborg company.

TESMAN   Yes, yes, Hedda dear, do.

TESMAN *and* BRACK *go into the inner room, sit, drink punch, smoke cigarettes, and carry on an animated conversation during the following.* LÖVBORG *remains standing by the stove.* HEDDA *goes to the writing table.*

HEDDA   [*Raises her voice a little*] Tesman and I did some sightseeing on our trip. Perhaps you'd like to see some photographs of our tour through the Tyrol on our way home.

She brings over an album, which she lays on the table by the sofa, in the farther corner of which she seats herself. LÖVBORG *approaches, stops, and looks at her. Then he takes a chair and seats himself to her left with his back to the inner room.*

HEDDA   [*Opens the album*] Do you see this range of mountains, Mr. Lövborg? It's the Ortler group—oh yes, Tesman has written underneath. "The Ortler group near Meran."

LÖVBORG   [*Who has never taken his eyes off her, says softly and slowly*] Hedda—Gabler!

HEDDA   [*Gives him a quick look*] Hush! Sh!

LÖVBORG   [*Repeats softly*] Hedda Gabler!

HEDDA   [*Looking at the album*] That was my name in the old days—when you and I knew each other.

LÖVBORG   Then I must learn never to say Hedda Gabler again?

HEDDA [*Turns the pages*] Yes, I'm afraid you must. The
sooner the better.

LÖVBORG [*Indignant*] Hedda Gabler married! And married
to—George Tesman!

HEDDA Yes. Well—that's how life goes!

LÖVBORG Oh, Hedda, Hedda—how could you throw yourself away like that?

HEDDA [*Looks at him sharply*] Stop it! I won't have you say
such things.

LÖVBORG Why shouldn't I?

TESMAN *enters and goes toward the sofa.*

HEDDA [*Hears him coming and says casually*] And this is a
view, Mr. Lövborg, from the Ampezzo Valley. Just look at
those peaks! [*Looks up at* TESMAN *affectionately.*] What's
the name of those curious peaks, dear?

TESMAN Let me see. Oh, those are the Dolomites.

HEDDA Oh yes, those are the Dolomites, Mr. Lövborg.

TESMAN Hedda, dear, wouldn't you like a little punch? For
yourself at any rate, eh?

HEDDA Yes, please. And perhaps a few biscuits.

TESMAN Cigarettes?

HEDDA No.

TESMAN Very well.

He goes to inner room and out to the right. BRACK *sits in
inner room, occasionally watching* HEDDA *and* LÖVBORG.

LÖVBORG [*Softly, as before*] Answer me, Hedda. How
could you do this?

HEDDA [*Apparently absorbed in the album*] If you continue
saying Hedda like that to me, I won't talk to you.

LÖVBORG Can't I say Hedda even when we're alone?

HEDDA No. You may think it, but you mustn't say it.

LÖVBORG I understand. It offends your love for George
Tesman.

HEDDA [*Glances at him and smiles*] Love? What an idea!
How funny you are!

LÖVBORG Then you don't love him!

HEDDA All the same, I don't intend to be unfaithful to him.
Remember that.

LÖVBORG   Hedda, answer me just one thing.
HEDDA   Sh!

TESMAN *enters from the inner room with a small tray.*

TESMAN   Here you are! Isn't this tempting? [*He sets tray on the table.*]
HEDDA   Why did you bring it yourself?
TESMAN   [*Fills the glasses*] Because I think it's such fun to wait on you, Hedda.
HEDDA   But you've poured out two glasses. Mr. Lövborg said he wouldn't have any.
TESMAN   I know. But Mrs. Elvsted will be here soon, won't she?
HEDDA   Oh yes. Mrs. Elvsted.
TESMAN   Had you forgotten her, eh?
HEDDA   We were so absorbed in these photographs. Do you remember this little village?
TESMAN   Oh, it's that one right below the Brenner Pass. We spent the night there—
HEDDA   —and met that lively party of tourists.
TESMAN   Yes, that was the place. Just think, if only we could have had you with us, Eilert, eh? [*Smiles good-naturedly.*]

He returns to inner room and sits beside BRACK.

LÖVBORG   Answer me this one thing, Hedda.
HEDDA   Well?
LÖVBORG   Was there no love in your feeling for *me,* either? Not a spark—not one glimmer of love?
HEDDA   I wonder. To me, we were two good comrades, two companions, two thoroughly intimate friends. [*Smiles.*] You were exceedingly frank!
LÖVBORG   It was you who made me so.
HEDDA   As I look back on it all, I realize there was something very beautiful, something fascinating, something daring—yes, daring—in that secret intimacy, that no living soul suspected.
LÖVBORG   Yes, yes, Hedda! Do you remember when I used to come to your house in the afternoon and the general sat

over by the window reading his paper, with his back to
us—

HEDDA   We sat on the corner sofa—

LÖVBORG   Always reading the same illustrated paper—

HEDDA   For want of an album, yes!

LÖVBORG   Do you remember, Hedda, all those wild things I
confessed to you? Things no one suspected at the time—
my days and nights of passion and frenzy, of drinking and
madness! How did you make me talk like that? What
power in you, Hedda, forced me to confess?

HEDDA   Power? In me?

LÖVBORG   Yes. How can I explain it? And all those devious
questions you asked—

HEDDA   Which you understood so perfectly—

LÖVBORG   How could you bring yourself to ask such questions? So frankly, so boldly?

HEDDA   In a devious way, you said.

LÖVBORG   But boldly all the same.

HEDDA   And how could you bring yourself to answer, Mr.
Lövborg?

LÖVBORG   That's what I can't understand. There must have
been love at the bottom of it, at the bottom of our friendship. Did you feel you would purge my sins by making me
confess that way?

HEDDA   No, not quite.

LÖVBORG   What was your motive, then?

HEDDA   Do you find it so surprising, so incredible, that a
young girl—if there's no chance of anyone else knowing—

LÖVBORG   Yes?

HEDDA   That she'd like some glimpse—should be tempted
to investigate—a forbidden world, a world she's not supposed to know about?

LÖVBORG   So that was it?

HEDDA   Partly. Partly, I think.

LÖVBORG   I see. Partners in a thirst for life. Then why did it
end?

HEDDA   That was your fault.

LÖVBORG   You broke it off.

HEDDA   Yes, when that intimacy of ours threatened to grow
more serious—to be dragged down to reality. Shame on
you, Eilert Lövborg! How could you abuse my trust when
I'd been so bold with my friendship?

LÖVBORG [*Clenches his fists*] Why didn't you do as you said? Why didn't you shoot me?

HEDDA Because I have a positive dread of scandal.

LÖVBORG Yes, Hedda, you are a coward at heart.

HEDDA A terrible coward. [*Changes her tone.*] But it was lucky for you. You've found ample consolation at the Elvsteds.

LÖVBORG I know Thea has confided in you.

HEDDA And perhaps you have confided in her—about us?

LÖVBORG Not a word. She's too stupid to understand that.

HEDDA Stupid?

LÖVBORG About that sort of thing—yes.

HEDDA And I am a coward. [*Leans toward him without looking him in the eye and says softly.*] Now I will confide something to you.

LÖVBORG [*Tensely*] Well?

HEDDA My not daring to shoot you—

LÖVBORG Yes?

HEDDA That wasn't my worst cowardice that evening.

LÖVBORG [*Looks at her for a moment, understands, and whispers passionately*] Oh, Hedda. Hedda Gabler! Now I begin to understand why we've been so close. You and I—! It *was* your craving for life—

HEDDA [*Softly, with a sharp glance*] Take care! Don't delude yourself.

It has begun to grow dark. BERTA *opens the hall door.* HEDDA *closes the album with a snap and smiles.*

HEDDA Ah, at last! Thea, dear—please come in!

MRS. ELVSTED *enters from the hall. She is in evening dress. The door is closed behind her.*

HEDDA [*On the sofa, stretches out her arms to her*] Darling little Thea—I thought you were never coming!

MRS. ELVSTED *in passing greets the gentlemen in the inner room, then goes up to the table and gives* HEDDA *her hand.* EILERT LÖVBORG *rises. He and* MRS. ELVSTED *greet each other with a silent nod.*

MRS. ELVSTED   Should I go and say good evening to your husband?

HEDDA   Oh, that's nonsense. We needn't bother about them. They're leaving soon.

MRS. ELVSTED   Are they going out?

HEDDA   Yes, to a men's party.

MRS. ELVSTED   [*Quickly to* LÖVBORG] You're not going with them?

LÖVBORG   No.

HEDDA   Mr. Lövborg is staying here with us.

LÖVBORG *sits again on the sofa.*

MRS. ELVSTED   [*Takes a chair and starts to sit beside him*] Oh, how nice it is to be here!

HEDDA   No, no, Thea dear! Not there! I want to be in the middle.

MRS. ELVSTED   Just as you like. [*She goes around the table and sits on the sofa to* HEDDA's *right.*]

LÖVBORG   [*To* HEDDA, *after a short pause*] Isn't she lovely to look at?

HEDDA   [*Lightly stroking her hair*] Only to look at?

LÖVBORG   Yes. Because we two—she and I—are true companions. We trust each other completely. We can talk frankly.

HEDDA   Not in a devious way, Mr. Lövborg.

LÖVBORG   Well—

MRS. ELVSTED   [*Clings to* HEDDA, *says softly*] Oh, I'm so happy, Hedda! Imagine—he says I've inspired him in his work!

HEDDA   [*Looks at her and smiles*] Does he really?

LÖVBORG   And then she has such courage, Mrs. Tesman.

MRS. ELVSTED   Good heavens, courage?

LÖVBORG   Absolute courage. Where I'm concerned.

HEDDA   Yes, courage! If one only had that!

LÖVBORG   Then what?

HEDDA   Then one might be able to live. In spite of everything. [*Changes her tone suddenly.*] But now, Thea darling, you must have a nice glass of cold punch.

MRS. ELVSTED   No, thank you. I never take anything like that.

HEDDA You, Mr. Lövborg?

LÖVBORG I don't either, thank you.

MRS. ELVSTED No, he doesn't either.

HEDDA [*Looks at him intently*] But if I want you to?

LÖVBORG It makes no difference.

HEDDA [*Laughs*] Poor me! Have I no power over you at all?

LÖVBORG Not in that area.

HEDDA But seriously, I think you ought to take it. For your own sake.

MRS. ELVSTED Why, Hedda—

LÖVBORG Why do you think so?

HEDDA People might suspect that you are not quite sure, quite confident of yourself.

MRS. ELVSTED [*Softly*] Oh, please, Hedda, don't—!

LÖVBORG People can suspect whatever they like.

MRS. ELVSTED [*Happily*] Yes, let them.

HEDDA Didn't you see Judge Brack's face a moment ago?

LÖVBORG What did you see?

HEDDA His contemptuous smile when you didn't dare to join them in there.

LÖVBORG Didn't dare! I simply wanted to stay here and talk to you.

MRS. ELVSTED That was only natural, Hedda.

HEDDA How could the judge know that? I saw him smile and glance at Tesman when you didn't dare go to their wretched little party.

LÖVBORG Didn't dare! You say I didn't dare!

HEDDA No, *I* don't say it. But that's the way the judge looks at it.

LÖVBORG Well, let him.

HEDDA So you're not going with them?

LÖVBORG No, I'm staying here with you and Thea.

MRS. ELVSTED Yes, Hedda, of course he is.

HEDDA [*Smiles and nods approvingly to* LÖVBORG] There, you see! Firm as a rock! A man of principle! That's how a man should be! [*Turns to* MRS. ELVSTED *and strokes her cheek.*] What did I tell you this morning, Thea, when you were so upset?

LÖVBORG [*Amazed*] Upset?

MRS. ELVSTED [*Terrified*] Hedda—! *Please*, Hedda!

HEDDA   You see? Now are you convinced? There's no reason for you to be deathly afraid that— [*Interrupts herself.*]
There! Now we can all three enjoy ourselves!

LÖVBORG   [*With a start*] What does all this mean, Mrs.
Tesman?

MRS. ELVSTED   Oh my God, my God, Hedda, what are you
saying? What are you doing?

HEDDA   Not so loud. That horrid judge is watching you.

LÖVBORG   So deathly afraid? For my sake?

MRS. ELVSTED   [*Softly, miserably*] Oh, Hedda, you've
ruined everything.

LÖVBORG   [*Looks at her intensely with a distorted face*] So,
that's how completely you trusted me.

MRS. ELVSTED   Eilert, dear, please listen to me—

LÖVBORG   [*Takes one of the glasses of punch, raises it, and
says in a low, husky voice*] Your health, Thea! [*Empties the
glass, puts it down, and takes the second one.*]

MRS. ELVSTED   [*Softly*] Hedda, Hedda, how could you do
this?

HEDDA   *I* do it? I? Are you crazy?

LÖVBORG   And here's to your health, too, Mrs. Tesman.
Thanks for the truth. Long live truth! [*Drains the glass
and is about to refill it.*]

HEDDA   [*Lays her hand on his arm*] All right. No more for
now. Remember, you're going to the party.

MRS. ELVSTED   No, no, no!

HEDDA   Sh! They're watching you.

LÖVBORG   [*Puts down his glass*] Now, Thea, be honest with
me.

MRS. ELVSTED   Yes?

LÖVBORG   Did your husband know you came after me?

MRS. ELVSTED   [*Wringing her hands*] Hedda, do you hear
what he is asking me?

LÖVBORG   You arranged between you that you should come
here and keep an eye on me? Perhaps he gave you the
idea? I suppose he needed my help in the office. Or he
missed me at the card table?

MRS. ELVSTED   [*Softly, sobbing*] Eilert! Eilert!

LÖVBORG   [*Seizes a glass and is about to refill it*] Skoal to
the old sheriff, too!

HEDDA   [*Lays her hand on his arm*] That's enough for now.
You have to read your manuscript to Tesman.

LÖVBORG [*Calmly, putting down the glass*] I'm behaving like a fool, Thea—I mean, taking it like this. Try and forgive me, my dear, dear friend. You'll see—you'll see—yes, and they'll see—though I stumbled and fell—I'm back on my feet again! With your help, Thea.

MRS. ELVSTED [*Radiant*] Oh, thank God!

In the meantime, BRACK *has looked at his watch. He and* TESMAN *stand and enter the drawing room.*

BRACK [*Takes his hat and overcoat*] Well, Mrs. Tesman, it's time for us to go.

HEDDA I suppose it is.

LÖVBORG I've decided to join you, Judge.

MRS. ELVSTED [*Softly, imploringly*] Oh, Eilert, don't!

HEDDA [*Pinching her arm*] Sh! They can hear you!

MRS. ELVSTED [*Gives a little cry*] Ow!

LÖVBORG [*To* BRACK] You were kind enough to ask me to join you.

BRACK You're coming after all?

LÖVBORG Yes, if you don't mind.

BRACK I'm delighted.

LÖVBORG [*To* TESMAN, *puts the manuscript in his pocket*] I should like to show you one or two things before I send it to the printers.

TESMAN Just think—how exciting! But, Hedda dear, how will Mrs. Elvsted get home, eh?

HEDDA Oh, we shall manage somehow.

LÖVBORG [*Looks toward the ladies*] Mrs. Elvsted? Of course, I'll come back and fetch her. [*Approaches.*] Around ten o'clock, Mrs. Tesman? Will that do?

HEDDA Yes, that will do admirably.

TESMAN Well, then, that's settled. But you mustn't expect *me* that early, Hedda.

HEDDA Oh, you may stay as long as you like, dear.

MRS. ELVSTED [*With suppressed anxiety*] Mr. Lövborg—I'll wait here until you come.

LÖVBORG [*His hat in his hand*] Pray do, Mrs. Elvsted.

BRACK So, gentlemen—the excursion train is leaving! I hope we'll have a "jolly time," as a certain fair lady puts it.

HEDDA Ah, if only the fair lady could be there, unseen, Judge.

BRACK   Why unseen?

HEDDA   To share in your unbridled fun.

BRACK   [*Laughs*] I should not advise the fair lady to try it.

TESMAN   [*Also laughs*] My, you're a nice one, Hedda! What an idea!

BRACK   Well, good-bye. Good-bye, ladies!

LÖVBORG   [*Bows*] About ten o'clock, then.

HEDDA   Yes, Mr. Lövborg.

BRACK, LÖVBORG, *and* TESMAN *exit through the hall door. At the same time,* BERTA *enters from the inner room with a lighted lamp, which she sets on the drawing room table and exits through the inner room.*

MRS. ELVSTED   [*Has risen and is pacing restlessly*] Hedda, what will come of all this?

HEDDA   At ten o'clock—he'll be here. I can see him—with vine leaves in his hair—flushed and fearless!

MRS. ELVSTED   Oh, I do hope so!

HEDDA   And then, you see, he'll be himself again! He'll be a free man forever and ever.

MRS. ELVSTED   Oh, God—if only he would come as you see him now!

HEDDA   He will come as I see him. [*Rises and approaches her.*] Doubt him as much as you like. *I* believe in him. Now—we shall find out—

MRS. ELVSTED   You have some hidden reason for this, Hedda.

HEDDA   Yes, I have. For once in my life, I want to have power to shape a human destiny.

MRS. ELVSTED   Haven't you that power already?

HEDDA   I haven't. I have never had it.

MRS. ELVSTED   What about your husband?

HEDDA   Him? Would it be worth the trouble? Oh, if only you could understand how poor I am. And you're allowed to be so rich! [*Flings her arms around* THEA *passionately.*] I think I'll burn your hair off after all!

MRS. ELVSTED   Let me go! Let me go! I'm afraid of you, Hedda!

BERTA   [*In the center opening*] Tea is laid in the dining room, ma'am.

HEDDA   Very well, we're coming. [BERTA *exits through inner room.*]

MRS. ELVSTED   No, no! I would rather go home alone! At once!

HEDDA   Nonsense! First, you're going to have some tea, you little fool. And then—at ten o'clock—Eilert Lövborg comes—with vine leaves in his hair— [*She drags* MRS. ELVSTED, *almost by force, toward the inner room.*]

ACT THREE

The same. The curtains are drawn across the middle doorway and also across the glass doors. The shaded lamp, turned down low, is burning on the table. The door of the stove is open and the fire is almost out.

MRS. ELVSTED, *wrapped in a large shawl, reclines in the armchair near the stove with her feet on a footstool.* HEDDA *lies asleep on the sofa covered with a blanket.*

MRS. ELVSTED   [*After a pause, suddenly sits upright in her chair and listens eagerly. Then she sinks back wearily, moaning to herself.*] Not yet — Oh, God!— Oh, God!— Not yet—

BERTA *slips cautiously in by the hall door. She has a letter in her hand.*

MRS. ELVSTED   [*Turns and whispers eagerly*] Well? Did someone come?

BERTA   [*Softly*] A servant just brought this letter.

MRS. ELVSTED   [*Quickly, stretching out her hand*] A letter! Give it to me!

BERTA   But it's for Dr. Tesman, ma'am.

MRS. ELVSTED   Oh.

BERTA   Miss Tesman's maid brought it. I'll leave it here on the table.

MRS. ELVSTED   Yes, do.

BERTA [*Puts down the letter*] I'd better put out the lamp. It's smoking.

MRS. ELVSTED Yes, put it out. It's nearly daylight.

BERTA [*Puts out the lamp*] It is daylight, ma'am.

MRS. ELVSTED Yes, broad day. And not home yet—

BERTA Lord bless you, ma'am—I guessed how it would be.

MRS. ELVSTED You guessed?

BERTA Yes, when I heard that a—certain gentleman—had returned to town and that he'd gone off with them. We heard plenty about him over the years.

MRS. ELVSTED Sh! Not so loud! You'll wake Mrs. Tesman.

BERTA [*Looks at sofa and sighs*] Yes, you're right—let her sleep, poor thing. Shall I put more wood on the fire, ma'am?

MRS. ELVSTED Thank you, not for me.

BERTA Oh, very well, ma'am. [*Goes quietly out through the hall door.*]

HEDDA [*Wakes as the door closes and looks up*] What's that?

MRS. ELVSTED It was just the maid—

HEDDA [*Looks around her*] What are we doing here? Oh, now I remember. [*Sits up on the sofa, stretches, and rubs her eyes.*] What time is it, Thea?

MRS. ELVSTED [*Looks at her watch*] It's past seven.

HEDDA When did Tesman get home?

MRS. ELVSTED He hasn't come.

HEDDA Not home yet?

MRS. ELVSTED No one has come.

HEDDA And we were fools enough to sit up until four in the morning—

MRS. ELVSTED [*Wrings her hands*] And how I've watched and waited for him!

HEDDA [*Yawns and says with her hand in front of her mouth*] Well, we might have spared ourselves the trouble.

MRS. ELVSTED Did you manage to get a little sleep?

HEDDA Yes, I believe I slept quite well—didn't you?

MRS. ELVSTED I couldn't, Hedda. I couldn't possibly!

HEDDA [*Rises and goes to her*] There, there! There's nothing to be alarmed about. I know what has happened.

MRS. ELVSTED What? Please tell me!

HEDDA Obviously, the party went on very late—

MRS. ELVSTED Yes—that's clear enough—but—

HEDDA   And Tesman didn't want to come home and wake
us in the middle of the night—[*Laughs*] probably didn't
want to show himself in the shape he was in, either.

MRS. ELVSTED   Where could he have gone?

HEDDA   To his aunts, of course! I expect he went there to
sleep it off. They keep his old room ready for him.

MRS. ELVSTED   No, he can't be with them. Miss Tesman just
sent that letter for him.

HEDDA   Letter? [*Looks at the address.*] Oh yes! It's Juliana
Tesman's handwriting. Well, then, he stayed at Judge
Brack's. As for Eilert Lövborg, he is sitting with a crown
of vine leaves in his hair reading his manuscript to
Tesman.

MRS. ELVSTED   Hedda, you're only saying that. You don't
believe it.

HEDDA   You really are a little blockhead, Thea.

MRS. ELVSTED   I suppose I am.

HEDDA   And how dreadfully tired you look!

MRS. ELVSTED   I am—dreadfully tired.

HEDDA   Go to my room and lie down for a while. Do as I tell
you.

MRS. ELVSTED   No, no, I couldn't sleep.

HEDDA   Of course you could.

MRS. ELVSTED   But your husband will be home soon. And I
have to know at once.

HEDDA   I'll call you the moment he comes.

MRS. ELVSTED   You promise me, Hedda?

HEDDA   Yes, you can count on me. Go in now, and have a
good sleep.

MRS. ELVSTED   Thanks. I will try. [*Exits through inner
room.*]

HEDDA *goes to the glass door and opens the curtains.
Bright daylight streams into the room. She takes a small
mirror from the writing table, looks at herself in it, and
arranges her hair. Then she goes to the hall door and rings
the bell-button. A few moments later* BERTA *appears at the
hall door.*

BERTA   Did you ring, ma'am?

HEDDA   Yes. Do something to the fire. I'm shivering.

BERTA   Bless me—we'll have it warm in no time. [*Rakes the

*embers together and puts on more wood, then stops and
listens.*] There's the front doorbell, ma'am.
HEDDA   Then go to the door. I'll look after the fire.

BERTA *exits by the hall door.* HEDDA *kneels on the
footstool and puts several pieces of wood in the stove.
After a few seconds,* TESMAN *enters from the hall. He
looks tired and rather worried. He tiptoes toward the
doorway of the inner room and is about to slip through the
curtains.*

HEDDA   [*At the stove, without looking up*] Good morning.
TESMAN   [*Turns*] Hedda! [*Comes nearer.*] Good heavens,
are you up so early, eh?
HEDDA   Yes, I'm up very early today.
TESMAN   And I was sure you'd be still sleeping. Fancy that,
Hedda!
HEDDA   Sh! Not so loud. Mrs. Elvsted is resting in my
room.
TESMAN   Mrs. Elvsted? Has she been here all night?
HEDDA   Yes, since no one came to escort her home.
TESMAN   Oh. No—I suppose not.
HEDDA   [*Closes the stove door and rises*] Well—did you
enjoy yourselves?
TESMAN   Did you worry about me, Hedda, eh?
HEDDA   No, that never occurred to me. I asked if you'd
enjoyed yourselves?
TESMAN   Yes, we really did, Hedda. Especially at first—you
see Eilert read me part of his book. We arrived more than
an hour too early—fancy that!—and Brack had so much to
get ready so Eilert read to me.
HEDDA   [*Sits to the right of the table*] Yes? Well?
TESMAN   [*Sits on a footstool near the stove*] Oh, Hedda,
you can't imagine what a book that is going to be! I believe
it's one of the most remarkable things that has ever been
written. Just think!
HEDDA   Yes, but I don't care about that—
TESMAN   I have a confession, Hedda. After he'd finished
reading, I had such a horrid feeling—
HEDDA   A horrid feeling?
TESMAN   Yes, I felt quite jealous of Eilert that he was able
to write such a book. Just think, Hedda!

HEDDA   Yes, yes, I am thinking.

TESMAN   It's really appalling, that—with all his gifts—he should be so utterly incorrigible!

HEDDA   I suppose you mean that he has more courage, that he's less afraid of life, than most men?

TESMAN   Good heavens, no. He just doesn't know the meaning of the word "moderation."

HEDDA   What happened?

TESMAN   Well, to tell the truth, Hedda, it was an orgy!

HEDDA   Had he vine leaves in his hair?

TESMAN   Vine leaves? No, I didn't see any vine leaves—but he made a long, rambling speech in honor of the woman who had inspired him in his work—yes, that was the phrase he used.

HEDDA   Did he mention her name?

TESMAN   No, he didn't; but it seems to me it has to be Mrs. Elvsted. Wait and see!

HEDDA   Where did you part from him?

TESMAN   On the way home. The party finally broke up so we left in a bunch, a few of us all together, and Brack came with us to get a breath of fresh air. And then we decided we had better take Eilert home—he was in pretty bad shape, you see.

HEDDA   Yes, I daresay.

TESMAN   But, now comes the strange part, Hedda—or I should say the tragic part. I'm almost ashamed to tell you—for Eilert's sake—

HEDDA   Oh, do go on!

TESMAN   Well—as we were nearing town, you see—I happened to drop behind for a minute. Only for a minute or two—er—you understand—

HEDDA   Yes, yes?

TESMAN   Well, then as I hurried after them, what do you think I found on the sidewalk, eh?

HEDDA   How should I know?

TESMAN   You mustn't tell anyone, Hedda! You hear me? Promise me—for Eilert's sake.

HEDDA   Yes!

TESMAN   [*Takes a parcel, wrapped in paper, from his coat pocket*] Just think—I found this.

HEDDA   Isn't that the parcel he had with him yesterday?

TESMAN   Yes. It's the whole of his precious, irreplaceable

manuscript. And he went and *lost* it! He didn't even notice it! What about that? By Jove! Tragic.

HEDDA Why didn't you give it back to him at once?

TESMAN I didn't dare do that, in the state he was in.

HEDDA Did you tell any of the others that you had found it?

TESMAN Certainly not! I didn't want them to know—for Eilert's sake, you see.

HEDDA Then no one knows that Eilert Lövborg's manuscript is in your possession?

TESMAN No—and no one must know it.

HEDDA What did you say to him afterward?

TESMAN I didn't have a chance to talk to him again. He and two or three of the others gave us the slip. Disappeared, by Jove!

HEDDA They must have taken him home.

TESMAN Yes, I suppose they did—and Brack went home, too.

HEDDA And what have you been doing with yourself since then?

TESMAN Well, I and some of the others went home with one of the fellows—he invited us—to have morning coffee, or perhaps it should be called a late supper, eh? And now, as soon as I've had a little rest and poor Eilert has had a chance to recover himself a bit, I must take this back to him.

HEDDA [*Reaches for the envelope*] No—don't give it to him! Not yet, I mean. Let me read it first.

TESMAN No, dearest Hedda. I daren't do that. I really dare not.

HEDDA You dare not?

TESMAN No. Think how desperate he'll be when he awakens and can't find his manuscript! There's no copy of it, Hedda—you know that! He said so himself.

HEDDA [*Looks at him searchingly*] Can't he rewrite it?

TESMAN No. I should think that would be impossible. I mean, the inspiration, you know—

HEDDA Yes, of course—the inspiration—I suppose it depends on that. [*Lightly.*] By the way, here's a letter for you.

TESMAN Oh, really? Imagine that!

HEDDA [*Hands it to him*] It came early this morning.

TESMAN It's from Auntie JuJu. What can it be? [*Puts parcel down on the other footstool, opens the letter, glances through it, and jumps up.*] Oh, Hedda—she says Auntie Rina is dying.

HEDDA Well, we were expecting that.

TESMAN And that I must hurry if I want to see her again— I'll run over and see them at once.

HEDDA [*Suppresses a smile*] Will you run?

TESMAN Oh, my dearest Hedda, if you could only bring yourself to come with me. What about it, eh?

HEDDA [*Rises and rejects the idea wearily*] No, no, don't ask me to do that! I'll have nothing to do with sickness or death. I loathe anything ugly.

TESMAN Well, then, in that case— [*In a dither.*] My hat? My overcoat? Oh, in the hall. I do hope I won't be too late, Hedda, eh?

HEDDA Oh, if you run—

BERTA *appears at the hall door.*

BERTA Judge Brack is here, sir, and wishes to know if you'll see him.

TESMAN At a time like this! No, I can't possibly see him now.

HEDDA But I can. [*To* BERTA.] Ask the judge to come in. [BERTA *exits.*] [*Quickly, in a whisper.*] Tesman! The manuscript! [*Snatches it from the stool.*]

TESMAN Yes, give it to me!

HEDDA No, no, I will keep it till you come back. [*Goes to writing table and puts it in the bookcase.* TESMAN *is in a frenzy of haste and can't get his gloves on.* BRACK *enters from the hall.*]

HEDDA [*Nods to him*] You're an early bird, Judge.

BRACK I am, aren't I? [*To* TESMAN.] Where are you off to in such a hurry?

TESMAN I must rush off to my aunts. Just think, Auntie Rina is dying, poor thing.

BRACK Good lord, she is? Then you mustn't let me detain you. Every moment is precious.

TESMAN Yes, I really must rush—good-bye! Good-bye! [*Hastens out hall door.*]

HEDDA [*Approaches* BRACK] I hear the party was more than usually jolly last night, Judge.

BRACK   I've been up all night—haven't even changed my clothes yet, Mrs. Hedda.

HEDDA   Not you, either?

BRACK   What has Tesman told you of last night's adventures?

HEDDA   Oh, some dreary tale about going to someone's house and having coffee and breakfast.

BRACK   Yes, I've heard about that breakfast party. Eilert Lövborg wasn't with them, was he?

HEDDA   No, they took him home first.

BRACK   Did Tesman go with him?

HEDDA   No, one or two of the others, he said.

BRACK   [*Smiles*] George Tesman is really a naive, simple soul, Mrs. Hedda.

HEDDA   Oh yes, God knows he is! But was there something else that happened?

BRACK   Yes, a number of things.

HEDDA   Then, sit down, my dear Judge, and tell me! [*Sits to the left of the table.* BRACK *sits near her, the long side of the table.*] Well?

BRACK   I had a special reason for keeping track of my guests—or rather of some of my guests—last night.

HEDDA   And among them Eilert Lövborg, perhaps?

BRACK   Frankly—yes.

HEDDA   Now you make me really curious—

BRACK   Do you know where he and some of my other guests spent the latter half of last night, Mrs. Hedda?

HEDDA   Tell me—if it's not unmentionable.

BRACK   Oh no, it's not at all unmentionable. Well, they showed up at a very animated soiree.

HEDDA   A very *jolly* party, Judge?

BRACK   An excessively jolly one!

HEDDA   Do go on!

BRACK   Lövborg, and the others also, had advance invitations. I knew all about it. But, Lövborg had begged off, because now, of course, he was supposed to have become a new man, as you know.

HEDDA   Up at the Elvsteds, yes. But he went anyway?

BRACK   Well, you see, Mrs. Hedda, last night at my house, unhappily, the "spirit" moved him.

HEDDA   Yes, I hear he became "inspired."

BRACK   Somewhat violently inspired. And so he changed

his mind. We men are not always as high-principled as perhaps we should be.

HEDDA   I'm sure you are an exception, Judge. But as to Lövborg—

BRACK   To make a long story short—he landed at last in Mademoiselle Diana's rooms.

HEDDA   Mademoiselle Diana?

BRACK   Yes. She was giving the soiree. For a selected circle of friends and admirers.

HEDDA   Is she that red-haired woman?

BRACK   Precisely.

HEDDA   A sort of a—singer?

BRACK   Yes—in her leisure moments. She is also a mighty huntress—of men, Mrs. Hedda. I'm sure you've heard of her. In the days of his glory, Eilert Lövborg was one of her most enthusiastic protectors.

HEDDA   And how did it all end?

BRACK   Far from amicably, it seems. She gave him a most tender welcome, with open arms, but before long she'd taken to fists.

HEDDA   Against Lövborg?

BRACK   That's right. He accused her or her friends of having robbed him. He kept insisting some valuable notebook had disappeared—as well as various other things. In short, he made a bloodthirsty scene. I understand it was quite frightful!

HEDDA   What did it come to?

BRACK   A general free-for-all, men and women as well. The police at last appeared on the scene.

HEDDA   The police?

BRACK   Yes, I'm afraid it may prove an expensive amusement for Eilert Lövborg—crazy fool that he is.

HEDDA   How?

BRACK   He made a violent resistance—hit one policeman— half killed him—and tore another one's coat off his back. So, they marched him off to the police station with the rest.

HEDDA   Where did you hear all this?

BRACK   From the police themselves.

HEDDA   [*Gazes straight in front of her*] So that is what happened. Then he had no vine leaves in his hair.

BRACK   Vine leaves, Mrs. Hedda?

HEDDA [*Changes her tone*] But tell me, Judge—why do
  you go around like this, spying on Eilert Lövborg?
BRACK In the first place, it's hardly a matter of no concern
  to me if it's brought out during the investigation that he'd
  come directly from my house.
HEDDA You mean, the case will go to court?
BRACK Naturally. However, that is not particularly serious.
  Still, I thought it my duty, as a friend of the family, to give
  you and Tesman a full account of his nocturnal adven-
  tures.
HEDDA Why?
BRACK Why? Because I have a shrewd suspicion that he
  intends to use you as a sort of—screen.
HEDDA What makes you think that!
BRACK Good heavens—we're not completely blind, Mrs.
  Hedda! You wait and see. This Mrs. Elvsted—she'll be in
  no great hurry to leave town—and return to her husband—
  not yet.
HEDDA Even if there were something between them, there
  are plenty of places where they could meet.
BRACK Not one single home. From now on, every respect-
  able home will be closed to Eilert Lövborg.
HEDDA So mine ought to be, too, is that what you mean?
BRACK Yes. I confess it would be painful to me if that
  gentleman were to be given free access of your house.
  How intrusive he would be, how superfluous, if he were to
  force his way into—
HEDDA —into the triangle?
BRACK Precisely. It would mean I should find myself home-
  less.
HEDDA [*Looks at him with a smile*] I see. The one cock-of-
  the-walk—that is your aim.
BRACK [*Nods slowly and speaks in a low voice*] Yes, that is
  my aim. And for that I will fight—with every weapon at
  my command.
HEDDA [*The smile vanishes*] You're a dangerous person,
  aren't you? When you want something.
BRACK You think so?
HEDDA I'm beginning to think so. And I'm exceedingly
  glad that you have no hold over me.
BRACK [*Laughs ambiguously*] Well, Mrs. Hedda—perhaps

you're right. If I had, who knows what I might be capable of.

HEDDA   Come, come, Judge Brack. That sounds almost like a threat.

BRACK   [*Rises*] Not at all! In the creation of a triangle, if possible, it should be spontaneously constructed.

HEDDA   There I agree with you.

BRACK   Well, I've said what I came to say. I better be off. Good-bye, Mrs. Hedda. [*Goes toward the glass door.*]

HEDDA   [*Rises*] Are you going through the garden, Judge?

BRACK   Yes, it's a shortcut for me.

HEDDA   And—it's the back way, isn't it?

BRACK   Very true. I've no objection to back ways. They're rather intriguing at times.

HEDDA   When there's shooting going on, you mean?

BRACK   [*At the glass door, laughing*] Oh, people don't shoot their tame poultry, I fancy.

HEDDA   [*Also laughs*] No, when there is only *one* cock-of-the-walk, Judge! Good-bye!

They exchange laughing nods of farewell. He goes. She closes the door behind him. HEDDA, *now serious, stands looking out. She goes and peeps through the curtains into the inner room. Then she goes to the writing table, takes* LÖVBORG'S *manuscript, and is about to look through it when* BERTA'S *voice is heard loudly in the hall.* HEDDA *turns and listens. Hurriedly, she locks the manuscript in the drawer and lays the key on the inkstand.* EILERT LÖVBORG, *with his overcoat on and his hat in his hand, tears open the hall door. He looks confused and excited.*

LÖVBORG   [*Looks toward the hall*] I must go in, I tell you! [*Closes door, turns, sees* HEDDA, *controls himself immediately, and bows.*]

HEDDA   [*At the writing table*] Well, Mr. Lövborg, this is rather a late hour to call for Thea.

LÖVBORG   And rather early to call on you. Forgive me.

HEDDA   How do you know that she is still here?

LÖVBORG   They told me at her lodging that she'd been out all night.

HEDDA [*Goes to the oval table*] Did you notice anything in
  their behavior when they told you?
LÖVBORG [*Looks at her, puzzled*] Notice anything?
HEDDA Didn't they seem to think it—a little—strange?
LÖVBORG [*Suddenly understands*] Oh, I see what you
  mean. I'm dragging her down with me. Actually, I didn't
  notice anything. Tesman is not up yet?
HEDDA No, I don't think so.
LÖVBORG When did he get home?
HEDDA Oh, very late.
LÖVBORG Did he tell you anything?
HEDDA He just said that it was an excessively jolly time at
  Judge Brack's.
LÖVBORG Anything else?
HEDDA No, I don't think so. As a matter of fact, I was so
  dreadfully sleepy.

  MRS. ELVSTED *enters through the curtains from the inner
  room.*

MRS. ELVSTED [*Goes toward him*] Eilert! At last!
LÖVBORG Yes—at last—and too late!
MRS. ELVSTED What is too late?
LÖVBORG Everything is too late. It's all over with me.
MRS. ELVSTED No, no! Don't say that!
LÖVBORG You'll say the same when you hear—
MRS. ELVSTED I don't want to hear anything!
HEDDA Perhaps you would rather talk alone. I'll leave you.
LÖVBORG No, stay, please. I beg of you.
MRS. ELVSTED But I don't want to hear anything, I tell you.
LÖVBORG I don't intend to talk about last night, Thea.
MRS. ELVSTED What is it, then?
LÖVBORG I just want to tell you that now we must part.
MRS. ELVSTED Part!
HEDDA [*Involuntarily*] I knew it!
LÖVBORG I have no more use for you, Thea.
MRS. ELVSTED How can you say that! No more use for me?
  I'm not to go on helping you now, as I have? We'll go on
  working together, won't we, Eilert?
LÖVBORG I shall do no more work.
MRS. ELVSTED Then what shall I do with my life?

LÖVBORG   You must try to live your life as if you had never known me.

MRS. ELVSTED   But you know I can't do that!

LÖVBORG   You must try, Thea. You must go home again.

MRS. ELVSTED   [*Protests vehemently*] Never! I will not leave you! Where you are, that's where I want to be! I want to be with you when the book comes out.

HEDDA   [*Half aloud, in suspense*] Ah yes—the book!

LÖVBORG   My book and Thea's—for that's what it is.

MRS. ELVSTED   Yes, I feel that, too! That's why we must be together when it is published. I want to see people respect and honor you again. I want to share the joy with you.

LÖVBORG   Thea—our book will not be published.

HEDDA   Ah!

MRS. ELVSTED   Not published?

LÖVBORG   No. It never can appear.

MRS. ELVSTED   [*Anxiously, with foreboding*] Lövborg— what have you done with the manuscript?

HEDDA   [*Watches him intently*] Yes—the manuscript?

MRS. ELVSTED   Where is it?

LÖVBORG   Oh, Thea—don't ask me that.

MRS. ELVSTED   Yes. I must know—I have a right to know.

LÖVBORG   Very well then. I've torn it into a thousand pieces.

MRS. ELVSTED   [*Screams*] No, no—!

HEDDA   [*Involuntarily*] But that's not—

LÖVBORG   [*Looks at her*] Not true, you think?

HEDDA   [*Controls herself*] Of course it must be—if you say so! But it sounds so utterly incredible!

LÖVBORG   It's true all the same.

MRS. ELVSTED   [*Wrings her hands*] Oh, God! Oh, God! Torn his own work to pieces! Oh, God, Hedda!

LÖVBORG   I have torn my own life to pieces. Why not my life's work as well—

MRS. ELVSTED   And you did this last night?

LÖVBORG   Yes, I tell you! I tore it into a thousand pieces and scattered them on the fjord. I watched them drift on the good, clean salt water. Let it carry them away in the current and the wind. After a while, they'll sink—deeper and deeper—as I shall, Thea.

MRS. ELVSTED   You know, Eilert, this thing you've done

with the book—for the rest of my life it will seem to me as if you've killed a little child.

LÖVBORG You're right. It was like killing a child.

MRS. ELVSTED But how could you do it? It was my child, too.

HEDDA [*Almost inaudibly*] Ah, the child—

MRS. ELVSTED [*Breathes heavily*] Then it *is* all over. I'll go now, Hedda.

HEDDA But you're not leaving town, are you?

MRS. ELVSTED Oh, I don't know what I'll do. There's nothing but darkness before me. [*Exits through hall door.*]

HEDDA [*Stands waiting a moment*] You're not going to see her home, Mr. Lövborg?

LÖVBORG I? Through the streets? You'd have her seen walking—walking with me?

HEDDA Of course I don't know what else may have happened last night, but is it so completely irreparable?

LÖVBORG It won't end with just last night—I know that well enough. But the curse of it is, I don't want to live that kind of life. I have no heart to start it again. It's the courage and daring for life—my defiant spirit—that's what she's broken in me.

HEDDA [*Looks straight ahead of her*] So that pretty little fool has had her fingers in a man's destiny. [*Looks at him.*] But how could you treat her so heartlessly?

LÖVBORG Don't call me heartless!

HEDDA What do you expect me to say? To go ahead and destroy what has filled her whole being for months and years! You don't call that heartless?

LÖVBORG To you I can tell the truth, Hedda.

HEDDA The truth?

LÖVBORG First promise me—give me your word—that Thea will never know.

HEDDA You have my word.

LÖVBORG Good. There was no truth in what I said just now.

HEDDA About the manuscript?

LÖVBORG Yes—I didn't tear it up—or throw it in the fjord.

HEDDA Where is it then?

LÖVBORG I have destroyed it, Hedda. Utterly destroyed it.

HEDDA I don't understand.

LÖVBORG Just now, Thea said I had killed our child.

HEDDA Yes—that's what she said.

LÖVBORG   But killing his child—that's not the worst a father can do.

HEDDA   What could be worse than that?

LÖVBORG   Hedda—suppose a man came home one morning after a frenzy of drinking and a night of debauchery and said to the mother of the child: "Look here. I took our child with me, dragged it around to all sorts of obscene places—and I lost our child—lost it! God only knows what's become of it—or who may have their clutches on it!"

HEDDA   When all is said and done—it was only a book.

LÖVBORG   Thea's pure soul was in that book.

HEDDA   Yes—I understand.

LÖVBORG   Then you must also understand why no future is possible for us.

HEDDA   What will you do now?

LÖVBORG   Nothing. I want to make an end of it. The sooner the better

HEDDA   [*Takes a step toward him*] Eilert Lövborg—listen to me. If you do make an end of it—do it beautifully!

LÖVBORG   Beautifully? [*Smiles.*] With a crown of vine leaves in my hair? The way you used to dream of me—in the old days?

HEDDA   No, I don't believe in vine leaves anymore. But beautifully nevertheless! For this once—! Good-bye! You must go now—and never come here again.

LÖVBORG   Good-bye, Mrs. Tesman. And give George Tesman my best.

HEDDA   No, wait! I want to give you a souvenir of me to take with you. [*Goes to the writing table, opens the drawer and the pistol case, and comes back to him with one of the pistols.*]

LÖVBORG   This? Is this the souvenir?

HEDDA   [*Nods slowly*] Do you recognize it? It was aimed at you once.

LÖVBORG   You should have used it then.

HEDDA   Here! Use it now!

LÖVBORG   [*Puts the pistol in his breast pocket*] Thanks.

HEDDA   And beautifully, Eilert Lövborg. Promise me that!

LÖVBORG   Good-bye, Hedda Gabler. [*Exits by the hall door.*]

HEDDA *listens for a moment at the door. Then she goes to the writing table, takes out the manuscript, peeps inside the cover, draws a few of the sheets half out, and looks at them. Next, she goes over to the armchair with the manuscript and sits with the manuscript in her lap. In a moment, she opens the stove door and takes the whole manuscript from the packet.*

HEDDA   [*Throws some of the sheets into the fire and whispers to herself*] I am burning your child, Thea—yours and Eilert Lövborg's! Burning it, darling little curlylocks. [*Throws more sheets on the fire.*] Burning your child. [*Throws the rest of the manuscript into the fire.*] I'm burning it—burning it—

ACT FOUR

The same rooms. It is evening. The drawing room is in darkness. The inner room is lit by the hanging lamp over the table. The curtains are drawn across the glass doors. HEDDA, *dressed in black, is pacing back and forth in the darkened room. Then, she goes to the inner room and crosses to the left. A few chords are heard on the piano. She appears again and returns to the drawing room.* BERTA *enters from the right through the inner room carrying a lighted lamp, which she sets on the table by the corner sofa in the drawing room. Her eyes are red from crying, and she has black ribbons on her cap. She exits by the hall door quietly.* HEDDA *goes to the glass doors, pulls the curtain slightly aside, and peers out into the darkness. Shortly afterward,* MISS TESMAN *enters from the hall. She is in mourning and wears a hat and a veil.* HEDDA *goes toward her, extending her hand.*

MISS TESMAN   Well, Hedda, here I am, all dressed in mourning. My poor sister has found peace at last.
HEDDA   As you see, I've already heard. Tesman sent me a note.

MISS TESMAN   Yes, he promised me he would. All the same, I thought I should bring the news of death to Hedda myself—here, in this house of life.

HEDDA   That was very kind of you.

MISS TESMAN   Ah, Rina ought not to have left us just now. This is not the time for Hedda's house to be a house of mourning.

HEDDA   [*Changes the subject*] It's good to know she died peacefully, Miss Tesman.

MISS TESMAN   Yes, her end was so calm, so beautiful. And she was so happy to see George again. And to say good-bye to him. Hasn't he come home yet?

HEDDA   No. He wrote that he might be detained. But please sit down.

MISS TESMAN   No, thank you, dearest Hedda. I'd love to, but I have much to do and little time. I have to dress her and make ready as best I can. She must go to her grave looking her sweetest and finest.

HEDDA   Can I help you with anything?

MISS TESMAN   Oh, you mustn't think of it! This is no time for Hedda Tesman to have a hand in death. Nor let her thoughts dwell on it. No, no, not at this time.

HEDDA   One cannot always control one's thoughts—

MISS TESMAN   Yes. How strange life is! At home we shall be sewing a shroud for Rina. And here, too, there will be sewing, I suppose—but of another sort, thank God!

GEORGE TESMAN *enters by the hall door.*

HEDDA   Here you are at last!

TESMAN   You here, Auntie JuJu? With Hedda? Fancy that!

MISS TESMAN   I was just going, dear boy. Well, did you get done all you promised you would?

TESMAN   No, I'm afraid I forgot half of it. I'll have to run over and see you in the morning. My brain's in a whirl today. I can't keep my thoughts together.

MISS TESMAN   George dear, you mustn't take it that way.

TESMAN   Oh? Well—er—how should I, then?

MISS TESMAN   You must rejoice in your grief—be glad that she has found rest.

TESMAN   Oh yes, of course—you're thinking of Auntie Rina.

HEDDA   It will be lonely for you now, Miss Tesman.

MISS TESMAN   At first, yes. But it won't last long, I hope. Poor dear Rina's room won't stay empty.

TESMAN   Indeed? Who will take it, eh?

MISS TESMAN   There's always some poor invalid who needs care and attention.

HEDDA   Would you really take such a burden on yourself again?

MISS TESMAN   Burden? Heaven forgive you, child—it's been no burden to me.

HEDDA   But it's different with a stranger!

MISS TESMAN   Oh, you soon make friends with an invalid. And I do so much need someone to live for. Perhaps soon there will be something in this house to keep an old aunt busy.

HEDDA   Please, don't trouble yourself about us!

TESMAN   By Jove, yes! What a splendid time the three of us could have together if—

HEDDA   If?

TESMAN   [*Uneasy*] Nothing. Let's hope things work out for the best, eh?

MISS TESMAN   Well, well, I expect you two have things to discuss. [*Smiles.*] And perhaps Hedda may have something to tell you, George. Good-bye! I must go home to Rina. Goodness me, how strange! Rina is now with my poor brother as well as with me!

TESMAN   Yes, fancy that, Auntie JuJu, eh!

MISS TESMAN *exits out the hall door.*

HEDDA   [*Follows* TESMAN *with a cold, probing look*] Aunt Rina's death seems to affect you more than Aunt Juliana.

TESMAN   Oh, it's not that alone. It's Eilert who has me so worried.

HEDDA   [*Quickly*] Have you heard anything new?

TESMAN   I looked in at his rooms this afternoon. I wanted to tell him the manuscript was safe.

HEDDA   Well? Did you see him?

TESMAN   No, he wasn't home. But later I met Mrs. Elvsted and she said he had been here early this morning.

HEDDA   Yes, directly after you left.

TESMAN And he said he'd torn the manuscript to pieces, eh?

HEDDA Yes, he claimed that he had.

TESMAN Good heavens, he must have gone completely mad! I suppose you didn't dare give it back to him, Hedda.

HEDDA No, he didn't get it.

TESMAN But of course you told him that we had it?

HEDDA No. [*Quickly.*] Did you tell Mrs. Elvsted?

TESMAN No. I thought I had better not. But you ought to have told him. He might go home and do something desperate. Give me the manuscript, Hedda. I will take it to him at once. Where is it?

HEDDA [*Cold and motionless, leaning against the armchair*] I haven't got it any longer.

TESMAN Haven't got it? What in the world do you mean?

HEDDA I've burnt it—every word of it.

TESMAN [*With a violent movement of terror*] Burnt! Burnt Eilert's manuscript!

HEDDA Don't shout. The servant might hear you.

TESMAN Burnt it! Why, good God—! No, no, no! It's impossible!

HEDDA It's true.

TESMAN Do you know what you've done, Hedda? It's illegal appropriation of lost property. Just think! You can ask Judge Brack; he'll tell you.

HEDDA It would be wise not to speak of it—to the judge or to anyone else.

TESMAN But how could you do such an incredible—unheard of—thing! What put it into your head? What possessed you? Answer me! Well?

HEDDA [*Suppressing an almost imperceptible smile*] I did it for your sake, George.

TESMAN For my sake?

HEDDA This morning when you told me he had read it to you—

TESMAN Yes, yes—what then?

HEDDA Then you confessed that you were jealous of his work.

TESMAN Good Lord, I didn't mean it literally!

HEDDA All the same, I couldn't bear the thought of your standing in someone else's shadow.

TESMAN [*In an outburst of mingled doubt and joy*] Hedda!
Is this true? But I've never known you loved me like that!
You've never shown it before! Fancy that!

HEDDA Well, then it's best you know that—that I'm going
to— [*Impatiently breaking off.*] No, no, ask Auntie JuJu.
She will tell you fast enough.

TESMAN Oh, I almost think I understand, Hedda. [*Clasps
his hands together.*] Good heavens, do you really mean it?
Is it really true, eh?

HEDDA Don't shout so. The servant might hear you.

TESMAN The servant? Oh, Hedda, how funny you are
sometimes. The servant! Why, that's Berta! I'll run out and
tell her myself.

HEDDA [*Clenching her fists in desperation*] Oh, God, I
shall die—I shall die of all this—

TESMAN Of what, Hedda? What is it, eh?

HEDDA [*Cold, controlled*] All this—absurdity—George.

TESMAN Absurdity? That I'm so happy? Oh, well, perhaps
I won't say anything to Berta.

HEDDA No, do. She might as well know, too.

TESMAN No, no, not yet. But Auntie JuJu—I must let her
know! And you—you called me George. For the first time!
Auntie JuJu will be so happy—so very happy.

HEDDA Will she be happy when she hears that I've burnt
Eilert Lövborg's manuscript for your sake?

TESMAN No. No one must know about the manuscript. But
I will certainly tell her how dearly you love me, Hedda.
She must share that joy with me. I wonder, now, if this sort
of thing is usual with young wives, eh?

HEDDA You might ask Auntie JuJu about that, too.

TESMAN I will indeed, some time or other. [*Looks uneasy
and downcast again.*] But the manuscript. Good God—
the manuscript. I can't bear to think what poor Eilert will
do now!

MRS. ELVSTED, *dressed as in Act One, with hat and coat,
enters by the hall door.*

MRS. ELVSTED [*Greets them hurriedly and speaks in agita-
tion*] Oh, dear Hedda, forgive me for returning so soon.

HEDDA Has something happened, Thea?

TESMAN Something about Eilert Lövborg, eh?

MRS. ELVSTED   Yes, I'm terribly afraid he's met with an accident.

HEDDA   Ah—you think so?

TESMAN   Why should you think that, Mrs. Elvsted?

MRS. ELVSTED   Because I heard them speaking of it at my boardinghouse, just as I came in. There are all sorts of strange rumors about him in town today.

TESMAN   Yes, I heard them, too! And yet I could swear that he went straight home last night. Imagine!

HEDDA   What did they say at the boardinghouse?

MRS. ELVSTED   Oh, I couldn't quite make it out. Either they knew nothing definite or else— Anyway, they stopped talking when they saw me, and I didn't dare ask.

TESMAN   We must only hope you misunderstood them, Mrs. Elvsted.

MRS. ELVSTED   No, no, I'm sure they were talking about him. And I heard something about a hospital or—

TESMAN   The hospital!

HEDDA   No, no, that's impossible!

MRS. ELVSTED   Oh, I became terribly afraid for him. I finally went to his rooms and asked to see him.

HEDDA   You went there yourself, Thea?

MRS. ELVSTED   What else could I do? I couldn't bear the suspense any longer.

TESMAN   But *you* didn't find him, either, eh?

MRS. ELVSTED   No. They had no idea where he was. They said he hadn't been home since yesterday afternoon.

TESMAN   Yesterday! Fancy that! Yesterday afternoon!

MRS. ELVSTED   There can only be one reason—something terrible has happened to him!

TESMAN   Hedda dear, suppose I went over and made a few inquiries?

HEDDA   No, no—don't you get mixed up in this affair.

JUDGE BRACK, *hat in hand, enters by the hall door, which* BERTA *opens and closes behind him. He looks grave and bows silently.*

TESMAN   Oh, it's you, my dear Judge, eh?

BRACK   Yes, it is imperative that I see you at once.

TESMAN   I can see Auntie JuJu has told you the news about Auntie Rina.

BRACK   Among other things, yes.

TESMAN   Isn't it sad, eh?

BRACK   My dear Tesman, that depends on how you look at it.

TESMAN   [*Looks at him doubtfully*] Has anything else happened?

BRACK   Yes.

HEDDA   [*Intently*] Something distressing, Judge?

BRACK   That, too, depends on how you look at it, Mrs. Tesman.

MRS. ELVSTED   Oh, it's something about Eilert Lövborg!

BRACK   [*Looks at her for a moment*] What makes you think that, Mrs. Elvsted? Perhaps you've heard something already?

MRS. ELVSTED   No, nothing at all, but—

TESMAN   Oh, for heaven's sake, tell us!

BRACK   Well—I'm sorry, but—Eilert Lövborg's been taken to the hospital. He's dying.

MRS. ELVSTED   [*Cries out*] Oh, God! God!

TESMAN   To the hospital! And dying!

HEDDA   [*Involuntarily*] So soon then—

MRS. ELVSTED   [*Tearfully*] And we parted in anger, Hedda!

HEDDA   [*In a whisper*] Thea—Thea—be careful!

MRS. ELVSTED   [*Ignores her*] I must go to him! I have to see him alive!

BRACK   It is useless, madam. No one will be admitted to see him.

MRS. ELVSTED   Oh, but at least tell me what has happened to him! What is it?

TESMAN   Don't tell me he tried to—! Eh?

HEDDA   Yes, he did. I'm sure of it.

TESMAN   Hedda, how can you—?

BRACK   [*Who has not taken his eyes from* HEDDA] I'm afraid, unhappily, you've guessed correctly, Mrs. Tesman.

MRS. ELVSTED   Oh, how horrible!

TESMAN   Killed himself! Think of that!

HEDDA   Shot himself!

BRACK   Again, exactly right, Mrs. Tesman.

MRS. ELVSTED   [*Tries to control herself*] When did it happen, Mr. Brack?

BRACK   This afternoon. Between three and four.

TESMAN   But, good Lord, where did he do it, eh?

BRACK   [*Hesitates slightly*] Where? Why, I suppose at his lodgings, of course.

MRS. ELVSTED   No, that's impossible. I was there myself between six and seven.

BRACK   Well, somewhere else, then. I don't know exactly. I only know that he was found. Shot himself—in the chest.

MRS. ELVSTED   How horrible! That he should die like that!

HEDDA   [*To* BRACK] In the chest you said?

BRACK   Yes—as I told you.

HEDDA   Not the temple?

BRACK   In the chest, Mrs. Tesman.

HEDDA   Well—well, the chest is just as good.

BRACK   Why, Mrs. Tesman?

HEDDA   [*Evasively*] Oh, nothing. Never mind.

TESMAN   And the wound is critical, you say, eh?

BRACK   Absolutely fatal. He's probably dead by now.

MRS. ELVSTED   Yes, yes, I feel it. Over—all over—oh, Hedda!

TESMAN   But, tell me, how did you manage to learn all this?

BRACK   [*Curtly*] From the police. A man I had some business with.

HEDDA   [*In a clear, bold voice*] At last, a deed worth doing!

TESMAN   [*Shocked*] My God, what are you saying, Hedda?

HEDDA   I'm saying there's beauty in all this.

BRACK   Hmm, Mrs. Tesman.

TESMAN   Beauty! Fancy that!

MRS. ELVSTED   Oh, Hedda, how can you talk of beauty in such an act?

HEDDA   Eilert Lövborg has settled his account with life—with himself. He had the courage to do—what *he* had to do—the one right thing!

MRS. ELVSTED   No, that isn't what happened! Don't believe it! He did it because he was in a delirium!

TESMAN   In despair, you mean.

HEDDA   No, he wasn't. I'm certain of that!

MRS. ELVSTED   He must have been delirious! The way he was when he tore up our manuscript.

BRACK   [*Startled*] His manuscript? His book, you mean? He tore it up?

MRS. ELVSTED   Yes. Last night.

TESMAN   [*Whispers*] Oh, Hedda, we'll never be able to forget this.

BRACK Hmm, how extraordinary.

TESMAN [*Paces the room*] To think of Eilert dying like that! And not leaving behind him the book that would have made him famous!

MRS. ELVSTED Oh, if only it could be put together again—

TESMAN Yes, if it only could! I'd give anything—

MRS. ELVSTED Perhaps it can, Mr. Tesman.

TESMAN What do you mean?

MRS. ELVSTED [*Searches in the pockets of her dress*] Look here. I've kept all these notes that he used to dictate from.

HEDDA [*Takes a step forward*] Ah—!

TESMAN You have kept them, Mrs. Elvsted, eh?

MRS. ELVSTED Yes, I have them here. I took them with me when I left home—they're here in my pocket.

TESMAN Let me see them!

MRS. ELVSTED [*Hands him a sheaf of small papers*] Here's some. But they are such a mess. All dreadfully mixed up, I'm afraid.

TESMAN I say, just fancy, if we could sort them out, decipher them—we could help each other—

MRS. ELVSTED Oh yes! At least we could try.

TESMAN We'll do it—we *must* do it—I'll devote my life to it!

HEDDA *You*, George? Your life?

TESMAN Yes, or rather all the time I can spare. My own work will simply have to wait. I owe this to Eilert's memory. You understand, Hedda, eh?

HEDDA Perhaps.

TESMAN Now, my dear Mrs. Elvsted, we must pull ourselves together. It's no good brooding over what has happened and can't be undone, eh? We must compose our thoughts as much as we can—

MRS. ELVSTED You're right, Mr. Tesman. I *will* try—

TESMAN Come on, then. Let's look over these notes right away. Where shall we sit? Here? No, in there, in the back room. Excuse me, Judge. Come along, Mrs. Elvsted!

MRS. ELVSTED If it were only possible—

TESMAN *and* MRS. ELVSTED *go into the inner room. She takes off her coat and hat. They sit at the table under the hanging lamp and become immersed in examining the papers.* HEDDA *crosses to the stove and sits in the arm-chair. After a moment,* BRACK *goes up to her.*

HEDDA [*Her voice lowered*] Ah, Judge—what a sense of liberation there is in this act of Eilert Lövborg's.

BRACK Liberation, Mrs. Hedda? Of course, it is for him.

HEDDA I mean for me. It's liberating to know that there can still be a free and courageous act in this world. Something that glows with spontaneous beauty.

BRACK [*Smiles*] Hmm—my dear Mrs. Hedda—

HEDDA Oh, I know what you are going to say. You're a kind of specialist, too, in a way, just like— Oh, well!

BRACK [*Looks at her*] Eilert Lövborg meant more to you than you're willing to admit—even to yourself. Or am I wrong?

HEDDA I don't answer such questions. I only know that Eilert Lövborg had the courage to live his life according to *his* principles. And to end it with beauty! That he had the will and the strength to break away from the banquet of life—so early.

BRACK I am sorry, Mrs. Hedda—but I fear I must dispel that charming illusion.

HEDDA Illusion?

BRACK Which couldn't have lasted long in any case.

HEDDA What do you mean?

BRACK Eilert Lövborg did not shoot himself—voluntarily.

HEDDA Not voluntarily?

BRACK No, the thing did not happen exactly as I told it.

HEDDA [*In suspense*] You've hidden something? What is it?

BRACK For poor Mrs. Elvsted's sake, I edited the facts somewhat.

HEDDA What?

BRACK First, he's already dead.

HEDDA At the hospital?

BRACK Yes, without regaining consciousness.

HEDDA What else did you hide?

BRACK That the incident didn't occur in his rooms.

HEDDA That makes no difference.

BRACK Doesn't it? Not even if I tell you that Eilert Lövborg was found shot in—in Mademoiselle Diana's boudoir?

HEDDA [*Attempts to rise but sinks back again*] That is impossible, Judge! He couldn't have been there again to-day!

BRACK He was there this afternoon. He went there, demanding something he said they had stolen. Kept raving about a lost child.

HEDDA Ah—so that was why—

BRACK I thought he must have meant his manuscript. But now I hear he destroyed that himself. So I suppose he must have meant his pocketbook.

HEDDA Yes, no doubt. He was found there?

BRACK Yes, there. With a discharged pistol in his breast pocket. The bullet had wounded him fatally.

HEDDA In the chest—yes.

BRACK No—in the bowels.

HEDDA [*Looks at him with an expression of loathing*] That, too! What is it, this—this curse—that everything I touch turns ludicrous and vile?

BRACK There's something else, Mrs. Hedda—something rather ugly.

HEDDA What?

BRACK The pistol he had—

HEDDA [*Breathless*] Well! What about it!

BRACK He must have stolen it.

HEDDA [*Leaps up*] Stolen it! That's not true! He didn't steal it!

BRACK No other explanation is possible. He must have stolen it— Sh!

TESMAN *and* MRS. ELVSTED *have risen from the table in the inner room and have come into the drawing room.*

TESMAN [*His hands full of papers*] Hedda dear, it's nearly impossible to see under that lamp. Just think!

HEDDA Yes, I am thinking.

TESMAN Do you think we could possibly use your writing table, eh?

HEDDA If you like. [*Quickly.*] No, wait! Let me clear it first!

TESMAN Oh, you needn't bother, Hedda. There is plenty of room.

HEDDA No, no, let me clear it, I say. I will take these things in and put them on the piano. There!

She has taken an object covered with sheet music from under the bookcase, places several other sheets of music upon it, and carries the whole thing into the inner room and off left. TESMAN *lays the scraps of paper on the writing table and moves the lamp there from the corner table. He and* MRS. ELVSTED *sit down and begin working again.* HEDDA *returns.*

HEDDA [*Behind* MRS. ELVSTED's *chair, gently ruffling her hair*] Well, my pretty, sweet Thea—how are you getting on with Eilert Lövborg's manuscript?

MRS. ELVSTED [*Looks up at her, disheartened*] Oh, it's going to be terribly hard to set these in order.

TESMAN We *must* do it. I am determined. And arranging other people's papers is rather my speciality, eh?

HEDDA *goes over to the stove and sits on one of the footstools.* BRACK *stands over her, leaning on the arm-chair.*

HEDDA [*Whispers*] What was that you said about the pistol?

BRACK [*Softly*] That he must have stolen it.

HEDDA Why stolen?

BRACK Because every other explanation is unthinkable, Mrs. Hedda, or ought to be.

HEDDA I see.

BRACK Of course Eilert Lövborg was here this morning, wasn't he?

HEDDA Yes.

BRACK Were you alone with him?

HEDDA Yes—for a little while—

BRACK You didn't leave the room while he was here?

HEDDA No.

BRACK Think again. Are you sure you didn't go out, perhaps just for a moment?

HEDDA Oh—yes, I might have gone into the hall—for just a moment.

BRACK And where was your pistol case during this time?

HEDDA It was locked in the—

BRACK [*Interrupting*] Er—Mrs. Hedda.

HEDDA It was over there on the writing table.

BRACK   Have you looked since to see if both pistols are there?

HEDDA   No.

BRACK   You needn't bother. I saw the pistol Lövborg had when they found him. I recognized it at once as the one I had seen yesterday. And other times, too.

HEDDA   Do you have it?

BRACK   No, the police have it.

HEDDA   What will they do with it?

BRACK   Try to trace the owner.

HEDDA   Do you think they'll succeed?

BRACK   [*Bends over her and whispers*] No, Hedda Gabler— as long as I say nothing.

HEDDA   [*Looks at him, frightened*] And if you do not say nothing—what then?

BRACK   [*Shrugs*] You could always say he'd stolen it.

HEDDA   I'd rather die!

BRACK   [*Smiles*] People say such things—but they don't *do* them.

HEDDA   And what then, if the pistol wasn't stolen? And they found the owner? What then?

BRACK   There will be a scandal, Hedda.

HEDDA   A scandal!

BRACK   Yes, a scandal—of which you're so terrified. Of course you'd have to appear in court—you and Mademoiselle Diana. She would have to explain how the thing happened—whether it was an accident or a murder. Was he about to take the pistol from his pocket to threaten her? And did the pistol go off? Or did she snatch it from his hand, shoot him, and put it back in his pocket? She might have done that, for she's a strong and resourceful woman, this Mademoiselle Diana.

HEDDA   But *I* have nothing to do with all this sordid business.

BRACK   No, but you will have to answer the question: Why did you give Eilert Lövborg the pistol? And what conclusion will people draw from the fact that you did give it to him?

HEDDA   [*Bows her head*] That is true. I didn't think of that.

BRACK   Well, luckily, there's no danger as long as I say nothing.

HEDDA [*Looks up at him*] In other words, I'm in your power, Judge. You have me at your beck and call from now on. You have your hold over me.

BRACK [*Whispers softly*] Dearest Hedda—believe me—I shall not abuse my advantage.

HEDDA All the same, I am in your power. Subject to your will and demands. Not free—not free—a slave! [*Rises impetuously.*] No, I couldn't bear that. Never!

BRACK [*Looks at her half mockingly*] Most people manage to adjust to the inevitable.

HEDDA [*Returns his look*] Yes. Perhaps. [*She crosses to the writing table. Suppressing an involuntary smile, she imitates* GEORGE's *intonation.*] Well, getting on with it, George, eh?

TESMAN Heaven knows, dear. It's going to mean months and months of work.

HEDDA [*As before*] Fancy that! [*Passes her hand softly through* MRS. ELVSTED's *hair.*] Doesn't it seem strange to you, Thea? Here you are, working with Tesman—just as you used to work with Eilert Lövborg?

MRS. ELVSTED Oh, if I could only inspire your husband in the same way!

HEDDA Oh, that will come, too—in time.

TESMAN You know, Hedda, I'm beginning to feel something like that. But you go back and sit with Judge Brack.

HEDDA Is there nothing you two need?

TESMAN No, nothing in the world. [*Turning his head.*] From now on, I trust you'll keep Hedda company, Judge.

BRACK With the greatest of pleasure!

HEDDA Thanks. But I'm tired this evening. I'll go and lie down on the sofa for a little while.

TESMAN Yes, do that, dear, eh?

HEDDA *goes into the inner room and draws the curtains. A short pause. Suddenly, she is heard playing a wild dance on the piano.*

MRS. ELVSTED [*Starts from her chair*] Oh— What's that?

TESMAN [*Runs to the doorway*] Hedda, dear, please! Don't play dance music tonight! Think of Auntie Rina! And of Eilert, too!

HEDDA　[*Puts her head between the curtains*] And Auntie JuJu. And all the rest of them. From now on, I'll be quiet. [*Closes curtains.*]

TESMAN　It distresses her to see us doing this. You know what, Mrs. Elvsted? You can move into the empty room at Auntie JuJu's. And then I'll come over in the evenings and we can sit and work *there,* eh?

MRS. ELVSTED　That might be best.

HEDDA　[*From the inner room*] I can hear what you are saying, Tesman. What will I do those long evenings—over here?

TESMAN　[*Turns over the papers*] Oh, I'm sure Judge Brack will be kind enough to come over and keep you company. [*To* JUDGE.] You won't mind my not being here, Judge?

BRACK　[*In the armchair, calls out gaily*] Every single evening. I shall be delighted to be here, Mrs. Tesman. I'm sure we shall have a jolly time together, you and I.

HEDDA　[*In a loud, clear voice*] Yes, that's what you hope, Judge, isn't it? Now that you are cock-of-the-walk— [*A shot is heard within.* TESMAN, MRS. ELVSTED, *and* BRACK *leap to their feet.*]

TESMAN　Now she's playing with those pistols again. [*He throws back the curtains and runs in, followed by* MRS. ELVSTED. HEDDA *lies stretched on the sofa, dead. Confusion and shouting.* BERTA *enters in alarm from right of inner room.*]

TESMAN　[*Cries out to* BRACK] Shot herself! Shot herself in the temple! By Jove! Fancy that!

BRACK　[*Sinks into the armchair, half fainting*] Good God! People don't do such things!

The Emperor Jones

BY
Eugene O'Neill

CHARACTERS

BRUTUS JONES, *Emperor*

HENRY SMITHERS, *a cockney trader*

AN OLD NATIVE WOMAN

LEM, *a native chief*

SOLDIERS, *adherents of Lem*

The Little Formless Fears; Jeff; The Negro Convicts; The Prison Guard; The Planters; The Auctioneer; The Slaves; The Congo Witch Doctor; The Crocodile God

The action of the play takes place on an island in the West Indies as yet not self-determined by white marines. The form of native government is, for the time being, an empire.

SCENE ONE

SCENE: *The audience chamber in the palace of the Em-*
peror—a spacious, high-ceilinged room with bare, white-
washed walls. The floor is of white tiles. In the rear, to the left
of center, a wide archway giving out on a portico with white
pillars. The palace is evidently situated on high ground, for
beyond the portico nothing can be seen but a vista of distant
hills, their summits crowned with thick groves of palm trees.
In the right wall, center, a smaller arched doorway leading
to the living quarters of the palace. The room is bare of
furniture with the exception of one huge chair made of uncut
wood which stands at center, its back to rear. This is very
apparently the Emperor's throne. It is painted a dazzling,
eye-smiting scarlet. There is a brilliant orange cushion on
the seat and another, smaller one is placed on the floor to
serve as a footstool. Strips of matting, dyed scarlet, lead
from the foot of the throne to the two entrances.

It is late afternoon but the sunlight still blazes yellowly
beyond the portico and there is an oppressive burden of
exhausting heat in the air.

As the curtain rises, a native Negro woman sneaks in
cautiously from the entrance on the right. She is very old,
dressed in cheap calico, barefooted, a red bandana hand-
kerchief covering all but a few stray wisps of white hair. A
bundle bound in colored cloth is carried over her shoulder on
the end of a stick. She hesitates beside the doorway, peering
back as if in extreme dread of being discovered. Then she
begins to glide noiselessly a step at a time, toward the
doorway in the rear. At this moment, SMITHERS *appears*
beneath the portico.

SMITHERS *is a tall, stoop-shouldered man about forty. His*
bald head, perched on a long neck with an enormous
Adam's apple, looks like an egg. The tropics have tanned his
naturally pasty face with its small, sharp features to a sickly

*yellow, and native rum has painted his pointed nose to a
startling red. His little, washy-blue eyes are red-rimmed and
dart about him like a ferret's. His expression is one of un-
scrupulous meanness, cowardly and dangerous. He is
dressed in a worn riding suit of dirty white drill, puttees,
spurs, and wears a white cork helmet. A cartridge belt with
an automatic revolver is around his waist. He carries a
riding whip in his hand. He sees the woman and stops to
watch her suspiciously. Then, making up his mind, he steps
quickly on tiptoe into the room. The woman, looking back
over her shoulder continually, does not see him until it is too
late. When she does* SMITHERS *springs forward and grabs
her firmly by the shoulder. She struggles to get away, fiercely
but silently.*

SMITHERS [*Tightening his grasp—roughly*] Easy! None o'
   that, me birdie. You can't wriggle out now. I got me 'ooks
   on yer.
WOMAN [*Seeing the uselessness of struggling, gives way to
   frantic terror, and sinks to the ground, embracing his
   knees supplicatingly*] No tell him! No tell him, mister!
SMITHERS [*With great curiosity*] Tell 'im? [*Then scornfully.*] Oh, you mean 'is bloomin' Majesty. What's the
   gaime, any 'ow? What are you sneakin' away for? Been
   stealin' a bit, I s'pose. [*He taps her bundle with his riding
   whip significantly.*]
WOMAN [*Shaking her head vehemently*] No, me no steal.
SMITHERS Bloody liar! But tell me what's up. There's somethin' funny goin' on. I smelled it in the air first thing I got
   up this mornin'. You blacks are up to some devilment. This
   palace of 'is is like a bleedin' tomb. Where's all the 'ands?
   [*The woman keeps sullenly silent.* SMITHERS *raises his
   whip threateningly.*] Ow, yer won't, won't yer? I'll show yer
   what's what.
WOMAN [*Coweringly*] I tell, mister. You no hit. They go—all
   go. [*She makes a sweeping gesture toward the hills in the
   distance.*]
SMITHERS Run away—to the 'ills?
WOMAN Yes, mister. Him Emperor—Great Father. [*She
   touches her forehead to the floor with a quick mechanical
   jerk.*] Him sleep after eat. Then they go—all go. Me old
   woman. Me left only. Now me go, too.

Blackshorts, weighed of clothes.

"Pink granite thrustup uncompromisingly through forest and terrace."

Shuffoson Ralph's body - really green.

Ralph's body - green - white

SMITHERS [*His astonishment giving way to an immense, mean satisfaction.*] Ow! So that's the ticket! Well, I know bloody well wot's in the air—when they runs orf to the 'ills. The tom-tom 'll be thumping out there bloomin' soon. [*With extreme vindictiveness.*] And I'm bloody glad of it, for one! Serve 'im right! Puttin' on airs, the stinkin' nigger! 'Is Majesty! Gawd blimey! I only 'opes I'm there when they takes 'im out to shoot 'im. [*Suddenly.*] 'E's still 'ere all right, ain't 'e?

WOMAN   Yes. Him sleep.

SMITHERS   'E's bound to find out soon as 'e wakes up. 'E's cunnin' enough to know when 'is time's come. [*He goes to the doorway on right and whistles shrilly with his fingers in his mouth. The old woman springs to her feet and runs out of the doorway, rear.* SMITHERS *goes after her, reaching for his revolver.*] Stop or I'll shoot! [*Then stopping— indifferently.*] Pop orf then, if yer like, yer black cow. [*He stands in the doorway, looking after her.*]

[JONES *enters from the right. He is a tall, powerfully-built, full-blooded Negro of middle age. His features are typically negroid, yet there is something decidedly distinctive about his face—an underlying strength of will, a hardy, self-reliant confidence in himself that inspires respect. His eyes are alive with a keen, cunning intelligence. In manner he is shrewd, suspicious, evasive. He wears a light blue uniform coat, sprayed with brass buttons, heavy gold chevrons on his shoulders, gold braid on the collar, cuffs, etc. His pants are bright red with a light blue stripe down the side. Patent-leather laced boots with brass spurs, and a belt with a long-barreled, pearl-handled revolver in a holster complete his makeup. Yet there is something not altogether ridiculous about his grandeur. He has a way of carrying it off.*]

JONES   [*Not seeing anyone—greatly irritated and blinking sleepily—shouts*] Who dare whistle dat way in my palace? Who dare wake up de Emperor? I'll git de hide frayled off some o' you niggers sho'!

SMITHERS   [*Showing himself—in a manner half-afraid and half-defiant*] It was me whistled to yer. [*As* JONES *frowns angrily.*] I got news for yer.

JONES [*Putting on his suavest manner, which fails to cover up his contempt for the white man*] Oh, it's you, Mister Smithers. [*He sits down on his throne with easy dignity.*] What news you got to tell me?

SMITHERS [*Coming close to enjoy his discomfiture*] Don't yer notice nothin' funny today?

JONES [*Coldly*] Funny? No, I ain't perceived nothin' of de kind!

SMITHERS Then yer ain't so foxy as I thought yer was. Where's all your court? [*Sarcastically.*] The generals and the cabinet ministers and all?

JONES [*Imperturbably*] Where dey mostly runs de minute I close my eyes—drinkin' rum and talkin' big down in de town. [*Sarcastically.*] How come you don't know dat? Ain't you sousin' with 'em most every day?

SMITHERS [*Stung but pretending indifference—with a wink*] That's part of the day's work. I got ter—ain't I—in my business?

JONES [*Contemptuously*] Yo' business!

SMITHERS [*Imprudently enraged*] Gawd blimey, you was glad enough for me ter take yer in on it when you landed here first. You didn' 'ave no 'igh and mighty airs in them days!

JONES [*His hand going to his revolver like a flash—menacingly*] Talk polite, white man! Talk polite, you heah me! I'm boss heah now, is you fergettin'? [*The cockney seems about to challenge this last statement with the facts but something in the other's eyes holds and cows him.*]

SMITHERS [*In a cowardly whine*] No 'arm meant, old top.

JONES [*Condescendingly*] I accept yo' apology. [*Lets his hand fall from his revolver.*] No use'n you rakin' up ole times. What I was den is one thing. What I is now 's another. You didn't let me in on yo' crooked work out o' no kind feelin's dat time. I done de dirty work fo' you—and most o' de brain work, too, fo' dat matter—and I was wu'th money to you, dat's de reason.

SMITHERS Well, blimey, I give yer a start, didn't I—when no one else would. I wasn't afraid to 'ire yer like the rest was—'count of the story about your breakin' jail back in the States.

JONES No, you didn't have no s'cuse to look down on me fo' dat. You been in jail you'self more'n once.

SMITHERS [*Furiously*] It's a lie! [*Then trying to pass it off by an attempt at scorn.*] Garn! Who told yer that fairy tale?

JONES Dey's some tings I ain't got to be tole. I kin see 'em in folks' eyes. [*Then after a pause—meditatively.*] Yes, you sho' give me a start. And it didn't take long from dat time to git dese fool, woods' niggers right where I wanted dem. [*With pride.*] From stowaway to emperor in two years! Dat's goin' some!

SMITHERS [*With curiosity*] And I bet you got yer pile o' money 'id safe some place.

JONES [*With satisfaction*] I sho' has! And it's in a foreign bank where no pusson don't ever git it out but me no matter what come. You didn't s'pose I was holdin' down dis emperor job for de glory in it, did you? Sho'! De fuss and glory part of it, dat's only to turn de heads o' de low-flung, bush niggers dat's here. Dey wants de big circus show for deir money. I gives it to 'em an' I gits de money. [*With a grin.*] De long green, dat's me every time! [*Then rebukingly.*] But you ain't got no kick agin me, Smithers. I'se paid you back all you done for me many times. Ain't I pertected you and winked at all de crooked tradin' you been doin' right out in de broad day? Sho' I has—and me makin' laws to stop it at de same time! [*He chuckles.*]

SMITHERS [*Grinning*] But, meanin' no 'arm, you been grab-bin' right and left yourself, ain't yer? Look at the taxes you've put on 'em! Blimey! You've squeezed 'em dry!

JONES [*Chuckling*] No, dey ain't *all* dry yet. I'se still heah, ain't I?

SMITHERS [*Smiling at his secret thought*] They're dry right now, you'll find out. [*Changing the subject abruptly.*] And as for me breakin' laws, you've broke 'em all yerself just as fast as yer made 'em.

JONES Ain't I de emperor? De laws don't go for him. [*Judicially.*] You heah what I tells you, Smithers. Dere's little stealin' like you does, and dere's big stealin' like I does. For de little stealin' dey gits you in jail soon or late. For de big stealin' dey makes you emperor and puts you in de Hall o' Fame when you croaks. [*Reminiscently.*] If dey's one thing I learns in ten years on de Pullman ca's listenin' to de white quality talk, it's dat same fact. And when I gits a chance to use it I winds up emperor in two years.

SMITHERS [*Unable to repress the genuine admiration of the small fry for the large*] Yes, yer turned the bleedin' trick, all right. Blimey, I never seen a bloke 'as 'ad the bloomin' luck you 'as.

JONES [*Severely*] Luck? What you mean—luck?

SMITHERS I suppose you'll say as that swank about the silver bullet ain't luck—and that was what first got the fool blacks on yer side the time of the revolution, wasn't it?

JONES [*With a laugh*] Oh, dat silver bullet! Sho' was luck! But I makes dat luck, you heah? I loads de dice! Yessuh! When dat murderin' nigger ole Lem hired to kill me takes aim ten feet away and his gun misses fire and I shoots him dead, what you heah me say?

SMITHERS You said yer'd got a charm so's no lead bullet'd kill yer. You was so strong only a silver bullet could kill yer, you told 'em. Blimey, wasn't that swank for yer—and plain, fat-'eaded luck?

JONES [*Proudly*] I got brains and I uses 'em quick. Dat ain't luck.

SMITHERS Yer know they wasn't 'ardly liable to get no silver bullets. And it was luck 'e didn't 'it you that time.

JONES [*Laughing*] And dere all dem fool, bush niggers was kneelin' down and bumpin' deir heads on de ground like I was a miracle out o' de Bible. Oh, Lawd, from dat time on I had dem all eatin' out of my hand. I cracks de whip and dey jumps through.

SMITHERS [*With a sniff*] Yankee bluff done it.

JONES Ain't a man's talkin' big what makes him big—long as he makes folks believe it? Sho', I talks large when I ain't got nothin' to back it up, but I ain't talkin' wild just de same. I knows I kin fool 'em—I *knows* it—and dat's backin' enough fo' my game. And ain't I got to learn deir lingo and teach some of dem English befo' I kin to talk to 'em? Ain't dat wuk? You ain't never learned ary word er it, Smithers, in de ten years you been heah, dough yo' knows it's money in yo' pocket tradin' wid 'em if you does. But you'se too shiftless to take de trouble.

SMITHERS [*Flushing*] Never mind about me. What's this I've 'eard about yer really 'avin' a silver bullet molded for yourself?

JONES It's playin' out my bluff. I has de silver bullet molded and I tells 'em when de time comes I kills myself wid it. I tells 'em dat's 'cause I'm de on'y man in de world big enough to git me. No use'n deir tryin'. And dey falls down and bumps deir heads. [*He laughs.*] I does dat so's I kin take a walk in peace widout no jealous nigger gunnin' at me from behind de trees.

SMITHERS   [*Astonished*] Then you 'ad it made—'onest?

JONES   Sho' did. Heah she be. [*He takes out his revolver, breaks it, and takes the silver bullet out of one chamber.*] Five lead an' dis silver baby at de last. Don't she shine pretty? [*He holds it in his hand, looking at it admiringly, as if strangely fascinated.*]

SMITHERS   Let me see. [*Reaches out his hand for it.*]

JONES   [*Harshly*] Keep yo hands whar dey b'long, white man. [*He replaces it in the chamber and puts the revolver back on his hip.*]

SMITHERS   [*Snarling*] Gawd blimey! Think I'm a bleedin' thief, you would.

JONES   No, 'tain't dat. I knows you'se scared to steal from me. On'y I ain't 'lowin' nary body to touch dis baby. She's my rabbit's foot.

SMITHERS   [*Sneering*] A bloomin' charm, wot? [*Venomously.*] Well, you'll need all the bloody charms you 'as before long, s' 'elp me!

JONES   [*Judicially*] Oh, I'se good for six months yit 'fore dey gits sick o' my game. Den, when I sees trouble comin', I makes my getaway.

SMITHERS   Ho! You got it all planned, ain't yer?

JONES   I ain't no fool. I knows dis emperor's time is sho't. Dat why I make hay when de sun shine. Was you thinkin' I'se aimin' to hold down dis job for life? No, suh! What good is gittin' money if you stays back in dis raggedy country? I wants action when I spends. And when I sees dese niggers gittin' up deir nerve to tu'n me out, and I'se got all de money in sight, I resigns on de spot and beats it quick.

SMITHERS   Where to?

JONES   None o' yo' business.

SMITHERS   Not back to the bloody States, I'll lay my oath.

JONES   [*Suspiciously*] Why don't I? [*Then with an easy laugh.*] You mean 'count of dat story 'bout me breakin' from jail back dere? Dat's all talk.

SMITHERS   [*Skeptically*] Ho, yes!

JONES [*Sharply*] You ain't 'sinuatin' I'se a liar, is you?

SMITHERS [*Hastily*] No, Gawd strike me! I was only thinkin' o' the bloody lies you told the blacks 'ere about killin' white men in the States.

JONES [*Angered*] How come dey're lies?

SMITHERS You'd 'ave been in jail if you 'ad, wouldn't yer then? [*With venom.*] And from what I've 'eard, it ain't 'ealthy for a black to kill a white man in the States. They burns 'em in oil, don't they?

JONES [*With cool deadliness*] You mean lynchin' 'd scare me? Well, I tells you, Smithers, maybe I does kill one white man back dere. Maybe I does. And maybe I kills another right heah 'fore long if he don't look out.

SMITHERS [*Trying to force a laugh*] I was on'y spoofin' yer. Can't yer take a joke? And you was just sayin' you'd never been in jail.

JONES [*In the same tone—slightly boastful*] Maybe I goes to jail dere for gettin' in an argument wid razors ovah a crap game. Maybe I gits twenty years when dat colored man die. Maybe I gits in 'nother argument wid de prison guard was overseer ovah us when we're wukin' de roads. Maybe he hits me wid a whip and I splits his head wid a shovel and runs away and files de chain off my leg and gits away safe. Maybe I does all dat an' maybe I don't. It's a story I tells you so's you knows I'se de kind of man dat if you evah repeats one word of it, I ends yo' stealin' on dis yearth mighty damn quick!

SMITHERS [*Terrified*] Think I'd peach on yer? Not me! Ain't I always been yer friend?

JONES [*Suddenly relaxing*] Sho' you has—and you better be.

SMITHERS [*Recovering his composure—and with it his malice*] And just to show yer I'm yer friend, I'll tell yer that bit o' news I was goin' to.

JONES Go ahead! Shoot de piece. Must be bad news from de happy way you look.

SMITHERS [*Warningly*] Maybe it's gettin' time for you to resign—with that bloomin' silver bullet, wot? [*He finishes with a mocking grin.*]

JONES [*Puzzled*] What's dat you say? Talk plain.

SMITHERS Ain't noticed any of the guards or servants about the place today, I 'aven't.

JONES [*Carelessly*] Dey're all out in de garden sleepin'

under de trees. When I sleeps, dey sneaks a sleep, too, and I pretends I never suspicions it. All I got to do is to ring de bell and dey come flyin', makin' a bluff dey was wukin' all de time.

SMITHERS [*In the same mocking tone*] Ring the bell now an' you'll bloody well see what I means.

JONES [*Startled to alertness, but preserving the same careless tone*] Sho' I rings. [*He reaches below the throne and pulls out a big, common dinner bell which is painted the same vivid scarlet as the throne. He rings this vigorously—then stops to listen. Then he goes to both doors, rings again, and looks out.*]

SMITHERS [*Watching him with malicious satisfaction. After a pause—mockingly*] The bloody ship is sinkin' an' the bleedin' rats 'as slung their 'ooks.

JONES [*In a sudden fit of anger flings the bell clattering into a corner*] Low-flung, woods' niggers! [*Then catching Smithers's eye on him, he controls himself and suddenly bursts into a low chuckling laugh.*] Reckon I overplays my hand dis once! A man can't take de pot on a bob-tailed flush all de time. Was I sayin' I'd sit in six months mo'? Well, I'se changed my mind den, I cashes in and resigns de job of emperor right dis minute.

SMITHERS [*With real admiration*] Blimey, but you're a cool bird, and no mistake.

JONES No use'n fussin'. When I knows de game's up I kisses it good-bye widout no long waits. Dey've all run off to de hills, ain't dey?

SMITHERS Yes—every bleedin' man jack of 'em.

JONES Den de revolution is at de post. And de Emperor better git his feet smokin' up de trail. [*He starts for the door in rear.*]

SMITHERS Goin' out to look for your 'orse? Yer won't find any. They steals the 'orses first thing. Mine was gone when I went for 'im this mornin'. That's wot first give me a suspicion of wot was up.

JONES [*Alarmed for a second, scratches his head, then philosophically*] Well, den I hoofs it. Feet, do yo' duty! [*He pulls out a gold watch and looks at it.*] Three-thuty. Sundown's at six-thuty or dereabouts. [*Puts his watch back—with cool confidence.*] I got plenty o' time to make it easy.

SMITHERS Don't be so bloomin' sure of it. They'll be after

you 'ot and 'eavy. Ole Lem is at the bottom o' this business an' 'e 'ates you like 'ell. 'E'd rather do for you than eat 'is dinner, 'e would!

JONES [*Scornfully*] Dat fool no-count nigger! Does you think I'se scared o' him? I stands him on his thick head mor'n once befo' dis, and I does it again if he come in my way . . . [*Fiercely.*] And dis time I leave him a dead nigger fo' sho'!

SMITHERS You'll 'ave to cut through the big forest—an' these blacks 'ere can sniff and follow a trail in the dark like 'ounds. You'd 'ave to 'ustle to get through that forest in twelve hours even if you knew all the bloomin' trails like a native.

JONES [*With indignant scorn*] Look-a-heah, white man! Does you think I'se a natural bo'n fool? Give me credit fo' havin' some sense, fo' Lawd's sake! Don't you s'pose I'se looked ahead and made sho' of all de chances? I'se gone out in dat big forest, pretendin' to hunt, so many times dat I knows it high an' low like a book. I could go through on dem trails wid my eyes shut. [*With great contempt.*] Think dese ign'rent bush niggers dat ain't got brains enuff to know deir own names even can catch Brutus Jones? Huh, I s'pects not! Not on yo' life! Why, man, de white men went after me wid bloodhounds where I come from an I jes' laughs at 'em. It's a shame to fool dese black trash around heah, dey're so easy. You watch me, man! I'll make dem look sick, I will. I'll be 'cross de plain to de edge of de forest by time dark comes. Once in de woods in de night, dey got a swell chance o' findin' dis baby! Dawn tomorrow I'll be out at de oder side and on de coast whar dat French gunboat is stayin'. She picks me up, take me to Martinique when she go dar, and dere I is safe wid a mighty big bankroll in my jeans. It's easy as rollin' off a log.

SMITHERS [*Maliciously*] But s'posin' somethin' 'appens wrong an' they do nab yer?

JONES [*Decisively*] Dey don't—dat's de answer.

SMITHERS But, just for argyment's sake—what'd you do?

JONES [*Frowning*] I'se got five lead bullets in dis gun good enuff fo' common bush niggers—and after dat I got de silver bullet left to cheat 'em out o' gittin' me.

SMITHERS [*Jeeringly*] Ho, I was fergettin' that silver bullet. You'll bump yourself orf in style, won't yer? Blimey!

JONES [*Gloomily*] You kin bet yo whole roll on one thing, white man. Dis baby plays out his string to de end and when he quits, he quits wid a bang de way he ought. Silver bullet ain't none too good for him when he go, dat's a fac'! [*Then shaking off his nervousness—with a confident laugh.*] Sho'! What is I talkin' about? Ain't come to dat yit and I never will—not wid trash niggers like dese yere. [*Boastfully.*] Silver bullet bring me luck anyway. I kin outguess, outrun, outfight, an' outplay de whole lot o' dem all ovah de board any time o' de day er night! You watch me! [*From the distant hills comes the faint, steady thump of a tom-tom, low and vibrating. It starts at a rate exactly corresponding to normal pulse beat—seventy-two to the minute—and continues at a gradually accelerating rate from this point uninterruptedly to the very end of the play.*]

[JONES *starts at the sound. A strange look of apprehension creeps into his face for a moment as he listens. Then he asks, with an attempt to regain his most casual manner.*] What's dat drum beatin' fo'?

SMITHERS [*With a mean grin*] For you. That means the bleedin' ceremony 'as started. I've 'eard it before and I knows.

JONES Cer'mony? What cer'mony?

SMITHERS The blacks is 'oldin' a bloody meetin', 'avin' a war dance, gettin' their courage worked up b'fore they starts after you.

JONES Let dem! Dey'll sho' need it!

SMITHERS And they're there 'oldin their 'eathen religious service—makin' no end of devil spells and charms to 'elp 'em against your silver bullet. [*He guffaws loudly.*] Blimey, but they're balmy as 'ell!

JONES [*A tiny bit awed and shaken in spite of himself*] Huh! Takes more'n dat to scare dis chicken!

SMITHERS [*Scenting the other's feeling—maliciously*] Ter-night when it's pitch black in the forest, they'll 'ave their pet devils and ghosts 'oundin' after you. You'll find yer bloody 'air 'll be standin' on end before termorrow mornin'. [*Seriously.*] It's a bleedin' queer place, that stinkin' forest, even in daylight. Yer don't know what might 'appen in there, it's that rotten still. Always sends the cold shivers down my back minute I gets in it.

JONES [*With a contemptuous sniff*] I ain't no chicken-liver like you is. Trees an' me, we'se friends, and dar's a full moon comin' bring me light. And let dem po' niggers make all de fool spells dey'se a min' to. Does yo' s'pect I'se silly enuff to b'lieve in ghosts an' ha'ants an' all dat ole woman's talk? G'long, white man! You ain't talkin' to me. [*With a chuckle.*] Doesn't you know dey's got to do wid a man was member in good standin' o' de Baptist church? Sho' I was dat when I was porter on de Pullmans, befo' I gits into my little trouble. Let dem try deir heathen tricks. De Baptist church done pertect me and land dem all in hell. [*Then with more confident satisfaction.*] And I'se got little silver bullet o' my own, don't forgit.

SMITHERS Ho! You 'aven't give much 'eed to your Baptist church since you been down 'ere. I've 'eard myself you 'ad turned yer coat an' was takin' up with their blarsted witch doctors, or whatever the 'ell yer calls the swine.

JONES [*Vehemently*] I pretends to! Sho' I pretends! Dat's part o' my game from de fust. If I finds out dem niggers believes dat black is white, den I yells it out louder 'n deir loudest. It don't git me nothin' to do missionary work for de Baptist church. I'se after de coin, an' I lays my Jesus on de shelf for de time bein'. [*Stops abruptly to look at his watch—alertly.*] But I ain't got de time to waste no more fool talk wid you. I'se gwine away from heah dis secon'. [*He reaches in under the throne and pulls out an expensive Panama hat with a bright multicolored band and sets it jauntily on his head.*] So long, white man! [*With a grin.*] See you in jail sometime, maybe!

SMITHERS Not me, you won't. Well, I wouldn't be in your bloody boots for no bloomin' money, but 'ere's wishin' yer luck just the same.

JONES [*Contemptuously*] You're de frightenedest man evah I see! I tells you I'se safe's 'f I was in New York City. It takes dem niggers from now to dark to git up de nerve to start somethin'. By dat time, I'se got a head start dey never kotch up wid.

SMITHERS [*Maliciously*] Give my regards to any ghosts yer meets up with.

JONES [*Grinning*] If dat ghost got money, I'll tell him never ha'nt you less'n he wants to lose it.

SMITHERS [*Flattered*] Garn! [*Then curiously.*] Ain't yer takin' no luggage with yer?

JONES I travels light when I want to move fast. And I got
   tinned grub buried on de edge o' de forest. [*Boastfully.*]
   Now say that I don't look ahead an' use my brains! [*With a
   wide, liberal gesture.*] I will all dat's left in de palace to
   you—and you better grab all you kin sneak away wid befo'
   dey gits here.
SMITHERS [*Gratefully*] Righto—and thanks ter yer. [*As
   JONES walks toward the door in rear—cautioningly.*] Say!
   Look 'ere, you ain't goin' out that way, are yer?
JONES Does you think I'd slink out de back door like a
   common nigger? I'se emperor yit, ain't I? And de Emperor
   Jones leaves de way he comes, and dat black trash don't
   dare stop him—not yit, leastways. [*He stops for a moment
   in the doorway, listening to the far-off but insistent beat of
   the tom-tom.*] Listen to dat roll call, will you? Must be
   mighty big drum carry dat far. [*Then with a laugh.*] Well, if
   dey ain't no whole brass band to see me off, I sho' got de
   drum part of it. So long, white man. [*He puts his hands in
   his pockets and with studied carelessness, whistling a
   tune, he saunters out of the doorway and off to the left.*]
SMITHERS [*Looks after him with a puzzled admiration*] 'E's
   got 'is bloomin' nerve with 'im, s'elp me! [*Then angrily.*]
   Ho—the bleedin' nigger—puttin' on 'is bloody airs! I 'opes
   they nabs 'im an' gives 'im what's what! [*Then putting
   business before the pleasure of this thought, looking
   around him with cupidity.*] A bloke ought to find a 'ole lot
   in this palace that'd go for a bit of cash. Let's take a look,
   'Arry, me lad. [*He starts for the doorway on right as*

                                   [*The curtain falls.*]

SCENE TWO

SCENE: *Nightfall. The end of the plain where the Great Forest begins. The foreground is sandy, level ground dotted by a few stones and clumps of stunted bushes cowering close against the earth to escape the buffeting of the trade wind. In the rear the forest is a wall of darkness dividing the world. Only when the eye becomes accustomed to the gloom can the outlines of separate trunks of the nearest trees be made out, enormous pillars of deeper blackness. A somber monotone of wind lost in the leaves moans in the air. Yet this sound serves but to intensify the impression of the forest's relentless immobility, to form a background throwing into relief its brooding, implacable silence.*

[JONES *enters from the left, walking rapidly. He stops as he nears the edge of the forest, looks around him quickly, peering into the dark as if searching for some familiar landmark. Then, apparently satisfied that he is where he ought to be, he throws himself on the ground, dog-tired.*]

Well, heah I is. In de nick o' time, too! Little mo' an' it'd be blacker'n de ace of spades heah-abouts. [*He pulls a bandana handkerchief from his hip pocket and mops off his perspiring face.*] Sho'! Gimme air! I'se tuckered out sho' nuff. Dat soft emperor job ain't no trainin' fo' a long hike ovah dat plain in de brilin' sun. [*Then with a chuckle.*] Cheah up, nigger, de worst is yet to come. [*He lifts his head and stares at the forest. His chuckle peters out abruptly. In a tone of awe.*] My goodness, look at dem woods, will you? Dat no-count Smithers said dey'd be black an' he sho' called de turn. [*Turning away from them quickly and looking down at his feet, he snatches at a chance to change the subject—solicitously.*] Feet, you is holdin' up yo' end fine an' I sutinly hopes you ain't blisterin' none. It's time you git a rest. [*He takes off his shoes, his eyes studiously avoiding the forest. He feels of the soles of his feet gingerly.*] You is still in de pink—on'y a little mite feverish. Cool yo'selfs. Remember you done got a long journey yit befo' you. [*He sits in a weary attitude, listening to the rhythmic beating of the tom-tom. He grumbles in a loud tone to cover up a growing uneasiness.*] Bush niggers! Wonder dey wouldn' git sick o' beatin' dat drum. Sound louder, seem like. I wonder if dey's startin' after me? [*He scrambles to his feet, looking back across the plain.*] Couldn't see dem now, nohow, if dey was hundred feet away. [*Then shaking himself like a wet dog to get rid of these depressing thoughts.*] Sho', dey's miles an' miles behind. What you gittin' fidgety about? [*But he sits down and begins to lace up his shoes in great haste, all the time muttering reassuringly.*] You know what? Yo' belly is empty, dat's what's de matter wid you. Come time to eat! Wid nothin' but wind on yo' stumach, o' course you feels jiggedy. Well, we eats right heah an' now soon's I gits dese pesky shoes laced up! [*He finishes lacing up his shoes.*] Dere! Now le's see. [*Gets on his hands and knees and searches the ground around him with his eyes.*] White stone, white stone, where is you? [*He sees the first white stone and crawls to it—with satisfaction.*] Heah you is! I knowed dis was de right place. Box of grub, come to me. [*He turns over the stone and feels under it—in a tone of dismay.*] Ain't heah! Gorry, is I in de right place or isn't I? Dere's 'nother stone. Guess dat's it. [*He scrambles to the next stone and turns it over.*] Ain't heah, neither! Grub, whar is you? Ain't heah. Gorry, has I got to go hungry into dem woods—all de night? [*While he is talking he scrambles from one stone to another, turning them over in frantic haste. Finally, he jumps to his feet excitedly.*] Is I lost de place? Must have! But how dat happen when I was followin' de trail across de plain in broad daylight? [*Almost plaintively.*] I'se hungry, I is! I gotta git my feed. Whar's my strength gonna come from if I doesn't? Gorry, I gotta find dat grub high an' low somehow! Why it come dark so quick like dat? Can't see nothin'. [*He scratches a match on his trousers and peers about him. The rate of the beat of the far-off tom-tom increases perceptibly as he does so. He mutters in a bewildered voice.*] How come all dese white stones come heah when I only remembers one? [*Suddenly, with a frightened gasp, he flings the match on the ground and stamps on it.*] Nigger, is you gone crazy mad? Is you lightin' matches to show dem whar you is? Fo' Lawd's sake, use yo' haid. Gorry, I'se got to be careful! [*He stares at the plain behind him apprehensively, his hand on his revolver.*] But how come all dese white stones? And whar's dat tin box o' grub I had all wrapped up in oil cloth?

[*While his back is turned, the* LITTLE FORMLESS FEARS *creep out from the deeper blackness of the forest. They are black, shapeless, only their glittering little eyes can be seen. If they have any describable form at all it is that of a grubworm about the size of a creeping child. They move noiselessly, but with deliberate, painful effort, striving to raise themselves on end, failing and sinking prone again.* JONES *turns about to face the forest. He stares up at the tops of the trees, seeking vainly to discover his whereabouts by their conformation.*]

Can't tell nothin' from dem trees! Gorry, nothin' 'round heah look like I evah seed it befo'. I'se done lost de place sho' 'nuff! [*With mournful foreboding.*] It's mighty queer! It's mighty queer! [*With sudden forced defiance—in an angry tone.*] Woods, is you tryin' to put somethin' ovah on me?

[*From the formless creatures on the ground in front of him comes a tiny gale of low mocking laughter like a rustling of leaves. They squirm upward toward him in twisted attitudes.* JONES *looks down, leaps backward with a yell of terror, yanking out his revolver as he does so—in a quavering voice.*]

What's dat? Who's dar? What is you? Git away from me befo' I shoots you up! You don't? . . .

[*He fires. There is a flash, a loud report, then silence broken only by the far-off, quickened throb of the tom-tom. The formless creatures have scurried back into the forest.* JONES *remains fixed in his position, listening intently. The sound of the shot, the reassuring feel of the revolver in his hand, have somewhat restored his shaken nerve. He addresses himself with renewed confidence.*]

Dey're gone. Dat shot fix 'em. Dey was only little animals—little wild pigs, I reckon. Dey've maybe rooted out yo' grub an' eat it. Sho', you fool nigger, what you think dey is—ha'nts? [*Excitedly.*] Gorry, you give de game away when you fire dat shot. Dem niggers heah dat fo' su'tin! Time you beat in de woods widout no long waits. [*He starts for the forest—hesitates before the plunge—then urging himself in with manful resolution.]* Git in, nigger! What you skeered at? Ain't nothin' dere but de trees! Git in! [*He plunges boldly into the forest.*]

SCENE THREE

SCENE: *Nine o'clock. In the forest. The moon has just risen. It beams, drifting through the canopy of leaves, makes a barely perceptible, suffused, eerie glow. A dense low wall of underbrush and creepers is in the nearer foreground, fencing in a small triangular clearing. Beyond this is the massed blackness of the forest like an encompassing barrier. A path is dimly discerned leading down to the clearing from left, rear, and winding away from it again toward the right. As the scene opens nothing can be distinctly made out. Except for the beating of the tom-tom, which is a trifle louder and quicker than in the previous scene, there is silence, broken every few seconds by a queer, clicking sound. Then gradually the figure of the Negro,* JEFF, *can be discerned crouching on his haunches at the rear of the triangle. He is middle-aged, thin, brown in color, is dressed in a Pullman porter's uniform, cap, etc. He is throwing a pair of dice on the ground before him, picking them up, shaking them, casting them out with the regular, rigid, mechanical movements of an automaton. The heavy, plodding footsteps of someone approaching along the trail from the left are heard and* JONES's *voice, pitched in a slightly higher key and strained in a cheering effort to overcome its own tremors.*

De moon's rizen. Does you heah dat, nigger? You gits more light from dis out. No mo' buttin' yo' fool head agin' de trunks an' scratchin' de hide off yo' legs in de bushes. Now you sees whar yo'se gwine. So cheer up! From now on you has a snap. [*He steps just to the rear of the triangular clearing and mops off his face on his sleeve. He has lost his Panama hat. His face is scratched, his brilliant uniform shows several large rents.*] What time's it gittin' to be, I wonder? I dassent light no match to find out. Phoo'. It's wa'm an' dat's a fac'! [*Wearily.*] How long I been makin' tracks in dese woods? Must be hours an' hours. Seems like fo'evah! Yit can't be, when de moon's jes' riz. Dis am a long night fo' yo', yo' Majesty! [*With a mournful chuckle.*] Majesty! Der ain't much majesty 'bout dis baby now. [*With attempted cheerfulness.*] Never min'. It's all part o' de game. Dis night come to an end like everything else. And when you gits dar safe and has dat bankroll in yo' hands you laughs at all dis. [*He starts to whistle but checks himself abruptly.*] What yo' whistlin' for, you po' dope! Want all de worl' to heah you? [*He stops talking to listen.*] Heah dat ole drum! Sho' gits nearer from de sound. Dey're packin' it along wid 'em. Time fo' me to move. [*He takes a step forward, then stops—worriedly.*] What's dat odder queer clickety sound I heah? Dere it is! Sound close! Sound like—sound like—fo' God sake, sound like some nigger was shootin' crap! [*Frightenedly.*] I better beat it quick when I gits dem notions. [*He walks quickly into the clear space—then stands transfixed as he sees* JEFF—*in a terrified gasp.*] Who dar? Who dat? It dat you, Jeff? [*Starting toward the other, forgetful for a moment of his surroundings and really believing it is a living man that he sees—in a tone of happy relief.*] Jeff! I'se sho' mighty glad to see you! Dey tol' me you done died from dat razor cut I gives you. [*Stopping suddenly, bewilderedly.*] But how you come to be heah, nigger? [*He stares fascinatedly at the other who continues his mechanical play with the dice.* JONES's *eyes begin to roll wildly. He stutters.*] Ain't you gwine—look up—can't you speaks to me? Is you—is you—a ha'nt? [*He jerks out his revolver in a frenzy of terrified rage.*] Nigger, I kills you dead once. Has I got to kill you again? You take it den. [*He fires. When the smoke clears away* JEFF *has disappeared.* JONES *stands trembling—then with a certain reassurance.*] He's gone, anyway. Ha'nt or no ha'nt, dat shot fix him. [*The beat of the far-off tom-tom is perceptibly louder and more rapid.* JONES *becomes conscious of it—with a start, looking back over his shoulder.*] Dey's gittin' near! Dey's comin' fast! And heah I is shootin' shots to let 'em know jes' whar I is. Oh, Gorry, I'se got to run. [*Forgetting the path he plunges wildly into the underbrush in the rear and disappears in the shadow.*]

SCENE FOUR

SCENE: *Eleven o'clock. In the forest. A wide dirt road runs diagonally from right, front, to left, rear. Rising sheer on both sides the forest walls it in. The moon is now up. Under its light the road glimmers ghastly and unreal. It is as if the forest had stood aside momentarily to let the road pass through and accomplish its veiled purpose. This done, the forest will fold in upon itself again and the road will be no more.* JONES *stumbles in from the forest on the right. His uniform is ragged and torn. He looks about him with numbed surprise when he sees the road, his eyes blinking in the bright moonlight. He flops down exhaustedly and pants heavily for a while. Then with sudden anger—*

I'm meltin' wid heat! Runnin' an' runnin' an' runnin'! Damn dis heah coat! Like a straitjacket! [*He tears off his coat and flings it away from him, revealing himself stripped to the waist.*] Dere! Dat's better! Now I kin breathe! [*Looking down at his feet, the spurs catch his eye.*] And to hell wid dese high-fangled spurs. Dey're what's been a-trippin' me up an' breakin' my neck. [*He unstraps them and flings them away disgustedly.*] Dere! I gits rid o' dem frippety emperor trappin's an' I travels lighter. Lawd! I'se tired! [*After a pause, listening to the insistent beat of the tom-tom in the distance.*] I must 'a put some distance between myself an' dem—runnin' like dat—and yit—dat damn drum sounds jes' de same— nearer, even. Well, I guess I a'most holds my lead anyhow. Dey won't never catch up. [*With a sigh.*] If on'y my fool legs stands up. Oh, I'se sorry I evah went in for dis. Dat emperor's job is sho' hard to shake. [*He looks around him*

suspiciously.] How'd this road evah git heah? Good level
road, too. I never remembers seein' it befo'. [*Shaking his
head apprehensively.*] Dese woods is sho' full o' de
queerest things at night. [*With a sudden terror.*] Lawd
God, don't let me see no more o' dem ha'nts! Dey gits my
goat! [*Then trying to talk himself into confidence.*] Ha'nts!
You fool nigger, dey ain't no such things! Don't de Baptist
parson tell you dat many times? Is you civilized, or is you
like dese ign'rent black niggers heah? Sho'! Dat was all in
yo' own head. Wasn't nothin' dere. Wasn't no Jeff! Know
what? You jus' get seein' dem things 'cause yo' belly's
empty and you's sick wid hunger inside. Hunger 'fects yo'
head and yo' eyes. Any fool know dat. [*Then pleading
fervently.*] But bless God, I don't come across no more o'
dem, whatever dey is! [*Then cautiously.*] Rest! Don't talk!
Rest! You needs it. Den you gits on yo' way again. [*Looking at the moon.*] Night's half gone a'most. You hits de
coast in de mawning! Den you'se all safe.

[*From the right forward a small gang of* NEGROES *enter.
They are dressed in striped convict suits, their heads are
shaven, one leg drags limpingly, shackled to a heavy ball
and chain. Some carry picks, the others shovels. They are
followed by a white man dressed in the uniform of a prison
guard. A Winchester rifle is slung across his shoulders
and he carries a heavy whip. At a signal from the* GUARD
they stop on the road opposite where JONES *is sitting.*
JONES, *who has been staring up at the sky, unmindful of
their noiseless approach, suddenly looks down and sees
them. His eyes pop out, he tries to get to his feet and fly,
but sinks back, too numbed by fright to move. His voice
catches in a choking prayer.*]

Lawd Jesus!

[*The* PRISON GUARD *cracks his whip—noiselessly—and
at that signal all the convicts start to work on the road.
They swing their picks, they shovel, but not a sound
comes from their labor. Their movements, like those of*
JEFF *in the preceding scene, are those of automatons—
rigid, slow, and mechanical. The* PRISON GUARD *points
sternly at* JONES *with his whip, motions him to take his
place among the other shovelers.* JONES *gets to his feet in
a hypnotized stupor. He mumbles subserviently.*]

Yes, suh! Yes, suh! I'se comin'.

[*As he shuffles, dragging one foot, over to his place, he curses under his breath with rage and hatred.*]

God damn yo' soul, I gits even wid you yit, sometime.

[*As if there were a shovel in his hands he goes through weary, mechanical gestures of digging up dirt, and throwing it to the roadside. Suddenly the* GUARD *approaches him angrily, threateningly. He raises his whip and lashes* JONES *viciously across the shoulders with it.* JONES *winces with pain and cowers abjectly. The* GUARD *turns his back on him and walks away contemptuously. Instantly* JONES *straightens up. With arms upraised as if his shovel were a club in his hands he springs murderously at the unsuspecting* GUARD. *In the act of crashing down his shovel on the white man's skull,* JONES *suddenly becomes aware that his hands are empty. He cries despairingly.*]

Whar's my shovel? Gimme my shovel till I splits his damn head! [*Appealing to his fellow convicts.*] Gimme a shovel, one o' you, fo' God's sake!

[*They stand fixed in motionless attitudes, their eyes on the ground. The* GUARD *seems to wait expectantly, his back turned to the attacker.* JONES *bellows with baffled, terrified rage, tugging frantically at his revolver.*]

I kills you, you white debil, if it's de last thing I evah does! Ghost or debil, I kills you again!

[*He frees the revolver and fires point blank at the* GUARD'S *back. Instantly the walls of the forest close in from both sides, the road and the figures of the convict gang are blotted out in an enshrouding darkness. The only sounds are a crashing in the underbrush as* JONES *leaps away in mad flight and the throbbing of the tom-tom, still far distant, but increased in volume of sound and rapidity of beat.*]

SCENE FIVE

SCENE: *One o'clock. A large circular clearing, enclosed by
the serried ranks of gigantic trunks of tall trees whose tops
are lost to view. In the center is a big dead stump worn by
time into a curious resemblance to an auction block. The
moon floods the clearing with a clear light.* JONES *forces his
way in through the forest on the left. He looks wildly about
the clearing with hunted, fearful glances. His pants are in
tatters, his shoes cut and misshapen, flapping about his feet.
He slinks cautiously to the stump in the center and sits down
in a tense position, ready for instant flight. Then he holds his
head in his hands and rocks back and forth, moaning to
himself miserably.*

Oh Lawd, Lawd! Oh Lawd, Lawd! [*Suddenly he throws
himself on his knees and raises his clasped hands to the
sky—in a voice of agonized pleading.*] Lawd Jesus, heah
my prayer! I'se a po' sinner, a po' sinner! I knows I done
wrong, I knows it! When I cotches Jeff cheatin' wid loaded
dice my anger overcomes me and I kills him dead! Lawd, I
done wrong! When dat guard hits me wid de whip, my
anger overcomes me, and I kills him dead. Lawd, I done
wrong! And down heah whar dese fool bush niggers raises
me up to the seat o' de mighty, I steals all I could grab.
Lawd, I done wrong! I knows it! I'se sorry! Forgive me,
Lawd! Forgive dis po' sinner! [*Then beseeching ter-
rifiedly.*] And keep dem away, Lawd! Keep dem away from
me! And stop dat drum soundin' in my ears! Dat begin to
sound ha'nted, too. [*He gets to his feet, evidently slightly
reassured by his prayer—with attempted confidence.*] De
Lawd'll preserve me from dem ha'nts after dis. [*Sits down
on the stump again.*] I ain't skeered o' real men. Let dem
come. But dem odders . . . [*He shudders—then looks
down at his feet, working his toes inside the shoes—with a
groan.*] Oh, my po' feet! Dem shoes ain't no use no more
'ceptin' to hurt. I'se better off widout dem. [*He unlaces
them and pulls them off—holds the wrecks of the shoes in*

his hands and regards them mournfully.] You was real, A-one patin' leather, too. Look at you now. Emperor, you'se gittin' mighty low!

[*He sits dejectedly and remains with bowed shoulders, staring down at the shoes in his hands as if reluctant to throw them away. While his attention is thus occupied, a crowd of figures silently enter the clearing from all sides. All are dressed in Southern costumes of the period of the fifties of the last century. There are middle-aged men who are evidently well-to-do planters. There is one spruce, authoritative individual—the* AUCTIONEER. *There is a crowd of curious spectators, chiefly young belles and dandies who have come to the slave-market for diversion. All exchange courtly greetings in dumb show and chat silently together. There is something stiff, rigid, unreal, marionettish about their movements. They group themselves about the stump. Finally a batch of slaves are led in from the left by an attendant—three men of different ages, two women, one with a baby in her arms, nursing. They are placed to the left of the stump, beside* JONES.

The white planters look them over appraisingly as if they were cattle, and exchange judgments on each. The dandies point with their fingers and make witty remarks. The belles titter bewitchingly. All this in silence save for the ominous throb of the tom-tom. The AUCTIONEER *holds up his hand, taking his place at the stump. The group strain forward attentively. He touches* JONES *on the shoulder peremptorily, motioning for him to stand on the stump—the auction block.*

JONES *looks up, sees the figures on all sides, looks wildly for some opening to escape, sees none, screams, and leaps madly to the top of the stump to get as far away from them as possible. He stands there, cowering, paralyzed with horror. The* AUCTIONEER *begins his silent spiel. He points to* JONES, *appeals to the planters to see for themselves. Here is a good field hand, sound in wind and limb as they can see. Very strong still in spite of his being middle-aged. Look at that back. Look at those shoulders. Look at the muscles in his arms and his sturdy legs. Capable of any amount of hard labor. Moreover, of a good disposition, intelligent and tractable. Will any gentleman start the bidding? The* PLANTERS *raise their fingers, make*

their bids. They are apparently all eager to possess JONES.
*The bidding is lively, the crowd interested. While this has
been going on,* JONES *has been seized by the courage of
desperation. He dares to look down and around him. Over
his face abject terror gives way to mystification, to gradual
realization—stutteringly.*]

What you all doin', white folks? What's all dis? What
you all lookin' at me fo'? What you doin' wid me, anyhow?
[*Suddenly convulsed with raging hatred and fear..*] Is dis a
auction? Is you sellin' me like dey uster befo' de war?
[*Jerking out his revolver just as the* AUCTIONEER *knocks
him down to one of the* PLANTERS—*glaring from him to
the purchaser.*] And *you* sells me? And *you* buys me? I
shows you I'se a free nigger, damn yo' souls! [*He fires at
the* AUCTIONEER *and at the* PLANTER *with such rapidity
that the two shots are almost simultaneous. As if this were
a signal the walls of the forest fold in. Only blackness
remains and silence broken by* JONES *as he rushes off,
crying with fear—and by the quickened, ever louder beat
of the tom-tom.*]

SCENE SIX

SCENE: *Three o'clock. A cleared space in the forest. The
limbs of the trees meet over it forming a low ceiling about
five feet from the ground. The interlocked ropes of creepers
reaching upward to entwine the tree trunks give an arched
appearance to the sides. The space thus enclosed is like the
dark, noisome hold of some ancient vessel. The moonlight is
almost completely shut out and only a vague, wan light
filters through. There is the noise of someone approaching
from the left, stumbling and crawling through the under-
growth.* JONES'S *voice is heard between chattering moans.*

Oh, Lawd, what I gwine do now? Ain't got no bullet left
on'y de silver one. If mo' o' dem ha'nts come after me, how

I gwine skeer dem away? Oh, Lawd, on'y de silver one
left—an' I gotta save dat fo' luck. If I shoots dat one I'm a
goner sho'! Lawd, it's black heah! Whar's de moon? Oh,
Lawd, don't dis night evah come to an end? [*By the
sounds, he is feeling his way cautiously forward.*] Dere!
Dis feels like a clear space. I gotta lie down an' rest. I don't
care if dem niggers does cotch me. I gotta rest.

[*He is well forward now where his figure can be dimly
made out. His pants have been so torn away that what is
left of them is no better than a breechcloth. He flings
himself full length, face downward on the ground, panting
with exhaustion. Gradually it seems to grow lighter in the
enclosed space and two rows of seated figures can be seen
behind* JONES. *They are sitting in crumbled, despairing
attitudes, hunched, facing one another with their backs
touching the forest walls as if they were shackled to them.
All are Negroes, naked save for loincloths. At first they
are silent and motionless. Then they begin to sway slowly
forward toward each other and back again in unison, as if
they were laxly letting themselves follow the long roll of a
ship at sea. At the same time, a low, melancholy murmur
rises among them, increasing gradually by rhythmic degrees which seem to be directed and controlled by the
throb of the tom-tom in the distance, to a long, tremulous
wail of despair that reaches a certain pitch, unbear-
ably acute, then falls by slow gradations of tone into
silence and is taken up again.* JONES *starts, looks up,
sees the figures, and throws himself down again to shut
out the sight. A shudder of terror shakes his whole body
as the wail rises up about him again. But the next time, his
voice, as if under some uncanny compulsion, starts with
the others. As their chorus lifts he rises to a sitting posture
similar to the others, swaying back and forth. His voice
reaches the highest pitch of sorrow, of desolation. The
light fades out, the other voices cease, and only darkness
is left.* JONES *can be heard scrambling to his feet and
running off, his voice sinking down the scale and receding
as he moves farther and farther away in the forest. The
tom-tom beats louder, quicker, with a more insistent, triumphant pulsation.*]

SCENE SEVEN

SCENE: *Five o'clock. The foot of a gigantic tree by the edge
of a great river. A rough structure of boulders, like an altar,
is by the tree. The raised riverbank is in the nearer background. Beyond this the surface of the river spreads out,
brilliant and unruffled in the moonlight, blotted out and
merged into a veil of bluish mist in the distance.* JONES's
*voice is heard from the left rising and falling in the long,
despairing wail of the chained slaves, to the rhythmic beat of
the tom-tom. As his voice sinks into silence, he enters the
open space. The expression of his face is fixed and stony, his
eyes have an obsessed glare, he moves with a strange deliberation like a sleepwalker or one in a trance. He looks
around at the tree, the rough stone altar, the moonlit surface
of the river beyond, and passes his hand over his head with a
vague gesture of puzzled bewilderment. Then, as if in obedience to some obscure impulse, he sinks into a kneeling,
devotional posture before the altar. Then he seems to come
to himself partly, to have an uncertain realization of what he
is doing, for he straightens up and stares about him hor-
rifiedly—in an incoherent mumble:*

What—what is I doin'? What is—dis place? Seems
like—seems like I know dat tree—an' dem stones—an' de
river. I remember—seems like I ben heah befo'. [*Trem-
blingly.*] Oh, Gorry, I'se skeered in dis place! I'se skeered!
Oh, Lawd, perfect dis sinner!
 [*Crawling away from the altar, he cowers close to the
ground, his face hidden, his shoulders heaving with sobs
of hysterical fright. From behind the trunk of the tree, as if
he had sprung out of it, the figure of the* CONGO WITCH
DOCTOR *appears. He is wizened and old, naked except for
the fur of some small animal tied about his waist, its bushy
tail hanging down in front. His body is stained all over a
bright red. Antelope horns are on each side of his head,
branching upward. In one hand he carries a bone rattle, in
the other a charm stick with a bunch of white cockatoo*

*feathers tied to the end. A great number of glass beads
and bone ornaments are about his neck, ears, wrists, and
ankles. He struts noiselessly with a queer prancing step to
a position in the clear ground between* JONES *and the
altar. Then with a preliminary, summoning stamp of his
foot on the earth, he begins to dance and to chant. As if in
response to his summons the beating of the tom-tom
grows to a fierce, exultant boom whose throbs seem to fill
the air with vibrating rhythm.* JONES *looks up, starts to
spring to his feet, reaches a half-kneeling, half-squatting
position, and remains rigidly fixed there, paralyzed with
awed fascination by this new apparition. The* WITCH DOC-
TOR *sways, stamping with his foot, his bone rattle clicking
the time. His voice rises and falls in a weird, monotonous
croon, without articulate word divisions. Gradually his
dance becomes clearly one of a narrative in pantomime,
his croon is an incantation, a charm to allay the fierceness
of some implacable deity demanding sacrifice. He flees,
he is pursued by devils, he hides, he flees again. Ever
wilder and wilder becomes his flight, nearer and nearer
draws the pursuing evil, more and more the spirit of terror
gains possession of him. His croon, rising to intensity, is
punctuated by shrill cries.* JONES *has become completely
hypnotized. His voice joins in the incantation, in the cries,
he beats time with his hands and sways his body to and fro
from the waist. The whole spirit and meaning of the dance
has entered into him, has become his spirit. Finally the
theme of the pantomime halts on a howl of despair, and is
taken up again in a note of savage hope. There is a
salvation. The forces of evil demand sacrifice. They must
be appeased. The* WITCH DOCTOR *points with his wand to
the sacred tree, to the river beyond, to the altar, and finally
to* JONES *with a ferocious command.* JONES *seems to sense
the meaning of this. It is he who must offer himself for
sacrifice. He beats his forehead abjectly to the ground,
moaning hysterically.*]

Mercy, Oh Lawd! Mercy! Mercy on dis po' sinner.

[*The* WITCH DOCTOR *springs to the riverbank. He
stretches out his arms and calls to some god within its
depths. Then he starts backward slowly, his arms remain-
ing out. A huge head of a crocodile appears over the bank
and its eyes, glittering greenly, fasten upon* JONES. *He*

stares into them fascinatedly. The WITCH DOCTOR *prances
up to him, touches him with his wand, motions with hideous command toward the waiting monster.* JONES
*squirms on his belly nearer and nearer, moaning con-
tinually.*]

Mercy, Lawd! Mercy!

[*The crocodile heaves more of his enormous hulk onto
the land.* JONES *squirms toward him. The* WITCH DOCTOR'S
*voice shrills out in furious exultation, the tom-tom beats
madly.* JONES *cries out in a fierce, exhausted spasm of
anguished pleading.*]

Lawd, save me! Lawd Jesus, heah my prayer!

[*Immediately, in answer to his prayer, comes the
thought of the one bullet left him. He snatches at his hip,
shouting defiantly.*]

De silver bullet! You don't git me yit!

[*He fires at the green eyes in front of him. The head of
the crocodile sinks back behind the riverbank, the* WITCH
DOCTOR *springs behind the sacred tree and disappears.*
JONES *lies with his face to the ground, his arms out-
stretched, whimpering with fear as the throb of the tom-
tom fills the silence about him with a somber pulsation, a
baffled but revengeful power.*]

SCENE EIGHT

SCENE: *Dawn. Same as Scene Two, the dividing line of forest
and plain. The nearest tree trunks are dimly revealed but the
forest behind them is still a mass of glooming shadows. The
tom-tom seems on the very spot, so loud and continuously
vibrating are its beats.* LEM *enters from the left, followed by
a small squad of his soldiers, and by the cockney trader,*
SMITHERS. LEM *is a heavy-set, ape-faced old savage of the
extreme African type, dressed only in a loincloth. A revolver
and cartridge belt are about his waist. His soldiers are in
different degrees of rag-concealed nakedness. All wear
broad palm-leaf hats. Each one carries a rifle.* SMITHERS *is*

the same as in Scene One. One of the soldiers, evidently a
tracker, is peering about keenly on the ground. He grunts
and points at the spot where JONES *entered the forest.* LEM
and SMITHERS *come to look.*

SMITHERS   [*After a glance, turns away in disgust*] That's
where 'e went in right enough. Much good it'll do yer. 'E's
miles orf by this an' safe to the Coast, damn 'is 'ide! I tole
yer yer'd lose 'im, didn't I!—wastin' the 'ole bloomin' night
beatin' yer bloody drum and castin' yer silly spells! Gawd
blimey, wot a pack!

LEM   [*Gutturally*] We cotch him. You see. [*He makes a*
motion to his soldiers who squat down on their haunches
in a semicircle.]

SMITHERS   [*Exasperatedly*] Well, ain't yer goin' in an' 'unt
'im in the woods? What the 'ell's the good of waitin'?

LEM   [*Imperturbably—squatting down himself*] We cotch
him.

SMITHERS   [*Turning away from him contemptuously*] Aw!
Garn! 'E's a better man than the lot o' you put together. I
'ates the sight of 'im but I'll say that for 'im. [*A sound of*
snapping twigs comes from the forest. The soldiers jump
to their feet, cocking their rifles alertly. LEM *remains sit-*
ting with an imperturbable expression, but listening in-
tently. The sound from the woods is repeated. LEM *makes*
a quick signal with his hand. His followers creep quickly
but noiselessly into the forest, scattering so that each
enters at a different spot.]

SMITHERS   [*In the silence that follows—in a contemptuous*
whisper] You ain't thinkin' that would be 'im, I 'ope?

LEM   [*Calmly*] We cotch him.

SMITHERS   Blarsted fat 'eads! [*Then after a second's*
thought—wonderingly.] Still an' all, it might 'appen. If 'e
lost 'is bloody way in these stinkin' woods 'e'd likely turn
in a circle without 'is knowin' it. They all does.

LEM   [*Peremptorily*] Sssh! [*The reports of several rifles*
sound from the forest, followed a second later by savage,
exultant yells. The beating of the tom-tom abruptly
ceases. LEM *looks up at the white man with a grin of*
satisfaction.] We cotch him. Him dead.

SMITHERS   [*With a snarl*] 'Ow d'yer know it's 'im an' 'ow
d'yer know 'e's dead?

LEM My mens dey got 'um silver bullets. Dey kill him
shore.

SMITHERS [*Astonished*] They got silver bullets?

LEM Lead bullet no kill him. He got 'um strong charm. I
cook 'um money, make 'um silver bullet, make 'um strong
charm, too.

SMITHERS [*Light breaking upon him*] So that's wot you was
up to all night, wot? You was scared to put after 'im till
you'd molded silver bullets, eh?

LEM [*Simply stating a fact*] Yes. Him got strong charm.
Lead no good.

SMITHERS [*Slapping his thigh and guffawing*] Haw-haw! If
yer don't beat all 'ell! [*Then recovering himself—scornfully.*] I'll bet yer it ain't 'im they shot at all, yer bleedin'
looney!

LEM [*Calmly*] Dey come bring him now. [*The soldiers come
out of the forest, carrying* JONES's *limp body. There is a
little reddish-purple hole under his left breast. He is dead.
They carry him to* LEM, *who examines his body with great
satisfaction.* SMITHERS [*leans over his shoulder—in a tone
of frightened awe.*] Well, they did for yer right enough,
Jonesey, me lad! Dead as a 'erring! [*Mockingly.*] Where's
yer 'igh an' mighty airs now, yer bloomin' Majesty? [*Then
with a grin.*] Silver bullets! Gawd blimey, but yer died in
the 'eight o' style, any'ow! [LEM *makes a motion to the
soldiers to carry the body out left.* SMITHERS *speaks to
him sneeringly.*]

SMITHERS And I s'pose you think it's yer bleedin' charms
and yer silly beatin' the drum that made 'im run in a circle
when 'e'd lost 'imself, don't yer? [*But* LEM *makes no reply,
does not seem to hear the question, walks out left after his
men.* SMITHERS *looks after him with contemptuous scorn.*]
Stupid as 'ogs, the lot of 'em! Blarsted niggers!

[*The curtain falls.*]

The following is a reading list of modern tragic plays that will supplement this selection of *Six Major Tragedies:*

EDWARD ALBEE:
Who's Afraid of Virginia Woolf? (1962)

JEAN ANOUILH:
Antigone (1944)

SAMUEL BECKETT:
Waiting for Godot (1953)
Krapp's Last Tape (1958)
Endgame (1958)

BERTOLT BRECHT:
The Threepenny Opera (1933)
Galileo (1937)
The Good Woman of Setzuan (1938)
Mother Courage (1941)
The Caucasian Chalk Circle (1948)

JEAN GENET:
The Balcony (1960)

JEAN GIRAUDOUX:
The Madwoman of Chaillot (1945)

FEDERICO GARCÍA LORCA:
Blood Wedding (1933)
The House of Bernarda Alba (1936)
Yerma (1935)

EUGENE IONESCO:
Rhinoceros (1960)

ARTHUR MILLER:
All My Sons (1947)
Death of a Salesman (1949)
The Crucible (1953)
After the Fall (1964)

JOHN OSBORNE:
The Entertainer (1957)

HAROLD PINTER:
The Caretaker (1960)
The Homecoming (1965)

LUIGI PIRANDELLO:
Six Characters in Search of an Author (1921)

GEORGE BERNARD SHAW:
Saint Joan (1923)

SAM SHEPARD:
True West (1980)

THORNTON WILDER:
Our Town (1938)
The Skin of Our Teeth (1942)

TENNESSEE WILLIAMS:
The Glass Menagerie (1944)
A Streetcar Named Desire (1947)
Summer and Smoke (1948)
Cat on a Hot Tin Roof (1955)
Sweet Bird of Youth (1959)
The Night of the Iguana (1961)

Selected Bibliography

The Art of the Playwright, William Packard. Paragon
    House: 1986.
The Classical Tradition in Poetry, Gilbert Murray.
    Vintage Books: 1957.
The Greeks, H.D.F. Kitto. Penguin Books: 1951.
Introduction to Classical Drama, Moses Hadas. Bantam
    Books: 1966.
Poetics, Aristotle (any edition).
Shakespearean Tragedy, Henry B. Charlton. AMS Pr:
    1949.

Bantam Drama Classics

☐ 21354   Sophocles: Complete Plays $3.95
☐ 21363   Euripides: Ten Plays $3.95
☐ 21343   Aristophanes: Complete Plays $4.50
☐ 21280   Henrik Ibsen: Four Great Plays $2.95
☐ 21360   Rostand: Cyrano De Bergerac $1.95
☐ 21211   Anton Chekhov: Five Major
                  Plays $2.95

Buy them at your local bookstore or use this page to order.

Bantam Books, Dept. CL5, 414 East Golf Road,
Des Plaines, IL 60016

Please send me the books I have checked above. I am enclosing
$_____ (Please add $2.00 to cover postage and handling.)
Send check or money order—no cash or C.O.D.s please.

Mr/Ms _____

Address _____

City/State _____ Zip _____

CL5—10/89

Please allow four to six weeks for delivery.
Prices and availability subject to change without notice.

Bantam Classics bring you the world's greatest literature— books that have stood the test of time—at specially low prices. These beautifully designed books will be proud additions to your bookshelf. You'll want all these time-tested classics for your own reading pleasure.

Titles by Charles Dickens:

☐ 21123	THE PICKWICK PAPERS	$4.95
☐ 21223	BLEAK HOUSE	$3.95
☐ 21265	NICHOLAS NICKLEBY	$4.95
☐ 21342	GREAT EXPECTATIONS	$2.95
☐ 21176	A TALE OF TWO CITIES	$2.50
☐ 21016	HARD TIMES	$1.95
☐ 21102	OLIVER TWIST	$2.50
☐ 21244	A CHRISTMAS CAROL & OTHER VICTORIAN TALES	$1.95

Titles by Thomas Hardy:

☐ 21191	JUDE THE OBSCURE	$2.95
☐ 21024	THE MAYOR OF CASTERBRIDGE	$2.25
☐ 21269	THE RETURN OF THE NATIVE	$2.25
☐ 21168	TESS OF THE D'URBERVILLES	$2.95
☐ 21331	FAR FROM THE MADDING CROWD	$3.50

Titles by Henry James:

☐ 21127	PORTRAIT OF A LADY	$3.50
☐ 21059	THE TURN OF THE SCREW	$1.95

Look for them at your bookstore or use this page to order:

Bantam Books, Dept. CL3, 414 East Golf Road, Des Plaines, IL 60016

Please send me the items I have checked above. I am enclosing $_____ (please add $2.00 to cover postage and handling). Send check or money order, no cash or C.O.D.s please.

Mr/Ms _____

Address _____

City/State _____ Zip _____

CL3–11/89

Please allow four to six weeks for delivery.
Prices and availability subject to change without notice.

Bantam Classics bring you the world's greatest literature—books that have stood the test of time—at specially low prices. These beautifully designed books will be proud additions to your bookshelf. You'll want all these time-tested classics for your own reading pleasure.

Titles by Fyodor Dostoevsky:

☐ 21216	THE BROTHERS KARAMAZOV	$3.95
☐ 21175	CRIME AND PUNISHMENT	$2.95
☐ 21352	THE IDIOT	$3.95
☐ 21144	NOTES FROM UNDERGROUND	$2.50

Titles by Leo Tolstoy:

☐ 21346	ANNA KARENINA	$3.50
☐ 21035	DEATH OF IVAN ILYICH	$1.95

Titles by Joseph Conrad:

☐ 21214	HEART OF DARKNESS & THE SECRET SHARER	$1.95
☐ 21361	LORD JIM	$2.25

Titles by George Eliot:

☐ 21180	MIDDLEMARCH	$4.95
☐ 21229	SILAS MARNER	$1.95

Titles by Ivan Turgenev:

☐ 21259	FATHERS AND SONS	$2.25

Look for them at your bookstore or use this page to order.

Special Offer
Buy a Bantam Book
for only 50¢.

Now you can have Bantam's catalog filled with hundreds of titles plus take advantage of our unique and exciting bonus book offer. A special offer which gives you the opportunity to purchase a Bantam book for only 50¢. Here's how!

By ordering any five books at the regular price per order, you can also choose any other single book listed (up to a $5.95 value) for just 50¢. Some restrictions do apply, but for further details why not send for Bantam's catalog of titles today!

Just send us your name and address and we will send you a catalog!
